What People are Saying About
20 World Religions & Faith Practices

One of our common interests is comparing religions. I studied the subject through the PhD level. I have never seen a more comprehensive study. Congratulations for a job well done! When we get past the words of any religion, we always find the same thing—a God who has spoken in a thousand tongues for all to hear. We have heard Your voice and feel You in our separate ways. But You, our Lord, You are One, although each of us may see you differently.

—Raphael A.
AngelPath, LLC

Normally, one might be suspicious about a book on world religions written by a minister's wife, but Robyn Lebron's effort here is to be lauded by the interfaith community. Her ability to sift through the complexities of the various doctrines of the various sects of the various denominations of the various religions of the world is impressive, to say the least. It's quite readable for the lay person and offers appropriate sources for those who wish to dig deeper.

—Fred Stella
President, Interfaith Dialogue Association

This book was read and reviewed by the church to see if it would be suitable for inclusion in the church in contributing to interfaith dialogue. We found it to be very insightful, and it is a useful book for the serious student of religion as well as for the person who simply wants to know what others believe. Great job, Robyn Lebron.

—Rev. RJ
Interfaith Seminary

Thank you to author, Robyn Lebron, for including the Bahá'í faith as a chapter in The Search for Peace in Times of Chaos. We appreciate the care she took to ensure the accuracy of the information presented. The book is a concise and enriching compilation of the history and faith practices of many of the world's religions. A wonderful reference book for spiritual seekers to have in their collection.

—Bahá'í US

Robyn's ambitious work is a divine and grace-filled d oorway t o realizing spiritual unity among the world's faith traditions and spiritual families. Her in-depth research, combined with a factual and unbiased tone, make for a wonderful tool to help anyone explore the common ground among the faith traditions. Effective as a reference guide or a comparative religion teaching aid, The S earch f or Peace i n T imes of Chaos is a spirit-filled effort that can serve as a beacon for unity and peace throughout the world.

—Rev. Robert Meagher
Interfaith Minister

20 WORLD RELIGIONS & FAITH PRACTICES

Volume 1

YorkshirePublishing
www.yorkshirepublishing.com
Write Now.

Complete your research by getting a copy of Volume 2 today.

20 More Religions & Faith Practices

Volume 2

Assemblies of God & Pentecostal Church of God
Bahá'í'
Baptist*
Church of Jesus Christ of Latter-day Saints(Mormon)
Congregationalist (United Church of Christ)
Episcopal
Lutheran*
Moravian (Unitas Fratrum)
Orthodox*
Quaker (Religious Society of Friends)
Seventh-day Adventists
Buddhist
Han
Jain
Sikh
Sôka Gakkai
Taoist (Daoist
Pagan
Traditional Religions of Africa*
Juche'

20
WORLD RELIGIONS
& FAITH PRACTICES

Volume 1

The Search for Peace in Times of Chaos

ROBYN LEBRON

ISBN: 978-1-947825-68-0 Hardback
        978-1-947825-67-3 Paperback
20 World Religions & Faith Practices—Volume 1
Copyright © 2017 by Robyn Lebron

Yorkshire Publishing
3207 South Norwood Avenue
Tulsa, Oklahoma 74135
www.YorkshirePublishing.com
918.394.2665

I dedicate this book to God's work on earth

Acknowledgments

I would like to express my love and appreciation to everyone for their patience with the endless hours I spent at the computer, sometimes to the exclusion of all else.

My thanks to my children, Christina and Nathaniel, and my mom, Lola, for their love and support. And to my friends Cynthia, Oyounne, and Patty who kept telling me I should publish these books.

I would be remiss if I didn't express my thanks for the people of Trinity Episcopal Church in Janesville, Wisconsin, who for two years faithfully attended the *Religions of the World* classes that evolved into the book you now have in your hands. Their enthusiasm and support helped convince me that the information needed to be shared.

I must also acknowledge all the help, advice, and input I received from the website owners as well. Many of them spent hours going through their particular faith to make sure it was accurate. Although I did receive some conflicting comments, as with any faith practices, there are variations from group to group and sometimes from individual to individual. Most of the websites were enthusiastic about the project and gave me much needed support.

I would also like to express the spiritual journey that I personally have taken during my research. I have come to understand that God (by whatever name) has shared the message to all humankind for thousands of years—the message of love, hope and inner peace.

Blessings and love to you all! I could not have done it without you.

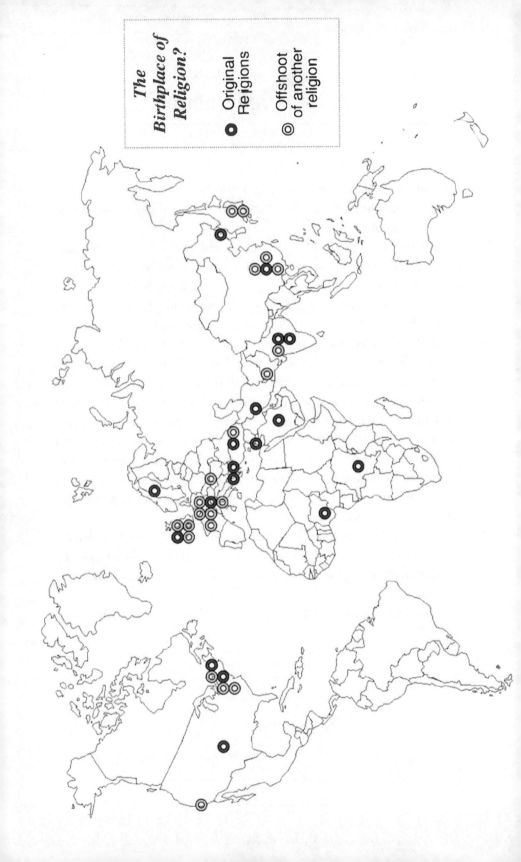

The
Birthplace of
Religion?

• Original
  Religions

◎ Offshoot
  of another
  religion

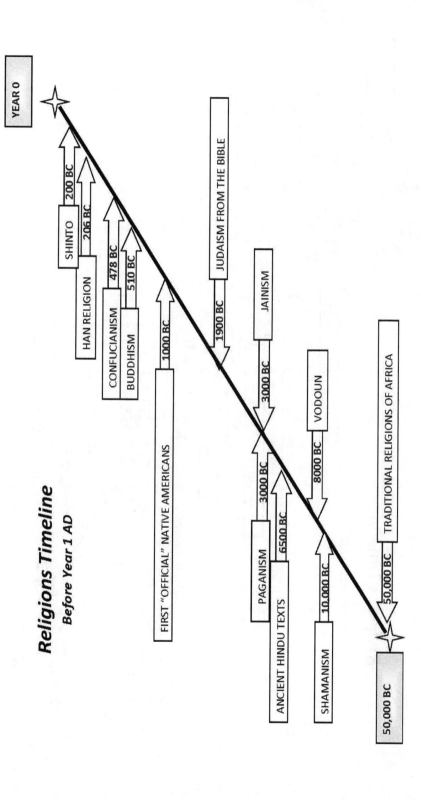

Religions Timeline
Before Year 1 AD

YEAR 0

SHINTO — 200 BC
HAN RELIGION — 206 BC
CONFUCIANISM — 478 BC
BUDDHISM — 510 BC
FIRST "OFFICIAL" NATIVE AMERICANS — 1000 BC
JUDAISM FROM THE BIBLE — 1900 BC
JAINISM — 3000 BC
PAGANISM — 3000 BC
ANCIENT HINDU TEXTS — 6500 BC
VODOUN — 8000 BC
SHAMANISM — 10,000 BC
TRADITIONAL RELIGIONS OF AFRICA — 50,000 BC

50,000 BC

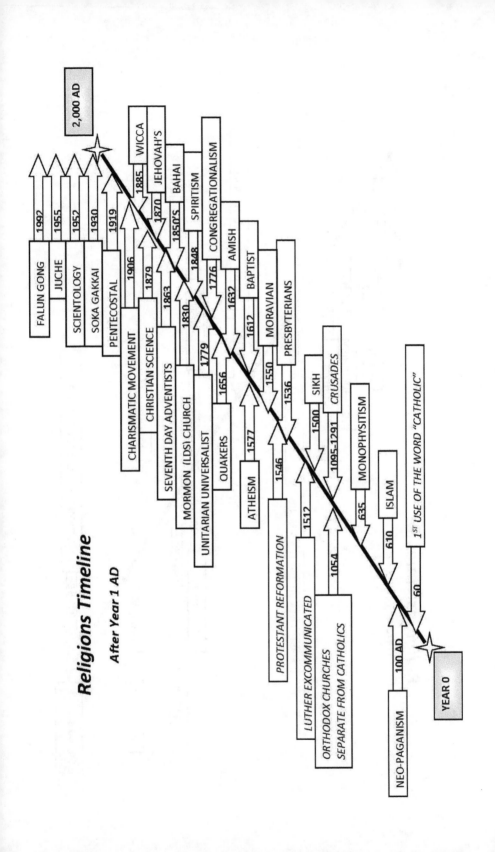

Religions Timeline

After Year 1 AD

Contents

Foreword

Having grown up as a Roman Catholic in the early 1950s, I was not exposed to any religions outside my tradition. Sadly, the prevailing attitude was that the other denominations were Christian but not Catholic, and even the study of their beliefs could harm your spiritual growth.

I loved the saints and had a devotion to St. Therese of the Child Jesus. She is called the Little Flower because she encouraged simple everyday spiritual practices. Because of my religious fervor, I thought I had a vocation to the religious life and joined a community of Franciscan sisters. But after four years, I grew to understand that I was following someone else's path and not my own, so I chose to leave the community, and my spiritual quest began in earnest.

Four decades later, after studying many traditions, I believe religion to be the external expression of our internal reality. Religion lives because it gives a voice to our personal spiritual truth. It is diverse because the human race is diverse. But there is only one spiritual truth hidden within the many voices. Finally, because it has the power to divide or unite humanity, depending on the attitude of the practitioner, it is the most important area of education.

Robyn Lebron has done an excellent job in encapsulating the major and many minor schools of religious thought. Beyond that, she has organized the material in a systematic way and presented the material in an easy-to-read format. Specifically, she examines the history; God/gods; Christ/Christ-figure; basic doctrine; their worship service; practices of baptism, confirmation, and marriage; how each group deals with the subject of death/afterlife; teachings on doctrines of judgment, salvation, and any other special doctrines. She highlights the minor differences between closely related religious groups and groups that have grown out of a previous, shared heritage.

The beauty of her work is in these facts: the material is current, unbiased, and easy to comprehend. Her extensive Internet sources are listed at the end of the book, and one can easily access further information in the pursuit of additional queries.

I strongly suggest reading Robyn Lebron's books as a small group and following up with discussion session. They are an ideal way to experience the multicolored dynamics of the prism effect that the religions of the world have had on the human experience. Some you will like, some you will smile benevolently at, and some are beyond your wildest imaginings. So enjoy the books. Theology is a means of enriching your life. I hope it enriches your life as it has added to mine.

—Sister Catherine Lohmann

Preface

One of the primary goals of these books is to bring knowledge and understanding of the world's religions and belief practices. The religions were originally selected by the number of members worldwide. Then the next criterion was the most unusual or misunderstood religions or spiritual practices. We have to keep in mind that as we read through the various chapters, some of them may seem over the top to us, but to the followers, it is a way of life, and they take it very seriously as we do with our faith practice. I feel that by understanding their faith, it may give us the ability to search for common ground. Another goal is to provide a source to people who might be searching for a spiritual practice that feels right for them.

When creating these books, every effort was made to be as accurate as possible with both research and documentation. I did try to be precise with dates and statistics, and it is important to understand how a faith developed. But the faith as it is today is what I was concentrating on. It is the core values and beliefs that I am trying to portray. There are literally hundreds of sources for research, and choosing among them was challenging. But more challenging was getting the important facts in while keeping the size manageable. If it appears that there is more detail on one religion versus another, it was purely based on the availability of information from different sources.

I also had some challenges getting permission to use some of my original research material, so there may be some faith practices that are not as detailed for that reason. In some cases, all attempts to obtain permission went unanswered, and in others, there was no contact information on the website or the e-mail address was invalid. If any permission was denied, their web address will still be listed for your future research, but their information was removed from the text. The comments in parenthesis are generally definitions, clarifications, or sometimes my effort to get the reader to think about the concept in comparison to a Christian faith practice. These comments are not the expressed feelings of the websites or their authors. *They are mine.*

I am not making any claim to the expertise of any of the websites, but I made efforts to find corroborating information whenever possible. In cases that the authors required specific recognition, I have tried to do so. In most instances, information was combined with all sources to create the final document. If any crucial information is not included in these studies, it is certainly not by design. The sources for these religions are listed should anyone like to pursue further study. The websites were wonderful sources, and their authors put a lot of work into them. I encourage you to visit them for more detailed information.

I would like to acknowledge all the people who posted the information on the Internet that I used in creating these texts for people to enjoy. I am in no way claiming credit for the information. In fact, the information on these pages is but a speck compared to what's available should one choose to go to the websites listed in the endnotes section. The reason for the extensive number of ellipses (…) is due to the fact that there was just not enough space to put the complete quotes in, but I tried to maintain the essence. The purpose of so many quotes was to preserve the core truths. For example, if someone paraphrased a Christian sacrament into "Christians eat bread on Sunday," the essence would be lost. Where there are direct quotes, there is a matching citation. If there is a citation without quotations, it is due to the fact that the information is not an exact quote. When the site's information was purely used for corroboration, and no direct quotes were taken, there is no citation given.

The fact that some sources are listed in the endnotes with details, and others are not, is not an attempt to show favoritism but was my effort to comply with that particular website's request for a specific citation. All of the websites were excellent resources, and I have listed only the home page that will lead into a world of information. I would encourage you to do additional research on your own. My only "claim to fame" will be that I spent over 4,000 hours searching, reading, and combining the information into a format that can be used by anyone— even those people who don't have access to the Internet. May these pages bring the world closer together in some small way!

Each religion has been broken down into the same specific categories to allow for comparison and additional insight:

- History
- God or gods
- Jesus Christ
- Basic Doctrine
- Basic Worship Service
- Infant Baptism or Blessing
- Initiation or Confirmation
- Marriage
- Death and Afterlife
- Judgment
- Special Doctrine

Throughout history, many of these religions have had moments in time when atrocities have been done in the name of righteousness. Keep in mind that these actions generally come about when the pure teachings are misinterpreted or manipulated by zealots and extremists of the time. It is with the desire to show the religions in their true, unadulterated light that these books were created.

Abrahamic Religions and Faith Practices

The first chapters we will go through are those religions that have some connection (no matter how small) to the Old and/or the New Testaments in the Bible. These religions have all sprung from the same basic roots of ancient faith practices and then evolved.

Amish and Mennonite

History

The Mennonite religious practice began with the sixteenth century Anabaptist movement in Europe. The Anabaptists were a group of religious reformers who felt the Protestant reformers of that time were not in line with their beliefs. A key difference was the issue of the baptism of infants. Anabaptists felt that one should be baptized after reaching an age of accountability, which was considered early adolescence, because they considered it paramount that the individual would be aware of the decision they were making. The name *Mennonite* came from a sixteenth century Dutch Anabaptist named Menno Simmons, who was originally a Catholic priest, who broke away after being disillusioned with the Catholic faith.

The Amish denomination or the Amish-Mennonite developed from a disagreement about the practice of shunning. It is a practice that had been adopted by the Mennonites in 1632, which demanded turning your back (literally and figuratively) on a fellow Mennonite who had transgressed their laws. A Swiss Mennonite by the name of Jacob Ammann had a stricter view of some of the practices that were developing, one being the laxity in the practice of shunning. He was also concerned about the belief that just being sympathetic to the faith but not joining it was enough to be saved. He stressed total simplicity and uniformity and an awareness of guarding against pridefulness. They also use nonmotorized vehicles as part of their call to simplicity and to discourage travel too far from the community. The group finally coalesced, and the first Amish group to settle in America was in 1727. The first Amish immigrants, for whom records are available—the Detweiler and Sieber families—settled in Berks County, Pennsylvania, in 1736. The bulk of this first wave of immigration had ceased by 1770.

During the religious revival that was spreading across the American colonies, the Amish were targeted by most of the other faith practices of that time.

The Amish have been shaped by a martyr tradition. Many of their religious forbears died for their faith. The persecution reinforced the biblical teaching of a cleavage between the church and the larger society. In Amish eyes, the kingdoms of this world, which use coercion, differ from the peaceable kingdom of God. Many Amish practices are based on the religious principle of separation from the world—that the practices of the church should be separate from the larger society.

The revivalists took a heavy toll on the Amish membership. By 1800, there were fewer than one thousand Amish in America.

A second wave of immigration from Europe lasted from 1817 to 1860. About three thousand Amish relocated to the United States. Most settled in Illinois, Indiana, Iowa, Missouri, New York, Ohio, and Ontario in Canada. A few went to Pennsylvania. The newcomers from Europe tended to be more progressive and liberal than those who were well-established in the United States. Some had partly abandoned the basic traditions of Amish life. Many were hardly recognizable to the Amish who were already here. Deviations included wearing buttons on their coats, owning a piano, dishes with decorations, decorated carriages, and fancy furniture, dressing their children in fancy clothes. Perhaps even more serious was the fact that many were more flexible on matters of doctrine and belief.

The church managed to remain united up until 1850, in spite of growing friction between liberals and conservatives. National meetings for Amish leaders were held in various settlements between 1862 and 1878. The intent was to strengthen church life and commitment. The attendance was small; and in spite of initial hope that they would bring harmony and a meeting of the minds, just the opposite occurred. All that transpired was a realization of the differences between the liberal and conservative factions within the Amish church. So the tensions worsened.

When separation came, it was not an event that one could point a date to or a specific event. Rather, it happened gradually, behind the scenes, over decades as individual families and congregations gradually sorted themselves out into the traditionalist and change-minded camps. The latter wanted change but could not reach a consensus on the details. By 1880, there were four Amish groups. All the groups operated independently from each other with variations in how they practice their religion, and religion dictated how they conduct their daily lives.

Over the years, there have been several issues that have affected the Amish population. Because they have continued to keep themselves separate from the rest of the world, and because they discouraged marriage outside the faith, they have a very small gene pool to work with. Due to this fact, they have started to develop some genetic issues within their communities. That being said, the percentage of people that leave the faith is extremely low. There have been a number of changes over the last few decades that have significantly impacted Amish culture. The rising cost of farm land has forced some Amish to take outside jobs while remaining in their community. Some developed home businesses, creating traditional Amish crafts for sale. Others founded commercial enterprises. Several Amish entrepreneurs operate health food stores that cater to the Amish as well as to their non-Amish neighbors.

"In the one-year period from 2009 to 2010, the Amish of North America show an estimated population growth of five percent, increasing from 237,500 in 2009 to 249,500 in 2010."[1] There are no more recent stats on line, however it is suggested that their birthrate alone would increase membership numbers approximately 20 percent per year. The Amish as a faith community were catapulted into the limelight in 2010 with the Lifetime Movie *Amish Grace*, based on the true story of the horrendous shooting of ten Amish school children in 2006. The emphasis on forgiveness and reconciliation in the response of the Amish community was widely discussed in the national media.

God or Gods

"Both Mennonites and Amish believe in one God eternally existing as Father, Son, and Holy Spirit. They believe that He is the Creator of all things visible and invisible; that He, in six days, created, made, and prepared, heaven and earth, and the sea, and all that in them is."[2] They believe that the Holy Spirit resides with them constantly and will give them a personal conviction of any sin they might commit. They also feel that the Holy Spirit prompts them and also empowers believers for service and holy living. They teach that salvation is by grace through faith in Christ, a free gift bestowed by God on those who repent and believe.

Christ

The Amish believe that Jesus Christ, God's only Son, who actually lived before John the Baptist, before Abraham, before the world, was and is the God of the whole world and the firstborn of every creature. Jesus shed His precious blood and died for all men, and by doing so, He destroyed the works of the devil, annulled the effects of the sin in the Garden of Eden, and obtained forgiveness of sins for all mankind. He is the cause of eternal salvation for all those who believe in and obey Him.

Basic Doctrine

The Amish support the basic Christian beliefs, but their overall spirituality and behavioral practices have been developed over time by their interpretation of the Bible as well as several other sources. The Bible is the inspired word of God, in addition to *Luther's German Bible*, the *Martyrs Mirror*, the *Ausbund*, and the *Dordrecht Confession of Faith*.

The *Ausbund* is the oldest Anabaptist hymnal and the oldest Christian song book in continuous use. It is used today by North American Amish congregations. The core of the *Ausbund* is based on fifty one songs written b y Anabaptists from Passau. Eleven of these songs were written by their leader, Michael Schneider. Twelve others may have been written by Hans Betz. The hymns were composed in the dungeon of Passau Castle, where the Anabaptists were imprisoned between 1535 and 1540 because of their convictions. Some—among them Hans Betz—did not survive the imprisonment. Many of these imprisoned Anabaptists were martyred."[3]

The *Dordrecht Confession of Faith* is a statement of religious beliefs adopted by Dutch Mennonite leaders at a meeting in Dordrecht, Netherlands, on April 21, 1632. Its eighteen articles emphasize belief in salvation through Jesus Christ, baptism, nonviolence, shunning those who leave the church, feet washing, and avoidance of taking oaths. It was an influential part of the Radical Reformation and remains an important religious document to many modern Anabaptist groups such as the Amish.

<u>Below are the eighteen articles:</u>

I. Of God and the Creation of All Things

II.   Of the Fall of Man

III.   Of the Restoration of Man Through the Promise of the Coming Christ

IV.   Of the Coming of Christ into This World, and the Purpose for Which He Came

V.   Of the Law of Christ, i.e., the Holy Gospel or the New Testament

VI.   Of Repentance and Reformation of Life

VII. Of Holy Baptism

VIII. Of the Church of Christ

IX.   Of the Election, and Offices of Teachers, Deacons, and Deaconesses in the Church

X.   Of the Holy Supper

XI.   Of the Washing of the Saints' Feet

XII. Of the State of Matrimony

XIII. Of the Office of the Secular Authority

XIV. Of Revenge

XV.   Of the Swearing of Oaths

XVI. Of the Ecclesiastical Ban, or Separation from the Church

XVII.   Of Shunning the Separated

XVIII.   Of the Resurrection of the Dead, and the Last Judgment

Luther's German Bible, The Martyrs Mirror, the *Ausbund,* and the *Dordrecht Confession of Faith* are the key sources for their beliefs. The Amish stress the importance of practicing their faith over teaching formal theological doctrines. They seek to follow the teachings of Jesus in daily life by loving their enemies and forgiving insults. They emphasize the teachings of Jesus in the *Gospel of Matthew,* especially the Sermon on the Mount. They also emphasize peace and justice while maintaining concern for the needs of others. They have a keen sense of missionary work with a theology of relief and material aid to people in want. "They believe that each congregation—called a "district"—is to remain autonomous. There is no centralized organization to enforce beliefs and behaviors."[5]

Each Amish congregation is served by a bishop, two ministers, and a deacon. Worship services are held in community members' homes where walls are designed to be moved aside for large gatherings. The Amish feel that traditions bind generations together and provide an anchor to the past.

They are taught to be separate from the outside world, citing scriptures such as *"Be not unequally yoked with unbelievers"* (2 Corinthians 6:14), *"Come out from among them and be ye separate, saith the Lord"* (2 Corinthians 6:17), and *"Be ye not conformed to this world, but be ye transformed by the renewing of your mind that ye may prove what is that good, and acceptable, and perfect, will of God"* (Romans 12:2). Even within the Amish communities, there is separation. More liberal Amish groups such as the Beachy Amish, who drive automobiles, are widely seen as non-Amish by other Amish groups and are considered outsiders. Smaller differences between groups such as how many suspenders to wear or how many pleats to put in a bonnet are considered minimal and inter-marrying between the two groups are allowed.[6]

Health care practices vary considerably across Amish communities and from family to family. Many Amish use modern medical services, but others turn to alternate forms of treatment. They cite no biblical injunctions against modern health care or the latest medicines, but they do believe that God is the ultimate healer. Compared to the non-Amish, Amish people are less likely to seek medical attention for minor aches or illnesses and more apt to follow folk remedies and drink herbal teas. Although they do not object to surgery or other forms of high-tech treatment, they are less inclined to use heroic life-saving interventions, and are reticent to intervene when their elderly face terminal illness. They are, in short, more willing to yield to the mysteries of divine providence. In addition to home remedies, members often seek other forms of unorthodox medical treatment. Their search for natural healing often leads them to vitamins, homeopathic remedies, health foods, reflexologists, and chiropractors.[7]

Basic Worship Service

An Amish worship service is devoted to prayer, to praising God, singing of hymns and to reading the word of God. The Bible of choice varies by congregation. It may be the *New International Version* or the *New Revised Standard Version.* The more conservative communities still use the *King James Version* or even the *German Luther Version.* The length of the service doesn't seem to be a concern for the members and can vary from thirty minutes to two and a half hours. They are always focused on Christ and living a Christlike life each day. The Holy Communion is only held twice a year. Held each autumn and spring, it frames the religious year and is considered a rite in which they receive the body and blood of Christ in the form of bread and wine, as an assurance the God has forgiven their sins.

These ritual high points emphasize self-examination and spiritual rejuvenation. Sins are confessed and members reaffirm their vow to uphold the *Ordnung* at a council meeting held prior to the communion service. Communion is held when the congregation is "at peace"; that is, when all members are in harmony. The eight-hour service includes preaching, a light meal during the service, and the commemoration of Christ's death with bread and wine. Pairs of members wash each another's feet as the congregation sings. At the end of the service, members give an alms offering to the deacon. This is the only time that offerings are gathered in Amish services.[8]

Infant Baptism or Blessing

Smaller, more conservative groups do not have a formal celebration for the birth of a child. Larger groups have a "child consecration," which can be held when the child is an infant or a toddler. During this service, the minister blesses the child and the parents; the congregation then responds to an invitation to help raise the child in a Christian environment.

Initiation, Baptism, or Confirmation

In most denominations, baptism is held for males and females in early adolescence but can occur anytime through adulthood. Prior to baptism,

Amish teenagers are encouraged to sample life in the outside world, in a period referred to as *rumspringa* (Pennsylvania Deutsch for "running around"). They still follow the beliefs and rules of their upbringing, but there is a relaxed attitude during this period of experimentation. During this time, many Amish teenagers use this time for a chance to date and take part in other wholesome fun, and some may dress "*English*" (what they call non-Amish people), smoke, talk on cell phones, or drive around in automobiles. Rumspringa ends when the youth requests baptism into the church or chooses to permanently leave Amish society.

Most young people take their baptismal vows between 18 and 22 years of age, during a Sunday morning service that follows several weeks of instruction for the candidates. The decision to join the church is the big decision for Amish youth. This lifelong romise before God and other members means that they will be accountable to the church for the rest of their lives. If they renege on vows and stray from the church, they face excommunication and shunning.[9]

At a service prior to the baptisms, the congregation agrees to accept the applicants as brothers and sisters. It is crucial that the candidates acknowledge that they are making a promise for life. This is one of the founding principles of waiting until the age of accountability. It is precisely because they join the church after they know the difference between right and wrong that they are expected to live up to their commitment and to the rules of the faith. They also accept th e fact that if they fail, church discipline will follow. During the ceremony, the candidate expresses their commitment to Christ in a kneeling position, while the minister sprinkles or pours water on their heads three times in the name of the Father, Son, and Holy Ghost.

Marriage

They believe that marriage was instituted by God for companionship, procreation, and the nurturing of children. The ceremony is considered an act of worship in which the couple confesses their love and commitment to each other before God and asks for His blessings on the union. A wedding is a particularly joyous occasion, for two baptized members of the church are joining in marriage, continuing the faith, and starting a new family together.

While parents do not select who their children will marry, approval must be given, and the deacon usually acts as the go-between. They involve the entire Amish community. A couple's engagement is usually kept secret until just a few weeks before the wedding, when their intentions are published in church. Amish marry Amish—no intermarriage is allowed. Divorce constitutes a basic violation of God's will and is not permitted, and separation is very rare.

In common with many conservative Christian faith groups, their family life has a patriarchal structure. Although the roles of women are considered equally important to those of men, they are very unequal in terms of authority. Unmarried women remain under the authority of their father. Wives are submissive to their husbands. Only males are eligible to be become Church officials.[10]

Death and Afterlife

Death is regarded as part of God's plan. Those who die obedient will share in the resurrection and be with Christ forever. At the resurrection, Christ will create a new heaven and a new earth in which righteousness will reign.

Judgment and Salvation

They believe that since the imagination of man's heart is evil from his youth, and, therefore, prone to all unrighteousness, sin, and wickedness, the first lesson of the precious New Testament of the Son of God is repentance and reformation of life, and that, therefore, those who have ears to hear and hearts to understand must bring forth genuine fruits of repentance, reform their lives, believe the Gospel, eschew evil and do good, desist from unrighteousness, forsake sin, put off the old man with his deeds, and put on the new man, which after God, is created in righteousness and true holiness.

For neither baptism, supper, church membership nor any other outward ceremony can, without faith, regeneration, change, or renewing of life, avail anything to please God or to obtain of Him any consolation or promise of salvation. But people must go to God with an upright heart, and in perfect faith, and believe in Jesus Christ, as the scripture says and testifies of Him—through which faith we obtain forgiveness of sins, are sanctified, justified, and made children of God.

Concerning the resurrection of the dead, they believe that in the last day, all men who shall have died shall be awakened and shall rise again through the power of God. And that they, together with those who then will still be alive and who shall be changed in the twinkling of an eye at the sound of the last trump, shall be placed before the judgment seat of Christ, and the good be separated from the wicked. Then everyone shall receive in his own body according to what he hath done, whether it be good or evil, and that the good or pious, as the blessed, shall be taken up with Christ and shall enter into life eternal and obtain that joy, which eye hath not seen, nor ear heard, neither hath entered into the heart of man to reign and triumph with Christ forever.

The unrighteous will suffer the anguish of eternal hell; the righteous will inherit the kingdom of God. For Evangelicals and other conservative Protestants, salvation is automatic when one trusts Jesus. The Amish are different.

They don't believe that anyone is guaranteed salvation as a result of a conversion experience, baptism, joining the church, etc…they would consider it arrogant or prideful to claim certainty of salvation. The Amish believe that God carefully weighs the individual's total lifetime record of obedience to the church and then decides whether the person's eternal destiny will be the reward of Heaven or the punishment in Hell.

If a person is baptized into the Amish church and later leaves the church or is excommunicated, they believe they have no hope of attaining heaven.

Special Doctrine

Biblical principles are applied in daily practice through the *Ordnung*. The Ordnung consists of district-specific regulations, usually unwritten, that are passed on by practice and oral tradition. The regulations apply the biblical principle of "separation from the world" to issues such as clothing, use of mass media, technology, and leisure activities. The regulations both require and suggest appropriate behavior. For example, as part of their Ordnung, the Old Order Amish forbid owning an automobile; tapping electricity from public utility lines; owning a television, radio, or personal computer; attending high school or college, joining the military; and initiating divorce.

They reject involvement with the military or warfare. They believe that Amish must never resort to violence or to take up arms in war. However, they do not generally view themselves as pacifists, because this would involve them in political action to promote peace. Their rejection of violence does not extend to the disciplining of their children.[11]

"The Amish emphasize the biblical teaching of mutual aid, urging church members to help each other in times of difficulty or disaster. Thus, they decline to participate in government-operated Social Security and commercial insurance coverage, which they view as undermining their faith in God and dependence on the church community."[12] The Amish believe strongly in education through the eighth grade and only in their own private schools. The Amish a e exempt from state compulsory attendance beyond the eighth grade based on religious principles, the result of a 1972 US Supreme Court ruling. One-room Amish schools are private institutions operated by Amish parents. Schooling concentrates on basic reading, writing, math, and geography, along with vocational training and socialization in Amish history and values. Education is also a big part of home life, with farming and homemaking skills considered an important part of an Amish child's upbringing.

All Amish groups expect men and women to wear prescribed clothing. Married men are expected to grow a beard but not a mustache and to wear an Amish-style hat and vest. Women are expected to wear a head covering and usually a three-piece dress that includes a cape and an apron. Unlike the broader American culture, where dress is often used to express personal preferences, dress among the Amish signals submission to the collective order and serves as a public symbol of group identity.

The Ordnung discourages members from joining public organizations or service clubs in their communities. Some of them, however, are members of local volunteer fire companies and emergency medical units. Members agree to obey the Ordnung at the time of baptism, with the clear understanding that they will be subject to church discipline, and perhaps excommunication, if they break that vow.

Major Differences Between Amish and Mennonite

Although there are no absolutes, generally speaking, the Amish lean toward the more conservative rules in all things. The Mennonites hold many of the same beliefs as the Amish, although they tend to be less conservative than their Amish neighbors. Most Mennonites have relaxed dress codes and have gotten away from farm-related occupations. While old-order Mennonites still drive their all-black carriages, most Mennonite groups do permit the use of cars and electricity. However, some groups do require that car bodies and trim be painted black.

Many people mistakenly think that all those who *look* Amish are Amish. In fact, many plain-dressing groups have Anabaptist roots but are not Amish. There are numerous plain-dressing Mennonite groups, including some who use horse-and-buggy transportation and others who use cars, tractors, electricity, and other forms of modern technology in their homes, farms, and businesses. Various Brethren groups such as the *Old German Baptist Brethren,* the *Old Brethren,* the *Dunkard Brethren,* and the *Old Order River Brethren* wear plain clothing and practice a traditional lifestyle.

Like some of the Plain Mennonites, members of these groups also own cars and tractors and use electricity and other forms of modern technology in their homes, farms, and businesses. The men in some of these Brethren groups wear beards, which easily leads to confusion with the Amish. Most of these plain groups forbid divorce and the ordination of women. They typically select laymen to lead their congregation. They do not use musical instruments in their worship services and seek to uphold traditional patterns of religious ritual. Most, but not all, of the plain groups worship in meetinghouses, but they are simple, modest buildings without steeples, stained glass, and ornate furnishings.

It is risky to talk about the Amish and to make generalized statements about all Amish groups in North America based on one

Amish community. Typically, most Amish groups forbid owning automobiles, tapping electricity from public utility lines, using self-propelled farm machinery, owning a television, radio, and computer, attending high school and college, joining the military, and initiating divorce. Members are expected to speak a German or Swiss dialect and to adhere to the dress standards of their group. Most groups have battery-powered lights on their carriages but the most conservative affiliations use kerosene lanterns.

The vast majority of Amish homes have indoor bathrooms but members in the most traditional groups walk to an outhouse. In some regions of the country, power lawn mowers are permitted but not in others. The women in one affiliation are permitted to use only treadle (foot-powered) sewing machines, but those in another group may power their sewing machines with batteries. Some communities are wealthy and others are rather poor. Clearly, diversity abounds even within affiliations and local church districts.[13]

Notes

Roman Catholic

History

<u>The Early Church:</u> The word catholic with a lower case "c" (Greek, *katholikos*) means "universal" and has been used to designate Christian churches since its earliest period, when it was the only Christian church. The Roman Catholic (capital "C") Church regards itself as the only legitimate inheritor of the commission and powers conferred by Jesus Christ on the twelve apostles.

As one of the oldest branches of Christianity, along with Eastern Orthodoxy, the history of the Roman Catholic Church plays an integral part of the history of Christianity as a whole. By its own reckoning, the Church began on the first Pentecost when the Holy Spirit descended on the apostles and disciples in the upper room. Jesus had earlier stated that He would entrust to Simon Peter the keys of the kingdom of heaven after being singled out and revealed by God the Father that upon the "rock" of Peter, Jesus would found His Church.

Christian tradition records that the Christian church in Rome was jointly founded by Saints Peter and Paul, and that Peter was its first bishop. It is on this foundational basis of scripture that the Catholic Church believes the pope is the successor of Saint Peter and the singular leader of the whole true church on earth. As the apostles of Jesus Christ spread the Gospel, they provided the beginning structure for the early Christian church. It is impossible to separate the initial stages of the Roman Catholic Church from that of the early Christian church. Saint Ignatius of Antioch (35–110 AD) is one of the chief apostolic fathers and early Christian authors who reportedly knew the apostles personally. He was the third bishop or patriarch of Antioch and a student of the apostle John.

The Roman authorities hoped to make an example of him and thus discourage Christianity from spreading. He was sentenced to die in the arena, but his journey to Rome offered him the opportunity to meet with and teach Christians along his route. En route to his martyrdom in Rome, Ignatius wrote a series of letters to the churches in the region and one to a fellow bishop, which have been preserved as an example of the theology of the earliest Christians. The letters of St. Ignatius have proved to be important testimony to the development of Catholic theology.

Ignatius is the first known Catholic writer to put great stress on loyalty to a single bishop in each city, who is assisted by both presbyters (elders/ priests) and deacons. Earlier writings only mention either bishops or presbyters. St. Ignatius stressed the value of the *Eucharist* (communion or sacrament), calling it a "medicine of immortality" in about 106 AD. He was also the first to coin the name *"Catholic Church"*: "Wherever the bishop appears, there let the people be; as wherever Jesus Christ is, there is the Catholic Church. It is not lawful to baptize or give communion without the consent of the bishop. On the other hand, whatever has his approval is pleasing to God. Thus, whatever is done will be safe and valid."[1]

In 380 AD, Roman Catholicism became the official religion of the Roman Empire. During the following one thousand years, Catholics were the only people recognized as Christians by the Catholic Church.

The Church Organizes and Builds Power: The First Council of Nicaea, held in Bithynia (present-day Iznik in Turkey), convoked by the Roman Emperor Constantine I in 325 AD, was the first ecumenical council of the Christian church, and most significantly resulted in the first uniform Christian doctrine, called the *Nicene Creed.* (See Creeds) A special prominence was also attached to this council because the persecution of Christians had just ended with the February 313 *Edict of Milan* by Emperors Constantine and Licinius. The long-term effects of the Council of Nicaea were significant. For the first time, representatives of many of the bishops in the Church convened to agree on doctrinal statements.

The Christian Church spent its first three centuries as an outlawed organization and was thus unable to hold or transfer property. Early Christian churches congregated in the audience halls of well-to-do individuals, and a number of Early Christian churches built around the edges of Ancient Rome were ascribed to patrons who held the property in custody for the Church. After the ban of property ownership was lifted by the Emperor Constantine I, the Church's private property grew quickly through the donations of the pious and the wealthy.

Other donations soon followed, mainly in mainland Italy but also in the provinces, but the Church held all of these lands as a private landowner, not as a sovereign entity. The seeds of the Papal States as a sovereign political entity were planted during this period.

With effective Byzantine power weighted at the northeast end of this territory, the Bishop of Rome, as the largest landowner and most prestigious figure i n Italy, began by default to take on much of the ruling authority in the area around the city of Rome. While the Bishops of Rome—now beginning to be referred to as the Popes—remained de jure Byzantine subjects, in practice, the Duchy of Rome became an independent state ruled by the Church; an area roughly equivalent to modern-day Latium (Latium was a region of ancient Italy, home to the original Latin people. Its area constituted a part of the much larger modern Italian Region of Lazio).

The cooperation between the papacy and the Carolingian dynasty climaxed in 800 AD , when Pope Leo III crowned Charlemagne the first emperor of the Romans. However, the precise nature of the relationship between the popes and emperors was not clear. Over the next two centuries, popes and emperors squabbled over a variety of issues. The major motivation for the Gregorian reform was to free the administration of the Papal States from this constant imperial interference. The Gregorian reform was a series of reforms initiated by Pope Gregory VII and the circle he formed in the papal curia, 1050–1080 AD, which dealt with the moral integrity and independence of the clergy. It was based on his conviction that the Church was founded by God and entrusted with the task of embracing all mankind in a single society in which divine will is the only law; that, in her capacity as a divine institution, she is supreme over all human structures, especially the secular state; and that the Pope, in his role as head of the Church under the petrine commission, is the vice-regent of God on earth, so that disobedience to him implies disobedience to God.[2]

Other Denominations Start to Break Away: In 1054 AD, a formal split occurred between the Roman Catholic and Eastern Orthodox churches largely over disagreements regarding papal primacy.

This division remains in effect today. By 1300, the Papal States, along with the rest of the Italian principalities, were effectively independent, but indeed it took until the sixteenth century for the pope to have any genuine control over all his territories. There was a large period in history after when corruption and atrocities were taking place and bishops were misusing their positions in the church to gain power and fortunes.

The Protestant Reformation was a movement in the Holy Roman Empire that began in 1517, though its roots lay further back in time. The Reformation involved cultural, economic, political, and religious aspects. The movement began as an attempt to reform the Catholic Church. Many western Catholics were troubled by what they saw as false doctrines and malpractices within the Church, particularly involving the teaching and sale of *indulgences* (buying your way into heaven).

Another major contention was the practice of buying and selling church positions and what was seen at the time as considerable corruption within the church's hierarchy. This corruption was seen by many at the time as systemic, even reaching the position of the pope. The Protestant Reformation took real hold with Martin Luther and ended with the *Peace of Westphalia* in 1648. Luther's spiritual predecessors were men such as John Wycliffe and Jan Hus. Other radicals, such as Ulrich Zwingli and John Calvin, soon followed Luther's lead.

Church beliefs and practices under attack by Protestant reformers included purgatory, particular judgment, devotion to Mary (*Mariology*), the intercession of and devotion to the saints, many of the sacraments, the mandatory celibacy requirement of its clergy (including monasticism), and the authority of the pope. The first denominations to emerge directly from the Reformation were the Lutherans, the Reformed Calvinists, Presbyterians, and the Anabaptists.

The Modern-Day Catholic Church: "Toward the latter part of the 17th century, Pope Innocent XI attempted to reform abuses by the Church, including simony (the buying and selling of church positions and indulgences), nepotism and the lavish papal expenditures. At that same time secular powers gained control of virtually all major Church appointments as well as many of the Church's properties."[3]

Direct attacks on the wealth of the church and associated grievances led to the wholesale nationalization of church property and attempt to establish a state-run church. Large numbers of priests refused to take an oath of compliance to the National Assembly, leading to the church being outlawed, and this ushered in a new era called the age of reason" (the era in which philosophy, logic, ethics, and politics grew in public consciousness). In this period, all monasteries were destroyed, thirty thousand priests were exiled, and hundreds more were killed. The pope was imprisoned by French troops and died in 1799 after six weeks of captivity. Just two years later, to win popular support for his rule, Napoleon reestablished the Catholic Church in France through the *Concordat of 1801.*[4]

In the Americas, the church expanded its missions in cooperation with the Spanish government and military. "Pope Gregory XVI, challenging Spanish and Portuguese sovereignty, appointed his own candidates as bishops in the colonies, condemned slavery and the slave trade and approved the ordination of native clergy in spite of government racism. In 1870, the First Vatican Council affirmed the doctrine of Papal infallibility when exercised in specifically defined pronouncements."[5]

During World War II, Pope Pius XI warned Catholics that anti-Semitism is incompatible with Christianity. However, the war presented challenges for the Catholic Church after historians such as David Kertzer accused it of encouraging centuries of anti-Semitism and Pope Pius XII of not doing enough to stop Nazi atrocities.

The Second Vatican Council (1962–65), initiated by Pope John XXIII, became one of the major influences on the Catholic Church in the second half of the twentieth century. It intended to engage the Church more closely with the present world, which was described by its advocates as an "opening of the windows." It led to changes in liturgy within the Latin Church such as worship in the vernacular (local language), changes to the Church's approach to ecumenism, and a call to improved relations with non-Christian religions.[6]

Pope John Paul II acknowledged past sins of the Church against Jews, and in 2000 formally apologized to the Jewish people by inserting a prayer at the Western Wall that read, "*We're deeply saddened by the behavior of those in the course of history who have caused the children of God to suffer, and asking your forgiveness, we wish to commit ourselves to genuine brotherhood with the people of the Covenant."*[7]

The nineteenth and twentieth century brought more challenges to the Catholic Church: people breaking away from traditional doctrine, abortion, contraception, capital punishment, homosexuality, ordination of women, sexual allegations, and the Pentecostal revival. Soon after the close of the Second Vatican Council, church teachings about sexuality became an issue of increasing controversy due to changing cultural attitudes in Europe and the United States. In his encyclical *Humanae Vitae* (1968), Pope Paul VI rejected all artificial contraception (though he permitted the regulation of births by means of natural family planning), contradicting those voices in the Church that saw at the time the birth control pill as an ethically justifiable method of contraception. This teaching was continued especially by John Paul II in his encyclical *Evangelium Vitae,* where he decried contraception and abortion as well as euthanasia as symptoms of a "culture of death"and called for a"culture of life." Efforts to ordain women have also caused controversy in the church. Opposition groups such as *Roman Catholic Women Priests* (an independent Catholic international group that asserts a connection to the Catholic Church) have performed alleged ordination ceremonies for women, claiming the aid of a Catholic bishop in performing the rites. The Roman Catholic Church's canon law bars ordination of women, stating that *"a baptized male alone receives sacred ordination validly."* The Church sees this as not merely a matter of changeable law, but something that it cannot alter. Pope John Paul II wrote in his *Apostolic Letter Ordinatio Sacerdotalis* of May 22, 1994: *"We declare that the Church has no authority whatsoever to confer priestly ordination on women and that this judgment is to be held by all the Church's faithful."* In 2007, the *Vatican Congregation for the Doctrine of the Faith* ,with the necessary authorization of the pope, decreed the penalty of automatic excommunication against anyone who attempts to confer a sacred order on a woman and the woman who attempts to receive a sacred order."

Another more damaging issue has been that of child abuse cases. Clerical sexual deviancy allegations have been made against a variety of religious groups including but not exclusively Roman Catholic priests, monks, and nuns. *The John Jay Report*, commissioned by the US Conference of Catholic Bishops, found accusations against 4,392 priests in the United States, equaling about four percent of all US priests between 1950 and 2002.

Figures supplied by the Catholic League promote the view that abuse statistics in the Catholic Church are similar to abuse in other institutions such as the preliminary estimate of education abuse statistics compiled by the US Department of Education. From a legal perspective, the most serious offense, aside from the incidents of child sexual abuse themselves, was the active institutional cover-up by the Roman Catholic Church's most senior church leaders, failing to report these felonies to the police and often moving the priests who had received complaints from church to church in order to protect them.

In response to the failure to report abuse, lawmakers have changed the law to make reporting of abuse to police compulsory in most states. Some incidents involved diocesan priests and members of the various Roman Catholic religious orders, with reports coming from the United States and Ireland, although there are cases cited in a total of nineteen countries. Cases involved seminaries, schools, orphanages, and other institutions where children were in the care of clergy. Criticism of the church and its leadership focused on the failure to act upon information; some allegations have led to successful prosecutions of the accused, as well as civil cases settling for millions of dollars.

The American Catholic Church has paid out $2 billion in abuse costs since 1950. In fact, there have been five dioceses in the United States that have had to file for either Chapter 11 or bankruptcy due to huge payouts. However, it is important to note that abuse by priests was occurring long before the start of Vatican II and that many of the Roman Catholic sex abuse cases did not involve pedophilia. For instance, the apostolic constitution that established general notice of the problem of sexual abuse amongst the clergy was published by Pope Benedict XIV in 1741.

he late Pope John Paul II took a number of steps to address the problem of priestly formation. On March 25, 1992, he completed an apostolic exhortation, one of the longest papal documents in history.

This explored the crisis of priestly identity, the renewal of priestly life, and the reform of seminaries in detail. Some have attributed the scant number of abuse allegations from the 1990s as evidence that the late pope's reform efforts were fruitful.

Philip Jenkins, a conservative Episcopalian and professor of history and religious studies at Penn State University, published the book *Pedophiles and Priests: Anatomy of a Contemporary Crisis* in 1996. His 2002 article *"The Myth of the 'Pedophile Priest'"* expresses his views: *"My research of cases over the past 20 years indicates no evidence whatever that Catholic or other celibate clergy are any more likely to be involved in misconduct or abuse than clergy of any other denomination–or indeed, than non clergy. However determined news media may be to see this affair as a crisis of celibacy, the charge is just unsupported."* During a recent visit to the United States, Pope Benedict admitted that he is "deeply ashamed" of the clergy sex abuse scandal that has devastated the church. Benedict pledged that pedophiles would not be priests in the Catholic Church.

The Church was propelled into the spotlight again in 2012 when they openly opposed the employer mandate in the *Patient Protection and Affordable Care Act*, requiring religious organizations to provide contraceptives for their employees, which they felt contradicted their religious beliefs. With the new pope Francis and his down-to-earth ways, the Catholic Church has seen a rejuvenation. He is deeply loved by Catholics and non-Catholics alike. The dignity of the human person is a central theme running throughout Catholic social teaching. Pope Francis said the church is "something else." The disciples do not make the church—they are the messengers sent by Jesus. And Christ was sent by the Father: *'The Church begins there ,"* he said, *"in the heart of the Father, who had this idea...of love. So this love story began, a story that has gone on for so long, and is not yet ended. We, the women and men of the Church, we are in the middle of a love story: each of us is a link in this chain of love. And if we do not understand this, we have understood nothing of what the Church is.* "9

Even with all the turmoil, the Catholic Church still remains the largest single body composed of Christians who acknowledge the supreme authority of the pope in matters of faith. There is no way to determine if membership has been affected since once you have been baptized, you remain a member for life. It is estimated that there are 1.29 billion Roman Catholics throughout the world today.

God or Gods

The Catholic Church is trinitarian since it believes that there is one eternal God who exists as a mutual indwelling of three persons: the Father, the Son, Jesus, and the Holy Spirit.

Roman Catholics believe Mary was without sin. Roman Catholics believe Mary remained a virgin after the birth of Jesus, that she did not have any other children. They believe Mary is queen over all things in heaven and on earth, and because Mary is the mother of God, prayers and petitions are to be made to her. Roman Catholics believe Mary is the mother of mercy, the all-knowing one; Mary is involved in saving us (Mary saves us in the sense that through her, Jesus Christ became incarnate and thus was able to do all that He did for our salvation). Because of this, they refer to Mary as the mediatrix for salvation because Chirst suffered the passion of the cross in the flesh that He assumed from her. And Mary's name is to be honored like God's name.

Christ

In an event known as the *Incarnation* , the Church teaches that, through the power of the Holy Spirit, God became united with human nature when Christ was conceived in the womb of the Blessed Virgin Mary. Christ is believed, therefore, to be both fully divine and fully human. It is taught that Christ's mission on earth included giving people His teachings and providing His example for them to follow as recorded in the four Gospels. The Church teaches that through the passion (suffering) of Christ and His crucifixion as described in the Gospels, all people have an opportunity for forgiveness and freedom from sin, and so can be reconciled to God. The Resurrection of Jesus, according to Catholic belief, gained for humans a possible spiritual immortality previously denied to them because of original sin. By reconciling with God and following Christ's words and deeds, the Church believes one can enter the Kingdom of God, which is the...Reign of God over people's hearts and lives.[10]

Basic Doctrine

"According to the Catechism, the Catholic Church professes to be the "sole Church of Christ," which is described in the Nicene Creed as the One, Holy, Catholic, and Apostolic Church."[14] Catholics believe that they are the continuing presence of Jesus's ministry on earth, and that the bishops are successors to the apostles. The Catholic Church believes that both the Bible and church are both necessary, and one cannot exist without the other. But they believe the church and the pope to have ultimate authority. Nowhere in the Bible does it say that the Bible is the only source of information available to a Christian.

Women in the Priesthood: The church has specified that they only will ordain male priests, but will in some congregations have female deaconesses, but they can only minister to other women. The Catholic Church defines its mission as spreading the message of Jesus Christ found in the four Gospels, administering sacraments that aid the spiritual growth of its members and the exercise of charity.

Satan and His Minions: Catholics believe that Satan is thriving in this world of materialism. His master plan is to fool everyone. He has even succeeded in fooling some religious people and clergy into believing he does not exist anymore. If no one believes he exists, he is free to use us as he pleases. It is time to look around and see Satan for who he is and, with Jesus Christ, fight back. Satan knows our weaknesses. He knows how to hurt us and how to get to us by customizing each attack.

He loves to use other people (as many as he can) to hurt us. He is the master of lies and deceit and uses and influences weaker people to lie and twist things to suit his needs. Evil spirits (the third of hosts cast out of heaven) like to get involved in the little things of the day because they can lead to bigger things. Small irritations can escalate into anger and frustration. Disappointment can become envy and self-pity. These sins can often have their roots in the demonic. Through them, evil spirits can keep Christian's lives off balance, stifle their relationships, and move them toward more opportunities to sin.

<u>Salvation</u>: Because of its roots in Christ's ministry, the Church teaches that the fullness of the "means of salvation" exists only in the Catholic Church but acknowledges that the Holy Spirit can make use of Christian communities separated from itself to bring people to salvation. It teaches that anyone who is saved is saved indirectly through the Church if the person has invincible ignorance of the Catholic Church and its teachings (as a result of parentage or culture, for example), yet follows the morals God has dictated in his heart and would, therefore, join the Church if he understood its necessity.[11]

<u>Confession</u>: One who desires to obtain reconciliation with God and with the church must confess to a priest all the grave sins he remembers after having carefully examined his conscience. The confession of venial faults, without being necessary in itself, is nevertheless strongly recommended by the church. Once an individual goes to confession and states the sin aloud with a contrite heart to one whom God has given authority, it is guaranteed that a cleansing will immediately follow, as well as a strong sense of forgiveness.

Confession gives the penitent a fresh start to work with a strong passion to never commit the sin. The Catholic Church advocates deathbed repentance and the granting of sacramental absolution. They consider it the first step in the process of preparation for death. It is the means of reconciliation with God and the most indispensable factor in helping the soul to qualify for its departure from the body.

<u>Transubstantiation</u>: The earliest known use, in about 1079, of the term *transubstantiation* to describe the actual change from bread and wine to the body and blood of Christ was by Hildebert de Savardin, Archbishop of Tours. This was long before the influence of Saint Thomas Aquinas. In 1215, the Fourth Lateran Council used the word transubstantiated in its profession of faith, when speaking of the change that takes place in the Eucharist. In 1551 the *Council of Trent* officially defined that "by the consecration of the bread and of the wine, a conversion is made of the whole substance of the bread into the substance of the body of Christ our Lord, and of the whole substance of the wine into the substance of His blood; which conversion is, by the holy Catholic Church, suitably and properly called Transubstantiation."[11]

His blood; which conversion is, by the holy Catholic Church, suitably and properly called Transubstantiation."[11]

In 1965, some Catholic theologians pushed to have the doctrine changed, but their request was rejected by Pope Paul VI. This belief is controversial to this day.

Basic Worship Service

The Catholic Mass revolves around the *Eucharist*—the bread that becomes Jesus on the altar and the wine that becomes His blood. When the priest places his hands over the bread and wine, He summons the Holy Spirit to make them holy and make these gifts into the literal flesh and blood of Jesus.

Roman Catholics believe the sacraments of the Roman Catholic Church are required for a person to have salvation and to be forgiven of their sins. Because the church teaches that Christ is present in the Eucharist, there are strict rules about its celebration and reception. The ingredients of the bread and wine used in the Mass are very specific. Also Catholics must abstain from eating for one hour before receiving Communion. Those who are conscious of having committed a sin are forbidden from this sacrament unless they have received absolution through the sacrament of confession and penance. "Catholics are not permitted to receive the Eucharist as celebrated in Protestant churches, which in the view of the Catholic Church lack the sacrament of *Holy Orders*. Likewise, Protestants are not normally permitted to receive communion in the Catholic Church."

During the service, scriptures from the Bible will be read and a sermon given that is generally related to the topic of the scriptures read. *The Nicene Creed* is always recited at Sunday Masses and is the core statement of Catholic Christian belief. Most Catholic Masses would qualify as high church. This basically means that it is not uncommon to have incense, bells, candles, and special attire for the priests, deacons, and anyone else who serves on the altar. Some churches do the whole service in Latin, but it is more common to see a mixture of Latin and English.

"According to the Council of Trent, Christ instituted seven sacraments and entrusted them to the Church. These are Baptism,

Confirmation, the Eucharist, Reconciliation (Penance), Anointing of the Sick (formerly called Extreme Unction, one of the "Last Rites"), Holy Orders and Holy Matrimony."[12]

Infant Baptism or Blessing

Before one can receive any other sacrament in the Catholic Church, they must receive the sacrament of Baptism. Holy Baptism is the basis of the whole Christian life. One must be baptized with both water and the Holy Spirit, and being baptized is what secures eternal salvation. Baptism occurs at six to eight weeks old, and the priest pours water over the infant's head and baptizes them in the name of the Father, the Son, and the Holy Ghost. It washes away all sins, both original sin (humanity's state of sin resulting from the Fall of Adam) and personal actual sins.

Initiation, Baptism, or Confirmation

Catholics are taught that Christ presented the first confirmation to His apostles on Pentecost when He gave them the Holy Spirit. In the same way that Christ strengthened His apostles to face the world through the Holy Spirit, confirmation also prepares us to go into the world armed with graces from above to preach and confirm their Catholic faith. Confirmation is sometimes called the "sacrament of Christian maturity" and is believed to increase and deepen the grace received at baptism and occurs generally between the ages of seven and eighteen. To be confirmed, Catholics must be in a state of grace, in that they cannot be conscious of having committed a mortal sin. They must also have prepared spiritually for the sacrament, chosen a sponsor or godparent for spiritual support, and selected a saint to be their special patron and intercessor.

Marriage

Catholics believe the consent by which the spouses mutually give and receive one another is sealed by God. The covenant between the spouses is integrated into God's covenant with man. Thus the marriage bond has been established by God himself and can never be dissolved. This bond is henceforth irrevocable. The Church does not have the power to contravene. However, Catholics are not excommunicated from the church if they get a divorce. The Catholic Church realizes that situations arise when a married man and woman can no longer live together, such as in the case of an abusive spouse or harm to the children of this union. The Church suggests in such cases that the two live apart, they are however still married in the eyes of the Church. It is possible for such a couple to have a divorce in the eyes of civil authorities but not in the eyes of God. Only through death is the sacramental marriage dissolved. If both spouses remain separated and do not marry they may receive all the sacraments of the church. If one spouse does remarry then he or she in turn is committing adultery and is not permitted to participate in the sacraments of the church. The Church, after an examination of the situation by the competent ecclesiastical tribunal, can declare the nullity of a marriage, i.e., that the marriage never existed. In this case the contracting parties are free to marry, provided the natural obligations of a previous union are discharged.[13]

Death and Afterlife

Roman Catholics believe *Purgatory* is a place in which people have to go to purge out their own sins, which the blood of Jesus Christ does not atone for. In other words, Christ can grant you eternal life, but you still must "pay for your sins." There are certain sins that people have to take care of themselves in order to be saved. All who die in God's grace and friendship but still imperfect are assured of salvation, but after death, they undergo purification so as to achieve the holiness necessary to enter the joy of heaven (Catechism paragraph 1030).

The Church gives the name purgatory to this final purification of the elect, which is entirely different from the punishment of the damned (Catechism paragraph 1031). Heaven is the state of everlasting life in which we see God face-to-face, are made like unto Him in glory, and enjoy eternal happiness. Those who have been purified will be rejoined with their bodies and join Christ and the angels in a celestial paradise. "Hell is a state to which the wicked are condemned, and in which they are deprived of the sight of God for all eternity, and are in dreadful torments."[14]

Judgment and Salvation

The teaching of the church affirms the existence of hell and its eternity. Immediately after death, the souls of those who die in a state of mortal sin descend into hell, where they suffer its punishments—eternal fire (*Catechism* paragraph 1035). The chief punishment of hell is eternal separation from God for which we long.

Catholics believe salvation is only available through the one true church, that being the Roman Catholic Church. Outside the church, there is no salvation. Basing itself on scripture and tradition, the council teaches that the church is necessary for salvation. They believe that if a person knows of the Catholic Church and either chooses not to join or joins and leaves, that person will not be saved. Those who, through no fault of their own, have never heard of the Gospel of Christ or His church, but who seek God with a sincere heart and try to do what's right as they understand it, through the dictates of their conscience, may achieve eternal salvation. Catholics do believe that works will get them to heaven accompanied by faith and God's grace.

Special Doctrine

Prayers to the Saints: Catholics ask the saints to mediate for them. A saint is someone who has lived their life so perfectly in the service of God that they changed others around them while they were alive on earth. Their example was exemplary. The logic is that the saints are closer to God than we are here on earth. They feel that the saints' prayers are a lot stronger than our own because they are perfected and in heaven with God.

The Pope: Roman Catholics believe that the pope is head over the church in all authority and power and is infallible when it comes to doctrine.

The office of the pope is known as the Papacy. His ecclesiastical jurisdiction is often called the *"Holy See"* or the *"Apostolic See"* (meaning the See of the Apostle Saint Peter). The pope is also head of state of Vatican City State. Following the death or resignation of a pope, members of the College of Cardinals...meet in the Sistine Chapel in Rome to elect a new pope. They will stay locked in the chapel until they get a majority vote for one man. The title Cardinal is a rank of honour bestowed by Popes on certain ecclesiastics, such as leaders within the Roman Curia, bishops serving in major cities and distinguished theologians. Although this election, known as a papal conclave, can theoretically elect any male Catholic as Pope, since 1389 only fellow Cardinals have been elevated to that position.[15]

The Rosary: The rosary is a prayer and meditation on the life of Christ. The early Christians did not have Bibles and by saying the Rosary they were meditating on Christ's life. The actual Rosary beads merely assist the individual reciting the prayer to help keep track of where they are in the meditation.

The Rosary consists of four mysteries. Prayer's recited are:

- *The Joyful Mysteries:* The Annunciation (Lk. 1:30–31); The Visitation (Lk. 1:42); The Birth of Jesus (Lk. 2:7); The Presentation of Jesus in the Temple (Lk. 1:22); The Finding of the Child Jesus in the Temple (Lk. 2:46)
- *The Sorrowful Mysteries:* The Agony in the Garden (Mk. 14:32); The Scourging of Jesus at the Pillar (Mk. 15:15); Jesus Crowned with Thorns (Mk. 15:17); Jesus Carries his Cross (Jn. 19:17); The Crucifixion (Mk. 15:24)
- *The Glorious Mysteries:* The Resurrection of Jesus (Mt. 28:5–6); The Ascension of Jesus (Acts 1:9); The Descent of the Holy Spirit (Acts 2:2); The Assumption of Mary in Heaven (1 Thes. 4:14); The Crowning of Mary (Rev. 12:1)
- *The Luminous Mysteries:* The Baptism of Jesus in the River Jordan (Mt. 3:17); The Wedding at Cana, Christ Manifested (Jn. 2:11); the Proclamation of the Kingdom of God (Mk. 1:15); The Transfiguration of Jesus (Mt. 17:2); The Last Supper, the Holy Eucharist (Mt. 26:26)[16]

<u>The Veneration of Mary:</u> Prayers and devotions to Mary are part of Catholic piety but are distinct from the worship of God. The Church holds Mary, as Perpetual Virgin and Mother of God, in special regard. Catholic beliefs concerning Mary include her Immaculate Conception without the stain of original sin and bodily assumption into heaven at the end of her life, both of which have been infallibly defined as dogma, by Pope Pius IX in 1854 and Pope Pius XII in 1950 respectively. *"Mariology"* deals not only with her life but also her veneration in daily life. Pope Paul VI called her Mother of the Church, because by giving birth to Christ, she is considered to be the spiritual mother to each member of the Body of Christ. Because of her influential role in the life of Jesus, prayers and devotions, such as the Rosary, the Hail Mary, the Salve Regina and the Memorare are common Catholic practices.[17]

<u>The Crucifix:</u> Non-Catholics believe that Christ is risen from the dead and does not belong on the cross. Catholics agree that Christ rose from the dead, but He did not want us to forget what He did for us and our miserable sins. Only because Jesus died upon the cross does the cross then become a sacred object. The crucifix is a reminder for us that it was our sins that nailed Him to the cross. May Christians wear crosses, but it is mostly Roman Catholics that wear crucifixes (a cross with Jesus still on it).

Notes

Charismatic Movement*

"We understand that the church of Jesus Christ is one that has a variety of expressions of Christian faith according to the values of the Kingdom of God. Each expression complements another. Accordingly, we understand that together with the people of the charismatic movements we are members of the body of Christ. As such it is crucial that we are willing to learn from one another, support each other, help each other and correct each other whenever necessary, about how we live as churches of Jesus Christ in our time in which the people and creation are crying for healing and salvation."

—Dr. Wilson Niwagila, United Evangelical Mission

History

Charis is, in English, derived from the Greek word for grace. *Mata* is the Greek word meaning gifts. *Charismata*, then, means "grace gifts," and the charismatic movement is the term given to the Christian movement that has swept across denominational lines, reaching its peak—at least in America—during the 1970s. What began on a corner at the turn of the twentieth century is now barreling down Main Street. The Charismatic movement is one of the most popular and growing forces within Christendom today. The major doctrinal distinctives of the Charismatic movement—the baptism in the Holy Spirit, tongues-speaking, prophecy, the gift of healing, and the emphasis on having a personal experience—are primary reasons for the movement's growth and popularity. The Charismatic movement is a twentieth-century phenomenon. While the Charismatic movement has taken on wings during the twentieth century, similar views and manifestations can be found on occasion throughout other periods in history.

---

* Within many of these religions there are subgroups. Because of space constraints, the subgroup with the highest number of members was the primary focus, and the other subgroups would be briefly described within the text of the religion.

In ancient times the practice of speaking in unintelligible languages during religious ecstasy was not unknown. From Egypt in the eleventh century BC, there is evidence of ecstatic speech, and later in the Greek world the prophetess of Delphi and the sibylline priestess spoke in unknown tongues. Amongst the Roman mystery religions, the Dionysian Cult was known for this practice. During the Middle Ages speaking in tongues was reported in monasteries of the Orthodox Church. Several of the early church fathers mention glossolalia in the church. Irenaeus and Tertullian speak favorably of it, Chrysostom disapproved, and Augustine declared that the gift was only for New Testament times. The Montanist movement of the late second century included prophetesses, claims of new revelation, speaking in tongues, and an ascetical and legalistic outlook; the movement was declared heretical by the official church and speaking in tongues seems to have been rare in the church after this time.[1]

In the seventeenth century, it seems to have been practiced in France amongst the Protestants and the pietistic Catholics.

Then the Azuza Street Revival of 1906–13 was the launching pad for a worldwide Pentecostal renewal. The main feature of this Pentecostal outpouring was the "baptism with the Holy Spirit," an experience subsequent to salvation, which is evidenced by speaking in other tongues. This Pentecostal movement arose mainly from within various Protestant churches, but they were soon forced out, either because of their unusual beliefs and practices or, in some cases, because they felt unhappy in churches that had become liberal theologically and worldly in position and practice. At least two things can be said for most of these early Pentecostals—they utterly repudiated the liberalism of the ecumenical movement and would not condone mixing the world with the church.

Pentecostal religion continued to span the globe through the 1930s, but by the mid-1940s, as the careers of many independent evangelists peaked, there was a "new" emphasis, the miraculous! "Spirit baptism" was still preached, but it was no longer the major focus of the revival meeting. Another one of the notably significant, yet controversial, phenomena to initially emerge with Pentecostalism is the doctrine and ministry of divine healing. Since the latter half of the nineteenth century, the practice of healing existed in America. This energized Pentecostalism nourished independent evangelists who brought a new emphasis to the healing arena that attracted a popular following. The shared heartbeat of "every service was the miracle—the hypnotic moment when the Spirit moved to heal the sick and raise the dead." The significance of the deliverance (healing) revival reached its zenith between 1947 and 1958.

Pentecostal denominations, such as the *Assemblies of God,* did not favor the revival and viewed the deliverance evangelists as independent extremists. Pentecostal leaders were disgusted by the lack of integrity among the revivalists, who often made claims marked by absurd exaggeration. The display of alleged miracles had become so outlandish that some revival meetings had turned into personality cults. Historian David Harrell quotes one Pentecostal leader who reported: *"The healing evangelists live in constant dialogue with angels and demons, the Holy Spirit and the spirits of diseases from the abyss; some experience electric currents through their hands when they pray with the sick, others have a halo around their heads when they are photographed, and others again have oil appearing on their hands when they pray."*

Up until the 1950s, this movement was on the fringes of religion in modern society. The few denominations that espoused this doctrine were not part of the mainstream of religious groups. Beginning in about 1960, interest in the biblical concept of spiritual gifts, including speaking in tongues, began spreading to congregations that had historically been in the mainstream, including the Roman Catholic Church and many Protestant groups. Rather than align themselves with the Pentecostal groups, they preferred to refer to themselves as a charismatic renewal within their own denominations. Even when some found themselves at odds with those in their old denominations and were forced to form new outside groups, most preferred to retain the designation charismatic. From the late 1950s, many charismatic Christians went on to form separate churches and denominations, for which the appropriate term is neocharismatic.[2]

Most historians date the beginning of the "official" Charismatic movement as April 3, 1960. On this day, Father Dennis Bennett of

St. Mark's Episcopal parish in Van Nuys, California, announced to his congregation that he had received the fullness and power of the Holy Spirit and how this accompanied "speaking in unknown tongues." After receiving much opposition, Bennett resigned from his position at St. Mark's and accepted an invitation to become vicar of St. Luke's Episcopal Church in Seattle, Washington, which grew to be one of the strongest charismatic churches in the northwest. For a decade, it was one of the major centers from which speaking in tongues would spread worldwide, especially in the mainline denominations.

Beliefs similar to Pentecostalism emerged in the historic Protestant denominations from 1960 onward, and in the Catholic Church, from 1967, opened up a Pandora's box in the Christian world. An important characteristic of the Charismatic movement at that time was willingness for the believer, after discovering the importance of spiritual gifts, to remain within their original denomination. Within the Charismatic movement, the commitment was embedded within the full variety of historic denominations, and so in each context, theology, culture, and acceptance varied enormously.

The movement, with all the holiness fever was now present within mainstream churches of traditional, upper-middle-class membership. Catholics, Episcopalians, Presbyterians, Methodists, and Baptists: all denominations began to experience, within their individual churches, the same phenomenon. It would typically begin with a few people feeling the need for a deeper, more fulfilling s pirituality w ithin t he context of the tradition in which they were raised. Meeting in living rooms—often without clergy, who were sometimes suspicious of the movement—people would pray together and suddenly find themselves speaking in tongues, gripped by a fever of emotional fulfillment and a sense of God's presence. It was as if the Holy Spirit had taken control of them. The feeling of being right with God, totally in the present and cleansed of all sin was one hardly ever experienced in formal church services. It was pure, simple, heartfelt religion, experienced rather than intellectualized. It swept the nation. *The PTL* (Praise the Lord) *Club* hosted by Jim Bakker started its two-hour daily television run. Pat

Robertson began *The 700 Club* and Jimmy Swaggart had a host of radio stations airing his show, and the Oral Roberts ministry aired once again.

Charismatic preachers and ministries dominated religious television in many parts of the country. Amazingly enough, the charismatic influence has reached even into the most traditional denominations, including the Episcopalians in the United States and Anglicans throughout the world. A Roman Catholic charismatic movement has thrived since the 1970s. More recently, questions of charismatic influence within the Southern Baptist Convention have been raised.

The Latter Rain Movement was a loosely directed and enthusiastic union of co-belligerents united by their fierce opposition to mainline denominations. This meteoric movement created quite a stir among Pentecostal denominations, like the Assemblies of God, and boasted of being a fresh revival displacing the apostatized Pentecostals. While its impact was on a small scale, its effects were nevertheless felt worldwide, and it became one of the several catalysts for the Charismatic movement of the 1960s, the *Independent Charismatic Movement* (Word-Faith/Positive Confession charismatics) of the 1970s, and the New Charismatics surfacing in the 1980s and 1990s. In reaction to the spiritual dryness existing in Pentecostal circles, the New Order of the Latter Rain viewed itself as a refreshing oasis returning to the full gospel of the first-century church.

During the period of 1975–2000, there were many charismatics within established denominations, but many have left or have been forced out and have joined either more progressive Pentecostal churches or formed their own churches or denominations. *The House Church Movement* in the UK and the *Vineyard Movement* in the USA are examples of a formal charismatic structure. *The Hillsong Church* in Australia is an example of a Pentecostal church that has embraced charismatic belief and practices, which has, in turn, influenced the Australian Assemblies of God denomination. They are heavily involved in the *Joyce Meyers Ministries*, which is also part of the Charismatic Christianity movement. In New Zealand, the preeminent Pentecostal movement has been the *New Life Churches*, although other local and international Pentecostal denominations are also well-established.

"Many clergy began to feel they had somehow missed the boat by failing to meet the spiritual needs of congregations who had grown used to a formal, spit-and-polish religion of the mind, not the emotional outburst of tongues-speaking Pentecostal power. Many clergy felt left out. They had prayed for so long that the church would be revived. Now it was happening, either in spite of them or without them."

In time, most evangelicals came to accept the Charismatic movement and many of its practices. It is no longer unusual to see charismatics of many faiths—Baptists, Catholics, Episcopalians, Lutherans, as well as nondenominationalists—raising their hands and arms in prayer, and singing, dancing, and shouting in the Spirit. They believe we are one of many congregations that represent the church of Jesus Christ. They are not part of a denomination in the traditional sense. There seems to be a consistent effort to have and value relationships with other pastors and Christian leaders in the community.

Although charismatic outpourings continued to spread through mainline churches, many denominational leaders left traditional churches to start independent churches. Before long, these mushrooming churches came under the influence of *Word-Faith/Positive Confession* teaching, propagated by independent charismatics. Their main emphasis was faith teaching, divine healing, and financial prosperity. Believers who consistently made a positive confession about their physical and spiritual situation and demonstrated great faith would receive abundant blessings from God.

Since the mid-1980s, the Charismatic movement has made some notable changes in its theology and emphases. This process has been termed the *Third wave of the Holy Spirit* and has been typified by the ministry of C. Peter Wagner, *Word of Faith* theology. There appears to be a great deal of evidence showing that, since 1975, these recent trends have been influenced heavily by the Latter Rain Movement of the 1950s within the Pentecostal churches—a movement that was officially declared heresy by the Assemblies of God at the time. This can be explained by the desire of charismatic Christians to enter into fellowship with those within the church who have experienced similar forms of religious ecstasy.

As a result of this, charismatics came into contact with both mainstream Pentecostalism as well as the Latter Rain Movement. It appears that modern-day charismatics and Pentecostals are far more united in experience and theology because both movements have adopted elements of Latter-Rain teachings.

The Charismatic movement now spans much of the globe, incorporating traditional Pentecostals, the Assemblies of God, the Vineyard Movement, and new-wave phenomena including purported prophets and apostles. Central to the movement is the claim that a new visitation of the Holy Spirit has brought back the apostolic gifts and manifestations of the New Testament. With an emphasis on a second blessing after conversion, the movement is calling all Christians to catch the wave.

Religious movements come and go. The American segment of the Charismatic movement peaked and began to level off. Worldwide, however, especially in Asia, Latin America, and Africa, Christianity with a charismatic cast is growing as rapidly as Islam and, in some cases, more rapidly. Since this movement is not an established church, but a movement working within the existing churches, it has raised many theological questions from the mainline churches.

In 2000, the Charismatic movement numbered 176 million; neo-Charismatics, 295 million; and Pentecostals, 66 million. This means that charismatics are the second largest branch of Christianity after the Roman Catholic Church. They are 27 percent of all Christians. As of 2008, according to Barna surveys, one out of every four Protestant churches in the United States, 23 percent is a charismatic congregation. A slight majority of all born-again Christians, 51 percent, are charismatic. Nearly half of all adults who attend a Protestant church, 46 percent, are charismatic. Charismatics are growing at the rate of 9 million per year making. Based on figures obtained from Adherents. com, the Charismatic Movement now encompasses approximately 631 million people.

God or Gods

They believe there is one God who lives forever in three persons: the Father, Son, and Holy Spirit. Because this is a movement that spans across many denominations, there will be variations.

Christ

They believe in the deity of Jesus Christ, in His virgin birth, in His sinless life, in His miracles, in His vicarious and atoning death through His shedding of blood, and in His bodily resurrection. It is the same Christ who, through His life, death, and resurrection, saves and forgives the lost, who also, through His exaltation to the right hand of the Father, sends forth the Holy Spirit upon the redeemed. So it is by the same faith that both turning from sin and empowering for ministry are to be received from Him.

Basic Doctrine

Because the Charismatic movement is not *monolithic* (consisting of a single denomination), it cannot easily be examined or judged as one entity. As a result, vast theological differences can be found in the movement, with some parts appearing to have quite orthodox beliefs while others seem to embrace more heterodox ideas. Virtually all charismatic Christians believe that the presence of God can be experienced in a supernatural way by believers, usually during times of intense spiritual reflection (such as during a worship service, a small group meeting, or personal prayer). The singing of praise songs is an important element in this belief.

Most of the theology behind the Charismatic movement comes from the apostle Paul. In *1 Corinthians 12*, he offers a list of the gifts of the Spirit given by God: wisdom, knowledge, faith, healing, miracles, prophecy, discernment, tongues, and interpretation of tongues. In *Romans 12*, he adds the gifts of serving, teaching, encouraging, contributing, leading, and showing mercy. An additional gift of self-control is referred to in *1 Corinthians 7:7*.

The term charismatic used in a Christian context primarily refers to a Christian theological position or doctrine. As secondary usage, the terms charismatic Christian and renewalist can be umbrella terms used to describe those modern Christians who are in agreement with this theological position and believe that the manifestations of the Holy Spirit seen in the first-century Christian church are available to contemporary Christians and may be experienced and practiced today. They include Pentecostalism, the Charismatic movement, and neo-Charismatics. The Charismatic movement has grown rapidly and has become more diversified, therefore, it would be misleading to place all under an identical banner.

The teachings of charismatic churches can vary from one to another. This is because it is a <u>movement</u>, not an organization. Also, sometimes it is difficult to ascertain what a particular church teaches since many don't have published confessions of faith. Thus, you can't be sure what is taught and believed till you're into the movement. It is because of this emphasis on feelings, rather than intellect, that it can sometimes be difficult to talk to people involved in these movements about their beliefs. The reason for this nonintellectual attitude relates to how people get involved in these movements in the first place. Many have come out of a "dead" Christian background. In other words, many in these movements came out of Christian backgrounds that they did not find emotionally fulfilling. So they are looking for an experience or a direct connection with the spiritual.

Many of the prominent Christians who are viewed as charismatic, like Oral Roberts, Larry Lea, Earl Paulk, Dick Iverson, Kenneth Copeland, Kenneth Hagin, Bob Tilton, etc., are proclaiming today that the Charismatic movement is over, and God's new move is underway. This new restorational movement advocated by most current charismatics has generated a groundswell of charismatic leaders to open themselves up to new spiritual revelations and deeper doctrinal truths. The theological menu served in most charismatic churches today is filled with novel ideas, new doctrinal teachings, and unusual practices. Most refer to this thriving new development expanding throughout the world as restorationism or Latter-Rain restorationism.

The doctrinal system of the Latter Rain included baptism of the Spirit with the evidence of speaking in tongues and the deliverance revivals' miraculous healing thrust. But the fiery movement had its own distinctives as well. There were primarily four new teachings that shaped the Latter Rain:

- The teaching that God is restoring apostles and prophets to the church to function with the three other gifted offices: evangelists, pastors, and teachers. Apostles and prophets provided direction with new revelations that would play a major role in paving the way for Christ's second coming.
- It views the practice of personal prophecy as being restored to the church. Prophecy would no longer be restricted to general words of exhortation but would include personal detailed revelations for guidance and instruction.
- The belief that God's manifested presence is dependent upon a certain order of worship, involving singing in tongues, clapping, shouting, singing prophecies, and a new order of praise dancing. This is considered to be true worship.
- Laying on of the hands is a ritual performed by modern apostles and prophets to impart the Holy Spirit and other spiritual blessings and gifts.

Most Christian groups would have no disagreement that many individuals among them have particular gifts—sometimes referred to as talents. These may be natural gifts they seem to have been born with. In addition, most groups will not dispute some such gifts may have been enhanced by God through the power of the Holy Spirit so that the person can use the gift more effectively to serve among the fellowship of Christians.

Specifically in the matter of speaking in tongues, a number of groups (but not all), which are historically defined as Pentecostal, have made this manifestation an absolute prerequisite to salvation. They do not view it as merely one of the spiritual gifts that may be given to a Christian. They believe it to be the sign of true conversion. On the other hand, most charismatic groups believe that it is the privilege of all

Christians to speak in tongues. Thus, a person who has not yet spoken in tongues but who has professed Christ, and perhaps even been baptized in water, would still be considered a brother or sister in Christ.

They believe that history is moving toward a spiritual climax, where God's power will be poured out on the church like never before. Restoration promoters believe that this new move could be the Lord's final move, where the church will be imbued with new power to Christianize the world before Jesus returns. Some contemporary restoration movements that fall under the umbrella term The New Charismatics are *Kingdom Theology,* the *Word-Faith/Positive Confession Movement,* and the *Third Wave or Signs and Wonders* movement. These groups have a common bond that promotes God's moving in a new supernatural way through signs and wonders that the church must be restored to first-century apostolic Christianity before Jesus returns, and that modern apostles and prophets will play a key role in this process.

The new Charismatics are proclaiming that a new supernatural move of God's Spirit is sweeping the entire globe. This new move will be so revolutionary that the entire course of human history will soon be changed. But in order for this glorious dream to work, the majority of the Christian churches must unite in philosophy and purpose. In other words, charismatics subscribing to new restoration ideas deeply desire that all believers will taste this new move of the Holy Spirit and unite with them in their efforts to supernaturally transform the world.

For the most part, Charismatics have an enthusiasm for the things of God. They have a freedom and a boldness to praise the Lord in public and in private. They are not ashamed to speak of the Lord before both Christians and non-Christians. They are usually excited about spiritual things. They are often enthusiastic about sharing what they have found with others: "My friend, I want you to have what I have."

They seem to have a spiritual dynamic which is sadly lacking among some Bible believers. When you think of Charismatic people you normally do not think of deadness. These people are lively and enthusiastic and excited and emotional and vibrant. They often have a zeal for serving the Lord, though, as we shall see, their zeal is often not according to knowledge. Often this is the way we were when we first came to know Christ as our personal Savior, but as the years pass by we tend to lose some of this. It is easy to leave our first love. As we grow in knowledge we must be very careful not to lose our zeal for Christ and our enthusiasm to make Him known to others. Often Charismatic people exhibit a type of joy and happiness. They seem to be enjoying what they are doing. Their religion is not a dead ritual. It is personal and real to them. They do what they do because it is meaningful to them and because they enjoy it. They often show a warmth and concern for one another. They are friendly and outgoing and are generally not afraid to talk to others about the Lord and what He has done for them. The Bible and prayer are important to them. They like to get together in their small prayer groups and Bible study times. They enjoy getting together for fellowship and prayer and praise and singing. Some question the fact that they sometimes let their personal experiences govern how they interpret the Bible, but they should be commended for their interest in the Scriptures and for their desire to have a personal and real relationship with the Savior.[3]

"Shared Beliefs: Pentecostals, the Charismatic Movement and neo-Charismatics share major narratives; among these are a common belief in the way God works in revival, and the power and presence of God, evidenced in the daily life of the Christian believer." Pentecostals and charismatics are characterized by their practice of speaking in other tongues and operating the gifts of the Spirit. A Pentecostal believer in an ecstatic religious experience may vocalize fluent unintelligible utterances or articulate an alleged natural language previously unknown to the speaker.

Differences: Many churches influenced by the Charismatic movement deliberately distanced themselves from Pentecostalism, however, for cultural and theological reasons. Foremost among theological reasons is the tendency of many Pentecostals to insist that speaking in tongues is necessary for Baptism in the Holy Spirit. Pentecostals are also distinguished from the Charismatic movement on the basis of style. Additionally, many in the Charismatic movement employ contemporary styles of worship and methods of outreach which differ from traditional Pentecostal practice."[4]

Basic Worship Service

Most charismatic groups have a tendency to have worship services, which are lively and quite interactive. Rather than just a message by one designated pastor, a variety of participants may contribute words of encouragement, prayer requests, praise reports, prophetic words they believe to have been inspired on the spot by God, and so on. The music that many charismatic congregations use for praise and worship may be loud and enthusiastic and very rhythmic at times, with an emphasis on contemporary music rather than the historical hymns of the more formal religious denominations.

With regards to the sacrament, the charismatic beliefs are fairly traditional. The feast, as it was celebrated in the Bible, was always eaten with two simple elements, bread and the fruit of the vine. Though the elements are only natural food, the Lord has made clear that they represent Christ's body and blood. They believe that we, who are saved, who are covered by the blood of the Lamb, and who are part of the Body of Christ, are instructed at this time to judge ourselves rightly so that we will not be judged (*1 Corinthians* 11:31). Thus, we are provided a special time for repentance. We should be examining our lives. We should not hesitate to set things right with our fellow believers and with the Lord.

The movement has been characterized by its acceptance of the importance of speaking in tongues, divine healing, and prophecies as part of the grace of the power of the Holy Spirit; most meetings are for prayer and spirited singing and shouting. Anointing the sick with oil is also often part of worship service.

Infant Baptism or Blessing

This may vary based on the denomination in question.

Initiation, Baptism, or Confirmation

One of the hallmarks of the Charismatic movement is what is called *Spirit-baptism* or the baptism in the Holy Spirit. The baptism in the Holy Spirit is regarded as an experience that usually happens after conversion. Most charismatics would say that at conversion, a Christian receives the Holy Spirit. But only at the subsequent baptism in the Holy Spirit does the Christian receive the fullness of the Spirit, the full empowerment for Christian service. (They believe the gifts of the Holy Spirit have never ceased and are operational today. These include the word of wisdom, the word of knowledge, faith, healing, miracles, prophecy, discerning of spirits, speaking in other tongues, and the interpretation of other tongues.)

Many but not all charismatics believe that Spirit-baptism is always accompanied with the gift of speaking in tongues as evidence for the baptism. Spirit-baptism is considered a second work of grace; that is, one can be a genuine Christian, yet not be baptized in the Holy Spirit. They believe Holy Spirit baptism is a separate experience and does not necessarily take place when a person is saved or is baptized in water.

Charismatics teach that believing in Jesus Christ is not enough for the fulfilled Christian life. They believe that the second work of grace is necessary for true spiritual fulfillment. The gift of the Holy Spirit, wherein Spirit baptism occurs, is understood as an act of God's sovereign grace. Accordingly, the gift may be received only through faith in Jesus Christ, who is the mediator of the gift and the baptism. Participants in the Charismatic movement emphasize the centrality of Christ (not the Holy Spirit) and the unique instrumentality of faith in Him. It is viewed as an event wherein the believer is filled with the presence and power of the Holy Spirit.

Baptism with the Holy Spirit is understood to result from the gift of the Holy Spirit, wherein the Spirit is freely poured out, falls upon, anoints, or endures the believer with power from on high. This experience is the moment of initiation into the Spirit-filled life. Spirit baptism is said to occur either at the time of conversion (through repentance and forgiveness) or subsequent thereto. Baptism with the Holy Spirit, accordingly, is not identified with conversion. It is viewed as a being filled with the Holy Spirit that brings about powerful witness to Jesus Christ. Charismatics generally hold that conversion and the gift of the Spirit, though they are both received by faith, may or may not happen at the same time.

Marriage

There m ay b e d enominational v ariations, b ut b asically t hey b elieve t he scriptures teach that marriage is the covenanting together of one man and one woman in a union to the exclusion of all others. This union is established by an authorized ceremony under God. Marriage is a unique reflection of God's faithful love for all humankind. The relationship of husband and wife, as family, reflects the covenanting self-giving love between Christ and His Bride, the Church. The pledge of mutual faithfulness is not tentative or conditional. The permanent nature of the marriage bond gives security and promotes the development of a trusting relationship. The church has a responsibility to care for, nurture, and prayerfully support the marriage relationship and the children of the union.

Death and Afterlife

This doctrine will vary based on denomination.

Judgment and Salvation

They t each the d octrine t hat the c hurch w ill a ttain u nity i n t he f aith before Christ returns. "The b elief t hat t hose b elievers m oving i n t he truth of Latter-Rain restoration, not necessarily all in the church will attain an immortal state before Jesus returns."[5]

The Word of God teaches that our salvation package is full and complete. When you received Christ by faith (*John* 1:12), you also received all that comes with Christ, including the following:

- Complete forgiveness of sins,
- Membership in the body of Christ,
- Entrance into the family of God,
- Peace with God, and
- The gift of eternal life.

Most charismatics believe that for salvation of the lost and sinful man, regeneration by the Holy Spirit is absolutely essential. They teach that Christians can lose their salvation because of sin. They find it hard to define which sins or how much sin causes one to lose his salvation, but they believe that Christians fall in and out of salvation based upon their behavior. What this basically teaches is that one's behavior must be changed or improved to get salvation back once it is lost, and this is salvation through works.

Special Doctrine

Prosperity and Health: A prominent teaching of the Charismatic movement is that Christians close to God are always physically blessed by God. Many other faiths teach the concept physically as God blessing His faithful servants with peace, joy, contentment, gratitude, etc. However, the Charismatic movement teaches that one's spirituality can be measured by his outward, physical circumstances. In other words, if one is healthy and/or physically prosperous, God is with him and vice versa.

"*For as he thinks in his heart, so is he*" (*Proverbs* 23:7). This verse is core to their teachings regarding positive thinking/confession. Healing comes as a direct result of perceiving ourselves as whole. Charismatics believe that the miraculous gifts, including faith healing, are available today. Therefore, they believe that dramatic miracles are still occurring in the church. The Bible teaches that signs are public, visible, miraculous events. Their purpose was not to give believers exciting worship services or a wonderful experience but to authenticate a divine message or messenger, to prove publicly that the person performing miracles was sent from God.

Speaking in Tongues: It is understood to be not irrational but suprarational (not listed in Webster's, but used in this context to mean transcending established boundaries) utterance. It is not the forsaking of the rational for the nonsensical, hence, gibberish, but the fulfillment and transcendence of the rational in the spiritual.

Charismatics are not disturbed by linguists who claim that glossolalia has no observable language structure, for if such were the case, speaking in tongues would not be spiritual but rational speech. Further, speaking in tongues is not viewed as ecstatic utterance, in the sense uncontrolled, highly emotional, perhaps frenzied activity. While containing a strong emotional element, glossolalia runs deeper than the emotions. Both reason and emotions are aspects of the human psyche, whether on the conscious or subconscious level. Speaking in tongues is thus understood to be transpsychical—it belongs to the realm of the spirit.

Most persons in the Charismatic movement view speaking in tongues as directly connected with the event of Spirit baptism. The scriptures in Acts, which specifically record speaking in tongues (2:4, 10:46, 19:6), state that it occurred with persons who had just received the gift of the Holy Spirit. Hence, most charismatics believe that there can be no speaking in tongues without prior Spirit baptism. The reason would seem to follow from the very nature of baptism in the Spirit: a fullness of the Spirit that overflows into transcendent prayer and praise. Also, these very tongues may thereafter become an ongoing part of the life of prayer and worship. Charismatics differ over whether or not tongues in the assembly are a form of direct revelation from God.

Prophecy: Thus far we have seen that most charismatics have redefined prophecy as something less revelational and authoritative than what occurred in the days of the apostles. By claiming that prophecy is less revelational and authoritative than scripture, they claim that they are not adding to scripture. Most charismatics also believe that God speaks to each Spirit-filled Christian directly. Phrases common in charismatic circles are "God told me to do this," "The Spirit led me to do that," and "Jesus spoke to me and told me such and such."

Other Denominations That Have Been Affected by the Charismatic Movement: While it is difficult to locate the place and time that Charismatic Christianity began to influence the mainstream churches, Dennis Bennett, an American Episcopalian, is often cited as the movement's seminal influence, when he announced to the congregation in 1960 that he had received the outpouring of the Holy Spirit. Soon after this he was ministering in Vancouver where he ran many workshops and seminars about the work of the Holy Spirit. This influenced tens of thousands of Anglicans world-wide and also began a renewal movement within the Roman Catholic and Orthodox churches.

In fact, if one is able to speak in tongues, or if he has experienced a supposed healing, he is accepted by the charismatics with little or no regard to his church affiliation or doctrinal deviation. When you hear Roman Catholics talk about how their baptism in the spirit has given them a greater love for the Mass, the mystic prayer chants of the Rosary, the pope and the worship of Mary, they believe that this can be attributed to the true Holy Spirit.

In the 1960s and 1970s there was a renewed interest in the supernatural gifts of the Spirit in mainstream churches such as the Episcopal, Lutheran and Catholic churches. The *Catholic Charismatic Renewal* was focused in individuals like Kevin Ranaghan and his group of followers at the University of Notre Dame in South Bend, Indiana. Dennis Bennett was Ranaghan's counterpart in the Episcopal Church.

On an international level, David du Plessis along with a host of others (including Lutheran and even Southern Baptist ministers) promoted the movement. The latter did not last long with their denominations, either volunteering to leave or being asked to do so. But in the Episcopal and Catholic churches, priests and ministers were permitted to continue on in their parishes, provided they did not allow these concerns to create major divisions within their congregations.

Lutherans: Larry Christenson, Lutheran charismatic theologian in California, did much in the 1960s and 1970s to interpret the Charismatic movement for Lutherans. A very large annual conference was held in Minneapolis during those years. Charismatic Lutheran congregations in Minnesota became especially large and influential. The next generation of Lutheran charismatics cluster around the *Alliance of Renewal Churches*. There is currently considerable charismatic activity among young Lutheran leaders in California, centered on an annual gathering in Huntington Beach.

Roman Catholics:

Since 1967, the Charismatic movement has been active within the Roman Catholic Church. In the USA, the Catholic Charismatic Renewal was focused at the University of Notre Dame. The Roman Catholic Duquesne University in Pittsburgh began hosting Charismatic revivals in 1977. Pope John Paul II, on many occasions, was reported as saying, *"Long life to the charismatics."* Cardinal Joseph Ratzinger (now Pope Emeritus Benedict XVI) has added his voice to Pope John Paul II in acknowledging the good occurring in the Charismatic Renewal but also providing some cautions.

In the Roman Catholic Church, the movement became particularly popular in the Filipino and Hispanic communities of the United States, in the Philippines itself, and in Latin America, mainly Brazil. Traveling priests and lay people associated with the movement often visit parishes and sing what are known as Charismatic masses. It is thought to be the second largest distinct sub-movement within Roman Catholicism (some 160 million members in 2013), along with traditional Catholicism. It presents a difficult situation for many church authorities, who, as always, must be careful to admit innovation only where it is clear the innovation is consistent with the Bible and the teachings of the Church.[6]

Seventh-day Adventist: A minority of Seventh-day Adventists today are charismatic. They are strongly associated with those holding more progressive Adventist beliefs. In the early decades of the church, charismatic or ecstatic phenomena was commonplace.

Anglican Communion (Episcopalians): As stated earlier in the beginning of this section, the beginning of the whole transition into mainline churches began with Dennis Bennett, an American Episcopalian and influenced tens of thousands of Anglicans worldwide and also began a renewal movement within the Roman Catholic and Orthodox churches.

Note: In doing the research, it must be noted that it was very difficult to find information in writing about the movement's doctrine.

That may be due to the fact that it is more of a philosophy or attitude and has been incorporated into many Christian religions within their own varied doctrines. It must also be noted that the volume of websites that were anti-Charismatic far surpassed those that were pro-Charismatic. I can only suggest that you follow up with your own research, study, and prayer.

Notes

Notes

_____

_____

_____

_____

_____

_____

_____

_____

_____

_____

_____

_____

_____

First Church of Christ, Scientists (Christian Science)

History

Christian Science was founded by a woman named Mary Baker Eddy. She was born Mary Ann Morse Baker in New Hampshire, in 1821. As a child, she was frequently ill. Her parents sought help from physicians for her ailments, but the treatments brought only temporary relief. In 1829, Mary Baker claimed to hear her name being called by an unseen voice. This recurs over a twelve-month period. In 1843, she married George Glover and accompanied him to his home in South Carolina. A year later she was widowed and with her infant son, George W. Glover, II, she returned to her family in New Hampshire.

In 1853, she is married to Daniel Patterson. She was often sick at this time, and Patterson arranged for the boy to live with a foster family. When he was seven, the family moved with him to North Dakota, and he did not see his mother again until he was thirty-five. Struggling with chronic illness compounded by personal loss, Mary Patterson was preoccupied with questions of health. Mary sought relief in various alternative treatments of the day, including the Graham diet and *hydropathy* (water cure). She studied homeopathy in-depth and experimented with unmedicated pellets (now known as placebos) and concluded that a patient's belief played a powerful role in the healing process. "In 1862, she visited a man named Phineas Quimby. He taught a system of healing dealing with the mind. He taught that the mind had the power to heal the body."[1] He had a significant influence on her thinking regarding physical healing matters. During these many years of illness, Mary consistently had a great love for the Bible and studied it often.

In 1866, she fell and was seriously injured and she was not expected to recover. She apparently read Matthew 9:2– *"And, behold, they brought to him a man sick of the palsy, lying on a bed: and Jesus seeing their faith said unto the sick of the palsy; Son, be of good cheer; thy sins be forgiven thee"* and a turning point occurred. She experienced a miraculous cure. It was this experience that convinced her of the truth."[2]

Mary could not explain to others what had happened, but she knew it was the result of what she had read in the Bible. Her belief grew in the coming months as her illness met with even stronger proofs of spiritual healing. Eventually, she referred to this as the moment she discovered *Christian Science.* Earlier that same year, her husband left her for another woman. That autumn, she began taking notes on the book of Genesis, writing hundreds of pages of biblical expositions, which later became part of the *Science and Health* text that the church uses today.

During the years between 1867 and 1872, Mary began teaching her beliefs and maintained a practice in healing. In 1872, she ceased all teaching and devoted herself to writing her first book. She published the first edition of *Science and Health with Key to the Scriptures* in 1875. She claimed it was the final revelation of God to mankind and asserted that her work was inspired of God. She felt strongly that she had been ordered by God to write down the revelations that she received, but she was only the scribe. This idea grew and expanded in her consciousness until it became the impelling motive of her entire life.

In the year 1866, she discovered the law of Spirit and named it Christian Science. This book is now recognized as the only textbook of Christian Science. Christian Scientists rely on the Bible and the Christian Science textbook, which is their key to the scriptures. The book reached its highest annual sales ever in 2000–2001, having sold over 10 million copies. It has also been cited by the *Women's National Book Association* as "one of the 75 books by women whose words have changed the world."

In 1876, Mary met and healed Asa Gilbert Eddy of a heart condition. He studied with her and became a Christian Science practitioner within three weeks. She married Asa Eddy in 1877, but he died five years later. In 1879, four years after the first publication of *Science and Health,* Mary Baker Eddy and some of her students, disappointed that existing Christian churches would not embrace her discovery, organized the *Church of Christ, Scientist* (the mother church), in Boston, Massachusetts, which would "commemorate the word and works of our Master, which should reinstate primitive Christianity and its lost element of healing."[3] Mary Baker Eddy is highly regarded by Christian Scientists as a revelator of God's word. Then in 1881, Mary Baker Eddy was ordained pastor by her church.

"In 1881 she opened a metaphysical college and taught healing lessons. The Church was reorganized in 1892, and the Church Manual was first i ssued i n 1895, w hich p rovided t he s tructure f or c hurch government and missions."[4]

She adopted Ebenezer J. Foster in 1888, but nine years later severed all ties with him. By the end of 1889, Mrs. Eddy dissolved her college and disorganized her church and moved to New Hampshire to complete a major new revision of *Science and Health with Key to the Scriptures.* She deeded her home in Boston on Commonwealth Avenue, to be the home for whoever was elected as *First Reader* of the Boston church. Mrs. Eddy's residence was made available for the First Reader to use while they are conducting the services at the church. (Similar to a rectory or home provided for a pastor in other Christian denominations.)

Typically, Readers are elected every three years by each church, so there is rotation in office. Christian Science churches maintain reading rooms in most major cities in the world, where Mary Baker Eddy's writings can be read, borrowed, or purchased. Most reading rooms have bound volumes that contain articles on Christian Science and verified testimonies of healing spanning more than 125 years. Then in 1892, the Church of Christ, Scientist, reorganized as the *First* Church of Christ, Scientist. And two years later, the newly organized church ordained the Bible and Science and Health as pastors of the mother church. The original mother church, built in 1894, was at the heart of the Christian Science Plaza and remains today as it was when first built.

The Manual of the Mother Church was published that year. The Manual continues to guide all the activities of the First Church of Christ, Scientist, such as classes on Christian Science healing, public lectures, and church services. It outlines the unique system of government Mary Baker Eddy established for her church and provides direction on the individual practice of Christian healing.

In 1906, the mother church was renovated and enlarged and now provides seating for approximately three thousand. The organ, built by the Aeolian-Skinner Company of Boston, is one of the largest in the world; it covers eight divisions and has a total of 13,290 pipes.

In 1907, the "next friends" (a phrase used for a person who represents an action for another person who is under disability or otherwise unable to maintain a suit on their own behalf) filed suit against church officials. The suit on behalf of Mary Baker Eddy but without her blessing, alleging incompetent misuse of her property and abuse of her person, is filed against church officials and others by George W. Glover, II (her son), George W. Baker (her nephew), and Ebenezer J. Foster Eddy (adopted son). The suit is unsuccessful. Senator Chandler, one of the committee who examined her, said, *"She's smarter than a steel trap."* Mary Baker Eddy died in 1910, aged 89. Her last written words are *"God is my life."* Upon Eddy's death in 1910, the administrative power was assumed, as laid down in the Manual, by the Christian Science board of directors.

Throughout the history of Christian Science there have been a small number of dissenting people, unacknowledged by the Boston organization. Such dissenters often point to certain "estoppel" clauses of the last Church Manual issued by Mary Baker Eddy before her death which, had they been interpreted literally, would have led to a radical decentralization of the Christian Science Church. The issue has involved the Church in repeated litigation brought by dissenters; most prominently from 1919-22, when a group of Trustees from the *Christian Science Publishing Society* filed a suit against the Christian Science Board of Directors.[5]

Although most Christian Scientists are in the United States, the religion is found in 130 countries with large Protestant populations. A great percentage of its adherents are women. The mother church does not publicly publish membership statistics because they feel that numbers are not important to their faith, but various undocumented sources have noted that membership has declined from its peak in the 1920s, of 400,000, down to 100,000 in 1992. However, the membership numbers on Adherents.com still shows 400,000 as of 2013.

God or Gods

They teach that God is omnipresent, the only creator, the only ruler of man and the universe, so that He fills all space and is in one place in exactly the same degree that He is in every other place. He has no personhood and no personality. God is the father-mother, and His universe is wholly spiritual. God is all that exists, and what we perceive as matter is an interpretation or illusion of our mind. There is not one material element in Him or in anything that He created. God created everything spiritually and not materially, and the only kind of man created by Him is the perfect spiritual man, not the *material man* (see Special Doctrine section), made in His own image and likeness. The Trinity in Christian Science is found in life, truth, and love and is supported by the unity of God, the Christ, and divine science.

Christ

Christian Science teaches that Jesus Christ was sent by God and that His history is factual, including the virgin birth, the Crucifixion, the resurrection, and the ascension. Jesus submitted to the Crucifixion of His body on the cross in order that He might be the *Way-shower.* He wanted to prove that spiritual man is immortal and that his immortality is brought to light not by the death of the physical body but by demonstrating the power of Truth. "Jesus' deed was for the enlightenment of men and for the salvation of the world from sin, sickness and death."[6]

Regarding Christ and the Trinity, to her students, Mrs. Eddy sent a definition of the Trinity (circa 1898), which read in part: *"Jesus in the flesh was the prophet or Way-shower to Life, Truth, and Love, and out of the flesh Jesus was the Christ, the spiritual idea, or image and likeness of God"* (*Christian Science Journal,* July 1915). This statement clearly reflects Mrs. Eddy's doctrine regarding the uniqueness, unity, and individuality of Christ Jesus's eternal, spiritual identity. They believe His physical body died on the cross, and He rose on the third day as the Bible teaches. He proved that God is life and that man is immortal and can never die and that even the belief in death, can be destroyed by the Truth. Sin is a state of mind that causes suffering, the atonement for sin is attained by following Truth and Christ's teachings.

Basic Doctrine

All sin, disease, and death come from the belief of life, intelligence, sensation, and substance in matter. If matter is an illusion, it follows that disease is also an illusion of diseased beliefs upon the human body. It then follows that the correct way to treat disease is not through matter, nor by giving material remedies and drugs to the body, but by destroying the images of disease out of the human mind. Christian Science aims to destroy erroneous beliefs by substituting knowledge of Truth in place thereof, which reveals the new man governed by God. It lays tremendous emphasis upon the necessity for "bringing into captivity every thought to the obedience of Christ," as the Bible commands.

Thus the human mind is renewed by the destruction of erroneous and sinful mental thoughts, and the substitution in their place of the qualities of Truth. As this renewing process goes on, sickness, suffering, and discordant conditions begin to disappear, and when it is finished, and every mortal thought has been brought into subjection to Christ, then man will be transformed from a sinning, suffering mortal into a state of peace and harmony.[7]

One must desire to be a good man and must love God in order for the transformation to occur. They believe in the Bible as spiritually interpreted by Mary Eddy. She wrote:

The decisions by vote of Church Councils as to what should and should not be considered Holy Writ; the manifest mistakes in the ancient versions; the thirty thousand different readings in the Old Testament, and the three hundred thousand in the New,—these facts show how a mortal and material sense stole into the divine record, with its own hue darkening to some extent the inspired pages.

These statements have brought much criticism by fundamentalists who believe that the Bible is both inerrant and free of internal contradictions.

And they believe that Christ Jesus was the promised Messiah, and that Jesus embodied the divinity of God but that he himself was not deity. And that Jesus's teachings and healing work expressed scientific Christianity or the application of the laws of God.[8] Jesus was the great demonstrator of Truth. In His efforts to heal the sick and cast out evil, He proved what could be done through the understanding and reliance upon the divine power, while He taught, He that believeth on me, the works that I do shall he do also. Christian Science is a simple scientific system of metaphysics and is the same process used by Jesus in the healing of sin, disease, and death.

The Christian Science Church does not oppose the teaching of evolution in schools. They regard participating in conflicts is only submitting to the illusion. For similar reasons, Christian Science does not take a position on homosexuality, abortion, or any other controversies that arise.

Above all, Christian Scientists believe in the saving, healing power of God's love—that no one is beyond redemption, that no problem is too entrenched or overwhelming to be addressed and healed. In other words, Christian Scientists don't believe that salvation occurs at some point in the future, but that the presence of God's goodness can be experienced here and now—and by everyone.

Basic Worship Service

Churches worldwide hold a one-hour service each Sunday, consisting of hymns, prayer, and currently, readings from the *King James Version* (KJV) of the Bible (although there is no requirement that this version of the Bible be used) and *Science and Health with Key to the Scriptures*. These readings are the weekly Lesson/Sermon, which is read aloud at all Sunday services in all Christian Science churches worldwide, and is studied by individuals at home throughout the preceding week. The Lesson, as it is informally called, is compiled by a committee at the Mother Church, and is made up of alternating passages from the Bible and Science and Health.

The topics follow each other in an unchanging, predetermined order, though the readings are new and different or each lesson, and the progression starts over midyear so that every week in the year has a topic devoted to it.

The churches have no individual pastors. Services are conducted by two readers, one reading from the scriptures, the other from Science and Health. All churches use the same lessons at the same time. The scriptures are read by lay members of the church. These readers are voted into their office by the members of the church for a limited period of time (usually for three years.) Most often, midweek public testimony meetings are held in their churches. This is a time when anyone can testify to what Christian Scientists believe is the healing power of the Christ in their life.

Christian Scientists celebrate the sacraments of baptism and Eucharist in an entirely nonmaterial way. *"Our baptism,"* wrote Eddy, *"is purification from all error. Our Eucharist is spiritual communion with the one God. Our bread, 'which cometh down from heaven,' is Truth. Our cup is the cross. Our wine the inspiration of Love, the draught the Master drank and commended to his followers"* (Science and Health, pg. 35)."[9] The only ritual in the Christian Science church is voluntary kneeling at the sacrament service twice a year while repeating the Lord's Prayer.

Infant Baptism or Blessing

Not applicable since the material body is an illusion, and so is sin; there is no need for the remission of sins or a rebirth. In The Science and Health, Mrs. Eddy defines baptism as "baptism of Spirit."

Initiation, Baptism, or Confirmation

To become a member of The Mother Church, The First Church of Christ, Scientist, in Boston, Mass., the applicant must be a believer in the doctrines of Christian Science, according to the platform contained in the Christian Science textbook and the Bible.

This Church will receive a member of another Church of Christ, Scientist, but not a church member from a different denomination until that membership is dissolved. Children who have arrived at the age of 12 years, who are approved, and whose applications are countersigned by one of Mrs. Eddy's loyal students, by a Director, or by a student of the Board of Education, may be admitted to membership with The Mother Church.[10]

At the age of twenty, the person graduates from Sunday school and may be presented with a copy of The Mother Church Manual.

Marriage

Since there are no clergy, there is no specific marriage ceremony. Marriage can be performed by anyone of the couples' choosing. Marriage is not a sacrament of the Christian Science church, but marriage does hold a special place in Christian Science as the moral and legal institution within which a man and woman can partner to help one another grow into a fuller demonstration, or lived understanding, of their spiritual completeness as expressions of the father-mother God. The church's bylaws require a legal, religious ceremony for marriage. If a Christian Scientist is to be married, the ceremony shall be performed by a clergyman who is legally authorized.

Death and Afterlife

Heaven is then a divine state of consciousness and not a locality, and people will be in the kingdom of heaven when they have within themselves the mind of the Christ—not as places or as part of an afterlife, but as a state of mind. Christian Science theology does not include a final judgment day. Every day, each individual can make a new choice that determines the path he or she is on—a path away from God or toward Him. Christian Science, like Buddhism, believes in the illusory nature of the world of the senses, but unlike Buddhism, it does not believe that aging and death are inevitable. Consequently, immortality is possible, and indeed in the long term, it is inevitable. The reality of each one of us is believed to be a spiritual idea only and not born of the flesh. Therefore, birth and death are illusions because the material body is considered an illusion.

Judgment and Salvation

Christian Science shows that all good comes to man from God through the operation of His laws, and that evil originates in the human carnal mind. Evil is not an entity. It has no kingdom and no king. It has no mind, no presence, and no laws. The only power it can ever exercise is what it derives from human belief in it and human acceptance of it. There is no such thing as an angry God waiting to smite you for sin, for God has no knowledge of sin.[11]

When the sin is destroyed and put away out of the human mind, the punishment stops, but as long as the sin remains, the sinner will suffer. Any thought or action contrary to our God-given goodness results in some kind of suffering, just as the misunderstanding of a mathematical principle results in incorrect answers. Thus, the forgiveness of sin is the destruction of wrong thinking as sin exists nowhere but in the carnal human mind.

Special Doctrine

Generally, a Christian Scientist's first choice is to rely on prayer for healing, and in most cases, this means that a medical remedy is unnecessary.

While there is no formal compulsion on Christian Scientists either to use Christian Science healing or to eschew medical means, Christian Scientists avoid using the two systems simultaneously in the understanding that they tend to contradict each other. Material medicine and Christian Science treatment proceed from diametrically opposite assumptions. Medicine asserts that something is physically broken and needs to be fixed, while Christian Science asserts that the spiritual reality is harmonious and perfect, and that the illness is an illusion and it is the belief that needs correction.

In support of that, The Christian Science Journal and the Christian Science Sentinel continually document Christian Science healing. These are sometimes supported by the observations of medical practitioners involved prior to the application of Christian Science healing and are always verified by three other parties.

Christian Scientists have been controversial for their failure to provide conventional health care for children (*Asser and Swan,* 1998). In the United States, the constitutional guarantee of protection of religious practice from intrusion by government has been used by Christian Scientists and other religious groups to seek exemption from legislative or regulatory requirements regarding child abuse and neglect, including medical neglect in more than three quarters of the states. There are now statutes in forty-four states that contain a provision stating that a child is not to be deemed abused or neglected merely because he or she is receiving treatment by spiritual means through prayer according to the tenets of a recognized religion. Although the Christian Science community wants to have religious freedom without discrimination against reasonably and effectively practiced spiritual healing, the church has stated that protection and welfare of children is and always has been paramount.

Some Christian Scientists, after having had instruction on how to heal effectively, become what are called *Christian Science practitioners.* These are lay persons who, after years of healing, go into the public practice of healing. These practitioners devote all their time to healing and to help people through the financial issues and personal problems; they are not counselors or do they advise those calling upon them. They provide treatment through prayer, which strengthens an individual's understanding of his or her relationship to God. Their services are available to help anyone for a fee.

You do not need to be a Christian Scientist or attend church to ask them for help. It should be noted that there is no manipulation or laying on of hands in a Christian Science healing treatment and that healings are often accomplished without the practitioner ever having met the patient who may live a great distance from the practitioner. Christian Science nurses are part of the worldwide healing mission and ministry of The First Church of Christ, Scientist. The Manual of The Mother Church contains the core standard for the men and women who represent a spiritual and practical model of care. CS nurses are experienced Christian Scientists whose proof of healing in their own lives have given them confidence in the Christian Science method of treatment through prayer. They do not offer any form of medical treatment, such as diagnosis, drugs, or physical therapy.

Christian Scientists believe that the material man is not the image of God, and in the second account of the creation, in the second chapter of Genesis, it is nowhere stated that Adam was made in God's image and likeness. Those statements are to be found in the first chapter, and are used in contrast to the real spiritual man. Since the material man is only the carnal mind's misconception of man, it follows that matter has no entity and is, in every case, nothing but a mental illusion. Christian Science believes that "there is no life, truth, intelligence, nor substance in matter." Everything in the material world, which appears to us as matter, is merely the visible manifestation of thought, formed in the carnal mind. The world as it appears to the senses is a distorted version of the spiritual world. Prayer can heal the distortion, bringing spiritual reality (the kingdom of heaven in biblical terms) into clearer focus in the human scene—not changing the spiritual creation, but giving a clearer view of it.

The Tenets of Christian Science: The church does not have a creed, but it does adhere to six tenets as found in *Science and Health with Key to the Scriptures* by Mary Baker Eddy (pg. 496–97).

As adherents of Truth,

- We take the inspired Word of the *Bible* as our sufficient guide to eternal Life.
- We acknowledge and adore one supreme and infinite God.
- We acknowledge His Son, one Christ; the Holy Ghost or divine Comforter; and man in God's image and likeness.
- We acknowledge God's forgiveness of sin in the destruction of sin and the spiritual understanding that casts out evil as unreal. But the belief in sin is punished so long as the belief lasts.

- We acknowledge Jesus' atonement as the evidence of divine, efficacious Love, unfolding man's unity with God through Christ Jesus the Way-shower; and we acknowledge that man is saved through Christ, through Truth, Life, and Love as demonstrated by the Galilean Prophet in healing the sick and overcoming sin and death.
- We acknowledge that the crucifixion of Jesus and His resurrection served to uplift faith to understand eternal Life, even the allness of Soul, Spirit, and the nothingness of matter.
- And we solemnly promise to watch, and pray for that Mind to be in us which was also in Christ Jesus; to do unto others as we would have them do unto us; and to be merciful, just, and pure.[12]

Note: You will notice several words that are capitalized in the middle of a sentence, such as Truth, Lesson, and Reader. This is the way this particular faith practice chooses to display these words that have special meaning to their members.

Notes

Islam* (Muslim)

History

In or about the year 570 AD, a child was born into a family in northwestern Arabia. His name was Muhammad, and he would become the prophet of one of the world's great religions, Islam.

"In his forties, he began to retire to meditate in a cave on Mount Hira, just outside Mecca, where the first of the great events of Islam took place. One day, as he was sitting in the cave, he heard a voice, later identified as that of the angel Gabriel, which ordered him to recite"[1, 2] his understanding of God. Finally, after three attempts, "Muhammad recited the words of what are now the first five verses of the 96th chapter of the *Qur'an*—words which proclaim God to be the Creator of man and the Source of all knowledge."[2] The word *Islam* means "submission" or the total surrender of oneself to God. An adherent of Islam is known as a *Muslim*, meaning "one who submits (to God)."

At first, Muhammad divulged his experience only to his wife and his immediate friends and family. But as he had more revelations to proclaim the oneness of God universally, his following grew, at first among the poor and the slaves, but later, also among the most prominent men of Mecca. The revelations he received at this time, and those that came later, are all incorporated in the Qur'an, the Scripture of Islam…Not everyone accepted God's message transmitted through Muhammad. Even in his own clan, there were those who rejected his teachings, and many merchants actively opposed the message. The opposition, however, merely served to sharpen Muhammad's sense of mission.

Because the Qur'an rejected polytheism and emphasized man's moral responsibility, it presented a grave challenge to the worldly people of the region. "After Muhammad had preached publicly for more than a decade, the opposition to him reached such a high pitch that, fearful

---

* Within many of these religions there are subgroups. Because of space constraints, the subgroup with the highest number of members was the primary focus, and the other subgroups would be briefly described within the text of the religion.

for their safety, he sent some of his adherents to Ethiopia. There, the Christian ruler extended protection to them...But in Mecca the persecution worsened. Muhammad's followers were harassed, abused, and even tortured."

There was even an assassination attempt on Muhammad's life, at which time he joined his followers. This was the *hijrah,* usually translated as "flight," from which the Muslim era is dated. "In fact, the Hijrah was not a flight, but a carefully planned migration that marks not only the beginning of the Islamic era, but also, for Muhammad and the Muslims, a new way of life. Henceforth, the organizational principle of the community was not to be of mere blood kinship, but the greater brotherhood of all Muslims."

There ensued a series of wars with the pagans; victories changing hands, until finally the Muslims, at the *Battle of the Trench,* took total control of Medina. "The Constitution of Medina, under which the clans accepting Muhammad as the Prophet of God formed an alliance, or federation, dates from this period. It showed that the political consciousness of the Muslim community had reached an important point; its members defined themselves as a community separate from all others."

Non-Muslims in the community, Jews, for example, were part of the community at that time. In fact, they were a protected people and were allowed religious freedom as long as they conformed to its laws and payment of a special tax. "This status did not apply to polytheists, who could not be tolerated within a community that worshipped the One God."

In 629 AD, Muhammad reentered and conquered Mecca. In one sense, Muhammad's return to Mecca was the climax of his mission. In 632, just three years later, he was suddenly taken ill, and on June 8 of that year, with his third wife in attendance, Muhammad died.

Abu Bakr, the first caliph of Muhammad (*caliph* means "successor of Muhammad"), "stood firm when some tribes, who had only nominally accepted Islam, renounced it in the wake of the Prophet's death. In what was a major accomplishment, Abu Bakr swiftly disciplined them."[3] Abu Bakr's immediate task was to put down a rebellion by Arab tribes in an episode known as the *Ridda* wars or Wars of Apostasy. These disputes over religious and political leadership would give rise to schism in the Muslim community. The majority believed in the legitimacy of the three rulers prior to Ali and became known as *Sunnis*. A minority disagreed and believed that Ali (Muhammad's cousin) was the only rightful successor: they became known as the *Shi'a* (or Shi'ites).

The second caliph, Umar, appointed by Abu, continued to demonstrate the ability to rule. Within four years after the death of the prophet, the Muslim state had extended its sway over all of Syria and, eventually, Persia; henceforth, it was to be one of the most important provinces in the Muslim Empire. His caliphate was a high point in early Islamic history. He was noted for his justice, social ideals, administration, and statesmanship. His innovations left an all-enduring imprint on social welfare, taxation, and the financial and administrative fabric of the growing empire.

Umar was stabbed by a Persian slave in 644. As He was lying on his deathbed, he appointed a committee of six people to choose the next caliph from among themselves. The members went about Medina asking the people for their choice. They finally selected Uthman as the new caliph, as the majority of the people chose him. One of the most important events of his reign "was Uthman's compilation of the text of the Qur'an as revealed to the Prophet. Realizing that the original message from God might be inadvertently distorted by textual variants, he appointed a committee to collect the canonical verses and destroy the variant versions. The result was the text that is accepted to this day throughout the Muslim world."[3]

Muslims consider the *Qur'an* to be the literal word of God; it is the central religious text of Islam. Muslims believe that the verses of the Qur'an were revealed to Muhammad by God through the angel Gabriel on many occasions between 610 and his death on June 8, 632. The Qur'an was reportedly written down by Muhammad's companions while he was alive, although the prime method of transmission was orally. It was compiled in the time of Abu Bakr, the first caliph, and was standardized under the administration of Uthman, the third caliph. The Qur'an is divided into 114 chapters, which, combined, contain 6,236 verses. The chronologically earlier chapters are primarily concerned with ethical and spiritual topics.

The Qur'an is m ore concerned with moral guidance than legal instruction and is considered the "sourcebook of Islamic principles and values." Muslim jurists consult the *Hadith,* or the written record of Muhammad's life, to both supplement the Qur'an and assist with its interpretation.[4]

During his caliphate, Uthman faced much hostility from new, nominal Muslims in newly Islamic lands, who started to accuse him of not following the example of the Prophet and the preceding caliphs in matters concerning governance. Uthman's enemies relentlessly made his governing difficult by constantly opposing and accusing him. His opponents finally plotted against him, surrounded his house, and encouraged people to kill him. Many of his advisors asked him to stop the assault but he did not, until he was eventually killed while reciting the Qur'an exactly as the Prophet had foretold. Uthman died as a martyr.[5]

In 656, after Uthman was killed, Ali assumed the position of caliph. After fighting off opposition in the first civil war, Ali was the next to be assassinated in 661. Following this, Mu'awiyah, who was governor of Levant, seized power and began the Umayyad Dynasty. After Mu'awiyah's death in 680, conflict over succession broke out again in the second civil war. Afterward, the Umayyad Dynasty prevailed for seventy years and was able to conquer large areas in the west as well as expand Muslim territory into Central Asia. While the Muslim-Arab elite engaged in conquest, some devout Muslims began to question the piety of indulgence in a worldly life, emphasizing rather poverty, humility, and avoidance of sin based on renunciation of bodily desires. Devout Muslim ascetic exemplars would inspire a movement that would evolve into *Sufism.*

Not strictly a denomination, Sufism i s a mystical-ascetic form of Islam. By focusing on the more spiritual aspects of religion, Sufis strive to obtain direct experience of God by making use of intuitive and emotional faculties that one must be trained to use. Sufism and Islamic law are usually considered to be complementary, although Sufism has been criticized by some Muslims for being an unjustified religious innovation. Most Sufi orders can also be classified as either Sunni or Shi'a.

For the Umayyad aristocracy, Islam was viewed as a religion for Arabs only; the economy of the Umayyad Empire was based on the *assumption that a majority of non-Muslims would pay taxes to the minority of Muslim Arabs.* Some of the descendants of one of Muhammad's uncles rallied a group of discontented Muslims, poor Arabs, and some Shi'a against the Umayyads and overthrew them with the help of their general Abu Muslim, inaugurating the Abbasid Dynasty in 750. Under the Abbasids, Islamic civilization flourished in the *"Islamic Golden Age,"* with its capital at the cosmopolitan city of Baghdad.[6]

The g olden age saw new legal, philosophical, and religious developments. The major *Hadith* collections were compiled, and the four modern Sunni *madhabs* (schools) were established. Islamic law was also advanced greatly by the efforts of al-Shafi'i; he codified a method to establish the reliability of Hadith, a topic which had been a subject of dispute among Islamic scholars. Finally, Sufism and Shi'ism both underwent major changes. Sufism b ecame a f ull-fledged mo vement that had moved toward mysticism and away from its ascetic roots, while Shi'ism split due to disagreements over the succession of *imāms* (a spiritual leader similar to a priest or rabbi).

By the late ninth century, the Abbasid caliphate began to fracture as various regions gained increasing levels of autonomy. During this time, expansion of the Muslim world continued by both conquest and peaceful proselytism even as both Islam and Muslim trade networks were extending into sub-Saharan West Africa, Central Asia, Volga Bulgaria, and the Malay Archipelago. It was during this time that Muslims began expressing belief that parts of the previously revealed scriptures, the *Torah* and the *Gospels*, had become distorted either in interpretation, in text or both. The spread of the Islamic dominion induced hostility among medieval ecclesiastical Christian authors who saw Islam as an adversary in the light of the large numbers of new Muslim converts. This opposition resulted in polemical treatises, which depicted Islam as the religion of the Antichrist.

Tāriqu l-Hākim was the sixth caliph in Egypt, ruling from 996 to 1021. His eccentric character, the inconsistencies and radical shifts in his conduct and policies, the extreme austerity of his personal life, the vindictive and sanguinary ruthlessness of his dealing with the highest officials of his government coupled with an obsession to suppress all signs of corruption and immorality in public life, his attempted annihilation of Christians and call for the systematic destruction of all Christian holy places in the Middle East culminating in the destruction of the most holy *Church of the Resurrection in Jerusalem*, which all combine to contrast his reign sharply with that of any of his predecessors and successors.[7]

From the eleventh century onward, alliances of European Christian kingdoms mobilized to launch a series of wars known as the *Crusades,* bringing the Muslim world into conflict with Christendom. Initially successful in their goal of taking the Holy Land and establishing the crusader states, crusader gains in the Holy Land were later reversed by subsequent Muslim generals who recaptured Jerusalem during the Second Crusade. In the East, the Mongol Empire put an end to the Abbasid Dynasty at the Battle of Baghdad in 1258 as they overran in Muslim lands in a series of invasions.

Mongol rule extended across the breadth of almost all Muslim lands in Asia, and Islam was temporarily replaced by Buddhism as the official religion of the land. Over the next century, many Mongols converted to Islam, and this religious and cultural absorption ushered in a new age of Mongol-Islamic synthesis that shaped the further spread of Islam in central Asia and the Indian subcontinent. After the invasion of Persia and sack of Baghdad by the Mongols in 1258, Delhi, India, became the most important cultural center of the Muslim East.

Beginning in the thirteenth century, Sufism underwent a transformation, largely as a result of the efforts of al-Ghazzali to legitimize and reorganize the movement. He developed the model of the Sufi order—a community of spiritual teachers and students. Also of importance to Sufism was the creation of the *Masnavi,* a collection of mystical poetry by the thirteenth-century Persian poet Rumi. The Masnavi had a profound influence on the development of Sufi religious thought; to many Sufis, it is second in importance only to the Qur'an.[8] After World War I losses, the remnants of the empire were parceled out as European protectorates or spheres of influence. Since then, most Muslim societies have become independent nations, and new issues such as oil wealth and relations with the State of Israel have assumed prominence.

Starting in the twentieth century, Muslim social reformers argued against veiling, seclusion, and other traditional practices such as polygamy, with varying success. Certain Islamist groups like the *Taliban* have sought to continue traditional law as applied to women. The twentieth century also saw the creation of many new Islamic revivalist movements. Groups such as the *Muslim Brotherhood* in Egypt and *Jamaat-e-Islami* in Pakistan advocate a totalistic and theocratic alternative to secular political ideologies. In countries like Iran and Afghanistan (under the Taliban), revolutionary movements replaced secular regimes with Islamist states, while transnational groups like Osama bin Laden's *al-Qaeda* engage in terrorism to further their goals. In 2015 and 2016, there was a new develpoment in the fundamentalists groups within Islam. There is increasing hatred of the "western ways," along with horrendous acts of terror in both the US and in Europe. The largest group of religious zealots call themselves *ISIS (Islamic State of Iraq and Syria).* The suicide bombers in the west and slaughtering of Christians, in addition to the brutal destruction of priceless ancient ruins, has brought Islam into full view of the world. Millions of Chrisitian refugees have started to seek refuge in other countries. But because ISIS is putting people in posing as refugees, there has been much contoversy over accepting these people in need. In contrast, liberal Islam is a movement that attempts to reconcile religious tradition with modern norms of secular governance and human rights. Every year in northern India, Muslims gather in Ajmer for the Urs festival to remember the death of Moinuddin Chishti, a Sufi Islamic cleric and scholar. In 2015, around seventy thousand clerics who attended issued a fatwa condemning terrorism. It was decided that a fatwa should be passed at the Urs this year, so the message went out loud and clear that the Muslim community condemns terrorism.[9]

According to Adherents.com, all sects of Islam combined have a total membership of 1.8 billion worldwide. A note of interest: there are fourteen countries in Africa and the Middle East that are 95 percent Muslim.

God or Gods

"Islam's fundamental theological concept is the belief that there is only one God. The Arabic term for God is *Allāh*. God is beyond all comprehension; Muslims are not expected to visualize God, but to worship and adore Him as a protector. God is described in a chapter of the Qur'an as *'...God, the One and Only; God, the Eternal, Absolute; He begetteth not, nor is He begotten; and there is none like unto Him.'*" He has no partners in His divinity.

The word *Allāh* is simply the Arabic word for "almighty God" and is the same word used by Arabic-speaking Christians and Jews. In addition, the word it is quite similar to the word for God in other Semitic languages. For example, the Hebrew word for God is *Elah*. For various reasons, some non-Muslims mistakenly believe that Muslims worship a different God than the God of Moses and Abraham and Jesus. This is certainly not the case since the pure monotheism of Islam calls all people to the worship of the God of Noah, Abraham, Moses, Jesus, and all the other prophets.

Belief in angels is crucial to the faith of Islam. The Arabic word for Angels means "messenger." According to the Qur'an, angels do not possess free will, and worship God in perfect obedience. Angels' duties include communicating revelations from God, glorifying God, recording every person's actions, and taking a person's soul at the time of death. They are also thought to intercede on man's behalf. The Qur'an describes angels as "messengers with wings–two, or three, or four (pairs): He [God] adds to Creation as He pleases."[10]

Christ

Although Muslims believe that Jesus was a prophet, they reject the Christian doctrine of the Trinity, comparing it to polytheism. In Islamic theology, Jesus was just a man and not the son of God. Islam considers Jesus to be one of the greatest and most forbearing of prophets, in addition to Noah, Abraham, Moses, and Muhammad. Jesus is also considered to be the Messiah as well.

Like Christians, Muslims believe that Mary was a chaste, virgin woman, who miraculously gave birth to Jesus. Jesus's birth in itself was a miracle in that he had no father. This fact, however, does not necessitate that Jesus is divine in essence or spirit, nor is he worthy of worship. "Muslims, like Christians, believe that Jesus performed miracles. These miracles were performed by the will and permission of God." As he was miraculously supported by God in his conception, birth, and childhood, he was also supported by numerous miracles to prove that he was a messenger from God.

God clarified in the Qur'an that Jesus was not crucified; rather, it was made to seem that way to the Jews, and that God raised him to the Heavens. As such, Islam denies that Jesus came to this earth with the purpose of sacrificing himself for the sin of Adam, Eve, and the rest of humanity, freeing them from its burden. Islam strictly rejects the notion that any person bears the sin of another.

Muslims believe in the generations after Jesus's departure from this world, his teachings were distorted, and he was elevated to the status of God. Six centuries later, with the coming of prophet Muhammad, the truth about Jesus Christ was finally retold and preserved eternally in the last book of divine revelation, the Qur'an. Love and respect of Jesus Christ is an article of faith in Islam, and Allāh stressed the importance of belief in Jesus in numerous places in the Qur'an.

As Christians do, Muslims also believe in the return of Jesus the Messiah to earth, although his role and reason for his return does differ from what the Christians propose. He will return to earth first and foremost to prove his mortality and refute the false beliefs people held about him. Jesus will also fight the false Christ, who will call people to the belief that he is God, and who will appear just before Jesus returns. Jesus will defeat the antichrist, and all people will accept the true religion of Allāh. The world will see a type of peace and serenity unfelt in history, all worshipping the same God, subservient to Him alone, and at peace with one another.[11]

Basic Doctrine

According to Islamic doctrine, Islam is the primordial religion of mankind professed by Adam. At some point, a religious split occurred, and God began sending prophets to bring his revelations to the people. In this view, Abraham, Moses, the Hebrew prophets, and Jesus were all prophets in Islam, but their message and the texts of the Torah and the Gospels were misinterpreted by Jews and Christians.

The idea of Islamic supremacy is encapsulated in the formula, "Islam is exalted, and nothing is exalted above it." Muslims believe that Allāh revealed his final message to humanity through the Islamic prophet Muhammad via the angel Gabriel. For them, Muhammad is God's final prophet, and the Qur'an is the revelations he received over a period of more than two decades. They do not regard Muhammad as the founder of a new religion but as the *restorer* of the original monotheistic faith of Abraham, Moses, Jesus, and other prophets.

Prophets are considered to be the closest to perfection of all humans and are uniquely the recipients of divine revelation—either directly from God or through angels. The Q ur'an mentions the names of numerous figures considered prophets in Islam, including Adam, Noah, Abraham, Moses, and Jesus, among others. Islamic theology says that all of God's messengers since Adam preached the message of Islam—submission to the will of God. Many Muslims believe that the prophet foretold of in Deuteronomy was not Jesus, but Muhammad.

Islam consists of a number of religious denominations that are essentially similar in belief but which have significant theological and legal differences. The primary division is between the Sunni and the Shi'a, with Sufism generally considered to be a mystical inflection of Islam rather than a distinct sect. According to most sources, approximately 85 percent of the world's Muslims are Sunni, and approximately 15 percent are Shi'a, with a small minority who are members of other Islamic sects.

The Shi'a, which constitute the second-largest branch of Islam, believe in the political and religious leadership of infallible imāms from the progeny of Ali ibn Abi Talib (fourth successor of Muhammad). They believe that he as the cousin and son-in-law of Muhammad, was his rightful successor, and they call him the first imām, rejecting the legitimacy of the previous Muslim caliphs. To them, the imām rules by right of divine appointment and holds spiritual authority among Muslims, having final say in matters of doctrine and revelation. Although the Shi'a shares many core practices with the Sunni, the two branches disagree over the proper importance and validity of specific collections of Hadith.

Adherents are generally required to observe the five pillars of Islam, which are five duties that unite Muslims into one community. In addition to the five pillars, Islamic law (sharia) has developed a tradition of rulings that touch virtually every aspect of life. The *sharia* (literally, "the path leading to the watering place") is Islamic law formed by traditional Islamic scholars. In Islam, sharia is the expression of the divine will and constitutes a system of duties that are incumbent upon a Muslim by virtue of his religious belief.

The Qur'an defines *hudud* as the punishments for five specific crimes: unlawful intercourse, false accusation of unlawful intercourse, consumption of alcohol, theft, and highway robbery. The Qur'an also contains laws of inheritance, marriage, and restitution for injuries and murder, as well as rules for fasting, charity, and prayer. However, these prescriptions and prohibitions may be broad, so their application in practice varies. Islamic scholars have elaborated systems of law on the basis of these rules and their interpretations.

The Five Pillars of Islam are five practices essential to Sunni Islam. Shi'a Muslims subscribe to eight ritual practices which substantially overlap with the Five Pillars. They are:

The *shahadah*, which is the basic creed or tenet of Islam: "I testify that there is none worthy of worship except God and I testify that Muhammad is the Messenger of God." This testament is a foundation for all other beliefs and practices in Islam. Muslims must repeat the shahadah in prayer, and non-Muslims wishing to convert to Islam are required to recite the creed.

Salāh, or *ritual prayer*, which must be performed five times a day. Each Salāh is done facing towards Mecca. Salāh is intended to focus the mind on God, and is seen as a personal communication with him that expresses gratitude and worship.

Salāh is compulsory but flexibility in the specifics is allowed depending on circumstances. In many Muslim countries, reminders called *Adhan* (call to prayer) are broadcast publicly from local mosques at the appropriate times. The prayers are recited in the Arabic language, and consist of verses from the Qur'an.

Sawm or *fasting* during the month of Ramadan. Muslims must not eat or drink from dawn to dusk during this month, and must be mindful of other sins. The fast is to encourage a feeling of nearness to God, and during it Muslims should express their gratitude for and dependence on him, atone for their past sins, and think of the needy. Sawm is not obligatory for several groups for whom it would constitute an undue burden. For others, flexibility is allowed depending on circumstances, but missed fasts usually must be made up quickly.

The Hajj, which is the pilgrimage to Mecca. Every able-bodied Muslim who can afford it must make the pilgrimage to Mecca at least once in his or her lifetime.

Zakāt or *alms-giving*. This is the practice of giving based on accumulated wealth, and is obligatory for all Muslims who can afford it. A fixed portion is spent to help the poor or needy, and also to assist the spread of Islam. The Zakāt is considered a religious obligation (as opposed to voluntary charity) that the well-off owe to the needy because their wealth is seen as a "trust from God's bounty." The Qur'an and the Hadith also suggest a Muslim give even more as an act of voluntary alms-giving.

Shi'a Muslims consider three additional practices essential to the religion of Islam. The first is *jihād*, which is also important to the Sunni but not considered a pillar. The word jihād translates as a noun, meaning "struggle." Jihād appears forty-one times in the Qur'an and frequently in the idiomatic expression "striving in the way of God."[12] Although the word has a different meaning within some extremist groups, its original meaning was the inner struggle with one's own demons.

The second is the *"enjoining to do good,"* which calls for every Muslim to live a virtuous life and to encourage others to do the same. The third is the *"exhortation to desist from evil,"* which tells Muslims to refrain from vice and from evil actions and to also encourage others to do the same.

Many practices fall in the category of Islamic etiquette. These include greeting others with "peace be unto you," saying "in the name of God" before meals, and using only the right hand for eating and drinking.

When someone converts to Islam, God forgives all of his previous sins and evil deeds. Since the consequences of following a false religion are so grave, the true religion of God must have been universally attainable from the beginning, and it must continue eternally to be understandable and attainable throughout the entire world. In other words, the true religion of God cannot be confined to any one people, place, or period of time (which would discount religions that are in their infancy, in the minds of Muslims). Within the central principle of Islam and its definition (the surrender of one's will to Allāh) lie the roots of Islam's universality. Whenever man comes to the realization that God is one and distinct from His creation and submits himself to God, he becomes a Muslim in body and spirit and is eligible for paradise.

Basic Worship Service

Salāh, or ritual prayer, mentioned earlier must be performed five times a day. Each salāh is done facing toward Mecca. Salāh is intended to focus the mind on God and is seen as a personal communication with him that expresses gratitude and worship. The time of prayer is announced by the call to prayer, which is called from the Muslim place of worship (mosque). On Fridays, there is a noon prayer service called *jumā,* which is congregational and recited in a central mosque designated for that purpose. The men and women form separate sections inside the mosque; the women are not to be seen by the men.

Infant Baptism or Blessing

Regular prayer is one of the most important fundamental practices in Islam. Muslim prayer, which is performed daily, can be performed almost anywhere—either individually or in a group. These beautiful words, which call the Muslim community to prayer five times a day, are also the first words the Muslim baby will hear. The father will recite these words to the baby immediately after its birth. Islam prescribes male circumcision with the sole purpose of facilitating cleanliness and carries no religious connotations. There can be a ceremony called the *Aikah* and is not universally practiced by all Muslims. The ceremony itself can vary, but generally, it is a way of welcoming the infant.

Initiation, Baptism, or Confirmation

At the *shahada* or "witnessing," a young Muslim repeats the Islamic declaration of faith. It is usually done at any age from midteens onward. It must be witnessed by either two males or eight female Muslims.

Marriage

The family is involved in the suggestion of candidates. They discuss all the potential prospects. And then one of the parents approaches the other family to suggest a meeting. The couple agrees to meet in a chaperoned or group environment. The family continues to talk with friends, family, Islamic leaders, coworkers, etc., to learn about the possible candidate. The couple prays for guidance to seek Allāh's help in making a decision. Then they agree to pursue marriage or part ways. Islam does allow freedom of choice to both young men and women—in most cases, they are not forced into a marriage that they don't want.

Marriage is the most ancient of human social institutions. Marriage came into existence with the creation of the first man and woman: Adam and Eve. Muslims hold marriage to be an integral part of their religious devotion. As mentioned before, the Prophet Muhammad explicitly stated that marriage is half of the Religion (of Islam). In other words, perhaps half of all Islamic virtues, such as fidelity, chastity, charity, generosity, tolerance, gentleness, striving, patience, love, empathy, compassion, caring, learning, teaching, reliability, courage, mercy, forbearance, forgiveness, etc., find their natural expression through married life. Marriage is a legal arrangement in Islam, not a sacrament in the Christian sense, and is secured with a contract. The contract is a civil contract which consists of an offer and acceptance between two qualified parties in the presence of two witnesses. The groom is required to pay a bridal gift tothe bride, as stipulated in the contract. Islamic marriage lays rights and corresponding responsibilities on each spouse.[13]

Although divorce, being allowed in Islam, is a sign of the lenience and practical nature of the Islamic legal system, keeping the unity of the family is considered a priority for the sake of the children. For this reason, divorce is always a last choice, after exhausting all possible means of reconciliation. For example, Allāh addresses men, asking them to try hard to keep the marriage even if they dislike their wives. Divorce comes in effect once the husband utters or writes down any of the legal formulae of divorce such as: "I divorce you," or "you are divorced," etc. The husband can do these either by himself or through a messenger.

Moreover the procedure of divorce in Islam is such as to encourage reconciliation where possible. After divorce the woman should wait three monthly cycles during which her husband remains responsible for her welfare and maintenance. He is not permitted to drive her out of the house during this period. She has been advised not to leave the house of the divorcing husband, in order to enhance the chances of reconciliation, as well as to protect her right of sustenance during the three months waiting period. The main purpose of this waiting period is to clarify whether the divorced wife is or is not expecting a child. Its second use is as a cooling-off p eriod d uring w hich t he r elatives a nd other members of the family or of the community may try to help toward reconciliation and better understanding between the partners.[14]

Death and Afterlife

Belief in the *Qiyāmah* or "Day of Resurrection," also known as "the Last Hour" is also crucial for Muslims. They believe that the time of Qiyāmah is preordained by God but unknown to man. The trials and tribulations preceding and during the Qiyāmah are described in the Qur'an and the Hadith, and also in the commentaries of Islamic scholars. The Qur'an emphasizes bodily resurrection, a break from the pre-Islamic Arabian understanding of death. It states that resurrection will be followed by the gathering of mankind, culminating in their judgment by God.[15]

Muslims view paradise as a place of joy and bliss, with qur'anic references describing its features and the physical pleasures to come. The Qur'an tells people about paradise, which God offers to them, describes its great blessings, and proclaims its beauties to everyone. It "shows that Paradise is a place where all blessings have been created perfectly and where people will be offered everything their souls and hearts will desire and that people will be far removed from want and need, anxiety or sadness, sorrow and regret…God has prepared such blessings there as a gift, and these will be offered only to people with whom He is pleased."[16]

When a believer is about to depart this world, angels come down from the heavens the soul peacefully passes out of the body, and the angels take hold of it; once extracted from the body, the angels wrap up the soul and ascend up to the heavens. As the gates of heaven open for the soul, the angels greet it. God commands his or her "book" to be recorded, and the soul is then temporarily returned to earth. The s oul then remains in limbo in its grave, awaiting the day of judgment.

Divine wrath and punishment is conveyed to the wicked soul by hideously ugly, dark angels who sit far away from it. The Angel of Death sits at the head of the disbeliever in his or her grave and says: *Wicked soul, come out to the displeasure of Allāh"* as he snatches the soul out of the body. The evil soul leaves the body with great difficulty…The Angel of Death then seizes the soul and puts it in a sack woven from hair which gives off a putrid stench…Then, when he is brought to the lowest heaven, a request is made that its gate be opened for him, but the request is denied. The cry will be heard from heaven *He has lied, so spread out carpets of Hell for him, and open for him a portal into Hell. "*…The disbeliever is then made to taste bitter remorse as he is shown what would have been his abode in Paradise—had he lived a righteous life—before a portal is opened for him every morning and evening showing him his actual home in Hell.[17]

Judgment and Salvation

The belief in the Oneness of God is paramount in Islam; from this all else follows. The verses of the Qur'an stress God's uniqueness, warn those who deny it of impending punishment, and proclaim His unbounded compassion to those who submit to His will. They affirm the Last Judgment, when God, the Judge, will weigh in the balance the faith and works of each man, rewarding the faithful and punishing the transgressor. So this is the only chance we have to win paradise and to escape from hell because if someone dies in disbelief, there will not be another chance to come back to this world to believe. "Islam teaches that Hell is a real place prepared by God for those who do not believe in Him, rebel against His laws, and reject His messengers. Hell is an actual place, not a mere state of mind or a spiritual entity. The horrors, pain, anguish, and punishment are all real, but different in nature than their earthly counterparts. Hell is the ultimate humiliation and loss, and nothing is worse.[18]

Special Doctrine

Predestination: Islam teaches predestination or divine preordainment. Allāh has full knowledge and control over all that occurs. For Muslims, everything in the world that occurs, good or evil, has been preordained and nothing can happen unless permitted by God. In Islamic theology, divine preordainment does not suggest an absence of God's indignation against evil, because any evils that do occur are thought to result in future benefits men may not be able to see. According to Muslim theologians, although events are pre-ordained, man possesses free will in that he has the faculty to choose between right and wrong, and is thus responsible for his actions. According to Islamic tradition, all that has been decreed by God is written in the *Preserved Tablet.* " The Shi'a understanding of predestination is called "divine justice,"[19] and stresses the importance of man's responsibility for his own actions. In contrast, the Sunni deemphasize the role of individual free will in the context of God's creation and foreknowledge of all things.

Several Areas in Which Islam Is Misunderstood

Terrorism and Oppression: Islam is a misunderstood religion in many parts of the world. Those who are unfamiliar with the faith often have misunderstandings about its teachings and practices. Common misconceptions include Islam is oppressive against women, or that it is a faith that promotes violence. Hopefully, some of these misconceptions can be clarified with additional study.

<u>Most Muslims are Arabs:</u> While Islam is often associated with Arabs, they make up only 15 percent of the world's Muslim population. The country with the largest population of Muslims is Indonesia. Muslims make up one fifth of the world's population, with large numbers found in Asia (69 percent), Africa (27 percent), Europe (3 percent), and other parts of the world.

<u>Islam Oppresses Women:</u> Most of the ill-treatment that women receive in the Muslim world is based on local culture and traditions, without any basis in the faith of Islam. Generally, it is practiced under the guise of sharia law by those who treat women less than fairly. In fact, practices such as forced marriage, spousal abuse, and restricted movement directly contradict Islamic law governing family behavior and personal freedom.

<u>Islam Promotes Jihād to Spread Islam by the Sword and Kill All Unbelievers:</u> Are there some verses of the Qur'an that condone "killing the infidel"? The word jihād stems from an Arabic word, which means "to struggle." Originally, jihād was an effort to practice religion in the face of oppression and persecution. The effort may come in fighting the evil in your own heart or in standing up to a dictator. Jihād in its broadest sense is classically defined as "exerting one's utmost power, efforts, endeavors, or ability in contending with an object of disapproval."

Depending on the object, being a visible enemy, the devil, an aspects of one's own self, different categories of jihād are defined. Jihād also refers to one's striving to attain religious and moral perfection. Within Islamic jurisprudence, jihād can be taken to mean military exertion against non-Muslim combatants in the defense or expansion of the Islamic state, the ultimate purpose of which is to universalize Islam. Jihād, the only form of warfare permissible in Islamic law, may be declared against apostates, rebels, highway robbers, violent groups, un-Islamic leaders or states, which refuse to submit to the authority of Islam. Military effort is a last resort and not "to spread Islam by the sword."

The Qur'an commands Muslims to stick up for themselves in a defensive battle (i.e., if an enemy army attacks, then Muslims are to fight against that army until they stop their aggression). All of the verses that speak about fighting/war in the Qur'an are in this context. There are some specific verses that are very often snipped out of context, either by those trying to malign the faith or by misguided Muslims themselves who wish to justify their aggressive tactics.[20] For example, one verse (in its snipped version) reads: *"slay them wherever you catch them"* (Qur'an 2:191). But who is this referring to? Who are "they" that this verse discusses? The preceding and following verses give the correct context:

> *Fight in the cause of God those who fight you, but do not transgress limits; for God loves not transgressors. And slay them wherever ye catch them, and turn them out from where they have turned you out; for tumult and oppression are worse than slaughter; but fight them not at the Sacred Mosque, unless they (first) fight you there; but if they fight you, slay them. Such is the reward of those who suppress faith. But if they cease, God is Oft-forgiving, most Merciful. And fight them on until there is no more tumult or oppression, and there prevails justice and faith in God; but if they cease, let there be no hostility except to those who practice oppression. (Qur'an 2:190–193).*

It is clear from the context that these verses are discussing a defensive war, when a Muslim community is attacked without reason, oppressed, and prevented from practicing their faith. In these circumstances, permission is given to fight back, but even then, Muslims are instructed not to transgress limits and to cease fighting as soon as the attacker gives up. Even in these circumstances, Muslim are only to fight directly against those who are attacking them, not innocent bystanders or noncombatants.

Any verse that is quoted out of context misses the whole point of the message of the Qur'an. Nowhere in the Qur'an can be found support for indiscriminate slaughter, the killing of noncombatants, or murder of innocent persons in payback for another people's alleged crimes.

In Islam, several things are clear:

- Suicide is forbidden. *"O ye who believe! [Do not] kill yourselves, for truly Allāh has been to you Most Merciful. If any do that in rancor and injustice, soon shall we cast him into the Fire..."* (Qur'an 4:29–30).
- The taking of life is allowed only by way of justice (i.e., the death penalty for murder), but even then, forgiveness is better. *"Nor take life-which Allāh has made sacred-except for just cause..."* (17:33).
- In pre-Islamic Arabia, retaliation and mass murder was commonplace. If someone was killed, the victim's tribe would retaliate against the murderer's entire tribe. This practice was directly forbidden in the Qur'an (2:178–179). Following this statement of law, the Qur'an says, *"After this, whoever exceeds the limits shall be in grave chastisement"* (2:178). No matter what wrong we perceive as being done against us, we may not lash out against an entire population of people.
- The Qur'an admonishes those who oppress others and transgress beyond the bounds of what is right and just. *"The blame is only against those who oppress men with wrongdoing and insolently transgress beyond bounds through the land, defying right and justice. For such there will be a chastisement grievous* (in the Hereafter)" (42:42).
- Harming innocent bystanders, even in times of war, was forbidden by the prophet Muhammad. This includes women, children, noncombatant bystanders, and even trees and crops. Nothing is to be harmed unless the person or thing is actively engaged in an assault against Muslims.[21]

The predominant theme in the Qur'an is forgiveness and peace. Allāh is merciful and forgiving and seeks that in His followers. Indeed, most people who spend time on a personal level with ordinary Muslims have found them to be peaceful, honest, hardworking, civic-minded people.

Islam and the West have had a rocky relationship for centuries, and in recent years the tension has only seemed to escalate. The ongoing conflict between Israel and Palestine is religiously charged, Western involvement in Middle Eastern affairs is resented, and various hijackers, suicide bombers and terrorists base their actions on their Muslim faith. With continue harassment and torture of non-Muslims by terrorist groups in Africa and the Middle East, the peaceful followers of Islam have a more difficult role than ever in proving their desire for peace. Many Muslims, however, have denounced this radical minority as violating both true Islam and the true meaning of Jihād.[22] Muslim leaders and scholars do speak out against terrorism in all its forms and offer explanations of misinterpreted or twisted teachings.

Polygamy: Islam is criticized for allowing polygamy, for popular culture in the West views polygamy as relatively backward and impoverished. For many Christians, it is a license to promiscuity, and feminists consider it a violation of women's rights and demeaning to women. A crucial point that needs to be understood is that for Muslims, standards of morality are not set by prevalent Western thought, but by divine revelation. The Qur'an limited the maximum number of wives to four. In the early days of Islam, those who had more than four wives at the time of embracing Islam were required to divorce the extra wives. Islam further reformed the institution of polygamy by requiring equal treatment to all wives. The Muslim is not permitted to differentiate be tween hi s wives in regards to sustenance and expenditures, time, and other obligations of husbands.

Also, marriage and polygamy in Islam is a matter of mutual consent. No one can force a woman to marry a married man. Islam simply permits polygamy; it neither forces nor requires it. Besides, a woman may stipulate that her husband must not marry any other woman as a second wife in her prenuptial contract. The point that is often misunderstood in the West is that women in other cultures—especially African and Islamic—do not necessarily look at polygamy as a sign of women's degradation ...Even though we see the clear permissibility of polygamy in Islam, its actual practice is quite rare in many Muslim societies. Some researchers estimate no more than 2% of the married males practice polygamy. Most Muslim men feel they cannot afford the expense of maintaining more than one family. Even those who are financially capable of looking after additional families are often reluctant due to the psychological burdens of handling more than one wife.[23] Most western men would agree, that one wife is sometimes more than they can handle!

<u>Diet:</u> According to the Qur'an, the only foods explicitly forbidden are meat from animals that die on their own, consumption of carnivores is prohibited and consumption of omnivores, such as pigs, monkeys, humans and dogs, is also prohibited. *Zabihah* is the prescribed method of ritual slaughter of all animals, excluding fish and mo st sea-life, per Islamic law. For such a method, the animal must be slaughtered by a Muslim or by the *People of the Book* (Christian or Jew) while mentioning the name of God (Allāh in Arabic).[24]

According to some, the animal must be slaughtered only by a Muslim. Food permissible for Muslims is known as *halāl* food (adherents to this philosophy maintain that in order for food to be considered halāl, it must not be a forbidden substance, and any meat must have been slaughtered according to traditional guidelines set forth by the law. This is the strictest definition of *halāl*.) Animals for food may not be killed by being boiled or electrocuted, and the carcass should be hung upside down for long enough to be blood free. Different rules apply to fish; for instance, fish with scales are always halāl, while it has been debated whether shellfish and scaleless fishes, such as catfish, are halāl. In Islam, alcoholic beverages or any intoxicant are forbidden, but alcohol is allowed to be used for medical and other purposes.

<u>Dress:</u> Islamic ethics considers modesty as more than just a question of how a person dresses, and more than just modesty in front of people; rather it is reflected in a Muslim's speech, dress, and conduct: in public in regards to people, and in private in regards to God. Any talk of modesty, therefore, must begin with the heart, not the hemline, as the Prophet of Mercy said, Modesty is part of faith, and that part of faith must lie in the heart. Take reservation in speech. As with everything in Islam, speech should be moderate. Raising one's voice in venting anger simply shows one lacks the ability to contain it, and only damage will ensue from it...Islamic scholars consider modesty to be a quality that distinguishes human beings from animals. Animals follow their

instincts without feeling any shame or a sense of right or wrong. Hence, the less modesty a person has, the more he resembles animals.

Islam has mandated certain legislations which induce this sense of modesty within humans. These legislation range from seeking permission before entering any room and distancing one from others while relieving oneself, to mandating certain manners of dress for men and women alike. Another way that modesty may be attained is by associating with modest people—people in whose presence a person feels embarrassed to do anything shameful ... Being shy of a stranger's gaze is one of the driving forces behind modesty in dress. In Islam, screening most of your body off from the gaze of a stranger, especially of the opposite sex, is actually mandated as a means to avoid falling into conduct that may lead to extra-marital or pre-marital sex. As seen from this verse, Islamic ethics view modesty not as a virtue for women only, but for men as well. Thus, men must also dress modestly, being careful to wear loose flowing and opaque clothes through which the area between their waist and knees is totally covered. Tight pants or translucent clothing is prohibited. This modesty is reflected upon Muslim male clothing throughout the world, long shirts reaching below the thighs, and loose flowing trousers. It may still seem, however, that women bear the main brunt of dressing modestly. When one reflects, however, about the predator and the prey in illegal relations between the sexes; the prey which is hidden escapes being a victim. Besides, another verse says modesty in dress actually identifies one as being a believing woman, a "target" which the devout Muslim, or any decent man, would be motivated to protect rather than abuse.[25]

Ahmadiyya Muslims: There are many sects of the Muslim faith, just as there are many denominations in other religions, but one that is worth noting in the search for peace is the sect call *Ahmadiyya*. The Ahmadiyya Muslim Community is an Islamic religious movement founded in Punjab, British India, near the end of the nineteenth century. Ahmadi thought emphasizes the belief that Islam is the final dispensation for humanity as revealed to Muhammad and feel it is crucial to restore it to its true essence and pristine form, which had been lost through the centuries. Ahmadiyya adherents believe that

Ahmad appeared in the likeness of Jesus, to end religious wars, condemn bloodshed and reinstitute morality, justice, and peace. They believe that upon divine guidance, he divested Islam of fanatical beliefs and practices by reverting back, in their view, to Islam's true and essential teachings as practised by Muhammad and the early Islamic community. Thus, Ahmadis view themselves as leading the revival and peaceful propagation of Islam.

These are the central beliefs constituting Ahmadi Muslim thought. The distinguishing feature of the Ahmadiyya Muslim Community is their belief in Mirza Ghulam Ahmad as the Promised Messiah and *Mahdi*, as prophesied by the Islamic prophet Muhammad. Summarising his claim, Ahmad writes:

"Through the proclamation of truth and by putting an end to religious conflicts, I should bring about peace and manifest the Divine verities that have become hidden from the eyes of the world. I am called upon to demonstrate spirituality which lies buried under egoistic darkness. It is for me to demonstrate by practice, and not by words alone, the Divine powers which penetrate into a human being and are manifested through prayer or attention. All this will be accomplished, not through my power, but through the power of the Almighty God, Who is the God of heaven and earth."

Ahmadi teachings state that all the major world religions had divine origins and were part of the divine plan towards the establishment of Islam as the final religion, because it was the most complete and perfected the previous teachings of other religions (but they believe that all other religions [including Islam] have drifted away from their original form and have been corrupted). The message which the founders of these religions brought was, therefore, essentially the same as that of Islam. Currently, the community is led by its Caliph, Mirza Masroor Ahmad, and is officially estimated to number between 10 and 20 million worldwide.[26]

Notes

Notes

Jehovah's Witness

History

Jehovah's Witnesses originated with the religious movement known as Bible Students, which was founded in the late 1870s by Charles Taze Russell when he organized a Bible study group. In 1876, Russell met Nelson H. Barbour and subsequently adopted Barbour's beliefs with regards to the end of the world. In 1877, Barbour and Russell jointly published the book *The Three Worlds*, detailing their views. In July 1879, Russell broke with Barbour after Barbour discounted the worth of Christ's atonement. He soon began publishing his own magazine, *Zion's Watch Tower and Herald of Christ's Presence* (now known as *The Watchtower*). He also maintained the Adventist rejection of the traditional view of hell and, by 1882, had rejected the doctrine of the Trinity. He also taught that after the death of the last of the twelve apostles, the church gradually diverged in a great apostasy from the original teachings of Jesus on several major points.

In 1881, he formed the legal entity that developed into the nonprofit organization: *The Watch Tower Bible and Tract Society of Pennsylvania* (currently headquartered in New York City). In 1884, it was incorporated with Russell as president. He authored the six-volume series: *Studies in the Scriptures*. Early editions predicted that Armageddon would culminate in the year 1914. Although the predictions did not come to fruition, Jehovah's Witnesses still stand today on the 1914 date as the defining point in man's history. Following Russell's death on October 31, 1916, an editorial committee of five was set up to supervise the writing of the Watchtower magazine as set forth in Russell's last will and testament. On January 6, 1917, Joseph Franklin Rutherford (also known as Judge Rutherford) was elected second president of the *Watch Tower Bible and Tract Society*. A power struggle soon developed between Rutherford and four of the seven-member board of directors of the Society. Rutherford announced to the staff that he was dismissing the four directors and replacing them with new members, claiming they had not been legally elected.

Dissension and schisms ensued in congregations worldwide as a result of these events. Matters reached a climax on July 17, 1917, as the book *The Finished Mystery* was released to the headquarters staff in Brooklyn. The Finished Mystery was controversial in its criticism of Catholic and Protestant clergy and Christian involvement in war. Citing this book, the United States federal government later indicted Rutherford and the new board of directors for violating the Espionage Act (a United States federal law, which made it a crime for a person to interfere with the operation or success of the military or naval forces of the United States).

On May 7, 1918, they were found guilty and sentenced to twenty years imprisonment. However, in March 1919, the judgment against them was reversed, and they were released from prison. The charges were later dropped. Those who remained supportive of the Watch Tower Society, in 1931 came to adopt the name *Jehovah's Witnesses* under Rutherford's leadership.[1]

By 1933, the Society was using 403 radio stations to broadcast Bible lectures. Later, the use of the radio was largely replaced by increased house-to-house visits by Witnesses with portable phonographs and recorded Bible talks. Home Bible studies were started with anyone who showed interest in biblical truth. Jehovah's Witnesses attest that they do not aim to convert everyone they visit, but rather they want to get their message out there—they want their beliefs to be heard and known. It is hard for people outside of the faith to understand why Witnesses persist in door-to-door sermonizing, but the truth is that the act of spreading the word is a requirement of the faith, so members are simply satisfying what they consider to be their obligation to Jehovah.

"The period from 1925–1933 saw many significant changes in doctrine. Attendance at their yearly memorial dropped from a high of 90,434 in 1925" down to 17,380 in 1928 due to the previous power struggle, the second series of failed predictions for the year 1925, and the evolving doctrinal changes that alienated those who sided with Russell's views. Hitler's Nazi Germany persecuted Jehovah's Witnesses in Europe, and many were imprisoned in concentration camps. Their identifying badge was a purple triangle.

In a book on Jehovah's Witnesses under the Nazi regime, Hans Hesse commented, "*Some five thousand Jehovah's Witnesses were sent to concentration camps where they alone were 'voluntary prisoners', so termed because the moment they recanted their views, they could be freed. Some lost their lives in the camps, but few renounced their faith.*"[2]

During this time period, Witnesses also experienced mob violence in America and were temporarily banned in Canada and Australia because they were perceived as being against the war effort.

In 1943, a special training school for missionaries, called the *Watchtower Bible School of Gilead,* was established. From that time onward, graduates from this school have been sent to lands all over the earth. New congregations have sprung up in countries where there had been none, and branches established internationally.

They do not salute the flag of any nation or sing nationalistic songs, believing it an act of false worship. Thus, t hey r efrain f rom s aluting the flag of any country. They believe that these acts are tantamount to worship. The political neutrality of Jehovah's Witnesses is also expressed by their refusal to participate in military service—even when it is compulsory—and by their detachment from secular politics. Voting in political elections is considered a compromise of their Christian neutrality. Jehovah's Witnesses believe their allegiance belongs to God's Kingdom, which is viewed as an actual government in heaven.

After the war, the Witnesses brought several suits in American courts dealing with their beliefs and practices, resulting in sixty Supreme Court rulings that were regarded as major judgments on the free exercise of religion and "have had a great impact on legal interpretation of these rights for others. In 1943, the United States Supreme Court ruled in *West Virginia State Board of Education vs. Barnette* that school children of Jehovah's Witnesses could not be compelled to salute the flag."[3] By 1988, the US Supreme Court had reviewed seventy-one cases involving Jehovah's Witnesses, two thirds of which were decided in their favor. Still, members are expected to obey all laws of their native governments, so long as these do not violate what they view as God's law.

They are reside, considering the government to be solely responsible for how they are used. They continue to face persecution in several countries, however, particularly for their refusal to serve in the military.

Five times in the history of Jehovah's Witnesses they have predicted the second coming of Christ and the end of the world, and each time the predictions did not come true. The last time was in 1975. Witnesses stopped teaching that the timing of Armageddon is tied to the literal generation of people alive in 1914 but were told not to lose confidence in "the nearness of Jehovah's day of judgment." "At the 2010 annual meeting, John Barr presented the latest understanding of the generation. Ninety-seven year old Barr was an apt choice to deliver this talk, being the last of the Governing Body born before 1914. He explained the generation is now to include two groups whose lives 'overlap' since 1914."[4] He further explained that the end will come while some are still alive who know someone born before 1914.

John Barr...twice read the comment: "*Jesus evidently meant that the lives of the anointed ones who were on hand when the sign began to be evident in 1914 would overlap with the lives of the other anointed ones who would see the start of the great tribulation. We do not know the exact length of 'this generation,' but it includes these two groups whose lives overlap. Even though the anointed vary in age, those in the two groups constituting the generation are contemporaries during the part of the last days. How comforting it is to know that the younger anointed contemporaries of those older anointed ones who discerned the sign when it became evident beginning in 1914 will not die off before the great tribulation starts!*" (Watchtower 2010 June 15, p. 5)[5]

In 2000, three new nonprofit corporations were organized: *Christian Congregation of Jehovah's Witnesses, Inc.* coordinates all service activities, including door-to-door preaching, circuit and district conventions, etc. *Religious Order of Jehovah's Witnesses, Inc.* coordinates the activities of those involved in full-time service, including pioneers, missionaries, and circuit and district overseers. *Kingdom Support Services, Inc.* controls construction of new kingdom halls and other facilities and holds the titles to society-owned vehicles. JWfacts.com states that as of 2016 there are approximately 20 million members in the world in over 235 different countries.

God or Gods

Jehovah's Witnesses believe that, according to the Bible, God has a personal name, *YHWH*, which is sometimes rendered in English as "Jehovah." The name Jehovah is mentioned 7,210 times in their version of the Bible. Some scholars have criticized the New World Translation, the translation of the Bible published by Jehovah's Witnesses, stating that the group has changed the Bible to suit their doctrine and that the translation contains a number of errors and inaccuracies. Jehovah is regarded as Almighty God, the Supreme Being and creator of everything, the sovereign of the universe. They believe that Jehovah's main qualities are love, justice, wisdom, and power, and that these qualities are consistently demonstrated throughout the Bible. There is one God Almighty—a Spirit Being with a body, but not a human body. There is no Trinity. The Holy Spirit is the name of God's active force in the world.

Christ

Jehovah's Witnesses believe that Jesus is the only—literally—begotten Son of Jehovah, His firstborn Son, created before anything else was created. They believe that Jehovah and Jesus Christ are separate beings. Christ (through His ransom sacrifice) is regarded as the only means by which to approach Jehovah in prayer and the means of salvation. They believe that Jesus is the head of the Christian congregation. For this and many other reasons Jehovah's Witnesses have been called guilty of the early-church heresy of *Arianism* (doctrine of the third century that Jesus was not fully divine). They believe that Jesus is also the Archangel Michael, as well as Abaddon/Appolyon from the book of Revelation.

Basic Doctrine

Their view of morality reflects some of the usual conservative Christian views. Bestiality, homosexuality, incest, fornication, and adultery are considered serious sins. Abortion is considered murder. They are instructed to marry only within their religion. Modesty in dress and grooming is frequently emphasized. Gambling is strictly forbidden, as are stealing and drunkenness. Free home Bible studies are offered to persons having questions or interest in their beliefs. Witnesses are instructed to devote as much time as possible in preaching activities.

They have made a dedication to God to do His will, and they apply themselves to fulfill this dedication. In all their activities they seek guidance from God's Word and His holy spirit. From this it is apparent that Jehovah's Witnesses believe in the Bible as the Word of God. They consider its 66 books to be inspired and historically accurate. What is commonly called the New Testament they refer to as the *Christian Greek Scriptures* and the Old Testament they call the *Hebrew Scriptures*. They rely on both of these, the Greek and the Hebrew Scriptures, and take them literally except where the expressions or settings obviously indicate that they are figurative or symbolic.[6]

They use Watchtower publications to explain their beliefs. Literature is published in many languages through a wide variety of books, magazines, and other publications, with some publications being available in as many as 410 languages. Members of a local congregation or "company" are known as "kingdom publishers" and are expected to spend four hours a week at kingdom hall meetings and to spend as much time as possible in doorstep preaching.

Pioneer publishers hold part-time secular jobs and try to devote 100 hours a month to religious service. Special pioneers are full-time salaried employees of the society, who are expected to spend at least 150 hours a month in this work. Each kingdom hall has an assigned territory, and each witness a particular neighborhood to canvass. Great pains are taken to keep records of the number of visits, return calls, Bible classes, and books and magazines distributed. Witnesses are perhaps best known for the efforts to spread their beliefs throughout the world.

They do this mainly by visiting people house-to-house. Members are required to participate in the preaching work and, if possible, to give voluntary donations to the *Watchtower Society's Worldwide Work* fund. Aid work to members after large natural disasters is considered an important part of their work, though secondary to their preaching effort.

Large sums of donated money are used in the affected areas to rebuild Kingdom Halls and provide aid to members of the church. The focus of relief efforts is primarily on helping fellow members and rebuilding Kingdom Halls, but usually, assistance is provided to nonmembers in need near the area in which they are working. Examples of relief work include that provided to Hutu and Tutsi victims rebuilding (Kingdom Halls) during the Rwandan genocide, as well as to Congo refugees. Witnesses have also had an active share in the relief work and rebuilding Kingdom Halls after Hurricane Katrina in the United States.[7]

Jehovah's Witnesses teach that Jesus acknowledged that humans are capable of wicked acts, but He pointed to the very cause and source of evil as Satan, the devil. Satan's evil influence even reached into the spirit realm, where he induced other angels to join him in rebellion. Like Satan, these wicked spirits took an improper interest in humans. As debased demons, they continued to oppose God and his righteous family of loyal angels and they have remained a potent force in human affairs...The Devil is maneuvering mankind into a tempest of increasing woes.

In fact, he is more determined than ever to do harm. Why? Because he and the demons were evicted from heaven because the devil has come down to you, having great anger, knowing he has a short period of time.

How, then, does Satan wield his influence over mankind today? Satan does so primarily by promoting a spirit that governs the way that people think and act. Instead of encouraging godly fear and goodness, this demonic "air" breeds rebellion against God and his standards. Satan and his demons thus promote and aggravate the evil perpetrated by humans.[8]

The forces of evil can appear formidable. The Bible points out that those striving to please God have a wrestling... against the wicked spirit forces, in addition to a struggle with their own imperfect flesh. Jehovah's Witnesses teach caffeine, alcohol, etc., are permitted, reasoning that moderate use of them has never been proved consistently dangerous to health. Alcohol is specifically allowed in the Bible. However, excessive alcohol consumption and drunkenness are condemned in scripture.

Abuse of alcohol and illegal drugs can result in disfellowshipping for members. The Watchtower has stated that smoking violates the principle in *2 Corinthians* 7:1 being a "defilement of the flesh."

Since 1973, smokers are not eligible for baptism, and Witnesses who persist in the habit are subject to being disfellowshipped or one of the less severe forms of discipline listed below:

Disfellowshipping is the most severe form of discipline. Congregation members, including family members, avoid social and/or spiritual association with disfellowshipped individuals. Disfellowshipped members can attend Kingdom Hall meetings but are not allowed to take an active part in meetings or the ministry. Reproof involves sins for which one could be disfellowshipped. But if true repentance is shown, the person may not be disfellowshipped but merely reproved. Reproof may be given before all who have knowledge of the transgression. In some cases, it is deemed necessary to make an announcement to the congregation that "(so and so) has been reproved."

Marking is employed when a member persists in conduct that is considered a clear violation of Scriptural principles, yet not of a sufficient seriousness to warrant disfellowshipping." Marking is based on their understanding of 2 *Thessalonian* 3:6. It is used only if the person repeatedly refuses counsel, and the elders feel that not addressing it would pose a spiritual danger to the members of the congregation. A talk may be given regarding the conduct (without naming the individual). Though such a person would not be shunned, social interaction outside of formal worship settings would be minimized.

The Jehovah's Witnesses do not have a system of clergy and laity. Rather, they see every baptized person as being an ordained minister who is able to teach and preach. All Jehovah's Witnesses are part of a congregation who are led by a body of elders. The elders a re m en who are chosen based on scriptural qualifications and appointed by the governing body as their direct representatives in the local congregation. Elders are prominent in congregational matters, particularly in religious instruction and spiritual counseling. Ministerial servants generally assist elders in a limited administrative capacity. Both roles are unpaid, but circuit and district overseers receive a small financial living allowance. Although they teach that the Bible and Jehovah show no prejudice to women, within local congregations, the role of women is minimal in terms of responsibility. They cannot serve as elders or ministerial servants, though they carry out a large proportion of the preaching work,[9] including missionary work, pioneering, and helping others in the congregation to become more regular in preaching.

Basic Worship Service

You can expect to hear discussion and encouragement about door-to-door practices when you attend a worship ceremony. Jehovah's Witnesses are known for their intense commitment to their faith, and in fact, they are encouraged to attend worship ceremonies two times a week, totaling approximately four hours. Worship ceremonies are held in Kingdom Halls, which are modest and simple buildings maintained by the congregation's members.

All members are referred to as either "Brother" or "Sister." Under normal circumstances, women cannot teach the congregation; though female Witnesses do participate in meeting programs. Prayer and songs are considered an important part of the meeting. Prayers at meetings or on other occasions are considered acceptable if directed to the Father Jehovah in the name of the Son. The use of idols is prohibited. They reject the veneration of Mary, the saints, or the cross.

There are three conventions held annually in facilities owned or maintained by the Watchtower Society or in rented stadiums or auditoriums. During the week, there are also meetings throughout the community to organize the preaching work. On Saturdays, the *Watchtower* and *Awake!* magazines are featured. On most days literature is offered based on monthly campaigns. Each month, a report is submitted to the congregation elders by active Witnesses, indicating the number of hours in the ministry, along with other details. This is required of or one to be officially counted as an active Jehovah's Witness. On a daily basis, Jehovah's Witnesses are encouraged to read the Bible and read publications such as *Examining the Scriptures Daily* , a booklet with a daily biblical scripture and commentary.

Their most important annual event is the commemoration of Jesus's death (referred to as "the Memorial") held after sundown, on the date corresponding to the date of the Hebrew Passover, Nisan 14 on the Hebrew calendar (usually in March or April).

Typically, in most congregations, no one partakes in drinking the wine or eating the bread during this annual event because only the members of the 144,000 or "the Anointed" partake of the emblems of the wine and unleavened bread. Instead, most Jehovah's Witnesses pass the wine and the bread around the congregation. Citing the words at 1 Corinthians 11:27, they believe that those who partake unworthily in the emblems will be judged by Jehovah. According to Witness publications, as of 2008, about nine thousand plus persons—an increase from the previous year—did partake of the emblems. These anointed ones anticipate being resurrected to heaven after their death.

"An important part of their worship is the 'family study.' Fathers are reminded of their responsibility to take the lead in instructing his wife and children in the Bible on a regular weekly schedule. Where there is no father that responsibility falls on the mother."[10]

Infant Baptism or Blessing

Not applicable.

Initiation, Baptism, or Confirmation

Baptism never tends to be something that is ever rushed into. Generally, a significant period of time passes whereby, in the meantime, the likely candidate will get through a fair amount of Watchtower literature and attend regular meetings. Before being recommended for baptism, one must answer over eighty questions to the satisfaction of local Kingdom Hall elders. Later, Jehovah's Witnesses entering into the baptism ceremony are asked the following questions:

1. On the basis of the sacrifice of Jesus Christ, have you repented of your sins and dedicated yourself to Jehovah to do His will?
2. Do you understand that your dedication and baptism identify you as one of Jehovah's Witnesses in association with God's spirit-directed organization?

Each must also declare any other prior baptism invalid. Baptisms are normally performed at assemblies and conventions and are always done by immersion.

Marriage

The family structure is patriarchal. The husband is considered the final authority on family decisions but is encouraged to solicit his wife's thoughts and feelings, as well as those of his children. Marriages are required to be monogamous. The Bible is clear: "God does not approve of or condone homosexual practices. He also disapproves of people who consent with those practicing them." And marriage cannot give homosexuality a cloak of respectability.

God's direction that "marriage be honorable among all" precludes homosexual unions, which he considers detestable. Still, with God's help, anyone can learn to abstain from fornication, which includes homosexual acts, and get possession of his own vessel in sanctification and honor. Admittedly, this is not always easy, but no problem is too big for Jehovah, who can provide the strength and help needed to meet His standards and receive His blessings.[11] Divorce is condemned for any reason other than adultery. Abuse and willful nonsupport of one's family is considered grounds for separation, but not divorce.

Death and Afterlife

"Jehovah's Witnesses believe that the earth will remain forever and that all people, living and dead, who will fit in with Jehovah's purpose for a beautified, inhabited earth may live on it forever."[12]

The vast majority of Jehovah's Witnesses expect to live on a renewed paradise on earth. The soul is the person itself, not an immortal immaterial entity that dwells inside the body. It expires with the body; thus, no soul exists after death, and death itself is a state of nonexistence with no consciousness. Hades is the designated common grave of all mankind. They do not believe in any hell of fiery torment. Soon, Jesus Christ will return to resurrect the dead, restoring soul and body. Those judged righteous will be given everlasting life on a paradise earth. Those judged unrighteous will not be tormented but will die a second time and eternally cease to exist.

Judgment and Salvation

Jehovah's Witnesses believe that Jesus' death was necessary to atone for the sin brought into the world by the first man, Adam, opening the way for the hope of everlasting life for mankind, and that 144,000 anointed Christians will receive immortal life in heaven as corulers with Christ, ruling over the rest of mankind during the millennial reign.

Witnesses believe that during the imminent war of Armageddon, the wicked will be destroyed, and survivors, along with millions of others who will be resurrected, will form a new earthly society ruled by a heavenly government and have the possibility of living forever in an earthly paradise. Armageddon is considered to be imminent. After false religion is destroyed, governments will also face destruction. After Armageddon, the majority of mankind who has died, both righteous and unrighteous, will be resurrected with the chance of being judged righteous and living forever in paradise.

There seems to be controversy on whether they believe that they are the only ones who will be saved. Publications of Jehovah's Witnesses have stated that only those serving Jehovah will survive God's judgment of the world. But there are statements on some of the JW websites that state:

Millions that have lived in centuries past and who were not Jehovah's Witnesses will come back in a resurrection and have an opportunity for life. Many now living may yet take a stand for truth and righteousness before the "great tribulation," and they will gain salvation. Moreover, Jesus said that we should not be judging one another. We look at the outward appearance; God looks at the heart. He sees accurately and judges mercifully. He has committed judgment into Jesus' hands, not ours.[13]

Special Doctrine

They believe only their religion represents true Christianity. They believe that all other religions fail to meet all the requirements set by God and will be done away with. Weddings, anniversaries, and funerals are typically observed; however, common celebrations or national holidays such as birthdays, Halloween, Easter, and Christmas are regarded as pagan holidays owing to their origins and are not celebrated.[14]

Higher education (equivalent to bachelor's degree or higher) is not a focus for most Witness youth. Jehovah's Witnesses are instructed to make spiritual matters the top priority in their life since the Witnesses view time as short for their global ministry. Higher education is considered a matter of conscience to be decided individually. If chosen, it should be kept secondary to spiritual responsibilities. Instead, Jehovah's Witnesses prefer various education programs provided for their members. Some examples are the *Theocratic Ministry School* (available for everyone), *Pioneer Service School, Ministerial Training School, Gilead School* (all by invitation only) and others, specifically focused on improving skills for their ministry.

The official teaching of Jehovah's Witnesses regards blood as sacred and rejects transfusions of whole blood, red cells, white cells, platelets, or plasma. This is based on an understanding of the biblical admonition to "abstain from...blood," "for the life of the flesh is in the blood...No soul of you shall eat blood," which they understand to be the first instance of "the Bible's clear prohibition against taking blood into the body. Baptized Witnesses who willingly violate the prohibition on blood are subject to being disfellowshipped.

"They highly value life, and they seek good medical care. But they are determined not to violate God's standard, which has been consistent. Those who respect life as a gift from the Creator do not try to sustain life by taking in blood."[15] They are willing to accept all medical treatments except blood. They have even been known to have major surgeries without any blood "assistance" during surgery. Many hospitals now are trying to come up with other ways to aide in the recovery of patients that refuse blood transfusions.

Whilst firmly against pedophilia, physical abuse of children or spouse, or any other anti-Christian behavior, the Watchtower policy has inadvertently buried these very practices amongst Jehovah's Witnesses, simply due to the fact that they teach separation between church and state. "Witnesses with problems are encouraged to go to the elders and discouraged from going to worldly experts or law enforcement agencies for fear of being influenced by people that do not understand Watchtower principles.

Many elders have no training in issues such as marriage, addictions and child abuse beyond limited information provided by the Watchtower Society."[16]

In the case of child abuse, for example, quite often, the child has been expected to face the accused and three male elders in a small Kingdom hall room. And to compound the problem even more, until the mid "1990s Watchtower policy dictated that two witnesses must be present at the actual sexual encounter or abuse for the perpetrator to be considered to have actually committed a scriptural offence." In most of these types of cases, "there are almost never two witnesses. This meant that even when several children made an accusation against the same offender, the elders were told to do nothing. Without two witnesses the only time action could be taken was when the accused confessed."[17]

"When a serial offender was found to have been a child molester, elders kept information discussed in judicial committees confidential under ecclesiastical privilege. This mimics the Catholic ideas on confessionals."[18] This included not reporting such matters to the police. Witnesses have regularly been discouraged from going to the police for fear of bringing reproach on Jehovah's name. Witnesses are expected to solve problems within the organization.

It was not until the late 1990s, and as a result of bad media publicity globally that Watchtower policy changes on child abuse finally started to come into effect. For a person to be considered to have acted inappropriately scripturally, collaborative evidence such as photos, or two children making a similar accusation in a short period of time can now be regarded as two witnesses. Elders are now to go to the secular authorities, though still only in States where they are legally required to do so. Prior to contacting the police, elders are expected to seek advice from the Watchtower legal department. The following proviso is stated in an October 10, 2002 *Confidential "Body of Elders"* Letter sent to all elders in Australia: "*If, after contacting the Society, it is determined that the elders should report a matter such as child abuse to the authorities, it would not be considered to be a breach of confidentiality to make such a report ... Elders should always contact the Society before providing any information on confidential matters to secular authorities.*"[19]

There was a settlement of sixteen child abuse cases in 2007. A number of abuse victims filed court cases against the Watchtower Society through the law firm Love and Norris. These were for up to $4 million per victim. "The Watchtower Society chose not to allow these cases to go to trial; rather they have settled out of court with nondisclosure agreements also known as 'gag orders,' which mean the victims receipt of compensation is dependant on them not speaking about the court cases. The settlements have been printed in newspapers around the world."[20]

The good that has come out of this is that the Church is much more mindful and has changed their handling of such situations.

Notes

Judaism

History

The book of Genesis describes the events surrounding the lives of the three patriarchs: Abraham, Isaac, and Jacob. (Joseph, who is recognized as a fourth patriarch by Christians, is not considered one of the patriarchs by Jews.) In 2000 BC, "the God of the ancient Israelites established a divine covenant with Abraham, making him the patriarch of many nations. The term Abrahamic Religions is derived from his name. These are the four major religions which trace their roots back to Abraham: Judaism, Christianity, Islam and the Bahá'í Faith."[1]

Abraham, hailed as the first Hebrew and the father of the Jewish people, rejected the idolatry that he saw around him and embraced monotheism (the belief in one God). As a reward for this act of faith in one God, he was promised many offspring. God sent the patriarch Jacob and his children to Egypt, where after many generations, they became enslaved. God later commanded Moses to redeem the Israelites from slavery, leading to the exodus from Egypt.

Moses was the next major leader of the ancient Israelites. He led his people out of captivity in Egypt and received the Mosaic law (the Ten Commandments) from God.[2] The Israelites gathered at Mount Sinai in 1313 BC and received the *Torah*—the five books of Moses: Genesis, Exodus, Leviticus, Numbers, and Deuteronomy. These books, together with *Nevi'im* and *Ketuvim,* are known as the written Torah, as opposed to the oral Torah, which refers to the *Mishnah* and the *Talmud.* Then God led the Israelites to the land of Israel. Eventually, Judaism dropped all associations with other gods and goddesses of the Canaanite pantheon and became monotheistic. When exactly this occurred, however, is also debated.

The original tribal organization was converted into a kingdom by Samuel; its first king was Saul. The United Monarchy was established under Saul and continued under King David and Solomon with its capital in Jerusalem. After Solomon's reign, the nation split into two kingdoms in 922 BC: the kingdom of Israel and the kingdom of Judah. The kingdom of Israel was conquered by the Assyrian ruler Sargon II in the late eighth century BC. The kingdom of Judah continued as an independent state until it was conquered by a Babylonian army in the early sixth century BC, destroying the First Temple that was at the center of ancient Jewish worship.

The Judean elite were exiled to Babylonia, and this is regarded as the first Jewish diaspora (a migration of people). During this captivity, the Jews in Babylon wrote what is known as the *Babylonian Talmud* while the remaining Jews in Judea wrote what is called the *Palestinian Talmud.* These are the first written forms of the *Torah,* and the Babylonian *Talmud* is the Talmud used to this day.[3]

A new Second Temple was constructed in 536 BC, and old religious practices were resumed. During the early years of the Second Temple, the highest religious authority was a council known as the *Great Assembly,* led by Ezra of the Book of Ezra. Among other accomplishments of the Great Assembly, the last books of the Hebrew Bible were written at this time and the canon sealed. Then Alexander the Great invaded the area in 332 BC From 300 to 63 BC, Greek became the language of commerce, and Greek culture had a major influence on Judaism. In 63 BC, the Roman Empire took control of Judea and Israel.

Around the first century AD there were several small Jewish sects: the Pharisees, Sadducees, Zealots, Essenes, and Christians. "In 30 AD some Jews, following the teachings of *Yeshua of Nazareth*" (known by Christians as Jesus Christ), formed a Jewish-Christian reform movement within Judaism. It was led by James, an apostle of Yeshua of Nazareth. The next development was in 55 AD, when "Paul, a Jewish persecutor of Christians, created an alternative religion involving the teachings and person of Yeshua. He started to organize Pauline Christian churches throughout much of the Roman Empire in conflict with the Jewish Christians."[4]

From 66–70 AD, the Great Jewish Revolt against Roman occupation ended with destruction of the Second Temple and the fall of Jerusalem.

After the destruction of the Second Temple in 70 AD, these sects vanished. Christianity survived, but by breaking with Judaism and becoming a separate religion; the Pharisees survived but in the form of Rabbinic Judaism (today, known simply as *Judaism* "). The Sadducees rejected the divine inspiration of the Prophets and the Writings, relying only on the Torah as divinely inspired. Consequently, a number of other core tenets of the Pharisees' belief system (which became the basis for modern Judaism), were also dismissed by the Sadducees.[5]

Following a second revolt, Jews were not allowed to enter the city of Jerusalem, and most Jewish worship was forbidden by Rome. "About a half-million Jews were killed; thousands were sold into slavery or taken into captivity. The rest were exiled from Palestine and scattered throughout the known world."[6] Following the destruction of Jerusalem and the expulsion of the Jews, Jewish worship stopped being centrally organized around the Temple, prayer took the place of sacrifice, and worship was rebuilt around rabbis, who acted as teachers and leaders of individual communities.

It was during that time that the first Jewish oral law was organized. Rabbinic tradition holds that the details and interpretation of the law, which are called the *Oral Torah* or oral law, were originally an unwritten tradition based upon what God told Moses on Mount Sinai. However, as the persecutions of the Jews increased and the details were in danger of being forgotten, these oral laws were recorded by Rabbi Judah haNasi in the *Mishnah* in 200 AD. Over the next four centuries, this law underwent discussion and debate in both of the world's major Jewish communities (in Israel and Babylonia), and the commentaries on the Mishnah from each of these communities eventually came to be edited together into compilations known as the two Talmuds. These have been expounded by commentaries of various Torah scholars during the ages. Over time, as practices develop, codes of Jewish law are written that are based on the responsa. In rabbinic literature, the *Responsa* are known as "questions and answers" and comprise the body of written decisions and rulings given by "decisors of Jewish law." Judaism's Responsa constitutes a special class of rabbinic literature, to be distinguished from the commentaries—devoted to the interpretation of the Hebrew Bible, the Mishnah, and the Talmud—and from the codes of law which delineate the rules for ordinary incidents of life.

The responsa literature covers a period of 1,700 years—the mode, style and subject matter have changed as a function of the travels of the Jewish people and of the development of other halakhic literature, particularly the codes. Responsa play a particularly important role in Jewish law. The questions forwarded are usually practical, and often concerned with new contingencies for which no provision has been made in the codes of law, and the Responsa thus supplement the codes. They therefore function as a source of law, almost as legal precedent, in that they are consulted by later decisors in their rulings; they are also, in turn, incorporated into subsequent codes.[7]

During the seventh century, the rise and domination of Islam among largely pagan Arabs in the Arabian Peninsula resulted in the almost complete removal and conversion of the ancient Jewish communities there. Some mark this as the beginning of the Golden Age of the Jewish culture that survived. Most Jews lived in the Muslim Arab realm (Andalusia, North Africa, Palestine, Iraq, and Yemen). Despite sporadic periods of persecution, Jewish communal and cultural life flowered in this period. The universally recognized centers of Jewish life were in Jerusalem and Syria, Sura, and Iraq.

Islam and Judaism have a complex relationship. Traditionally, Jews living in Muslim lands, known as *dhimmis*, were allowed to practice their religion and to administer their internal affairs, but subject to certain conditions. They had to pay the *jizya* (a per capita tax imposed on free adult non-Muslim males) to Muslims. Dhimmis had an inferior status under Islamic rule. They had several social and legal disadvantages such as prohibitions against bearing arms or giving testimony in courts in cases involving Muslims. Many of the limitations were highly symbolic.[8]

At this point in history, the final separation of the two great religions was complete. Judaism in its rabbinical form, centered in local synagogues, was scattered throughout the known world, and Christianity, the spiritual successor of Pauline Christianity, had incorporated fragments of gnostic Christianity and Jewish Christianity. In 1054 AD, this Christianity split to become Roman Catholicism and Eastern Orthodoxy. Relations between the two religions became strained.

The Christian Scriptures include many examples of anti-Judaism. One of the gospels, written during the last third of the first century, included the accusation that all Jews, (past, present, and future), are responsible for *Deicide* the killing of God. This form of religious propaganda (from a Jewish perspective) was serious enough in its original setting, when Christianity remained a small reform movement within Judaism"[9] but became even more damaging as Christianity grew.

Then from 1095 to 1291, Christian Crusades began, sparking warfare with Islam in Palestine. Crusaders temporarily captured Jerusalem in 1099. In the year 1144, a hoax about St. William of Norwich began to circulate, accusing Jews of killing a boy and using his blood. The myth shows a complete lack of understanding of mainline Judaism. Aside from the prohibition of killing innocent persons, the Torah specifically forbids the drinking or eating of any form of blood in any quantity. However, reality never has had much of an impact on "blood libel myths." This rumor lasted for many centuries; even today it has not completely disappeared. Pope Innocent IV ordered a study in 1247. His investigators found that the myth was a Christian invention used to justify persecution of the Jews. At least four other popes subsequently vindicated the Jews. However, the accusations, trials and executions continued. In 1817, Czar Alexander I of Russia declared that the blood libel was a myth. Even that did not stop the accusations against Jews in that country.[10]

The vicious cycle continued to spiral. Many believe now it was used to justify actions during the Crusades. Tens of thousands of Jews were killed by European crusaders throughout Europe and in the Middle East. Anti-Semitism arose during the Middle Ages in the form of persecutions, forced conversion, expulsions, social restrictions, and ghettoization.

During the years 1290 and 1496, the Jews were expelled from England, France, Spain, Italy, Portugal, and many German cities. The expelled Jews relocate to the Netherlands, Turkey, Arab lands, and Judea; some eventually went to South and Central America. However, most Jews immigrated to Poland. In later centuries, more than 50 percent of Jewish world population lived in Poland. Many Jews remained in Spain after publicly converting to Christianity, becoming crypto-Jews. *Crypto-Judaism* is the secret adherence to

Judaism while publicly professing to be of another faith. The term *crypto-Jew* is also used to describe descendants of Jews who still (generally secretly) maintain some Jewish traditions, often while adhering to other faiths.

Attacks on Jews became motivated instead by theological considerations specifically deriving from Christian views about Jews and Judaism. Rabbi Moses Ben Maimon lived at a time when both Christianity and Islam were developing active theologies. Jewish scholars were often asked to attest to their faith by their counterparts in other religions. *Maimonides's 13 Principles of Faith* were formulated in his commentary on the Mishnah. By the time of Maimonides, centers of Jewish learning and law were dispersed geographically. Judaism no longer had a central authority that might bestow official approval on his principles of faith.

Detailed constructions of articles of faith did not find favor in Judaism before the medieval era, when Jews were forced to defend their faith from both Islamic and Christian inquisitions, disputations and polemics. The necessity of defending their religion against the attacks of other philosophies induced many Jewish leaders to define and formulate their beliefs. *Emunot ve-Deot* is an exposition of the main tenets of Judaism. They are listed as: The world was created by God; God is one and incorporeal; belief in revelation; man is called to righteousness and endowed with all necessary qualities of mind and soul to avoid sin; belief in reward and punishment; the soul is created pure; after death it leaves the body; belief in resurrection; Messianic expectation, retribution, and final judgment.[11]

The most important code, the *Shulchan Aruch* (a written catalogue of Jewish law) was composed in the sixteenth century. It, together with its commentaries, is considered by the vast majority of Orthodox Jews to be the most authoritative compilation since the Talmud and largely determines Jewish Orthodox religious practice today.

A Ukrainian Cossack led a massacre of Polish gentry and Jewry that left an estimated one hundred thousand Jews dead and a similar number of gentry between the years of 1648 and 1655.

In 1729, Moses Mendelssohn, the founder of the enlightenment movement, strove to bring an end to the isolation of the Jews so that they would be able to embrace the culture of the western world and, in turn, be embraced by gentiles as equals. This opened the door for the development of all the modern Jewish denominations and the revival of Hebrew as a spoken language, but it also paved the way for many who, wishing to be fully accepted into Christian society, converted to Christianity or chose to assimilate or to emulate it.

Then in 1790, in the USA, President George Washington sent a letter to the Jewish community taking a stand against the constant persecution received by the Jews. He wrote that he envisions a country "which gives bigotry no sanction...persecution no assistance." Despite the fact that the United States was a predominantly Protestant country, theoretically Jews are given full rights.[12] But the persecution in Europe continues in 1881–1884, 1903–1906, and 1918–1920 in the form of *pogroms* (pogrom is a form of riot directed against a particular group, whether ethnic, religious or other, and characterized by destruction of their homes, businesses, and religious centers. Historically, the term as used in English has very often been used to denote extensive violence against Jews—either spontaneous or premeditated). These three major waves killed tens of thousands of Jews in Russia and Ukraine. In February of 1917, Jews got equal rights in Russia, but the Russian civil war led to over two thousand more pogroms with tens of thousands murdered and hundreds of thousand made homeless.

In 1933, Hitler took over Germany; his anti-Semitic sentiments were well-known, prompting numerous Jews to emigrate. Shortly after that, in 1938, the Holocaust began.

The *Holocaust* is the term generally used to describe the genocide of approximately six million European Jews during World War II, as part of a program of deliberate extermination planned and executed by the *National Socialist German Workers' Party* (Nazi) regime in Germany led by Adolf Hitler. Other groups were persecuted and killed by the regime, including the Roma; Soviets, particularly prisoners of war; Communists; ethnic Poles; other Slavic people; the disabled; gay men; and political and religious dissidents. Many scholars do not include these groups in the definition of the Holocaust, defining it as the genocide of the Jews, or what the Nazis called the *"Final Solution of the Jewish Question."*

Taking into account all the victims of Nazi persecution, the death toll rises considerably: estimates generally place the total number of victims at 9 to 11 million.[13]

Because of the magnitude of the Holocaust, many people have reexamined the classical theological views on God's goodness and actions in the world. Some question whether people can still have any faith after the Holocaust. Some theological responses to these questions are explored in Holocaust theology. It refers to a body of theological and philosophical debate, soul-searching, and analysis, with the subsequent related literature, that attempts to come to grips with various conflicting views about the role of God in this human world and the events of the European Holocaust that occurred during World War II.

Within all the monotheistic faiths, many answers have been proposed. However, in light of the magnitude of evil seen in the Holocaust, many people have reexamined classical views on this subject. The aftermath it had on the faith of some Jews varied. There have been writings stating everything from "God is dead; He turned away from humanity, and is therefore no longer relevant" to "the European Jews were sinful and needed to be punished."

In most industrialized nations with modern economies, such as the United States, Israel, Canada, United Kingdom, Argentina, and South Africa, a wide variety of Jewish practices exist, along with a growing plurality of secular and nonpracticing Jews. For example, in the world's second largest Jewish community, that of the United States, according to the 2001 edition of the National Jewish Population Survey, 4.3 million out of 5.1 million Jews had some sort of connection to the religion. Of that population of connected Jews, 80 percent participated in some sort of Jewish religious observance, but only 48 percent belonged to a synagogue.

Religious (and secular) Jewish movements in the United States and Canada perceive this as a crisis situation and have grave concern over rising rates of intermarriage and assimilation in the Jewish community. Since American Jews are marrying later in life and are having fewer children. Intermarriage rates range from 40–50 percent in the United States, and only about a third of children of intermarried couples are raised as Jews.

Due to intermarriage and low birth rates, the Jewish population in the United States declined between 1990 and 2001. But to be fair, there has been a decline in many other mainline religions as well. Today's Jewish population is difficult to define. The numbers found online range from fourteen million to eighteen million worldwide. The reason for this may vary, from secular Jews who consider it as their culture instead of their religion, to the fact that some Jews are wary to identify themselves due to a long history of prejudices.

Basic Doctrine

Judaism is a *monotheistic* religion based on principles and ethics embodied in the Hebrew Bible (books of the Bible originally written in biblical Hebrew and closely corresponds to contents of the Protestant Old Testament), and the Talmud and other texts. According to Jewish tradition, Judaism begins with the covenant between God and Abraham. Historically, Judaism has considered belief in the divine revelation and acceptance of the *Written* and *Oral Torah* as its fundamental core belief, but Judaism does not have a centralized authority dictating religious dogma. This gave rise to many different formulations as to the specific theological beliefs inherent in the *Torah* and *Talmud*. While some rabbis have at times agreed upon a firm formulation, others have disagreed, many criticizing any such attempt as minimizing acceptance of the entire Torah.

13 Principles of Faith:

1. *I believe with perfect faith that the Creator, Blessed be His Name, is the Creator and Guide of everything that has been created; He alone has made, does make, and will make all things.*
2. *I believe with perfect faith that the Creator, Blessed be His Name, is One, and that there is no unity in any manner like His, and that He alone is our God, who was, and is, and will be.*
3. *I believe with perfect faith that the Creator, Blessed be His Name, has no body, and that He is free from all the properties of matter, and that there can be no (physical) comparison to Him whatsoever.*

4. *I believe with perfect faith that the Creator, Blessed be His Name, is the first and the last.*
5. *I believe with perfect faith that to the Creator, Blessed be His Name, and to Him alone, it is right to pray, and that it is not right to pray to any being besides Him.*
6. *I believe with perfect faith that all the words of the prophets are true.*
7. *I believe with perfect faith that the prophecy of Moses our teacher, peace be upon him, was true, and that he was the chief of the prophets, both those who preceded him and those who followed him.*
8. *I believe with perfect faith that the entire Torah that is now in our possession is the same that was given to Moses our teacher, peace be upon him.*
9. *I believe with perfect faith that this Torah will not be exchanged, and that there will never be any other Torah from the Creator, Blessed be His Name.*
10. *I believe with perfect faith that the Creator, Blessed be His Name, knows all the deeds of human beings and all their thoughts, as it is written, "Who fashioned the hearts of them all, Who comprehends all their actions" (Psalms 33:15).*
11. *I believe with perfect faith that the Creator, Blessed be His Name, rewards those who keep His commandments and punishes those that transgress them.*
12. *I believe with perfect faith in the coming of the Messiah; and even though he may tarry, nonetheless, I wait every day for his coming.*
13. *I believe with perfect faith that there will be a revival of the dead at the time when it shall please the Creator, Blessed be His name, and His mention shall be exalted for ever and ever.[14]*

The basis of Jewish law and tradition is the Torah. According to rabbinic tradition, there are 613 commandments in the Torah. Some of these laws are directed only to men or to women, some only to the ancient priestly groups (members of the tribe of Levi), and some only to farmers within the land of Israel. Many laws were only applicable when the Temple in Jerusalem existed, and fewer than 300 of these commandments are still applicable today. While there have been Jewish groups whose beliefs were claimed to be based on the written text of the Torah alone, most Jews believed in what they call the Oral Law as well.

Maimonides's thirteen principles were controversial when first proposed. These were ignored by much of the Jewish community for the next few centuries. Over time, two poetic restatements of these principles became canonized in the Jewish prayer book. Eventually, *Maimonides's Thirteen Principles of Faith* became the most widely accepted statement of belief. As noted, however, neither Maimonides nor his contemporaries viewed these principles as encompassing all of Jewish belief, but rather as the core theological underpinnings of the acceptance of Judaism.

God or Gods

Fundamentally, Judaism believes that God, as the creator of time, space, energy and matter, is beyond them and cannot be born or die or have a son. Every Jew must believe and know that there exists a First Being, without beginning or end, who brought all things into existence and continues to sustain them. This being is God. He is everywhere. He has no spatial boundaries. He fills the universe and beyond. God is all knowing. He knows all man's thoughts and deeds in the past, present, and future.

God's name is treated with unusual care in Jewish tradition. The divine name Yhwh is never pronounced. Traditionally, Jews read the word Adonai (often translated as "the Lord") whenever reading God's holiest name in Torah or in prayer. However, Adonai is not God's name. While Judaism's traditional beliefs about God are clear, Jews today vary greatly in their beliefs about God. Did God write the Torah or inspire the Torah? What does God want from people? How could God let the Holocaust happen?

Christ

While Judaism has no special or particular view of Jesus, and very few texts in Judaism directly refer to or take note of Jesus, Judaism takes a strong stand against many views expressed by Christian theology. One of the most important Jewish principles of faith is the belief in one God, and one

God only, with no partnership of any kind. And belief in Jesus as a deity, part of a deity, son of God, or Christ, is incompatible with Judaism.

The belief that Jesus is the Messiah or a prophet of God is also incompatible with traditional Jewish tenets. For this reason, related issues such as the historical existence of Jesus and whatever his life involved are likewise not considered relevant in Judaism. "The idea of the Jewish Messiah is different from the Christian Christ because Jews believe Jesus did not fulfill Jewish Messianic prophecies that establish the criteria for the coming of the Messiah. Authoritative texts of Judaism reject Jesus as God, Divine Being, intermediary between humans and God, Messiah or saint."[15]

Basic Worship Service

Traditionally, Jews recite prayers three times daily, with a fourth prayer added on *Shabbat* (also known as Sabbath in non-Jewish circles) and holidays. At the heart of each service is the *Amidah*. Another key prayer in many services is the declaration of faith, the *Shema Yisrael*. The Shema is the recitation of a verse from the Torah (*Deuteronomy* 6:4): *"Hear, O Israel! The Lord is our God! The Lord is One!"* Most of the prayers in a traditional Jewish service can be said in solitary prayer, although communal prayer is preferred. Communal prayer requires a quorum of ten adult Jews, called a *minyan*. In nearly all Orthodox and a few conservative circles, only male Jews are counted toward a minyan; but most conservative Jews and members of other Jewish denominations count female Jews as well.

In addition to prayer services, traditional Jews recite prayers and benedictions throughout the day when performing various acts. Prayers are recited upon waking up in the morning, before eating or drinking different foods, after eating a meal, and so on. Approach to prayer varies among the Jewish denominations. Differences can include the texts of prayers, the frequency of prayer, the number of prayers recited at various religious events, the use of musical instruments and choral music, and whether prayers are recited in the traditional liturgical languages or the vernacular. In general, Orthodox and Conservative congregations adhere most closely to tradition, and Reform and Reconstructionist synagogues are more likely to incorporate translations and contemporary writings in their services.

Also, in some Conservative synagogues, and all Reform and Reconstructionist congregations, women participate in prayer services on an equal basis with men, including roles traditionally filled only by men, such as reading from the Torah. In addition, many Reform temples use musical accompaniment such as organs and mixed choirs.

Shabbat, the weekly day of rest lasting from shortly before sundown on Friday night to shortly after sundown Saturday night, commemorates God's day of rest after six days of creation. It plays a pivotal role in Jewish practice and is governed by (a large amount) of religious law. At sundown on Friday, the woman of the house welcomes the Shabbat by lighting two or more candles and reciting a blessing. The evening meal begins with a blessing recited aloud over a cup of wine, and a blessing recited over the bread. It is customary to have two braided loaves of bread on the table. During Shabbat Jews are forbidden to engage in any activity that falls under 39 categories of work. In fact the activities banned on the Sabbath are not "work" in the usual sense: They include such actions as lighting a fire, writing, using money and carrying anything in the public domain. The prohibition of lighting a fire has been extended in the modern era to driving a car which involves burning fuel and using electricity.[16]

Infant Baptism or Blessing

Brit Milah (covenant of circumcision) or *bris* (Yiddish) is a religious ceremony within Judaism to welcome infant Jewish boys into a covenant between God and the Children of Israel through ritual circumcision performed by a *mohel* (the man qualified to perform the ceremony), on the eighth day of the child's life in the presence of family and friends, followed by a celebratory meal. *Zeved habat* or *simchat bat* are terms for the ritual for naming infant Jewish girls. These rituals are parallel to the Brit Milah ceremony for Jewish boys, albeit without the circumcision. In the last century, both Modern Orthodox and non-Orthodox Jews have revived interest in these little-known traditional ceremonies for welcoming baby girls and have developed innovative ceremonies. These ceremonies are often known under the newly coined terms *simchat bat* or a *brit bat.*

Initiation, Baptism, or Confirmation

Boys reach the status of *Bar Mitzvah* on their 13th birthday; girls reach *Bat Mitzvah* on their 12th birthday. This means that they are recognized as adults and are personally responsible to follow the Jewish commandments and laws. Males are allowed to lead a religious service; they are counted in a minyan (a quota of men necessary to perform certain parts of religious services). Following their Bar Mitzvah or Bat Mitzvah they can sign contracts; they can testify in religious courts; theoretically, they can marry, although the Talmud recommends 18 to 24 as the proper age for marriage.[17]

Marriage

According to the Talmud, forty days before a male child is conceived, a voice from heaven announces whose daughter he is going to marry, literally a match made in heaven! In Yiddish, this perfect match is called *bashert* (meaning, fate or destiny). The idea has a strong hold within the Orthodox Jewish community, and there is a resurgence of "matchmaking" today. As part of the wedding ceremony, the husband gives the wife a marriage contract. It spells out the husband's obligations to the wife during marriage, conditions of inheritance upon his death, and obligations regarding the support of children of the marriage. It also provides for the wife's support in the event of divorce. There are standard conditions; however, additional conditions can be included by mutual agreement.

Because marriage under Jewish law is essentially a private contractual agreement between a man and a woman, it does not require the presence of a rabbi or any other religious official. It is common, however, for rabbis to officiate, partly in imitation of the Christian practice and partly because the presence of a religious or civil official is required under United States civil law. Judaism has always accepted divorce as a fact of life, albeit an unfortunate one, and permits divorce for any reason but discourages divorce.

Death and Afterlife

Although Judaism concentrates on the importance of the earthly world, all of classical Judaism suggests an afterlife. Jewish tradition affirms that the human soul is immortal, and thus, survives the physical death of the body. The hereafter is known as *Olam Ha-Ba* (the world to come) *gan eden* (paradise) and *gehinnom* (purgatory). Only the very righteous go directly to gan eden. "Although there are a few statements to the contrary in the Talmud, the predominant view of Judaism is that the righteous of all nations have a share in the Olam Ha-Ba."[18]

The average person descends to a place of punishment and/or purification, generally referred to as *gehinnom*. Some views see gehinnom as one of severe punishment, a bit like the Christian hell of fire and brimstone. Other sources merely see it as a time when we can see the actions of our lives objectively, see the harm that we have done and the opportunities we missed, and experience remorse for our actions. The period of time in gehinnom does not exceed twelve months and then ascends to take his place on Olam Ha-Ba. Only the utterly wicked do not ascend at the end of this period. Sources differ on what happens at the end of those twelve months: some say that the wicked soul is utterly destroyed and ceases to exist while others say that the soul continues to exist in a state of consciousness of remorse.

There are some mystical schools of thought that believe resurrection is not a one-time event, but is continual. The souls of the righteous are reborn in to continue the ongoing process of mending of the world. Some sources indicate that reincarnation is a routine process, while others indicate that it only occurs in unusual circumstances, where the soul left unfinished business behind. Belief in reincarnation is also one way to explain the traditional Jewish belief that every Jewish soul in history was present at Sinai and agreed to the covenant with God. (Another explanation: that the soul exists before the body, and these unborn souls were present in some form at Sinai).

According to Judaism, there is little material on this subject of what happens in the next world.

Traditional Judaism firmly believes that death is not the end of human existence. However, because Judaism is primarily focused on life here and now rather than on the afterlife, Judaism does not have much dogma about the afterlife, and leaves a great deal of room for personal opinion. It is possible for an Orthodox Jew to believe that the souls of the righteous dead go to a place similar to the Christian heaven, or that they are reincarnated through many lifetimes, or that they simply wait until the coming of the Messiah, when they will be resurrected. Likewise, Orthodox Jews can believe that the souls of the wicked are tormented by demons of their own creation, or that wicked souls are simply destroyed at death, ceasing to exist.[19]

All attempts to describe heaven and hell are, of course, speculative. Because Judaism believes that God is good, it believes that God rewards good people; it does not believe that Adolf Hitler and his victims share the same fate. Beyond that, it is hard to assume much more. They are asked to leave afterlife in God's hands.

Judgment and Salvation

Judaism does not believe that salvation or repentance from sin can be achieved through sacrifice on another's behalf and is instead focused on the requirements of personal repentance. In addition, Judaism focuses on understanding how one may live a sacred life according to God's will in this world, rather than the hope of, or methods for, finding spiritual salvation in a future one. Judaism views Jews' divine obligation to be living as a holy people in full accordance with divine will, as a light unto the nations, and Judaism does not purport to offer the exclusive path to salvation or the one path to God. Judaism is not focused on the question of how to get into heaven. Judaism is focused on <u>this life</u> and how to live it.

Special Doctrine

Orthodox Judaism: holds that both the Written and Oral Torah were divinely revealed to Moses, and that the laws within it are binding and unchanging. Most Orthodox Jews holds to one particular form of Jewish theology, based on *Maimonides's Thirteen Principles of Faith*. Orthodox

Judaism broadly shades into two main styles, Modern Orthodox Judaism and Haredi Judaism. The philosophical distinctions are often reflected in styles of dress and rigor in practice. According to most Orthodox Jews, Jewish people who do not keep the laws of Shabbat and *Yom Tov* (the holidays), kashrut, and family purity are considered "non-religious."

Haredi Judaism: (Also known as ultra-Orthodox Judaism, although some find this term offensive.) It is a very conservative form of Judaism. The Haredi world revolves around study, prayer, and meticulous religious observance. Some Haredi Jews are more open to the modern world, perhaps most notably the *Lubavitch Hasidim,* but their acceptance of modernity is more a tool for enhancing Jewish faith than an end in itself.

Modern Orthodox Judaism: It emphasizes strict observance of religious laws and commandments but with a broad, liberal approach to modernity and living in a non-Jewish or secular environment. Modern Orthodox women are gradually assuming a greater role in Jewish ritual practice, which is not acceptable in the Haredi community.

Conservative Judaism: It developed in Europe and the United States in the 1800s as Jews reacted to the changes brought about by the Enlightenment and Jewish emancipation. It is characterized by a commitment to following traditional Jewish laws and customs, including observance of Shabbat and *kashruth* (Jewish dietary law), a deliberately nonfundamentalist teaching of Jewish principles of faith, a positive attitude toward modern culture, and an acceptance of both traditional rabbinic modes of study along with modern scholarship and critical text study when considering Jewish religious texts.

Conservative Judaism teaches that Jewish law is not static but has always developed in response to changing conditions. It holds that the Torah is a divine document written by prophets inspired by God but rejects the Orthodox position that it was dictated by God to Moses. Similarly, conservative Judaism holds that Judaism's Oral Law is divine and normative but rejects some orthodox interpretations of the Oral Law. Accordingly, conservative Judaism holds that both the Written and Oral Law may be interpreted by the rabbis to reflect modern sensibilities and suit modern conditions, although great caution should be exercised in doing so.

Reconstructionist Judaism: It started as a stream of philosophy by Mordechai Kaplan, a conservative rabbi, and later became an independent movement emphasizing reinterpreting Judaism for modern times. Like Reform Judaism, Reconstructionist Judaism does not hold that Jewish law as such requires observance, but unlike Reform, Reconstructionist thought emphasizes the role of the community in deciding what observances to follow.

Reform Judaism: It is called liberal or progressive in many countries and originally formed in Germany in the late eighteenth century AD in response to the Enlightenment. Its defining c haracteristic w ith respect to the other movements is its rejection of the Jewish ceremonial law and belief. Instead, individual Jews should exercise an informed autonomy about what to observe. Reform Judaism initially defined Judaism as a religion rather than as a race or culture, rejected most of the ritual ceremonial laws of the Torah while observing moral laws, and emphasized the ethical call of the prophets.

Hasidic Judaism: It is a stream of Haredi Judaism based on the teachings of Rabbi Yisroel ben Eliezer. Hasidic philosophy is rooted in the *kabbalah*. Kabbalah is an esoteric system of interpretation of the scriptures and is based on the belief that every word, letter, number, and even accent contained mysteries interpretable by those who knew the secret. The two principal sources of the kabbalists are the *Book of Creation* and the *Book of Splendor*. Hasidic Jews accept the kabbalah as canonical sacred scripture. They are distinguished both by a variety of special customs and practices, including reliance on a supreme religious leader and a special dress code particular to each Hasidic group. Hasidic Judaism eventually became the way of life for many Jews in Europe. Waves of Jewish immigration in the 1880s carried it to the United States.[20]

Jewish Renewal: It is a recent North American movement that was begun by Rabbi Zalman Schachter-Shalomi, a Hasidic rabbi, in the 1960s.

Jewish Renewal focuses on spirituality and social justice but does not address issues of Jewish law. Men and women participate equally in prayer.

There are some organizations th at combine elements of Ju daism with those of other religions. The most well-known of these is the *Messianic Judaism* movement (closely related to Hebrew Christianity), groups of ethnic Jews and gentiles, historically sponsored by Christian organizations that promote the belief that Jesus is the Messiah. These groups typically combine Christian theology and Christology with a thin veneer of Jewish religious practices. The most controversial of these groups is the American Jews for Jesus, which actively proselytizes ethnic Jews through numerous missionary campaigns in major American cities. Other examples of syncretism include Judeo-Paganists, a loosely organized set of Jews who incorporate Pagan or Wiccan beliefs. Jewish Buddhists is another loosely organized group that incorporates elements of Asian spirituality in their faith, and some Renewal Jews who borrow freely and openly from Buddhism, Sufism, Native American religion, and other faiths. It should be noted here, that these "syncrenistic Jews" are not considered Jews by those that are more traditional. But the practicioners themselves believe that they are still Jews, and honor their Jewish heritage and culture.[21]

Beliefs on Homosexuality: The issue has been a subject of contention within modern Jewish denominations and has led to debate and division. More liberal branches of Judaism are allowing the ordination of gay and lesbian rabbis and performing or hosting same-sex union ceremonies. Traditional Judaism believes that even someone born with homosexual preferences may be able to find sexual fulfillment in a heterosexual marriage. And it is the heterosexual marriage that most benefits the community.

The role of women in the Jewish faith has been a subject of debate within the Jewish community since 1946. The reform movement was the first to ordain women rabbis in 1972. The reconstructionist movement followed suit by graduating their first woman rabbi in 1977. The conservative movement lagged slightly behind, ordaining their first woman rabbis from its rabbinical school in 1983.

<u>Religious Clothing:</u> A *kippah* (plural kippot) is a slightly rounded brimless skullcap worn by many Jewish men while praying, eating, reciting blessings, or studying Jewish religious texts, and at all times by some Jewish men. In non-Orthodox communities, some women have also begun to wear kippot. The kippot range in size, from a small round beanie that covers only the back of the head to a large snug cap that covers the whole crown.

Tzitzit are special knotted fringes or tassels found on the four corners of the *tallith* or prayer shawl. The tallith is worn by Jewish men and some Jewish women during the prayer service. Customs vary regarding when a Jew begins wearing a tallith. In some communities, boys wear a tallith from bar mitzvah age. In others, it is customary to wear one only after marriage. A *tallith katan* (small tallith) is a fringed garment worn under the clothing throughout the day.

Tefillin, known in English as *phylacteries* (meaning fortress or protection), are two square-leather boxes containing biblical verses, attached to the forehead or wound around the left arm by leather straps. They serve as a sign and remembrance that God brought the children of Israel out of Egypt. According to Jewish law, they should be worn during weekday morning prayer services. There are four specific verses that are always used:

- *Exodus* 13:1–10: the duty of the Jewish people to always remember the redemption from Egyptian bondage,
- *Exodus* 13:11–16: the obligation of every Jew to inform his children on these matters,
- *Deuteronomy* 6:4–9: pronouncing the unity of the one God, and
- *Deuteronomy* 11:13–21: expressing God's assurance to us of reward that will follow our observance of the Torah's precepts and warning of retribution for disobedience to them.

A *kittel*, a white knee-length overgarment, is worn by prayer leaders and some observant traditional Jews on the high holidays. It is traditional for the head of the household to wear a kittel at the Passover

Seder, and some grooms wear one under the wedding canopy. Jewish males are buried in a tallith and sometimes also a kittel, which are part of the burial garments.

<u>Diet:</u> The laws of *Kashrut* (keeping kosher) are the Jewish dietary laws. Food in accord with Jewish law is termed *kosher* (similar to the halāl requirements of Islam, but with fewer preparation requirements). The Torah cites no reason for the laws of kashrut, but the rabbis have offered various explanations, including ritual purity, teaching people to control their urges, and health benefits. Kashrut involves the abstention from consuming birds and beasts that prey on other animals, and creatures that roam the sea floor eating the excretions of other animals (such as shrimp or crab). Major prohibitions exist on eating pork, which is considered an unclean animal. Meat is ritually slaughtered, and meat and milk are not eaten together, based on the biblical injunction against cooking a kid in its mother's milk...The deeper purpose of Kashrut is to lend a spiritual dimension to the physical act of eating. The idea is that Jews should not put anything into their mouths that involves spiritual "negatives" such as pain, sickness, uncleanliness.[22]

Notes

Monophysitist

History

Monophysitism (mon-nah'-fuh-site-izm) is based on the concept of Christ having only one nature—this being purely divine. The early Christians were often divided among themselves about how much of a "god" Jesus was supposed to be. Definitions can be hard to understand; they deal with the following challenge: How to define Christ with full divine qualities, yet preserve the concept of God walking among men as a man. The issue of the divine and the human nature of Christ was no mere theological polemic. The issue would be, and indeed still is, important in Western Christianity. In fact, this doctrine alone has caused splits within the Christian faith. But in Greek patristic thought, the relationship between the human and the divine, both actually and symbolically represented in the person of Jesus Christ, takes on added significance.

In the East, it was expressed in mystical terms of deification and a new life in God: *"God became man, so that man may become God"* as Athanasius once declared. If Jesus is not truly man, then there is no special relationship between Jesus and mankind, and hence, no deification. Conversely, if Jesus is not God, then there is no bridge between mankind and God, and no hope of deification as well. Thus, for Eastern Christians in particular, both the humanity and the divinity need to be present in Christ to achieve mankind's salvation. The question of the Christological debates, then, was how that relationship was to be conceived and developed.

The Council of Nicaea in 325 AD stated that Jesus Christ was God, coequal, coeternal, and of one nature with the Father. After Nicaea, all Orthodox Christians could agree that the Son was fully divine, but Jesus of Nazareth was nevertheless an historical person, a man who lived and breathed and even died within the context of history. How could this finite man also be the all-powerful God of the Judeo-Christian tradition? The Christian scriptures had no definitive answer, and therefore, the relationship between this historical figure of Jesus of Nazareth and the divine Son of God was open to debate.

The controversy emerging out of Nicaea tended to divide along opposing schools of thought. Theologians of the Antiochian school emphasized the humanity of Christ; their counter-parts at Alexandria, Egypt, emphasized his divinity and his role as teacher of divine truth. The debate intensified when the subject of Mary came into discussion. One group called Mary the Mother of God, which was contrary to the other group's philosophy that Mary was the Mother of Christ, suggesting that Mary was the mother of only Christ's human nature, but that Christ's divine nature was separate and eternal and did not come through his human mother because they believed that Christ needed to be fully and truly human if he were to be the savior of human beings.

Apollinarius of Antioch (now in present-day Turkey) had in the late fourth century declared that Christ did have a human body, but that the divine had taken place of the "thinking principle"(the human consciousness). Apollinarianism was condemned at the Second Ecumenical Council in 381. Apollinarianism was not a Monophysite concept, but within it laid the seeds for Monophysite ideas.

Eutyches, a fifth-century leader of a monastery in Constantinople, was the first who began the doctrine. In response to the controversy, Eutyches taught that Jesus's humanity was essentially absorbed by His divine nature, describing it as being "dissolved like a drop of honey in the sea."[1] An analogy that might help explain what he meant can be seen if you would put a drop of ink in a glass of water. The result is a mixture that is not pure water or pure ink. Instead, you would have some type of <u>third</u> substance that is a mixture of the two in which both the ink and water are changed in some way. In essence, that is what Eutyches taught about the two natures of Christ. He taught that both natures were changed to some degree, which resulted in a third and unique nature being formed— the essential principal of Monophysitism.

During the same period, the Alexandrians were convinced that God had a single divine nature, and that He "emptied Himself" to become human—without losing any of His divinity. But how this relationship between the divine and the human was to be conceived was not made clear. How can one speak of God being incarnate within Jesus and still equally assert Jesus's full manhood? Eutyches was there to share his answers to those questions. Eutyches's energy and imprudence with which he asserted his opinions brought him the accusation of heresy in 448, leading to his excommunication in 449, at the controversial Second Council of Ephesus.

"Leo's Tome" refers to a letter in 449 AD from Pope Leo I to the patriarch of Constantinople, expounding the orthodox Christology of the West. In this letter, Leo maintains that Jesus Christ is one person of the divine Trinity with two distinct natures that are permanently united. These two natures unite properties through the sharing of attributes between the divine and human natures of Christ. Alexandrian theologians favored this concept. Leo's statement was written specifically to discredit the heresy of Eutyches's teachings. Only two years after the council had made its pronouncement, another ecumenical council was called, the Council of Chalcedon in 451 AD, to deal with the issue at hand. Pope Leo's letter was recognized by the Council of Chalcedon as a statement of orthodox Christology and was soon to formulate for the doctrine of the Church in the West.

Chalcedon attempted to establish a common ground between the Monophysitists and the Orthodox, but it did not work. The doctrine of the hypostatic union (the two natures of Jesus) was adopted as the Orthodox doctrine at the council. The creed asserted two distinct natures, human and divine, and affirmed the one person of Jesus Christ.

More moderate Monophysitism was put forward by Severus, patriarch of Antioch. It was less rigid and in many ways differed only nominally from the doctrines of the Council of Chalcedon. Nonetheless, all Monophysites rejected the dogmatic formulas of Chalcedon, and all efforts to reach an acceptable compromise failed. Even after the Council of Chalcedon, the citizens of Alexandria refused to give up their belief, which became a symbol of resistance to the central imperial authority. A riot was the result. The soldiers who attempted to quell it were driven into the ancient temple of Serapis, which was now a church, and it was burnt over their heads. Two thousand soldiers reinforced the garrison and committed scandalous violence. The people were obliged to submit, but the patriarch was safe only under military protection. Edicts were issued by Emperor Theodosius II against the Eutychians in 452, forbidding them to have priests or assemblies to make wills or inherit property or to do military service. Priests who were obstinate in error were to be banished beyond the limits of the empire.[2]

Pope Dioscorus I of Alexandria was patriarch of Alexandria at the time. He was deposed by the Council of Chalcedon in 451 but was recognized as patriarch by the Coptic Church. When the death of Dioscurus (September 454) in exile at Gangra was known, two bishops consecrated Timothy Ælurus as his successor. Henceforward, almost the whole of Egypt acknowledged the Monophysite patriarch. In February 457, Archdeacon Proterius was murdered in a riot, and Catholic bishops everywhere were replaced by Monophysites. Antioch, the other great rival of Constantinople, also embraced Monophysitism. By the sixth century, Monophysitism had a strong institutional basis in three churches: the Armenian Church, the Coptic Church, and the Jacobite Church, all of which remain nominally Monophysite today. Divisions arose in the Eastern Church, which caused Rome to eventually excommunicate the Monophysitists in 519 AD.

But they didn't care about Rome or Greece. The response on the part of the people seems to have been one of complete loyalty to the emperor. But in 516, the monks and people of Alexandria rioted against Emperor Anastasius's choice of patriarch, and more than a few monasteries in Egypt refused to bow to the Orthodox emperor Heralius, the heretic. Each of the provinces had maintained their own distinctive heritage and traditions, and because the Monophysite position seems to have attached itself to the vernacular language of these areas, it was popular among the common people. The Monophysite controversies continued the theological, political, social, and philosophical tensions between the Christians at Alexandria and the Christians at Antioch. It was condemned as heresy at the sixth ecumenical council in 680–81AD. The Alexandrian Monophysites ultimately separated to become the Egyptian Coptic Orthodox Church in Syria and Armenia, Monophysitism dominated a permanent schism resulted in the creation of the Jacobite, Coptic, and Armenian Churches.

The Byzantine emperors tried to eradicate Monophysitism from their empire in an effort to achieve civil and religious unity, but Empress Theodora, wife of Justinian I, promoted its spread throughout all of Syria, Mesopotamia, and other countries by sending Jacob Baradai into Syria to secretly consecrate twenty-seven bishops and some two thousand priests, thus giving a strong hierarchy to the Syrian Monophysite Church. The Coptic Church asserted its independence from the empire, which it saw as hostile and alien. It became a national church and survived the Arab conquests, in part because it was strongly supported by the desert monks.

The Coptic churches, both in Egypt and in Ethiopia, remained the dominant form of African Christianity from the Muslim invasion up to the coming of the missionaries in the nineteenth century. There are at present between twelve and thirteen million Christians worldwide who have, to a lesser or greater extent, identified themselves with one or another of the many variant forms of Monophysitism. Generally, it is possible to speak of four main Monophysite churches: the *Syrian Orthodox Church* of Antioch (the *West Syrian* or *Jacobite Church*), the *Armenian Church*, the *Egyptian (Coptic) Church*, and the *Ethiopian Church*.

God or Gods

The Trinity is God the Father, and His Son, and His Holy Spirit. The Trinity is one in essence and is undivided. Saint Gregory Nazianzen says, "*It is necessary both to maintain the one God and confess the three Persons, each in his own individuality.*" According to Saint Gregory, the God is three persons without division, and the three persons are united but with distinctions. Because of this, both the division and the union are paradoxical. So you can say they are one with three distinct (not different) personalities.

God the Father is the Creator of heaven and earth and all seen and unseen. He created the world through the Son (the Word) in the Holy Spirit. From the Father, the Son is begotten, not created; He is the Word of God. Through the Son, we come to know the Father. The Holy Spirit proceeds from the Father, is the Spirit of God, and is one in essence with the Father just as is the Son. The Holy Spirit is the inspirer of the holy scriptures. He empowers the church for service to God and imparts spiritual gifts and virtues for Christian life and witness.

Christ

In a basic sense, Monophysitism is the doctrinal position that Jesus Christ had only one nature. The name itself is of modern construction: literally, *mono,* meaning one, and *physis*, meaning nature.

One of the controversies was the activity of Christ as man and the purely divine activity, will, and knowledge, which the Son has in common with the Father and the Holy Spirit. In speaking of one activity, one will, and one knowledge in Christ, Monophysitism refused to distinguish between the human faculties of Christ-activity, will and intellect, and the divine nature itself. Christ's humanity was not a mere fleshly s hell that God rented and used for a temporary amount of time. God did not just come to live in flesh as a man, but the "Word became flesh."

God incorporated human nature into His eternal being. In the incarnation, humanity has been permanently incorporated into the Godhead. God is now a man in addition to being God. At the virgin conception, God acquired an identity He would retain for the rest of eternity. His human existence is both authentic and permanent. Jesus's humanity is not something that can be discarded or dissolved back into the Godhead, but He will always and forever exist in heaven as a glorified man, albeit God at the same time. Upon His ascension, Jesus was not deified but, rather, was glorified.

Some Monophysites thought it necessary for Christ to retain His human nature but tended to view that nature as being mixed with the divine. One parallel to the Word being in double being is that of the bread and the wine in the Eucharist. The actual bread and wine remain by their nature bread and wine, but in power and by a miracle, they become in truth the body and blood of Christ for the believer.

Basic Doctrine

Vocabulary

Catholicism: The union in Christ is not a union of two natures directly with one another, but a union of the two in one hypostasis; thus they are distinct yet inseparable, and each acts in communion with the other.

Dyophysitism: This is the belief that Christ had two natures: both divine and human. This concept won out after extensive debate at the church council at Chalcedon in 451 AD. It is imbedded in the Chalcedonian Creed.

Eutychianism: It holds that the human and divine natures of Christ were fused into one new single (mono) nature. His human nature was dissolved like a drop of honey in the sea. This view essentially absorbed the human nature into the divine nature. In an attempt to unify the person of Jesus, Eutychianism denied the two natures of Jesus and affirmed a new, or third, nature.

Nestorianism: Jesus to be two distinct persons, closely and inseparably united. He was banished for maintaining that Mary was the mother of the man Jesus only, and therefore should not be called the mother of God.

Monophysitism: It is the Christological position that Christ has only one nature (human that was divine), as opposed to the Chalcedonian position, which holds that Christ maintains two natures: one divine and one human. Monophysitism and its antithesis, Nestorianism, were both hotly disputed and divisive competing tenets in the maturing Christian traditions during the first half of the fifth century.

Another comparison:
- Nestorians: one person, two beings or entities, two natures.
- Catholics: one person, one being or entity, two natures.
- Monophysites: one person, one being or entity, one nature.

There are four branches of the Monophysites: the Syrian Jacobites; the Copts, including the Abyssinians; the Armenians; and the less ancient Maronites.

<u>The Coptic Church of Egypt:</u> The name *Coptic* is derived from the Greek word for "Egyptian." The Copts in Egypt are the genuine descendants of the ancient Egyptians, though with a mixture of Greek and Arab blood. The Coptic Church is the major Christian church in Egypt and goes back to the origins of Christianity. Unsubstantiated tradition attributes to the apostle Mark the initial preaching of Christianity in Egypt. Recent scholarship suggests that the origins of Egyptian Christianity are to be found among the Jews living in Alexandria in the first century AD.

When the Christian church was torn apart by the fifth-century controversies on the identity of Christ, most Egyptian Christians refused to follow the decrees of the Council of Chalcedon. The doctrine of two natures appeared to them to imply the existence of two Christs, divine and human. They upheld t he terminology o f Cyril, w ho h ad spoken of "one incarnate nature of God the Word." Soon after the Council of Chalcedon, they chose their own patriarch in opposition to the patriarch Proterius. They have since had their own patriarch of Alexandria, who accounts himself the true successor of the evangelist Mark, St. Athanasius, and St. Cyril. His jurisdiction extends over the churches of Egypt, Nubia, and Abyssinia, or Ethiopia. He is also responsible for choosing and anointing the patriarch for the Abyssinian Church. Under him are twelve bishops, some with real jurisdiction, some titular; and under these again are other clergy, down to readers and exorcists.

The Coptic Church is the major Christian community in Egypt today, numbering approximately 20 million in 2016. There are continued and increasing complaints of discrimination and attacks against the church. Between 2011 to 2107, the Coptic Church has been under extreme assault by a terroist organization called ISIS. The slaughter of Christians and the desecration of religious sites continues today.

The Coptic Church has in recent times, encouraged the development of a modern school system in an effort to improve their situation. The Church has also been in fruitful communication with the Ethiopian,

Armenian, Jacobite, and Malabar communities. Recent discussion between Coptic and Eastern Orthodox theologians has indicated that the controversies of the past, provoked mainly by verbal differences, could possibly be overcome and communion restored between the two.[3] (see "An effort toward Union" in Special Doctrine.)

The Ethiopian Orthodox Church—Abyssinian Church: The Abyssinian Church is a daughter of the Coptic, and was founded in the fourth century, by two missionaries...from Alexandria. It presents a strange mixture of barbarism, ignorance, superstition, and Christianity. Its *Ethiopic Bible*, which dates perhaps from the first missionaries, includes in the Old Testament, the apocryphal *Book of Enoch*. The Chronicles of Axuma (the former capital of the country), dating from the fourth century, receive almost the same honor as the Bible...The Abyssinian Church has retained even more Jewish elements than the Coptic. It observes the Jewish Sabbath together with the Christian Sunday...Singularly enough it honors Pontius Pilate as a saint, because be washed his hands of innocent blood. The endless controversies respecting the natures of Christ, which have died out elsewhere still rage there.[4]

The Syrian Orthodox Church: The Jacobites reside mostly in Syria, Mesopotamia, and Babylonia. Their name comes down from their ecumenical metropolitan Jacob Baradai. His followers teach that this remarkable man, in the middle of the sixth century, devoted himself for thirty-seven years (511–578), with unwearied zeal to the interests of the persecuted Monophysites. In the garb of a beggar, he journeyed across the region amid the greatest dangers and privations; revived the patriarchate of Antioch; ordained bishops, priests, and deacons; organized churches; healed divisions; and thus saved the Monophysite body from impending extinction. A part of the Jacobites have united with the Church of Rome. Lately, some Protestant missionaries from America have also found entrance among them.

The Armenian Orthodox Church: These are the most numerous, interesting, and hopeful of the Monophysite sects, and now the most accessible to evangelical Protestantism. Their nationality reaches back into antiquity, like Mount Ararat, at whose base lays their original home.

They were converted to Christianity in the beginning of the fourth century...*The Armenian Canon* has four books found in no other Bible; in the *Old Testament*, the *History of Joseph and Asenath*, and the *Testament of the 12 Patriarchs,* and in the *New Testament*, the *Epistle of the Corinthians* to Paul and a third, but spurious, *Epistle of Paul* to the Corinthians...The Armenians fell away from the church of the Greek Empire in 552, from which year they date their era...*The Confessio Armenica*, which in other respects closely resembles the Nicene Creed, is recited by the priest at every morning service...Since 1830, the Protestant Missionary, Tract, and Bible societies of England, Basle, and the United States, have labored among the Armenians especially among the Monophysite portion, with great success, *The American Board of Commissioners for Foreign Missions*, in particular, has distributed Bibles and religious books in the Armenian and Armenia-Turkish language, and founded flourishing churches and schools in the area.[5]

The Maronite Orthodox Church: The youngest sect of the Monophysites and the solitary memorial of the Monothelite controversy, are the Maronites, so called from St. Maron, and the eminent monastery founded by him in Syria (400 AD). They inhabit the range of Lebanon...and amount at most to half a million people. They have also small churches in Aleppo, Damascus, and other places. They are pure Syrians, and still use the Syriac language in their liturgy, but speak Arabic in conversation. They are subject to a patriarch, who commonly resides in the monastery of Kanobin on Mt. Lebanon. They were originally Monophysites, even after the doctrine of "one will (nature) of Christ"...had been rejected at the sixth Ecumenical Council in 680. But after the Crusades (1182), and especially after 1596, they began to go over to the Roman Church, although retaining the communion under both kinds, their Syriac missal, the marriage of priests, and their traditional fast-days, with some saints of their own, especially St. Maron.[6]

Note: The next sections are based on specifics of the *Coptic Church* since it is considered the largest group within the Monophysitist faith.

Basic Worship Service

"The Holy Bible is considered as an encounter with God and an interaction with Him in a spirit of worship and piety...Worship is a practical entrance to the Gospel, and the study of the Bible is a true experience of worshipping. Every type of worship outside the Bible is fruitless, and every Bible study without the spirit of worship distorts the soul."[7] All church worship includes readings from the Old and New Testaments, particularly from the *Book of Psalms*, the *Epistles of St. Paul*, the *Catholic Epistles*, and from the four *Gospels*. Such readings are included in the liturgy of catechumens, the liturgy of blessing the water, the celebration of Holy matrimony, blessing the baptismal water, funeral services, for blessing new homes as well as at the daily Canonical Hour. Thus the church offers thanksgiving to God in every occasion in a spirit of worship through reciting verses of the Holy Bible, and at the same time urges her children to sit with God's word, enjoy and meditate on it. Church life is not only a life of worship in an evangelic way or a biblical life in a spirit of worship, but it is one, inclusive and integral life, which includes the practical daily life with good behavior, the ascetic practice and the desire of the heart to witnessing and preaching

Liturgy does not mean some hours spent by believers— clergymen and laity—in participating in rituals, but it is the true communion with Christ. This liturgical life is not lived only when a believer participates in common worship, but it dwells within his heart. In fact, they use the word liturgy for common worship because the believer participates in this worship with or without the members of the community. He is a member even when he is alone speaking with God in his own room. The holy community is *in the heart* of the real believer, and the believer is within the heart of the church community. In other words, when a believer prays in his room, he realizes that all the church is within his heart, praying in her name, calling God: "Our Father" and not "My Father who art in heaven." At the same time, when the community prays it endows its members, present and absent with love.[8] The divine liturgy is a spiritual journey of thanksgiving, traveled by your mind, emotions, and all your senses.

It is concluded by the ultimate expression of the *Holy Eucharist,* which means "Thanksgiving, the Holy Mystery," referred to as communion. If it is practiced as a duty or routine work, performed literally without understanding or penitent heart, it becomes an obstacle to the evangelic spiritual life. In the Coptic rite, not only the whole body participates in worshipping God, but also the creation shares in glorifying the Creator. In other words, the believer, realizing the sanctity of the creation, appears before God offering incense, wood (icons), bread, wine, etc., to God, declaring that all creation glorifies God. Thus, the inanimate objects are not evil, nor do they hinder worship, but are good tools, which the believer can use to express the sanctity of all creatures.

Feasts and Worship: Moses's law arranged seven major feasts, which had their rites and sanctity, as a living part of the common worship. The aim of these feasts was to revive the spirit of joy and gladness in the believers' lives and to consecrate certain days for the common worship in a holy assembly and to remember God's promises and actions with His people to renew the covenant with Him on both common and personal levels. The feasts were a way leading to enjoy Christ, "the continuous feast," and the source of eternal joy.

Almost all the days are feasts to the Coptic Church. They are eager to have their members live, through the midst of sufferings, in spiritual gladness. In other words, the Coptic Church is continuously suffering and joyful at the same time.

One of the main characteristics of the Coptic Church is "joy," even in her ascetic life…St. Jerome informs us about an abbot called Apollo who was always smiling. He attracted many to the ascetic life as a source of inward joy and heartfelt satisfaction in our Lord Jesus. He often used to say: "Why do we struggle with an unpleasant face?! Aren't we the heirs of the eternal life?! Leave the unpleasant and the grieved faces to Pagans, and weeping to the evil-doers. But it befits the righteous and the saints to be joyful and pleasant since they enjoy the spiritual gifts."[9]

The Seven Major Feasts of our Lord:

- *The Annunciation* (April 7) recalls the fulfillment of the Old Testament prophecies.
- *The Nativity of Christ* (Christmas) (January 7). It is preceded by a fast of forty-three days to confirm when God sent His only-begotten Son incarnate.
- *The Epiphany* or the Baptism of Christ (January 19). In this feast, the liturgy of blessing the water is conducted, and the priest blesses the people by the water on their foreheads and hands to commemorate baptism.
- *Palm Sunday.* The Sunday that precedes Easter. The church commemorates the entrance of our Lord Jesus into our inward Jerusalem to establish His Kingdom in us and gather all in Him.
- *Easter* (the Christian Passover). It is preceded by Great Lent (a fast of fifty-five days. There is no abstention from food on Sundays after the celebration of the Eucharist, even during Great Lent).
- *Pentecost.* It represents the birthday of the Christian Church.[10]

The Seven Minor Feasts of Our Lord:

- The Circumcision of our Lord (January 14)
- The Entrance of our Lord into the Temple (February 15)
- The Escape of the Holy family to Egypt (June 1)
- The First Miracle of our Lord Jesus at Cana (January 12)
- The Transfiguration of Christ (August 19)
- Maundy Thursday. This is the Thursday of the Holy Week.
- Thomas's Sunday. This is the Sunday that follows Easter.[11]

St. Mary's Other Feasts: The Coptic Church venerates St. Mary as the Mother of God. She is exalted above heavenly and earthly creatures. Therefore, the church does not cease glorifying her and celebrating her feasts in order that they may imitate her and ask her intercessions on their behalf. Her main feasts are:

- The Annunciation of her birth (August 13)
- Her Nativity (May 9)
- Her Presentation into the Temple (December 12)

- Her Dormition (January 29)
- The Assumption of her body (June 28)
- Her apparition over the church of Zeitoon (April 2)
- And the Apparition of her body to the Apostles (August 22)

The Fasting Order in the Coptic Church: The Coptic Church is an ascetic church that believes in the power of fasting in the life of the believers. Fasting is not considered a physical exercise, but rather, it is an offering of inward love given by the heart as well as the body. Consequently, the church requests believers to fast cumulatively for over six months a year. While fasting, they pray to be liberated from our ego. Thus they fast and abstain from selfishness as much as abstain from food.

We practice loving God through loving our brothers and all humanity. Therefore, fasting should be associated with the witness to God's love through giving alms and striving for the salvation of souls. Strangely enough, the Coptic Church desires of its own free will to spend its whole life fasting, while most churches in the world increasingly tend to reduce the fasting periods from one generation to the next. In fact, during confession, many of the Coptic youth request to increase the days of fasting. Very few, indeed, complain of the many fasting periods.

Fasting is not merely abstention from food, drink, or delicacies. It is essentially an expression of our love to God who has given His only begotten Son to die for us. Thus, fasting and abstention from food is closely connected with abstention from all that is evil or has a semblance of evil. It is, moreover, connected with continuous spiritual growth. The days of fasting are days of repentance and contrition. At the same time, they are periods of joy and cheer as believers experience victory and power in their innermost self. This is the experience of the Coptic Church, particularly during the Holy Week. At that time, believers practice asceticism more than at any other time of fasting.

Lent is considered one of the richest periods of wholehearted devotion demonstrated by practical offerings to the poor and the needy. Believers undertake this in obedience to scripture: *"Is not this the fast that I have chosen? ...*

Is it not to deal by bread to the hungry and that you bring the poor that are cast out to your house?" (Is. 58:37). In the first centuries of Christianity, praying and fasting were integrated with almsgiving (our love to God interpreted by our love to our neighbors). This is explained in the book The Shepherd of Hermas, urging believers to offer their savings resulting from fasting to widows and orphans. Origen Adamantius (a scholar, ascetic, and early Christian theologian) blesses those who fast and feed the poor, and St. Augustine has written a whole book on fasting, as he feels that a person who fasts without offering his savings to the poor has fasted for the wrong reason and has in fact practiced greed rather than charity and spirituality.

<u>Private Worship in the Coptic Church</u>: In his daily life, conduct and worship, the believer bears an integral indivisible life, either life "in Christ" or "out of Christ." When he enjoys his life "In Christ," his fellowship in public worship is complimented by practicing his unseen private worshipping; as both represent a life devoted to Christ. In other words, while sharing the church liturgies with the congregation, a believer fortifies his spiritual life when he goes into his "private room" and shuts the doors of his senses.

Thus, when he is among the group physically, his heart, mind, and soul are conversing intimately and privately with God. In the light of this concept, they do not draw a dividing line that separates between church life and private worshipping life because the church is every believer holding firmly together with his brethren.

That is why in the present time, due to housing problems in Egypt, when a believer does not find a private room to pray in solitude, he stands or bows in prayer in the presence of the family members. He does not abstain from praying because he does not have a private locked room. His room is already inside him if he chooses to shut out his senses.[12]

The canonical hours that are part of many Coptic worship schedules take after the Jewish Church in the system of dividing the days into hours of prayers. In every hour, the church offers the memory of a certain phase of God's redeeming work.

- The *Matin* (morning prayer) reminds us of the resurrection of our Lord Jesus Christ and our daily resurrection to begin a new life in Him.
- The *Terce* (praise of the third hour) reminds us of the coming upon the church of the Holy Spirit of God, the giver of perpetual renewal and holiness.
- In the *Sext,* we remember the crucifixion of our Lord Jesus Christ.
- The *None* (ninth hour), we remember the death in the flesh of our Lord and the acceptance of the right-hand thief in paradise.
- In the *Vespers* (sunset), we remember the removing of our Lord's Body from the cross, giving thanks for concluding the day, and asking Him that we might spend the night in peace.
- In *Compline*, we remember the burial of the body of our Lord, watching for the end of our sojourn on earth; yet, in the three midnight prayers, we await for the advent of our Lord Jesus Christ.
- *"Prayer of calling Jesus' name"* (arrow prayer) in which the believer cries out whenever they feel the enemy upon them with a short prayer, calling the name of our Lord Jesus Christ as an arrow to strike the snares of our enemy, Satan. This action, simple as it is, has its own effectiveness in the life and worship of the believer.[13]

"Some believers practice church hymns daily or on feasts as a private worship in their bedrooms. Here we need to mention that some Copts prefer setting up a special corner for prayer. If this is not easy to do they use many icons decorating their homes as a sign of their longing for holy life in God and fellowship with the saints."

They venerate the icons of saints and put them on a stand. Church walls and doors are hung with icons also in homes, etc., as a sign of communion with them in the Lord Jesus Christ. The saints are brothers who have struggled like us and have departed to paradise. They are not dead but are sleeping, as our Lord said, and as St. Paul called them. The saints in paradise are the triumphant members of the same church. They departed from earth but did not leave the church; their love toward their brothers did not cease by their departure and dwelling in paradise. The death of their bodies does not sever the bond of mutual love between them and us; on the contrary, it increases in depth and strength. Their prayers for the salvation of the entire world never cease. They believe that the icons pray for us, and they venerate them as they are holy and dear friends.[14]

Baptism

When God grants a family a baby, the church prays a special liturgy for washing the babe on the eighth day of his/her birth. The priest, deacons, the family and their friends participate in giving thanks and praise to God, asking Him to act in the baby that he/she might grow in the grace of God as a saintly member of the church. They believe that infants are born carrying the original sin, and they are concerned about their eternal life; *"Unless one is born of water and the Spirit, he cannot enter the kingdom of God. "* In this rite, the church deposits the newly baptized into the hands of a godparent giving him firm commandments, to be responsible of, and do his best to present the evangelic church life to the newly baptized. The Coptic Church insists that baptism is performed by immersion; whereas the baptized person is buried with Christ and also risen with Him to enjoy the new risen life. Water baptism by immersion is a requirement for salvation.

The words of the Lord *"He who believes and is baptized will be saved "* are meant for adults who are capable of understanding the significance of faith. Therefore, they do not baptize adults unless they profess their belief. In the sacrament of Baptism, we attain the rebirth, not of our own merit nor by a human hand but by the Holy Spirit. We also receive God's adoption; attain the remission of sins and sanctification. For example, "the believer who receives rebirth in baptism, looks to the church as his mother who begot him by the Holy Spirit as a son of God. This gift of adoption unites him spiritually with other members so that he will not feel isolation nor live in individualism. In the Coptic rite of Baptism there are two essential principles; denying Satan and the acceptance of God's work. In other words, in baptism the believer is transferred from belonging to Satan through subjection to his works, to receiving God's adoption, and being His."[15]

Initiation, Baptism, or Confirmation

Chrismation (sometimes called chrism or confirmation) is the holy mystery by which a baptized person is granted the gift of the Holy Spirit through anointing with oil. As baptism is a personal participation in the death and resurrection of Christ, so chrismation is a personal participation in the coming of the Holy Spirit at Pentecost. The Christian is anointed with this oil in the sign of the Cross on his forehead, eyes, nostrils, mouth, ears, breast, hands and feet.[16]

Each time the priest, administering the sacrament, says, "*The Seal and Gift of the Holy Spirit, as a symbol of the sanctification of the soul and body together, so that man in his wholeness, becomes a temple of the Holy Spirit.*"[17] The Coptic Orthodox Church does not accept many of the doctrines of the Roman Catholic, such as the Immaculate Conception, the filioque, the purgatory, the supremacy of the pope of Rome, etc. When one is baptized in a certain denomination, he/she is baptized according to the faith of that particular church, vowing to accept and embrace all her teachings. Consequently, a person baptized in another church does not hold the same faith as one baptized in the Coptic Orthodox Church. Therefore, his/her baptism is invalid in the Coptic Church.

Marriage

Through the sacrament of marriage, the couples are united together, and the Holy Spirit sets their home as the holy church of God. In his conjugal life, a husband meets his wife as one with him through the loving church, looking at his relation with her as an image of the relation of Christ and the church. Putting on a crown or wreath made of cloth in the shape of lemon blossoms, with which the priest crowns the newlyweds during the sacrament, representing the power that is given to the newlyweds to become king and queen of their home. The crowns are white, signifying a pure and heavenly life.

"In the sacrament of marriage, the rite is concentrated on revealing the heavenly crown, that the hearts of all who are present may be lifted up to the heavenly marriage, and that the couple acknowledge that their conjugal life is a shadow of the church in heaven."[18]

An Orthodox Christian must marry in the Orthodox Church in order to achieve unity of the family because the Lord taught that the two shall become one. This unity is unachievable in the absence of unity of faith. That is why both partners must be baptized Orthodox. If an Orthodox marries a newly baptized Orthodox, then it is the utmost responsibility of the former to encourage the latter to attend the divine liturgy on a regular basis and to teach him or her the principles of the Orthodox faith so that both partners may enjoy the full benefits of church life and pass on these principles to their children.

"Polygamy is illegal, even if recognized by the civil law of the land. Divorce is not allowed except in the case of adultery, annulment due to bigamy, or other extreme circumstances, which must be reviewed by a special council of Bishops. Divorce can be requested by either husband or wife. Civil divorce is not recognized by the Church."[19] There is a requirement of a single marriage for priests and deacons but bishops are not allowed to marry.

<u>Women in the Priesthood:</u> In the Old Testament, God chose His priests from the sons of Levi. In the New Testament, although women worked in the service, Our Lord chose men for the establishment and continuation of the new order of priesthood. Of all the female righteous or martyrs, no woman is to have the office of priest because it is not in God's good will for them to do so. Each of God's children has a distinct calling, role, and purpose.

<u>Homosexuality:</u> Orthodoxy distinguishes between a homosexual orientation and a homosexual expression of one's sexuality. While denouncing same-sex sexual relations, they affirm the basic human dignity and rights of the person with a homosexual orientation. In short, homosexual acts are condemned, not homosexual people. The homosexual man or woman, then, is faced with a particular struggle with his/her sexuality that, by the grace of God and guidance of His Church, he or she can find a healthy, Christ-centered means of life.

Death and Afterlife

Grace is the center of the Alexandrian theology, for God first loved us, foreknew us, chose us, predestined us, called us, justified us and glorified us. He wills, decides, and acts for our salvation, but we never enjoy this free salvation unwillingly. God wills that all men might be saved and come to the knowledge of the truth, for He has no pleasure in the death of the wicked. He offered His Son as the sacrifice for the whole world. Nevertheless, God asked us to choose the way we desire and to declare this choice through practical faith. Thus, the good deeds that we practice by the divine grace are necessary and essential.

Judgment and Salvation

The Coptic Church teaches the principle of penance and confession. The priest and the confessor feel that they are together under the guidance of the Holy Spirit, which convicts men of sins and forgives sins in order to obtain a communion with the Holy Trinity. According to their doctrine, all men after death go into Hades, a place without sorrow or joy. After the general judgment, they enter into heaven or are cast into hell; and meanwhile, the intercessions and pious works of the living have an influence on the final destiny of the departed. There are three heavens: the first one is the heaven of birds, the second one is the space, and the third one is the paradise of joy. St. Paul caught a glimpse of paradise when he described the third heaven. After the restoration of humanity, the faithful who kept God's commandments will enjoy the eternal presence of God.

Special Doctrine

An Effort toward Union: For over 1,500 years, the Eastern (Byzantine) Orthodox churches and the Oriental Orthodox churches have remained separated. Only thirty years ago they came together for the first of four unofficial theological consultations: Aarhus (1964), Bristol (1967), Geneva (1970), and Addis Ababa (1971). These were followed by the establishment of a *Joint Commission of the Theological Dialogue* between the Orthodox Church and the Oriental Orthodox

Churches, which has held four meetings: Chambesy, Geneva (December 1985), Anba Bishoy monastery, Egypt (June 1989), Chambesy II (September 1990), and Chambesy III (November 1993).

Ignorance of the remarkable advance toward the reunion of the two families is still widespread, and it is a sad reflection on the lack of understanding that some journals, commenting on the recent reception of the *British Orthodox* Church by the Coptic Orthodox Patriarchate, are still impugning the orthodoxy of the *Oriental Orthodox* churches with accusations of the Monophysite heresy. "The outcome of this latter meeting was of historical dimensions, since in this meeting the two families of Orthodoxy were able to agree on an Christological formula, thus ending the controversy regarding Christology which has lasted for more than fifteen centuries."[20]

Notes

Presbyterian

History

In Western Europe, the authority of the Roman Catholic Church remained largely unquestioned until the Renaissance in the fifteenth century. The invention of the printing press i n Germany a round 1440 made it possible for common people to have access to printed materials including the Bible. This, in turn, enabled many to discover religious thinkers who had begun to question the authority of the Roman Catholic Church which started the movement known as the Protestant Reformation. Some twenty years later, a French/Swiss theologian, John Calvin, further refined the reformers' new way of thinking about the nature of God and God's relationship with humanity in what came to be known as Reformed theology.

Calvin also developed the Presbyterian pattern of church government, which vests governing authority primarily in elected laypersons known as elders. The word *presbyterian* comes from the Greek word for elder.

John Knox, a Scotsman who studied with Calvin in Geneva, Switzerland, took Calvin's teachings back to Scotland. Other Reformed communities developed in England, Holland and France. The Presbyterian Church traces its ancestry back primarily to Scotland and England in the sixteenth century.

Presbyterians have featured prominently in United States history. The Rev. Francis Makemie, who arrived in the US from Ireland in 1683, helped to organize the first American Presbytery at Philadelphia, PA in 1706. In 1726, the Rev. William Tennent founded a ministerial "log college" in Pennsylvania. Twenty years later, the *College of New* Jersey (now known as Princeton University) was established.

Rev. Jonathan Edwards, although a Congregational minister, actually preached at a Presbyterian pulpit in New Yourk City, his first year out of college. He and another Presbyterian minister, Rev. Gilbert Tennent, were driving forces in the "Great Awakening," a revivalist movement in the early eighteenth century.

One of the signers of the *Declaration of Independence*, the Rev. John Witherspoon, was a Presbyterian minister and the president of Princeton University from 1768-1793.[1]

In America, the first general assembly was held in 1789. The *Presbyterian Church (USA)* or PCUSA is the largest Presbyterian denomination in the United States and was established by the 1983 merger of the former Presbyterian Church in the United States, whose churches were located in the Southern and Border States, and the *United Presbyterian Church* in the United States of America, whose congregations could be found in every state.

In the twentieth century, some Presbyterians have played an important role in the ecumenical movement, including the *World Council of Churches*. Many Presbyterian denominations have found ways of working together with other Reformed denominations and Christians of other traditions, especially in the *World Alliance of Reformed Churches*. Some Presbyterian churches have entered into unions with other churches, such as Congregationalists, Lutherans, Anglicans, and Methodists. However, others are more conservative, holding rigid interpretations of traditional doctrines and shunning, for the most part, relations with non-Reformed bodies. Because of these doctrinal differences, the Presbyterian Church in the United States has split, and parts have reunited several times.

Other Presbyterian bodies in the United States include the *Presbyterian Church in America* (PCA), the *Orthodox Presbyterian Church* (OPC), the *Evangelical Presbyterian Church* (EPC), the *Reformed Presbyterian Church*, the *Bible Presbyterian Church*, the *Cumberland Presbyterian Church*, the *Westminster Presbyterian Church in the United States* (WPCUS), and the *Reformed Presbyterian Church in the United States* (RPCUS). All the latter bodies, with perhaps the exception of the Cumberland Presbyterians, are theologically conservative and profess some degree of evangelicalism.

Calvinism is no longer emphasized in some contemporary branches. Many branches of Presbyterianism are remnants of previous splits from larger groups. Some of the splits have been due to doctrinal controversy, while some have been caused by disagreement concerning the degree to which those ordained to church office should be required to agree with the *Westminster Confession of Faith,* which historically serves as an important confessional document— second only to the Bible, yet directing the standardization and translation of the Bible in Presbyterian churches.[2]

The territory within about a fifty-mile radius of Charlotte, North Carolina, is historically the greatest concentration of Presbyterianism in the southern United States, while an almost-identical geographic area around Pittsburgh, Pennsylvania, contains probably the largest number of Presbyterians in the entire nation. With their members' traditional stress on higher education, the largest Presbyterian congregations can often be found in affluent, prestigious uptown suburbs of American cities. The Presbyterian denomination currently has declined to 1.7 million members worldwide as of 2014. It has been estimated that 58 percent of the members of the Presbyterian Church (USA) did not grow up in the denomination. As is true with all the mainline Christian denominations, they have had a drop in membership over the last decade.

God or Gods

"We trust in the one triune God, the Holy One of Israel, whom alone we worship and serve." There is one essence of God; the emphasis is on oneness, not three-ness. The Father is God, the Son is God, and the Holy Spirit is God—but they are one God. They teach that through the Holy Spirit, God empowers us to grow in faith, make more mature decisions, and live more faithful lives. The Spirit gives us the will, as Jesus said, to *"be perfect, therefore, as your heavenly Father is perfect."* The Holy Spirit gives believers the authority to accurately interpret the Bible, just as the Spirit enabled the original writers of scripture to tell truthfully about God, Jesus, and everything else we need to know. The Spirit also gives authority to the church to act in God's name for the good of humanity. The Spirit gives every person a sense of calling to a special function in the world, in keeping with God's providence and Jesus's summons to follow him. Among the fruits of the spirit identified by the apostle Paul are love, joy, peace, patience, kindness, goodness, faithfulness, gentleness, and self-control.

Christ

Presbyterians believe that Jesus Christ is fully human and fully divine, one person with two natures, without confusion and without change, without separation and without division. They "believe that Jesus is as alive today as He was on the first Easter morning and that He is present with us today, even though we cannot see Him or physically touch Him. (They) call Jesus 'Lord' because He has saved us from the power of death and the power of sin and because, through His sacrifice, we are able to know the fullness of God's love for us."[3]

Basic Doctrine

Some of the principles articulated by John Calvin remain at the core of Presbyterian beliefs. Among these are the sovereignty of God, the authority of the scripture, justification by grace through faith and the priesthood of all believers. What they mean is that God is the supreme authority throughout the universe. Our knowledge of God and God's purpose for humanity comes from the Bible, particularly what is revealed in the New Testament through the life of Jesus Christ. Our salvation (justification) through Jesus is God's generous gift to us and not the result of our own accomplishments. It is everyone's job—ministers and lay people alike—to share this Good News with the whole world. That is also why the Presbyterian Church is governed at all levels by a combination of clergy and laity, men and women alike[4] in a system known as Presbyterian polity. Presbyterian polity is a method of church governance typified by the rule of assemblies of presbyters or elders. Each local church is governed by a body of elected elders usually called the session or consistory, though other terms, such as church board, may apply. They are elected by the congregation and in one sense are representatives of the other members of the congregation. On the other hand, their primary charge is to seek to discover and represent the will of Christ as they govern. Presbyterian elders are both elected and ordained.

Through ordination they are officially set apart for service. They retain their ordination beyond their term in office. Ministers who serve the congregation are also part of the session. Groups of local churches are governed by a higher assembly of elders known as the *presbytery* or classis; presbyteries can be grouped into a *synod*, and synods nationwide often join together in a General Assembly.

Presbyterian polity was developed as a rejection of governance by hierarchies of single bishops (*Episcopal polity*), but also differs from the *Congregationalist polity* in which each congregation is independent. In contrast to the other two forms, authority in the Presbyterian polity flows both from the top down (as higher assemblies exercise considerable authority over individual congregations) and from the bottom up (as all officials ultimately owe their elections to individual church members). This theory of government developed in Geneva under John Calvin and was introduced to Scotland by John Knox after his period of exile in Geneva. It is strongly associated with Swiss and Scottish Reformation movements and with the Reformed and Presbyterian churches.

The Presbyterian Church USA has adopted the *Book of Confessions*, which reflects the inclusion of other Reformed confessions in addition to the *Westminster documents*. These other documents include ancient creedal statements, (the Nicene Creed, the Apostles' Creed), sixteenth century Reformed Confessions...(all of which were written before Calvinism had developed as a particular strand of Reformed doctrine), and twentieth century documents.[5]

In 1983, the two largest Presbyterian churches in the United States reunited. The plan for reunion called for the preparation of a brief statement of the Reformed faith for possible inclusion in the Book of Confessions. This tatement is therefore not intended to stand alone apart from the other confessions of the church. It is not a complete list of all their beliefs, nor does it explain any of them in detail. It was designed to be confessed by the whole congregation in the setting of public worship, and it may also serve pastors and teachers as an aid to Christian instruction.

Presbyterians believe it is through the action of God working in us that they become aware of their sinfulness and the need for God's mercy and forgiveness. Just as a parent is quick to welcome a wayward child who has repented of rebellion, God is willing to forgive our sins if we but confess them and ask for forgiveness in the name of Christ.

While resisting anything that might sound at all like works righteousness—doing good to earn salvation—Presbyterians believe that the grace that comes to us is never easy and surely not superficial. While forgiveness has sometimes sounded like our debts are simply forgiven and our slate is wiped clean through the atoning death of Jesus Christ, forgiveness and atonement have never been that simple. Grace is defined as favor, blessing, or goodwill offered by one who does not need to do so. With this understanding of grace, we are all predestined to be saved if we repent of our sins and accept by faith the relationship of love that God offers to us, and behave accordingly.

A covenant is a binding agreement between two parties. In the covenant God established with the people of Israel, we see the plan of grace:

> *"Now therefore, if you obey my voice and keep my covenant,*
> *you shall be my treasured possession out of all the peoples...*
> *You shall be for me a priestly kingdom and a holy nation."*

They compare God's grace in terms similar to marriage. *Covenant grace* is the period of courtship prior to the commitment to marriage. *Justifying grace* is the marriage ceremony—the moment when the commitment is made and the relationship is sealed. *Sanctifying grace* is life after the marriage —is the work of the Spirit in our lives the way we live out our part of the covenant relationship.

They believe that the faith they confess unites them with the one universal church. They teach that churches should learn to accept, and even to affirm, diversity without divisiveness since the whole counsel of God is more than the wisdom of any individual or any one tradition. The Spirit of truth gives new light to the churches when they are willing to become pupils together of the Word of God. This statement therefore intends to confess the catholic faith (lower case c representing the universal church of God).

They are convinced that to the Reformed churches, a distinctive vision of the catholic faith has been entrusted to them for the good of the whole church. Accordingly, *"A Brief Statement of Faith"* includes the major themes of the Reformed tradition without claiming them as their private possession, and they hope to learn and to share the wisdom and insight given to other traditions. And as a confession that seeks to be both catholic and Reformed, the statement is a *Trinitarian confession* in which the grace of Jesus Christ has first place as the foundation of our knowledge of God's sovereign love and our life together in the Holy Spirit.

<u>A Brief Statement of Faith:</u> In life and in death we belong to God. Through the grace of our Lord Jesus Christ, the love of God, and the communion of the Holy Spirit, we trust in the one triune God, the Holy One of Israel, whom alone we worship and serve. We trust in Jesus Christ, Fully human, fully God.

Jesus proclaimed the reign of God: preaching Good News to the poor and release to the captives, teaching by word and deed and blessing the children, healing the sick and binding up the brokenhearted, eating with outcasts, forgiving sinners, and calling all to repent and believe the gospel.

Unjustly condemned for blasphemy and sedition, Jesus was crucified, suffering the depths of human pain and giving His life for the sins of the world.

God raised Jesus from the dead, vindicating His sinless life, breaking the power of sin and evil, delivering us from death to life eternal. We trust in God, whom Jesus called Abba, Father.

In sovereign love God created the world good and makes everyone equally in God's image male and female, of every race and people, to live as one community. But we rebel against God; we hide from our Creator. Ignoring God's commandments, we violate the image of God in others and ourselves, accept lies as truth, exploit neighbor and nature, and threaten death to the planet entrusted to our care.

We deserve God's condemnation. Yet God acts with justice and mercy to redeem creation.

In everlasting love, the God of Abraham and Sarah chose a covenant people to bless all families of the earth. Hearing their cry, God delivered the children of Israel from the house of bondage. Loving us still, God makes us heirs with Christ of the covenant. Like a mother who will not forsake her nursing child, like a father who runs to welcome the prodigal home, God is faithful still. We trust in God the Holy Spirit, everywhere the giver and renewer of life.

The Spirit justifies us by grace through faith, sets us free to accept ourselves and to love God and neighbor, and binds us together with all believers in the one body of Christ, the Church. The same Spirit who inspired the prophets and apostles rules our faith and life in Christ through Scriptures engages us through the Word proclaimed, claims us in the waters of baptism, feeds us with the bread of life and the cup of salvation, and calls women and men to all ministries of the church. In a broken and fearful world the Spirit gives us courage to pray without ceasing, to witness among all peoples to Christ as Lord and Savior, to unmask idolatries in church and culture, to hear the voices of peoples long silenced, and to work with others for justice, freedom, and peace.

In gratitude to God, empowered by the Spirit, we strive to serve Christ in our daily tasks and to live holy and joyful lives, even as we watch for God's new heaven and new earth, praying, Come, Lord Jesus! With believers in every time and place, we rejoice that nothing in life or in death can separate us from the love of God in Christ Jesus our Lord. Glory be to the Father, and to the Son, and to the Holy Spirit. Amen. (From A Brief Statement of Faith)[6]

The General Assembly affirms its conviction that neither the Church as the body of Christ, nor Christians as individuals, can be neutral or indifferent toward evil in the world; affirms its responsibility to speak on social and moral issues for the encouragement and instruction of the Church and its members, seeking earnestly both to know the mind of Christ and to speak always in humility and love; reminds the churches that their duty is not only to encourage and train their members in daily obedience to God's will, but corporately to reveal God's grace in places of suffering and need, to resist the forces that tyrannize, and to support the forces that restore the dignity of all men as the children of God, for only so is the gospel most fully proclaimed. (See Special Doctrine section on Middle East)

Alcohol: The PCUSA in the 1940s and 1950s supported the goal of voluntary abstinence as a worthy goal in relation to alcohol. The 1961 statement of the assembly on *"The Church and the Problem of Alcohol"* provided the first comprehensive statement on the subject to recognize the fact that many Presbyterians do drink and suggests that the problems of alcohol could be resolved by responsible drinking for those who choose to drink and abstinence for others that have a problem with alcohol. The General Assembly encourages and supports personal decision to abstain from alcohol. For those who choose to drink and can do so without becoming dependent, the general assembly urges a pattern of moderate and responsible drinking behavior.

Gambling: The The Presbyterian Church also has a long history of opposition to all forms of gambling as an abdication of stewardship. A 1950 statement described gambling as "an unchristian attempt to get something for nothing or at another's expense." Twenty-five years later, a Presbyterian General Assembly adopted a statement calling upon its members to exert influence on local, state, and national legislative bodies to oppose all forms of legalized gambling (e.g., lotteries, bingo, pari-mutuel betting, dog racing, horse racing, betting on sports games, casino games and numbers.[7]

Homosexuality: In 1978, a Presbyterian General Assembly adopted the following statement:

> *Persons who manifest homosexual behavior must be treated with the profound respect and pastoral tenderness due all people of God. Homosexual persons are encompassed by the searching love of Christ. The church must turn from its fear and hatred to move toward the homosexual community to welcome homosexual inquirers to its congregations. It should free them to be candid about their identity and convictions, and it should also share honestly and humbly with them in seeking the vision of God's intention for the sexual dimensions of their lives..."*

Although they teach tolerance of alternate lifestyles, in 1993, the General Assembly stated that "current constitutional law in the

Presbyterian Church is that self-affirming, practicing homosexual persons may not be ordained as ministers of the Word and Sacrament, elders, or deacons."

Then in 1997, the approval by a majority of presbyteries of an amendment to the *Book of Order* known as *"Amendment B"* makes constitutional the following language:

> *"Those who are called to office in the church are to lead a life in obedience to Scripture and in conformity to the historic confessional standards of the church. Among these standards is the requirement to live either in fidelity within the covenant of marriage between a man and a woman, or chastity in singleness. Persons refusing to repent of any self-acknowledged practice which the confessions call sin shall not be ordained and/or installed as deacons, elders, or ministers of the Word and Sacrament."* (Book of Order -G-6.0106b)[8]

Several attempts have been made to remove this from the Book of Order, but no attempt has received both the necessary votes at the General Assembly and approval of enough presbyteries. They do, however, welcome women into ordained positions. There were a total of 21,360 ministers in 2006; of active ministers, approximately 30 percent are female.

The denomination has set four mission priorities for the twenty first century of the Presbyterian Church (USA):

Evangelism and Witness—We are called to invite all people to faith, repentance and the abundant life of God in Jesus Christ, to encourage congregations in joyfully sharing the gospel, and through the power of the Holy Spirit to grow in membership and discipleship.

Justice and Compassion—We are called to address wrongs in every aspect of life and the whole of creation, intentionally working with and on behalf of poor, oppressed and disadvantaged people as did Jesus Christ, even at risk to our corporate and personal lives.

Spirituality and Discipleship—We are called to deeper discipleship through Scripture, worship, prayer, study, stewardship and service and to rely on the Holy Spirit to mold our lives more and more into the likeness of Jesus Christ.

Leadership and Vocation—We are called to lead by Jesus Christ's example, to identify spiritual gifts and to equip and support Christians of all ages for faithful and effective servant leadership in all parts of the body of Christ.[9]

Basic Worship Service

The order of a Sunday worship service in a Presbyterian church is determined by the pastor and the session, the church's governing body.

The Session of the local congregation has a great deal of freedom in the style and ordering of worship, within the guidelines set forth in the *"Directory of Worship"* section of the Book of Order. Worship varies from congregation to congregation. The order may be very traditional and highly liturgical, or it may be very simple and informal. This variance is not unlike that seen in the *"High Church"* and *"Low Church"* styles of the Anglican Church. The Book of Order suggests a worship service ordered around five themes:

- Gathering around the Word,
- Proclaiming the Word,
- Responding to the Word,
- The sealing of the Word, and
- Bearing and following the Word into the world.[10]

The pastor has certain responsibilities that are not subject to the authority of the session. In a particular service of worship, the pastor is responsible for:

> (a) the selection of scripture lessons to be read, The minister of Word and Sacrament should exercise care so that over a period of time the people will hear the full message of Scripture. It is appropriate that in the Service for the Lord's Day there be readings from the Old Testament and the Epistles and Gospels of the New Testament. The full range of the Psalms should be also used in worship.

Selections for reading in public worship should be guided by the seasons of the church year, pastoral concerns for a local congregation, events and conditions in the world, and specific program emphases of the church. Lectionaries offered by the church ensure a broad range of readings as well as consistency and connection with the universal Church.

(b) the preparation and preaching of the sermon or exposition of the Bible,

(c) the prayers offered on behalf of the people and those prepared for the use of the people in worship,

(d) the music to be sung,

(e) the use of drama, dance, and other art forms. The pastor may confer with a worship committee in planning particular services of worship.[11]

Prayer is central to the service and may be silent, spoken, sung, or read in unison (including the Lord's Prayer). In prayer, through the Holy Spirit, people seek after and are found by the one true God who has been revealed in Jesus Christ. They listen and wait upon God, call God by name, remember God's gracious acts, and offer themselves to God. Prayer grows out of the center of a person's life in response to the Spirit.

Music plays a large role in most worship services and ranges from chant to traditional Protestant hymns, to classical sacred music, to more modern music, depending on the preference of the individual church and should be offered prayerfully and not "for entertainment or artistic display. Care should be taken that it not be used merely as a cover for silence." They teach that music is a response, which engages the whole self in prayer. Songs unite the faithful in common prayer wherever they gather for worship whether in church, home, or other special place.

Through the ages and from varied cultures, the church has developed additional musical forms for congregational prayer. Congregations are encouraged to use these diverse musical forms for prayer as well as those that arise out of the musical life of their own cultures. To lead the congregation in the singing of prayer is a primary role of the choir and other musicians. They also may pray on behalf of the congregation with responses and other musical forms. Instrumental music may be a form of prayer since words are not essential to prayer.

The Presbyterian Church believes there are two sacraments. The sacraments of Baptism and the Lord's Supper are signs of the real presence and power of Christ in the Church, symbols of God's action. Through the sacraments, God seals believers in redemption, renews their identity as the people of God, and marks them for service.

An altar is a place where a sacrifice is offered, and it is often viewed with special reverence. In the traditional Roman Catholic understanding, the priest reoffers Christ on the altar as a sacrifice to God. In contrast, Presbyterians believe the sacrifice of Christ has already been offered once for all, it needs no repetition, and the action of a priest cannot make it occur again. In the Presbyterian view, therefore, the Lord's Supper takes place at a table rather than an altar. Although many communion tables are rather ornate, the table itself holds no particular significance or holiness; it is simply a supper table.

Presbyterians argue that Christ is genuinely present in these elements, but it is a spiritual presence rather than a physical presence. That is, it is not a question of molecules of bread becoming molecules of human flesh. Instead, it is Christ coming to dwell within us as He promised to do. The Lord's Supper is the sign and seal of eating and drinking in communion with the crucified and risen Lord. Around the table of the Lord, God's people are in communion with Christ and with all who belong to Christ. Reconciliation with Christ compels reconciliation with one another. All the baptized faithful are to be welcomed to partake in the Lord's Supper. However, prior to coming to the Lord's table, the believer is to confess sin and brokenness and must seek reconciliation in every instance of conflict or division between them and their neighbors, trusting in Jesus Christ for cleansing and renewal.[12]

Infant Baptism or Blessing

The baptism of children witnesses to the truth that God's love claims people before they are able to respond in faith. Baptism, therefore, usually occurs during infancy, though a person may be baptized at any age. Parents bring their baby to church, where they publicly declare their desire that he or she be baptized, and they are sprinkled with water in the name of the Father, of the Son, and of the Holy Spirit.

When an infant or child is baptized, the church commits itself to nurture the child in faith. When adults are baptized, they make a public profession of faith. Baptism is God's gift of grace and also God's summons to respond to that grace. Baptism calls to repentance, to faithfulness, and to discipleship. The water that is used symbolizes three accounts from the Bible's Old Testament: the waters of creation, the flood described in the story of Noah, and the Hebrews' escape from slavery in Egypt by crossing the Red Sea. All three stories link humanity to God's goodness through water. Unlike some denominations, Presbyterians do not require a person to be entirely immersed in water during baptism. Baptism is received only once. The Presbyterian Church believes that persons of other denominations are part of one body of Christian believers; therefore, it recognizes all baptisms with water in the name of the Father, of the Son, and of the Holy Spirit administered by other Christian churches.

Initiation, Baptism, or Confirmation

Thirty-five-week confirmation classes provide youth in early adolescence with a consistent standard of education regarding Presbyterian beliefs and a Reformed understanding of scripture. Confirmation is the time when young people claim the promises that were made on their behalf in baptism. Without that public profession of faith, baptism is like a gift that remains unopened. When confirmation is done with integrity, it can convey to our young people that membership in the church of Jesus Christ is a serious core commitment of their lives.

Marriage

Presbyterians consider the marriage ceremony sacred, but it is not considered a sacrament. They teach that a Christian marriage performed in accordance with the Directory for Worship can only involve a covenant between a woman and a man, it would not be proper for a minister of the Word and sacrament to perform a same-sex union ceremony that the minister determines to be the same as a marriage ceremony.

Many Presbyterian scholars, pastors, and theologians have been heavily involved in the debate over homosexuality. Officially, the church does permit clergy-performed blessing ceremonies for same-sex unions as long as it is clear that the blessing ritual is not a marriage ceremony.[13]

As recently as 2008, the *Permanent Judicial Commission of the Presbyterian Church* stated that:

> By the definition in (the Book of Order), a same-sex ceremony can never be a marriage. One cannot characterize same-sex ceremonies as marriages for legal or ecclesiastical purposes. We do hold that the liturgy should be kept distinct for the two types of services, it said. We further hold that officers of the PCUSA authorized to perform marriages shall not state, imply or represent that a same-sex ceremony is a marriage.

Death and Afterlife

Presbyterians teach that in heaven, souls behold the face of God and wait for the full redemption of their bodies. When we die, our souls leave the body and go to be with God. They do not agree with the doctrine of purgatory as taught by the Catholic Church (a place where the remainders of our sinfulness would be purged away). Presbyterians believe it is not necessary. God will indeed redeem us and cleanse us from all our sins, and we will be readied for heaven without our needing to postulate a third possible place to go when we die. Presbyterians do not believe that sins can be graded by their severity. Sin is sin. Forgiveness is God's free gift in Christ.[14]

Judgment and Salvation

Presbyterians believe God has offered us salvation because of God's loving nature. It is not a right or a privilege to be earned by being good enough. "No one of us is good enough on our own—we are all dependent upon God's goodness and mercy. From the kindest, most devoted churchgoer to the most blatant sinner, we are all saved solely by the grace of God."[15]

They believe that "Jesus shall visibly return for this Last Judgment as He was seen to ascend. And then the time of refreshing and restitution of all things shall come, so that those who from the beginning have suffered violence, injury, and wrong, for righteousness' sake, shall inherit that blessed immortality promised them from the beginning."[16] They teach that at this final judgment, there will be a reuniting of the soul with the body and the giving of eternal rewards to the elect, with the casting into hell of the wicked. "The only official Presbyterian statement that includes any comment on hell is a 1974 paper on universalism adopted by the *General Assembly of the Presbyterian Church in the United States.* It warns of judgment and promises hope, acknowledging that these two ideas seem to be 'in tension or even in paradox.'"

In the end, the statement concedes, "how God works redemption and judgment is a mystery."They feel that the Bible does not give clear and detailed answers to our questions about what happens after death, so they put their trust in God's love and grace. "Presbyterians have always insisted that no one is truly good enough. We are saved only by grace. Despite our failure, God decided to save us through the incarnation, death and resurrection of Jesus."[17]

Special Doctrine

Book of Order: This is the rule book for the Presbyterian Church. It contains the guidelines for church life, including structure, worship, and collective action. It not only tells them how to do things but also explains why. It was developed and can be modified by the General Assembly, with the ratification of a majority of the presbyteries. Presbyterians have always had a very strong doctrine of biblical authority, but historically most have shied away from calling that doctrine inerrancy with regards to individual scriptures. The doctrine of authority, in contrast, focuses on the whole Bible rather than particular texts. With regard to topics like healing or inclusiveness or final judgment, this doctrine prompts us to ask, "What are all the verses that talk about this? How do they fit together to form one cohesive biblical teaching? And how do I follow that teaching and live it out in my life?"

<u>Predestination:</u> The father of Presbyterianism, John Calvin (1509–64), is most famous for his doctrine of predestination. Calvin defines predestination in this way:

> *"By predestination we mean the eternal decree of God, by which he determined with himself whatever he wished to happen with regard to every man. All are not created on equal terms, but some are preordained to eternal life, others to eternal damnation; and, accordingly, as each has been created for one or other of these ends, we say that he has been predestined to life or to death. We say, then, that Scripture clearly proves this much, that God by his eternal and immutable counsel determined once for all those whom it was his pleasure one day to admit to salvation, and those whom, on the other hand, it was his pleasure to doom to destruction. We maintain that this counsel, as regards the elect, is founded on his free mercy, without any respect to human worth, while those whom he dooms to destruction are excluded from access to life by a just and blameless, but at the same time incomprehensible judgment."*[8]

Other theologians have seen in predestination only a positive calling to eternal life. Still others have seen it as God's foreknowledge of who would choose faith. This word, similar to election, often raises questions for people of other denominations.

The starkness of affirming that God has pre-selected some for heaven and others for hell has moved people to try to put the puzzle together in several ways. Over the centuries many long theological essays have been written, presenting different efforts to make it all fit together smoothly, and criticizing the failures of other attempts.

Below is just one of those attempts to explain the Presbyterian view on predestination, but there is no way to know if this is what Calvin actually had in mind:

> *"Some believe that every event may be caused by previous events. If so, it is an illusion to suppose that your decisions actually change anything. If you do a good deed…that is what you were fated to do. If you do something evil, that is just the outworking of your predetermined fate. This is different from the Presbyterian doctrine of predestination, which says God chose to redeem us, long before we could even understand what that might mean."*

Because God chose us before the foundation of the world, that means we are predestined to life. That does not take away our ability to choose; we make many trivial-but-free choices every day. Beyond that, predestination teaches us that God has given us a new and bigger freedom: the freedom to fulfill our destiny."[19]

Outreach: As far back as 1837 the General Assembly declared that the church, by its very nature, is a missionary society whose purpose is to share the love of God in Jesus Christ in word and deed with the entire world. Witnessing to the Good News of Jesus Christ throughout the world, Presbyterians engage in mission activities, seek to alleviate hunger, foster self-development, respond to disasters, support mission works, preach the gospel, heal the sick and educate new generations for the future. In partnership with more than 165 churches and Christian organizations around the world, the missionary efforts of the Presbyterian Church (USA) involve nearly 300 volunteers and compensated personnel...Besides annual receipts from congregations and income from endowments, additional special funds are received each year that make particular ministries possible. These include funds received through *Selected Giving Programs* and the *Special Gifts Program*, through the *Hunger Fund*, *Presbyterian Women's Birthday Offering* (spring) and *Thank Offering* (fall), and through four special Churchwide offerings: *One Great Hour of Sharing*, divided among *Presbyterian Disaster Assistance, Self-Development of People*, and the *Presbyterian Hunger Program*; the *Christmas Joy Offering*, which supports racial ethnic schools and assistance programs of the Board of Pensions; the *Peacemaking Offering* to support peace education and peacemaking efforts throughout the denomination; and the *Pentecost Offering* to support ministries with youth and young adults and children at risk.[20]

<u>Presbyterians and the Middle East:</u> "In June of 2004, the PCUSA General Assembly met in Richmond, Virginia and adopted by a vote of 431-62 a resolution that called on the church's committee on *Mission Responsibility Through Investment* (MRTI) to initiate a process of selective divestment in corporations operating in Israel." The resolution also said "the occupation...has proven to be at the root of evil acts committed against innocent people on both sides of the conflict." The church statement at the time noted that "divestment is one of the strategies that US churches used in the 1970s and '80s in a successful campaign to end apartheid in South Africa." They hoped that a similar strategy would work in the Middle East.

A second resolution, calling for an end to the construction of a wall by the state of Israel, passed. The resolution opposed the construction of the West Bank barrier, regardless of its location, and opposed government contribution to the construction. The General Assembly also adopted policies rejecting Christian Zionism and rejected allowing the continued funding of conversionary activities aimed at Jews. Together, the resolutions caused tremendous dissent within the church and a sharp disconnect with the Jewish community. Leaders of several American Jewish groups communicated to the church their concerns about the use of economic leverages that apply specifically to companies operating in Israel. Some critics of the divestment policy accused church leaders of anti-Semitism.

In June 2006, after the Presbyterian Church (USA) General Assembly in Alabama changed the policy, both pro-Israel and pro-Palestinian groups praised the new resolution. Pro-Israel groups, who had written General Assembly commissioners to express their concerns about a corporate engagement/divestment strategy focused on Israel, praised the new resolution, saying that it reflected the church stepping back from a policy that singled out companies. Pro-Palestinian groups said that the church maintained the opportunity to engage and potentially divest from companies that support the Israeli occupation.[21]

Notes

Spiritist

History

Mediumship and other phenomena studied by Spiritism weren't created by Allan Kardec. They have existed since the dawn of mankind, having manifested in most primitive religions, but being more closely related to Shamanism.

The belief in, and practice of communication with Spirits has existed in all nations. Spiritual phenomenons have occurred throughout human history, with people being entranced, inspired and influenced by Spirit intelligences. In fact, mankind's history, literature, folk law and fairy tales are full of mystical Spiritual beings both good and bad. In ancient times, primitive man had no doubt that his ancestors survived death, and ancestor-worship was a form of religion. Some people had psychic abilities, similar to modern mediums, and were aware of psychic forces of the Spirit world, and could communicate with Spirit peoples.[1]

Asian Shamans claimed to have fully accomplished the ability to communicate with the dead and the gods and served as intermediates between them and the living people. Native American medicine men also claimed the same ability. Even today, some cultures have their witch-doctors and Shamans, who invoke the powers of the Spirit for healing and giving guidance.

The Roman Catholic worship of the saints, for instance, is likened to the veneration of the enlightened spirits. The manifestation of the Holy Ghost in Pentecost is explained by Spiritism as a mass manifestation of mediumship. The Catholic Church has, in every age since the redemption, encountered spirits, but it has uniformly associated them with Satan and his angels.

In the fourth century, Christian leaders decided that the use of psychic and mediumship abilities was wrong unless performed by the Christian priesthood. All others who demonstrated Spiritual abilities were denounced as false prophets, evil sorcerers, heretics and were liable to punishment. In 1484 the Pope strongly denounced mediums.

The Church also sanctioned the publication of a book entitled, *"Hammer of the Witches,"* that described all people who communicated with Spirits as witches and stated that they should be severely punished. After this, there was a long period of persecution where people suspected of using psychic abilities were in danger of trial, torture and execution. During these times thousands of mediums were put to death by the church-sanctioned witch-hunters.[2]

The first to begin the development of what would become modern Spiritism was Emanuel Swedenborg (1688–1772) a Swedish scientist, philosopher, seer and theologian. Swedenborg had a prolific career as an inventor and scientist. Then at age 56 he entered into a Spiritual phase of his life, where he experienced visions of the Spiritual world and claimed to have talked with angels, devils, and Spirits by visiting heaven and hell. He claimed of being directed by God, the Lord Jesus Christ to reveal the doctrines of His second coming.[3]

Leon Rivail (the man considered to be the founder of the modern-day Spiritism movement), better known by his alias of Allan Kardec, was born in 1804. He "acquired at an early age the habit of investigation and the freedom of thought of which continued into his later life... Born in a Catholic country, but educated in a Protestant one, he began, while yet a boy, to mediate on the means of bringing about a unity of belief among the various Christian sects—a project of religious reform at which he labored in silence for many years."[4]

Then the most striking development was brought on by the Fox Sisters of Hydesville, New York. Catherine (1838–92), Leah (1814–90) and Margaret (1836–93) played an important role in the acceptance of Spiritism and Spiritualism. (Although *Webster's Dictionary* defines them as one and the same, there is some question as to whether or not that is accurate. In *Wikipedia,* they have two different sites although they do reference one another. Some say that they should not be confused since the adherents of each section were opposed to the tenets of the other. My understanding is that *Spritualism* is the basic understanding that there is "something more than matter within us," which may or may not include contact with spirits. The doctrine of *Spiritism* goes further and believes there is a relationship between the spiritual world and the material world, with much information to be shared. The website that I obtained my Spiritualism information from did not want to be included as an "also ran" in the chapter on Spiritism.)

In 1848, the Fox family began to hear unexplained rapping sounds. Catherine and Margaret conducted channeling sessions in an attempt to contact the presumed. The Fox girls became instant celebrities. They demonstrated their communication with the spirit by using taps and knocks, automatic writing, and later, even voice communication as the spirit took control of one of the girls. Skeptics suspected this was nothing but clever deception and fraud. Nonetheless, belief in the ability to communicate with the dead grew rapidly, becoming a religious movement and contributing greatly to the embracing of Spiritism.[5] People love the idea of spirits and angels, because it gives them hope of an afterlife.

The tale of the Fox sisters spurred immediate interest, and the beginning of Spiritism was underway. Four years later, in 1852, a spiritualist convention was held in Cleveland with additional impetus, with the help of Horace Greeley, the editor of the *New York Tribune*. Much of this activity was motivated by mere curiosity and the fascination of the supernatural, but it had a more serious intention. Many inquirers wished to convince themselves as to human survival of bodily death; others felt comfort to communicate with their departed love ones; others wanted information about the future life.

Following the communication with rapping spirits by the Fox sisters and others, communication through the phenomena of moving objects became much more common. It was clear that the cause was not purely physical and, based upon the principle, "to every effect a cause is associated, then to every intelligent effect there is an intelligent cause," and spiritual intelligence was appointed as the cause. The way to ascertain this was quite simple: a discussion with such an entity would be necessary. Interrogated in this way about their nature, all the beings declared themselves to be spirits and belong to an invisible world. As the phenomena were produced in different locations through several different people and observed by serious and intelligent people, it was decided that they were not an illusion.[6]

In the beginning, communication with the spirits presented by means of human channeling was too slow and cumbersome, so a new one was devised, supposedly from a suggestion by the spirits themselves—the talking board. The energy channeled from the spirits through their hands made the board spin around and find letters which, once written down by a scribe, would form intelligible words, phrases, and sentences. The system was an early, and less effective, precursor of the *Ouija* boards that later became so popular.[7]

Allan Kardec first became interested in Spiritism when he learned of the Fox sisters, but his first contact with what would become the doctrine was by means of talking boards.

Experience had shown that the Spirit who acted upon an unanimated body could in the same way control the arms or the hands and leads the pencil. Writing mediums then appeared, that is, people who could write in an involuntary manner under the impulse of the Spirits, being their interpreters and instruments. Thenceforth the communications had no limits, and the exchange of thoughts was as fast and easy as among the living.[8]

The phenomenon spread from the United States to the rest of Europe, where for several years, it became a popular and even fashionable form of entertainment for many curious observers.

Despite its popularity, however, Spiritism was not without its many critics. Materialists, who believed only in the visible and tangible, and had no belief in life after death, would not even consider the idea of invisible Spirits and mocked those who did believe, calling them madmen. Some critics admitted the physical effects but attributed them to the devil; which had the effect of scaring some and exciting others. (The Roman Catholic Church still maintains that people shouldn't open the door to spirits as you never know whom you will let in. They consider it very dangerous.)

"Foreseeing the vast importance, to science and to religion, of such an extension of the field of human observation, (Kardec) entered at once upon a careful investigation of the new phenomena. A friend of his had two young, giggly daughters who had become what are now called "mediums."[9] Whenever Kardec "was present, the messages transmitted through these young ladies were of a very grave and serious character; and on his inquiring of the invisible intelligences, he was told that 'Spirits of a much higher order than those who habitually communicated through the two young mediums came expressly for him, and would continue to do so, in order to enable him to fulfill an important religious mission'."

Much astonished at the announcement, he at once proceeded to test its truthfulness by drawing up a series of progressive questions in relation to the various problems of human life and the universe in which we find ourselves, and submitted them to his unseen interlocutors, receiving their answers through the instrumentality of the two young mediums, who willingly consented to devote a couple of evenings every week to this purpose, and who thus obtained the replies which have become the basis of the Spiritist theory...When these conversations had been going on for nearly two years, he one day remarked to his wife, in reference to the unfolding of these views ..."*"It is a most curious thing! My conversations with the invisible intelligences have completely revolutionized my ideas and convictions. The instructions thus transmitted constitute an entirely new theory of human life, duty, and destiny, that appears to me to be perfectly rational and coherent, admirably lucid and consoling, and intensely interesting. I have a great mind to publish these conversations in a book; for it seems to me that what interests me so deeply might very likely prove interesting to others."* His wife approving the idea, he next submitted it to his unseen interlocutors, who replied that their communications had been made to him for the express purpose of being given to the world as he proposed to do, and that the time had now come for putting this plan into execution. "To the book in which you will embody our instructions," continued the communicating intelligences, "you will give, as being our work rather than yours, the title of *Le Livre des Esprits* (The Spirits' Book); and you will publish it, not under your own name, but under the pseudonym of Allan Kardec (allegedly the Spirits told him about a previous incarnation of his as a Druid by that name). Keep your own name of Rivail for your own books already published; but take and keep the name we have now given you for the book you are about to publish by our order, and, in general, for all the work that you will have to do in the fulfillment of the mission which, as we have already told you, has been confided to you by Providence, and which will gradually open before you as you proceed in it under our guidance."[10]

Similar medium experiences were occurring all over the world. Many of these mediums published periodicals in support of the new doctrine. "An enormous mass of Spirit teaching, unique both in quantity and in the variety of the sources from which it was obtained, thus found its way into the hands of Allan Kardec, who studied, collated, coordinate it all, with unwearied zeal and devotion, over a period of fifteen years."[11]

From the material furnished to him from every quarter of the globe, he completed *The Spirits' Book,* under the direction of the spirits by whom it was originally dictated. Thebook then produced and published, sold with great rapidity, making converts all over the Europe, and rendering the name of Allan Kardec a household word. "The Spirits' Book comprised a series of 1,018 questions exploring matters concerning the nature of Spirits, the Spirit world, and the relationship between the Spirit world and the material world. This was followed by a series of other books, the most important being *'The Gospel According to Spiritism,'* and by a periodical, the *Revue Spirite,* which Kardec published until his death."[12]

Following Spiritism's initial codification by Allan Kardec, one of its most prominent followers was another Frenchman, Léon Denis, who is often referred to as the "consolidator of the doctrine," or the Apostle of Spiritism. Léon Dénis lived during approximately the same time period as Allan Kardec (Kardec 1804-1869, Denis 1846-1927). From an early age, he felt the influence and guidance of "invisible friends" and was always interested in the pursuit of meaningful study …sought answers to questions of philosophic and religious issues. He studied with enthusiasm both History and Social Sciences…From the moment he purchased his first copy of *The Spirits' Book,* at 18 years of age, he took great interest in Spiritism, whereby he continued his studies of Kardec's works and soon became one of Spiritism's greatest students, defenders, and propagators. As a seeing and writing medium, Denis received communications from Sorella (who he later claimed to be Joan of Arc, about whom he wrote a book), from a Spirit nicknamed Blue Spirit, and from his own Spirit guide, Jerônimo de Praga. As a disseminator of Spiritism, Denis developed several conferences in which he demonstrated and shared his profound knowledge of the doctrine.

He spoke at several *International Spiritists Conferences*, in which he defended the doctrine's philosophy and objective, and he wrote several books[13] on the subject.

All this while Kardec was compiling four other works: *The Mediums' Book,* a practical treatise on medianimity and evocations on 1861, *The Gospel as Explained by Spirits*, an exposition of morality from the Spiritist point of view on 1864, *Heaven and Hell*, a vindication of the justice of the divine government of the human race on 1865, and *Genesis*, showing the concordance of the Spiritist theory with the discoveries of modern science and with the general tenor of the Mosaic record as explained by Spirits on 1867. He also published two short treatises entitled *What is Spiritism?* and *Spiritism Reduced to its Simplest Expression*.

It is to be noted, in connection with the works just mentioned, that Allan Kardec was not a medium and was consequently obliged to avail himself of the skills of others in obtaining the spirit communications from which the writings were compiled through many thousands of mediums, unknown to each other, belonging to different countries, and to every variety of social position.

Having suffered for many years from heart disease, in 1869, Allan Kardec drew up the plan of a new Spiritist organization, which should carry on the work after his death. But Allan Kardec was not destined to witness the realization of the project in which he took so deep an interest. He passed away on in 1869 by the rupture of the aneurysm.

Allan Kardec refers to Spiritism as a science involving the relationship between spirits and human beings. Because of that, some Spiritists see themselves as not adhering to a religion, but to a doctrine with a scientific cornerstone with moral teachings. On the other hand, many Spiritists consider it a religion as well. "Spiritism is now studied and practiced in many countries around the world. For example, the countries that belong to the *International Spiritist Council* include Angola, Argentina, Belgium, Bolivia, Brazil, Chile, Colombia, El Salvador, Spain, France, Guatemala, Italy, Japan, Mexico, The Netherlands, Norway, Paraguay, Peru, Portugal, Sweden, Switzerland, United Kingdom, United States of America, and Uruguay."[14]

In many of these countries, there are multiple Spiritist Centres. "In addition to the centers themselves, there are also several Spiritist-run humanitarian projects and organizations that bring material and spiritual support to the poor, the sick, and others in need of social assistance. In addition, there are Spiritist associations of professionals, such as doctors, lawyers, etc."[15] It is estimated that there are approximately 40 million people in Brazil alone who believe and/or practice some form of Spiritism although another website touted total believers at 70 million.

God or Gods

1. "God is the supreme intelligence and primary cause of all things. God is eternal, immutable, unique, omnipotent, supremely just and good."[16]
2. The universe is a creation of God. It encompasses all things.
3. All the laws of nature are divine laws because God is their author. They cover both the physics and moral laws.
4. Beyond the physical world, which is the habitation of incarnate spirits (mankind), there exists the spiritual world, which is the habitation of discarnate spirits.
5. God created matter, which constitutes the worlds. He also created intelligent beings called spirits, which are in charge of these worlds. By improving themselves, the spirits approach the likeness of God.[17]

As a good father, God does not leave people to themselves during their earth atonements but offers them guides. These are firstly the protecting spirits or guardian angels, who watch over people and try to make them follow the good way. Secondly, there are the great incarnated spirits which, sometimes appear on earth in order to illuminate human paths and make mankind walk forward.

Christ

Spiritism believes Jesus was on earth as a special envoy from God. He was (and still is) the most elevated spirit to incarnate on earth. His preaching was intended to prepare the ground for the evolution of the planet to a higher state. In light of these theses, Spiritism explains the teachings of Christ as veiled hints of what would later be revealed to the world as Spiritism. According to Spiritism, the teachings of Christ are eternal because they are the very law given by God.

The origin of this law is not the Earth. When He said *"My kingdom is not of this world"* He was hinting on the heavenly origin of His teachings and the heavenly nature of the work He was doing. He did not come as a human Messiah to save physical lives and restore a temporal kingdom, but to spread the truth about the afterlife so that the Spirits of people could evolve faster during their incarnations on Earth. Christ also hinted on the plurality of inhabited planets, millennia before such a notion became widespread, when He said *"In my Father's house are many mansions."*[18] Christ, the greatest moral example for humankind, is deemed to have incarnated here to show us, through His example, the path that we have to take to achieve our own spiritual perfection. Jesus is the guide and model for all humanity. His teachings and examples are the most pure expression of God's laws.

Basic Doctrine

Spiritism is a science because it studies all Spiritual phenomena by the light of reason and within scientific criterion. There is nothing of the supernatural within Spiritism. Even the strangest phenomena can be explained scientifically and therefore, are in the order of natural occurrences.

Spiritism is a philosophy because it investigates the true nature of life by answering questions such as "where have I come from," "what am I doing in this world" and "'where will I go after death"? Every doctrine that offers an explanation of life is a philosophy.

Spiritism is a religion because it has the transformative capabilities of all other religions. It advocates a return to the basics of Jesus Christ's teachings in our daily lives. Spiritism is not a traditional organized religion with a clerical structure. It is in fact profoundly different from all traditional religions.

It does not accept the concept that priests or ministers are necessary mediators between God and man, or that there is any need for religious offices, temples, or churches.

It adopts no kinds of ceremonies, nor does it perform any rituals. It doesn't advocate the use of special clothing, symbolism, ornamentation for its services, reverent gestures, or incense. The spiritism religion is an act of devotion that is performed within each heart. It is the elevation of one's sentiments, of love for one's fellow beings, and of constant work in favor of one's neighbor. Spiritism, then, seeks to revive the teachings of Jesus in all their simplicity and sincerity, without luxury or social conventions, without pomp or ceremony. (It is possible, for this reason, that mainline churches have had a negative concept of Spiritism since the philosophy could make them obsolete.)

From a religious point of view, however, Spiritism is based on the fundamental truths of every religion: God, the soul, immortality, future punishments, and rewards. Its goal is to prove to those who negate the soul's existence that the soul survives after the body, that it experiences after death the consequences of the good or evil practiced during its corporeal life. These concepts are common to most religions.

One can, therefore, be a Catholic or Protestant, a Greek or a Roman, a Jew or a Muslim and yet believe in the manifestations of the spirits and, consequently, be a Spiritist.[19] The essential aim of Spiritism is human improvement. It is useless to believe if this faith does not make one progress positively and also do the utmost for one's fellow creatures. Spiritism's faith is only useful for those who can say "we are better today than yesterday."

Under the natural laws of evolution and progress, our Creator has ordained that each of His children, all spirits created in equal states of simplicity and ignorance, will one day reach the ultimate goal of relative perfection. The spirit, having been given free will, has total control over its own destiny. In all, we have the possibility of developing, evolving, and perfecting ourselves just like a student in school who learns and progresses through each year of study. Spiritual evolution requires learning and growth, which can only be achieved by living in a material world.

Spirits acquire knowledge through the experiences offered with each physical life and will continue to reincarnate periodically for as many times as is necessary. Earth afflictions are remedies to the soul. The y are salve for the future, like a painful surgical treatment, which relieves a sick person's life and brings back health. For this reason, Christ said, *"Blessed are the afflicted for ye shall be comforted."* It is for this very purpose that reincarnation exists. Perhaps we are correcting past mistakes that we made against others; on the other hand, perhaps we are being helped and upheld by those who, in the past, caused us harm.

The progress achieved by each spirit during the many experiences it has passed through is not only intellectual but, most of all, moral. It is exactly this aspect of growth that permits the spirit to approach ever closer to God. As we evolve, we gradually awaken to new levels of understanding about life and the meaning of our existence. Like growing children, we develop a hunger for knowledge, and at each stage of development, we ask questions that demand a new level of explanation. Those who are more advanced have more desire to learn and grow. Every communication, no matter of what type, should not be accepted blindly. It is imperative to regard all communications with a certain reserve and examine them with care so that we do not become victims of spirits who wish to deceive and mislead us.

The Spiritist doctrine alerts people to the dangers of untruths within communication and to be aware of false mediums or mediums of poor moral character who attract spirits of a different nature.[20]

The basic doctrine of Spiritism is defined in five books written and published by Allan Kardec, collected communications received from enlightened spirits:

The Spirit's Book. It defines the guidelines of the doctrine and clarifies its roots and relationship to similar or namesake doctrines.

The Book on Mediums. It details the mechanics of the spiritual world, the processes involved in channeling spirits, techniques to be developed by would-be mediums, etc.

The Gospel According to Spiritism. It is intended to demonstrate that Spiritism clarifies and extends the most important teachings of Jesus. The book attracted a lot of reaction from the Catholic Church and was indexed (added to the list of prohibited books).

Followers consider this to be one of the most influential of his writings. Kardec was a devoted Catholic and a dedicated teacher. He looked forward to basing his teachings in solid biblical knowledge as well as the messages he received from his guiding spirits. Kardec also argues that what makes the Spiritist doctrine reliable is that it is not self-contradictory; the elevated spirits, channeled by mediums of goodwill, all gave the same message, and this message was consistent both among the mediums and with what Christ taught.

Heaven and Hell. An enlightening series of interviews with spirits of deceased people, intending to establish a correlation between the lives they lead and their conditions in the beyond.

Genesis According to Spiritism . It tries to reconcile religion and science, dealing with the three major points of friction between the two: the origin of the universe (and of life, as a consequence) and the concepts of miracle and premonition.

Despite being published from 1857 to 1865, these books remain the core of the Spiritist doctrine today.[21]

<u>Charity is the supreme law</u>: *"Love each other as brothers and sisters—Love your neighbor as yourself—forgive your enemies—Do unto others as you would have them do unto you"*; all this is summed up in the word charity. God makes some persons strong and powerful in order for them to help the weak; the greater their strength, the more that is expected of them. Powerful people who oppress the weak are warned by God. The affluent will be severely called to account for the use of their wealth. Charity is not only alms-giving, for there can be charity in thought, in words and in acts. He who is charitable in thoughts is lenient toward his fellowman's mistakes; he who is charitable in words says nothing against his fellowman, and he who is charitable in acts helps his fellow sisters and brothers according to his capacity. A poor person who shares his bred with someone even poorer is more charitable and has much more merit in God's eyes than those who, lacking for nothing, give only that which is superfluous to them.

He who declares himself a Christian and, at same time, feeds evil feelings and lack of charity toward his neighbor, is offending God. It is of no use to say that you belong to this or that religion. It is of little use to remain praying all the time.

The important thing is to practice what you believe every day of your life. We can do all of this by looking after our own attitudes better, by being vigilant about our daily behavior, by being more attentive and polite, by seeing only the good qualities in others and finally, by being ever more demanding of ourselves in the battle toward perfection. For this reason, Christian Spiritism exhorts the maxim: *"Without charity there is no salvation."[22]*

Basic Worship Service

"Kardec's works do not establish any rituals or formal practices for followers. Instead, the doctrine suggests that followers adhere to some principles, which are regarded as common to all religions. Based on the actual content of Kardec's works and further elaborations by early adepts" like Léon Dénis, Spiritism was organized as a religion with the following characteristics:

- All practical Spiritism is free of any charge. Spiritists are never asked for any contribution.
- A Spiritist center has no exterior mark of its use. They do not use icons, idols, crosses, pictures, etc.
- Although Spiritists have no special place or form of worship, Spiritists gather to study the spiritist doctrine and discuss how they can morally contribute to the betterment of the world around us.
- Spiritist mediumship is only that which is practiced based upon the principles of the spiritist doctrine and within Christian morality, which means that it mustn't be done for money, fame, or vanity.
- "Spiritism respects all religions, values all efforts towards the practice of goodness and recognizes that "a true person of goodness is one who fulfils the laws of justice, love and charity

in their greatest form of purity." Therefore, they accept as "perfect Spirits" people from other religions as well."

- There is a strong campaign against abortion and suicide. Spiritists believe abortion is murder and suicide is cowardice, which leads to worsening of the conditions of a future life.
- "Doing charity work is of utmost importance. According to the doctrine, we should be willing to donate not only material resources, but also our better share of love and care for the less fortunate."
- Spiritists are prompted to read a lot. Spiritist centers usually have libraries and spiritist authors are often expected to donate their copyright to works of charity or charge low amounts for it.[23]

All groups carry on mediunic meetings, in which they either invoke or receive the Spirits of deceased persons, which is done nowadays exclusively for charitable reasons. Such reasons include bringing relief to the family of a recently deceased person, sending away some evil influence that is lurking about someone and, quite usually, allow Spirits of people that died an unfortunate or unexpected death and are unaware of their state.[24]

<u>Prayer:</u> Prayer is an act of adoration toward God. It is contained within the natural law and is innate in man just as the idea of the existence of a Creator is also innate in man. Prayer helps man to become better. Those who pray with fervor and confidence find themselves to be stronger against the temptations of evil, and God sends them good spirits to assist them. This is help that is never denied to those who ask with true sincerity. Sincerity and pureness of purpose is essential. Praying a lot is unimportant, but one must pray well. The principal quality of prayer is clarity. Each word should be of value in expressing an idea and in touching a fiber of the soul. In short, it should cause you to reflect. The first duty of all human beings is prayer. In the morning hours, open your channels to God. You should also pray constantly without seeking your chapel or falling on your knees.

It is an act of gratitude to lift up your thoughts to Him when something happy occurs, when you avoid an accident, or even when some simple triviality grazes our soul. This is quite apart from regular morning and evening prayer and those for sacred days. As you see, prayer can be for all moments without interrupting your activities ...You can be sure that just one of these thoughts, if sent from the heart, is listened to by our Celestial Father even more than those long repetitive prayers said out of habit and almost always without any determined motive behind them only because the habitual hour is calling mechanically.[25]

<u>Spiritism in the Home:</u> The *Study Meeting of the Gospel at Home* is the gathering of the family for the study of the Gospel under the light of Spiritism and their joint prayers. It is of vital importance for the spiritual balance of the family and the harmony of the domestic atmosphere. In this meeting, in addition to the study and vibrations carried out together, there is also the opportunity for the Spiritual friends to provide spiritual assistance to the home, and in particular, to each one of its members...The entire family should be motivated to participate in the Study Meeting of the Gospel at Home, including the children...However, one person alone can accomplish it, with the certainty that the home, as well as other relatives, will benefit from it.

Spiritism was accused of lax morality because of its tolerance toward women. Not only did Kardec accept them as equal to men long before it was acceptable, but effectively published that the Spirits said that a man may choose to live as woman or vice-versa to attain greater improvement. Sex, in Spiritism, is a transitional biological trait that exists among humans, but may be different or absent in other intelligent species of the Universe. Most of the mediums that channeled for Kardec were women, as well as some of the early leaders of Spiritism.

The tolerance extended to marriage as well. When Christ said *"Shall man not divide what God has united "* is not seen as binding. God has established marriage, it is important for the improvement of mankind now, but it will eventually cease to be. Man cannot break a union that is united by God, so, any union that ends was not united by Him. Therefore, the permanence of marriage is relative because there are marriages based on misrepresentation of love, coercion on any or both the nubents or simply by mistake (when a person marries someone and later discovers a sound reason why the wedding should have never taken place).

Spiritism accepts divorced people without any discrimination and accepts that they have the right to marry again (although it states that divorce should be an exception, not a rule).

Infant Baptism or Blessing

Not applicable.

Initiation, Baptism, or Confirmation

Not applicable.

Death and Afterlife

Kardec argues that if we assumed that we only live once, the apparent injustice of the world must be a reflection of God's injustice. On the other hand, considering that through reincarnations, we live many times and that we carry from one life to the next the missions we left unfulfilled, t he guilt f or t he wrongs we did against others, etc., the apparent injustice of the world reflects the compensation of the wrong done in previous lives. Kardec proposes the "Law of Cause and Effect" (an interpreted version of the Hindu concept of karma) and reinforces the monstrosity of homicide and suicide as the greatest sins against the law of God.

Death is simply the destruction of the crude shell of the spirit; only the body dies, not the spirit. But the spirit gives up only the material body, keeping the perispirit, which a kind of ethereal body, vaporous and very subtle to us. It has the human form, which seems to be the standard one. By using the perispirit, the spirit can act upon matter and produce the several phenomena of raps, movements, writing, etc.

Deathbed repentance is okay if sincere because we will have another life to pay for the wrong we did, and if we have enough time to repair some of the evil we spread, our future may be less demanding. The spirit's improvement is a consequence of its own effort. It cannot acquire all the intellectual and moral qualities that will bring it to the end in only one existence. It reaches its goal through a series of several lives. In each one of them, the spirit walks a little farther in the path of progress. In each corporeal existence, the spirit has to fulfill a mission proportional to its degree of development.

The rougher and harder it is, the greater the spirit's merit in fulfilling it. It depends on the spirit's will to shorten it by working harder for its moral improvement, in much the same way a laborer's diligence shortens the time to complete a job. The Gospel proposed the notion that adhering to Christ's teachings was a way to get rid of suffering, if not immediately, in a later life. Relying solely on the morality proposed by God, we fulfill our missions in the world, stop accumulating guilt by doing wrong to others, and start repairing our past sins. Kardec believed that following the teachings of Christ is much easier and leads us to more comfort than refusing them; all suffering comes from denying in doing what God wants us to. That's why Christ's yoke is light.

During the intermissions of its lives, the spirit state has no definite duration. In it, the spirit is happy or sad according to the good or bad use of its previous life. The spirit studies the causes that quickened or delayed its progress and takes proper decisions, which it will try to put into practice in its next incarnation. It also chooses the most adequate tests for its improvement. Sometimes, however, the spirit makes a mistake and falls, not fulfilling as a human, the decisions it had made as a spirit. In its successive incarnations, the spirit, little by little, loses its impurities and improves itself through work until the end of its corporeal lives. Then the spirit belongs to the pure spirit or angel order and fully enjoys God's complete life and endless, unshakable happiness. In a sense, everyone will achieve salvation; it will just take some people a lot longer.[26]

Judgment and Salvation

"The Spirits gladly describe their impressions after leaving the earth, their new situation, the origin of their happiness and suffering in their new world. Some are happy, others are unhappy; suffering terrible torments according to the way in which they lived and the good or bad use they made of their lives." Such knowledge enables us the explanation of our future state and to foresee the happy or sad destiny that waits for us there.

Spiritists don't believe in heaven or hell as depicted by other more traditional religions. They also do not have teachings about angels or devils, only superior or inferior spirits, who also are on their way toward perfection. All the time, good spirits are getting better, and bad spirits are regenerating themselves. It is generally believed that a single life is not sufficient for us to reach enlightenment as to God's plans. Many people have a struggle just to survive. Many have never been exposed to any spiritual teaching, and others die very early. Assuredly, no one is lost. Everyone has the opportunity they deserve. They believe that when Christ said, *"No one may see the Kingdom of Heaven if they are not born again,"* He was making a reference to the physical rebirth and moral rebirth of human beings. By this, we need to understand that each life is always a new opportunity to grow spiritually. In this way, reincarnation is the perfect mechanism of divine justice. It also explains why there exists so much inequality in the destinies of our fellow creatures on earth.

Through the mechanism of reincarnation, we can verify that God does not punish. We ourselves are the cause of our suffering because, as yet, we have not accepted the law of cause and effect. The guilty spirit is punished through moral sufferings in the spirit world and physical penalties during its corporeal lives. Its afflictions are consequence of its faults, that is, of its violation of God's law. These sorrows constitute both atonement for the past and a test for the future. In this way, the proud can have a life of humiliations; the tyrant, a servant life; and the wealthy oppressor, an incarnation in misery.

Being sovereignly just and good, God does not punish His creatures to endless penalties as a consequence of their limited mistakes. He provides correction and repairs for them at any moment. God forgives but also waits for regret, repair, and return to good in such a way that punishment is proportional to the spirit's insistence in the evil. Consequently, penalties would be eternal only for those who forever remained on the evil side. As soon as a sign of regret appears in the guilty heart, God holds out His mercy. Therefore, eternal punishments should be understood in relative sense only and not in an absolute one.

According to this belief, we are destined for perfection; there are other planets hosting more advanced life forms, and happier societies, where the Spirit has the chance to keep evolving both on the moral and intellectual sense. Although not clear from Kardec's works, later writers explain this point a little bit better; it seems that we cannot detect more advanced life forms in other planets, as they are living in a slight different plane from ours, in the same way the Spiritual plane is superimposed over our own plane.[27]

Since the time for the earth to become home to peace and happiness has arrived, God does not wish that bad spirits continue to disturb it at the sacrifice of the good ones. Consequently, bad spirits will have to leave earth at some designated time; they will atone for their heartlessness on less-developed worlds where they will work again on their improvement during several more painful and less happy lives than those on earth. They will only go to a better world when they deserve it and will continue there until they are completely refined. I f the earth represents a purgatory to these spirits, these new world will be their hell, but a hell with ever-existing hope.[28]

Special Doctrine

The Mission of Spiritists: "Fortify your phalanx with decision and courage! Hands to work! The plough is ready! The land awaits; plough! Go forth and thank God for the glorious task which He has entrusted to you; but pay attention! Amongst those called to Spiritism many will go astray; so then, mark well your pathway and follow the truth" (Erastus, *The Gospel According to Spiritism*, ch. 20, item 4).

The Workers of the Lord: The time approaches when those things that have been announced for the transformation of humanity will be accomplished.

Blessed are those who have said to their fellowmen, "Let us work together and unite our efforts so that when the Lord arrives He will find His work finished." Seeing that, the Lord will say to them, "Come unto me, you who have been good servants, you who knew how to silence your rivalries and discords so that no harm should come to the work" ("The Spirit of Truth" in *The Gospel According to Spiritism*, ch. 20, item 5).

No instances were found where Spiritism is referred to as a new religion or a church. Quite to the contrary as clearly attested below:

Spiritism is the new science which has come to reveal to mankind, by means of irrefutable proofs, the existence and nature of the Spiritual world and its relationship with the physical world. Spiritism is a philosophical doctrine with religion effects, as is any Spiritualist philosophy, because it inevitably reaches to the roots of all religions: God, soul, and future life. But it is not a constituted religion, since it has no services, no rituals, no temples, and no one among its adherents received the title of priest or high priest. (*The Gospel According to Spiritism*, ch. 1, item 5)

Notes

Notes

_____

_____

_____

_____

_____

_____

_____

_____

_____

_____

_____

_____

_____

Creeds of the One Catholic and Apostolic Church

In many of the previous chapters, there are references made to several creeds of belief used by the denominations. Although the verbiage may not be exact when comparing one denomination to another, these are the basic creeds for clarification and further understanding. When the term catholic is used in the creeds, it refers to the true universal Christian church of all times and all places. It is not necessarily a reference to the Roman Catholic Church.

The Apostle's Creed
(200 AD; current version, 542 AD)

I believe in God, the Father almighty,
creator of heaven and earth.
I believe in Jesus Christ,
His only Son, our Lord.
He was conceived by the power of the Holy Spirit
and born of the Virgin Mary.
He suffered under Pontius Pilate, was crucified, died, and was buried.
He descended to the dead.
On the third day He rose again.
He ascended into heaven and sits at the right hand of God, the
Father Almighty.
From thence He shall come to judge the living and the dead.
I believe in the Holy Spirit,
the holy catholic Church,
the communion of saints,
the forgiveness of sins,
the resurrection of the body,
and the life everlasting. Amen.

The Nicene Creed
(325 AD)

We believe in one God, the Father,
the Almighty, maker of heaven and
earth of all that is seen and unseen.
We believe in one Lord, Jesus Christ,
the only Son of God, eternally begotten
of the Father, God from God, Light
from Light, true God from true God,
begotten, not made, one in Being
with the Father. Through him all things
were made. For us men and our
salvation he came down from heaven:
by the power of the Holy Spirit he was
born of the Virgin Mary, and became
man. For our sake he was crucified
under Pontius Pilate; he suffered, died,
and was buried. On the third day he
rose again in fulfillment of the
Scriptures; he ascended into heaven
and is seated at the right hand of the
Father. He will come again to judge
the living and the dead, and his
kingdom will have no end. We
believe in the Holy Spirit, the Lord,
the giver of life, who proceeds from
the Father and the Son. With the
Father and the Son he is worshipped
and glorified. He has spoken through
the Prophets. We believe in one holy
catholic and apostolic Church. We
acknowledge one baptism for the
forgiveness of sins. We look for the
resurrection of the dead, and the life
of the world to come. Amen.

The Athanasian Creed
(415 AD)

Whosoever will be saved, before all things it is necessary that he hold
the catholic faith.

Which faith except every one do keep whole and undefiled; without
doubt he shall perish everlastingly.

And the catholic faith is this: That we worship one God in Trinity, and
Trinity in Unity; Neither confounding the Persons; nor dividing
the Essence.

For there is one Person of the Father; another of the Son; and another
of the Holy Ghost.

But the Godhead of the Father, of the Son, and of the Holy Ghost, is
all one; the Glory equal, the Majesty coeternal.

Such as the Father is; such is the Son; and such is the Holy Ghost.

The Father uncreated; the Son uncreated; and the Holy
Ghost uncreated.

The Father unlimited; the Son unlimited; and the Holy
Ghost unlimited.

The Father eternal; the Son eternal; and the Holy Ghost eternal.

And yet they are not three eternals; but one eternal. As also there are not
three uncreated; nor three infinites, but one uncreated; and one infinite.

So likewise the Father is Almighty; the Son Almighty; and the Holy
Ghost Almighty. And yet they are not three Almighties; but
one Almighty.

So the Father is God; the Son is God; and the Holy Ghost is God.

And yet they are not three Gods; but one God.

So likewise the Father is Lord; the Son Lord; and the Holy Ghost Lord.

And yet not three Lords; but one Lord.

For like as we are compelled by the Christian verity; to acknowledge
every Person by himself to be God and Lord;

So are we forbidden by the catholic religion; to say, There are three
Gods, or three Lords. The Father is made of none; neither created,
nor begotten. The Son is of the Father alone; not made, nor created;
but begotten.

The Holy Ghost is of the Father and of the Son; neither made, nor
created, nor begotten; but proceeding.

So there is one Father, not three Fathers; one Son, not three Sons; one
Holy Ghost, not three Holy Ghosts.

And in this Trinity none is before, or after another; none is greater, or
less than another. But the whole three Persons are coeternal, and
coequal. So that in all things, as aforesaid; the Unity in Trinity, and
the Trinity in Unity, is to be worshipped.

He therefore that will be saved, let him thus think of the Trinity.
Furthermore it is necessary to everlasting salvation; that he also
believe faithfully the Incarnation of our Lord Jesus Christ.

For the right faith is, that we believe and confess; that our Lord Jesus
Christ, the Son of God, is God and Man;

God, of the Essence of the Father; begotten before the worlds;

and Man, of the Essence of his Mother, born in the world.

Perfect God; and perfect Man, of a reasonable soul and human
flesh subsisting.

Equal to the Father, as touching his Godhead; and inferior to the
Father as touching his Manhood.

Who although he is God and Man; yet he is not two, but one Christ.

One; not by conversion of the Godhead into flesh; but by assumption
of the Manhood into God.

One altogether; not by confusion of Essence; but by unity of Person.

For as the reasonable soul and flesh is one man; so God and Man is
one Christ; Who suffered for our salvation; descended into hell;
rose again the third day from the dead.

He ascended into heaven; he sitteth on the right hand of the God the Father
Almighty, from whence he will come to judge the quick and the dead.

At whose coming all men will rise again with their bodies;

And shall give account for their own works. And they that have done
good shall go into life everlasting; and they that have done evil,
into everlasting fire.

This is the catholic faith; which except a man believe truly and firmly,
he cannot be saved.

Eastern Philosophy Religions and Faith Practices

Within the next chapters, we will investigate the uniqueness of the more philosophically based religions. Many of these faith practices have specific thoughts regarding the nature of God and the universe. Others are less direct. Many just stress on one's life and how it is to be lived. Because of the blend of religion and secular life practices, the distinction is often blurred and can be hard to comprehend to a person with a different background. Delving more deeply can lead to enlightenment. Keep in mind that some of these faith practices may in fact also fit into another category. This category was chosen as the primary source of the early years of the religion or practice. But during the process of evolving into what it is today, you will find some blending that is most interesting.

Confucianist

History

Confucianism, a religion of optimistic humanism, has had a monumental impact upon the life, social structure, and political philosophy of China. The founding of the religion goes back to one man, known as Confucius, born a half millennium before Christ. *K'ung Fu Tzu* (commonly pronounced Confucius in English) was born in 551 BC, the youngest of eleven children, in what is now Shantung Province. "His parents, while not wealthy, belonged to the superior class. His father was a warrior, distinguished no less for his deeds of valor than for his noble ancestry."[1]

Confucius was, in fact, a relatively ordinary person; his family was from the lesser aristocracy that had fallen on extremely hard times when he was born. His father died when Confucius was only three years old. Instructed first by his mother, Confucius then distinguished himself as a passionate learner in his teens. He was a contemporary of the Buddha (although they probably never met) and lived immediately before Socrates and Plato.

It is important to understand life in China at the time of Confucius in order to develop a better appreciation of the reforms he was attempting to institute. The age in which Confucius lived was characterized by social anarchy. The in terminable warfare had degenerated toward the undiluted horror of the period of the Warring States. Instead of nobly holding their prisoners for ransom, conquerors put them to death in mass executions. Soldiers were paid upon presenting the severed heads of their enemies. Whole populations unlucky enough to be captured were beheaded, including women, children, and the aged. We read of mass slaughters of 60,000, 80,000, 82,000, and even 400,000. There are accounts of the conquered being thrown into boiling cauldrons, and their relatives forced to drink the human soup. It is easy to see how the need arose for someone like Confucius to provide answers for how the people should live together harmoniously. Although the conduct of

Chinese officials was exceedingly corrupt, Confucius believed the situation was not hopeless, for the general population had not reached the point of total corruption. Confucius believed China could be saved if the people would seek for the good of others, a practice of their ancestors. The role Confucius would play was not as a savior or messiah, but as one who would put the people back in touch with the ancients.

Confucius had served in minor government posts, managing stables and keeping books for granaries. He became a teacher in his early twenties, and that proved to be his calling in life.

He made such progress that at the age of twenty-two years he opened a school that produced statesmen with a strong sense of state and duty, known as *Rujia*, the "School of the Literati"; to which many were attracted by the fame of his learning. His ability and faithful service merited for him promotion to the office of Minister of Justice. Under his wise administration the State attained a degree of prosperity and moral order that it had never seen before. But through the intrigues of rival states the Marquis of Lu was led to prefer ignoble pleasures to the preservation of good government. Confucius tried by sound advice to bring his liege lord back to the path of duty, but in vain. He thereupon resigned his high position and left the state...For thirteen years, accompanied by faithful disciples, he went about from one state to another, seeking a ruler who would give heed to his counsels.[2]

But Confucius was no special religious leader, nor did he claim any special divine status. Confucius's love of antiquity was motivated by his strong desire to understand why certain rituals, such as the ancestral cult, reverence for heaven, and mourning ceremonies, had survived for centuries. He had faith in the cumulative power of culture. Confucius's sense of history was so strong that he saw himself as a conservationist responsible for the continuity of the cultural values and the social norms that had worked so well for the civilization of the Chou Dynasty[3] (the longest dynasty in Chinese history, which lasted approximately 1,200 years).

At last he returned to Lu, where he spent the last five years of his life encouraging others to the study and practice of Virtue. At the age of sixty-seven, Confucius returned home to teach and to preserve his cherished classical traditions by writing and editing.[4] He died in Chfou, Shantung, in 479 BC, having established himself as the most important teacher in Chinese culture. His lifetime almost exactly coincided with that of Buddha, who died two years earlier in India.

Another of the central figures in Confucianism is Meng-tzu, who became second only to Confucius in the history of Confucian thought. Mencius was born in 371 BC and studied with a disciple of Confucius's grandson, Tzu-Ssu. Meng-tzu, Tzu-Ssu, and others sustained Confucianism after Confucius, but it was not influential until Dong Zhongshu emerged in the second century BC. Confucianism was then recognized as the state cult during the Han Dynasty, and the Five Classics became the core of education.[5]

The impact Confucianism has had on China can hardly be overestimated. For over two thousand years, his teachings have profoundly affected a quarter of the population of this globe. During the Han Dynasty (206 BC–AD 20), Confucianism became, in effect, China's state religion. In 130 BC, it was made the basic discipline for the training of government officials, a pattern that continued until the establishment of the Republic of China in 1912. In 59 AD, sacrifices (a practice of giving food to ancestors in a ceremonial style) were ordered for Confucius in all urban schools and universities. In 492, he was canonized as "the Venerable, the Accomplished Sage," and in the seventh and eighth centuries, temples were erected in every prefecture of the empire as shrines to him and his principal disciples.

Sometime during the period from 1068–1086, Confucius was posthumously raised to the full rank of emperor. And in 1914, the worship of Confucius was continued by the first p resident o f t he Republic of China, Yuan Shi Kai. Through the second half of the twelfth century, his book *The Analects* (a collection of aphorisms, which was compiled many years after his death) remained one of the classics. But in the Sung Dynasty, it became not merely a school book but the school book, the basis of all education.

In 1530 AD, a Ming emperor reformed the Confucian cult to focus more on Confucius' teachings than the sage himself (e.g. images of Confucius were replaced with inscribed tablets).

The works of Confucius were translated into European languages through the agency of Jesuit scholars stationed in China. It is thought that such works had considerable importance on European thinkers of the period, particularly among the Deists and other philosophical groups of the Enlightenment who were interested by the integration of the system of morality of Confucius into Western civilization.[6]

The cult of Confucius declined after the founding of the Chinese Republic in 1912, but the influence of Confucianism continues.[7]

Despite its loss of influence during the Tang Dynasty, Confucianist doctrine remained a mainstream Chinese orthodoxy for two millennia until the beginning of the twentieth century, when it was vigorously repressed by Chinese Communism. Some contend there is no use trying. China's...people know Confucius as well as America's millions know Jesus Christ.

There are recent signs of a revival of Confucianism in mainland China. The cultures most strongly influenced by Confucianism include Chinese, Japanese, Korean, and Vietnamese. Confucianism, as passed down to the twentieth and twenty-first century, derives primarily from the school of the Neo-Confucians, led by Zhu Xi, who gave Confucianism renewed vigor in the Song and later dynasties.[8]

In China, and some other areas in Asia, Neo-Confucianism combines the social ethics and moral teachings of Confucius with the Taoist communion with nature and Buddhist concepts of the afterlife, to form a set of complementary, peacefully co-existent and ecumenical religions.[9]

There are approximately 6.1 million people in the world who follow Confucianism exclusively. However, because there are several faith practices that have become a blend of Confucianism and something else, the total number has been quoted as high as 350 million.

God or Gods

Representing a relatively traditionalist-humanist viewpoint of Catholic thought, the 1913 Catholic Encyclopedia declares: *"In Confucianism there is much to admire."* The Encyclopedia praises its "noble conception of the supreme Heaven-god" as well as the high standard of morality and the "refining influence of literary education and of polite conduct"[10] it credits Confucianism to have brought about.

There are numbers of texts that show plainly that Confucius did not depart from the traditional belief in the supreme heaven-god and subordinate spirits, in divine providence and retribution, and in the conscious existence of souls after death. These religious convictions on his part found expression in many recorded acts of piety and worship. The religion of ancient China, to which Confucius gave his reverent adhesion, was a form of nature worship, very closely approaching to monotheism.

While numerous spirits associated with natural phenomena were recognized—spirits of mountains and rivers, of land and grain, of the four quarters of the heavens, the sun, moon, and stars—they were all subordinated to the supreme heaven-god, *T'ien* (heaven) also called *Ti* (Lord) or *Shang-ti* (Supreme Lord). All other spirits were but his ministers, acting in obedience to his will. T'ien was the upholder of the moral law, exercising a benign providence over men. Nothing done in secret could escape his all-seeing eye. His punishment for evil deeds took the form either of calamities and early death or of misfortune laid up for the children of the evildoer.

Confucius said, *"A virtuous man has three awes. Awe for Heaven's decree, Awe for great men. Awe for saints' words...When worshipping God, one must feel as if He were visibly present."*

Christ

Not applicable

Basic Doctrine

Confucianism is a way of life. Sometimes viewed as a philosophy, sometimes as a religion, Confucianism is perhaps best understood as an all-encompassing humanism that neither focuses on nor denies heaven. Confucianism has been followed by the Chinese for more than two millennia. It has deeply influenced spiritual and political life in China; its influence has also extended to Korea, Japan, and Vietnam.

East Asians may profess themselves to be Shintōists, Taoists, Buddhists, Muslims, or Christians—but seldom do they cease to be Confucians.

In numerous passages of the *Shu Ching* (Book of History), we find a motive to right conduct. That it was not ignored by Confucius himself is shown by his recorded saying that "he who offends against Heaven has no one to whom he can pray." Another quasi-religious motive to the practice of virtue was the belief that the souls of the departed relatives were largely dependent for their happiness on the conduct of their living descendants.

The Confucian canon achieved its present form in the Sung Dynasty under the direction of Chu Hsi (1130–1200). It consists of the Five Classics and the Four Books. During his teaching career, Confucius collected ancient manuscripts, which he edited and on which he wrote commentaries. He arranged these manuscripts into four books to which he also added a fifth book of his own. These works are known as the *Five Classics*. The Classics as we have them today have gone through much editing and alteration by Confucius's disciples, yet there is much in them that can be considered the work of Confucius.

The Five Classics are:

1. *"The Book of Changes"* ("I Ching"[*]). This is the same text that has been lauded for its accurate predictions and shows life as we know it, ending on December 21, 2012 --the exact same day as the Mayan calendar ends. The "I Ching" is a collection of eight trigrams and sixty-four hexagrams that reflect the relationship between yin and yang in nature and society. These lines were supposed to have great meaning if the key were discovered.

2. *"The Book of History"* ("Shu Ching"). This is a work of the history of the five preceding dynasties (23–220 AD), "a religious and moral work, tracing the hand of Providence in a series of great events of past history, and inculcating the lesson that the

---

[*] The "I Ching" may be one of the oldest books in the world. It is said to have originated thousands of years ago among the courtly shaman diviners of ancient China. Traditionally, it was believed that the principles of the "I Ching" originated with the mythical Fu Xi, an early culture hero, one of the earliest legendary rulers of China (traditional dates 2800–2737BC, reputed to have had the trigrams revealed to him supernaturally. Through technical manipulations, a skilled psychic reader can use the book as an oracle. In fact, the book has been used for fortune-telling from its earliest days.

Heaven-god gives prosperity and length of days only to the virtuous ruler who has the true welfare of the people at heart.

3. *"The Book of Poetry"* ("Shih Ching"). The book of ancient poetry and songs from the early Chou Dynasty (1027–402 BC), was assembled by Confucius because he believed the reading of poetry would aid in making a man virtuous.

4. *"The Book of Ceremonies"* ("Li Chi"). This work taught the superior man to act in the right or traditional way. Again, Confucius stressed doing things in the same way as the ancients. In its present form it dates from the second century of our era, being a compilation from a vast number of documents, most of which date from the earlier part of the Chow Dynasty. It gives rules of conduct down to the minute details for religious acts of worship, court functions, social and family relations, dress—in short, for every sphere of human action. It remains today the authoritative guide of correct conduct for every cultivated Chinese.[11]

5. *"The Annals of Spring and Autumn"* ("Chun Chiu"). This book, supposedly written by Confucius, gave a commentary on the events and history of the state of Lu at Confucius's time.

None of the works listed on the following page contain the unique teachings of Confucius alone but are rather an anthology of works he collected and from which he taught.

Confucius's own teachings have come down to us from four books written by his disciples. They include[:]

1. *The Analects.* This is the most important revered sacred scripture in the Confucian tradition. The Analects are sayings of both Confucius and his disciples preserved in both oral and written transmissions.

2. *The Great Learning.* This work, which deals with the education and training of a gentleman, comes not from the hand of Confucius but rather from a later period (about 250 BC). In the Great Learning, Confucius revealed the process, step-by-step, by which self-development is attained and by which it flows over into the common life to serve the state and bless mankind.

The order of development that Confucius set forth is as follows: investigation of phenomena, learning, sincerity and rectitude of purpose, self-development, family discipline, local self-government, and universal self-government.

3. *The Doctrine of the Mean.* This work deals with the relationship of human nature to the order of the universe. This is considered by many to be one of its most valuable treatises. It consists of a collection of sayings of Confucius characterizing the man of perfect virtue. Authorship is uncertain but part of it may be attributed to Confucius's grandson Tzu-Ssu.

4. *The Book of Mencius.* Mencius wrote the first exposition of Confucian thought about 300 BC, by collecting earlier teachings and attempting to put them down systematically. This work, which has had great influence and gives an idealistic view of life, stresses the goodness of human nature.

Confucianism's doctrines can be summarized by six key terms or ways:

1. *Jen is the golden rule.* All those virtues that help maintain social harmony and peace, like benevolence, charity, magnanimity, sincerity, respectfulness, altruism, diligence, loving kindness, goodness, are included in Jen. The rule of reciprocity, that is to say, do not do anything to others that you would not have them do to you. Tzu-Kung asked, *"Is there a single word that can be a guide to conduct throughout one's life?"* The master said, *"It is perhaps the word shu. Do not impose on others what you yourself do not desire."* The nearest equivalent to this difficult word is social virtue.

2. *Chun-tzu the gentleman.* Chun-tzu can be translated as true manhood, the superior man, and man-at-his-best. The teachings of Confucius were aimed toward the gentleman, the man of virtue. Confucius had this to say about the gentleman: *"He who in this world can practice five things may indeed be considered man-at-his-best: Humility, magnanimity, sincerity, diligence, and graciousness. If you are humble, you will not be laughed at. If you are magnanimous, you*

will attract many to your side. If you are sincere, people will trust you. If you are gracious, you will get along well with your subordinates. It is this type of man who can transform society into the peaceful state it was meant to be."

3. Cheng-ming is the role-player. Another important concept according to Confucius was cheng-ming, or the rectification of names. For a society to be properly ordered, Confucius believed everyone must act his proper part. Consequently, a king should act like a king, a gentleman like a gentleman, etc.

4. Te is virtuous power. The word te literally means power, but the concept has a far wider meaning. The power needed to rule, according to Confucius, consists of more than mere physical might. It is necessary that the leaders be men of virtue, who can inspire their subjects to obedience through example. This concept had been lost during Confucius's time with the prevailing attitude being that physical might was the only proper way to order a society. If the rulers would follow the example of the past, then the people would rally around the virtuous example. Confucius knew but one form of government: the traditional monarchy of his native land. It was the extension of the patriarchal system to the entire nation. The king exercised an absolute authority over his subjects as the father over his children. He ruled by divine right. He was providentially set up by heaven to enlighten the people by wise laws and to lead them to goodness by his example and authority; hence, his title, the son of heaven. To merit this title, he should reflect the virtue of heaven. It was only the high-minded king who won heaven's favor and was rewarded with prosperity. The unworthy king lost divine assistance and came to naught. The Confucian texts abound in lessons and warnings on this subject of right government. The value of good example in the ruler is emphasized most strongly. The principle is asserted again and again that the people cannot fail to practice virtue and to prosper when the ruler sets the high example of right conduct. On the other hand, the implication is conveyed in more than one place that when crime and misery abound, the cause is to be sought in the unworthy king and his unprincipled ministers.

5. *Li is the standard of conduct.* One of the key words used by Confucius is Li. The term has a variety of meanings, depending upon the context. It can mean propriety, reverence, courtesy, ritual, or the ideal standard of conduct.

6. *Wen encompasses the arts of peace.* The concept of wen Confucius held in high esteem. These include music, poetry, and art. Confucius felt that these arts of peace, which came from the earlier Chou period, were symbols of virtue that should be manifest throughout society. Confucius condemned the culture of his day because he believed it lacked any inherent virtue and only did things for show.

To judge from the sayings of Confucius that have been preserved, he laid chief stress on the love of virtue for its own sake. To make oneself as good as possible, this was with him the main purpose of life. Everything that was conducive to the practice of goodness was to be eagerly sought and made use of. To this end, right knowledge was to be held indispensable. He believed principles of morality and their concrete application to the varied relations of life were embodied in the sacred texts, which in turn represented the teachings of the great sages of the past raised up by heaven to instruct mankind. The sages were born with wisdom meant by heaven to enlighten the children of men. To follow the path of duty was within the reach of all men, provided that their nature, good at birth, was not hopelessly spoiled by vicious influences.[12] Confucius did not believe in evil spirits causing us to misbehave, nor did he teach of divine grace to save us. We have the tools to become men of virtue on our own.

Confucianism is characterized by a highly optimistic view of human nature. The faith in the possibility of ordinary human beings to become awe-inspiring sages and worthies is deeply rooted in the Confucian heritage, and the insistence that human beings are teachable, improvable, and perfectible through personal and communal endeavor is typically Confucian. In his view, like Socrates, what spoiled men was bad environment, evil example, an inexcusable yielding to evil appetites.

His motto was, to associate with the truly great and to make friends of the most virtuous.

Besides association with the good, Confucius urged on his disciples the importance of always welcoming the correction of one's faults. Then, too, the daily examination of conscience was inculcated. As a further aid to the formation of a virtuous character, he valued highly a certain amount of self-discipline. He recognized the danger, especially in the young, of falling into habits of softness and love of ease.

As a foundation for the life of perfect goodness, Confucius insisted chiefly on the four virtues of sincerity, benevolence, filial piety, and propriety. Sincerity was with him a cardinal virtue. As used by him it meant more than a mere social behavior. To be truthful and straightforward in speech, faithful to one's promises, conscientious in the discharge of one's duties to others—this was included in sincerity and something more. The sincere man in Confucius's eyes was the man whose conduct was always based on the love of virtue, and who in consequence sought to observe the rules of right conduct in his heart as well as in outward actions, when alone as well as in the presence of others.

Benevolence, showing itself in a kindly regard for the welfare of others and in a readiness to help them in times of need, was also a fundamental element in Confucius's teaching. It was viewed as the characteristic trait of the good man...We read that when a disciple asked him for a guiding principle for all conduct, the master answered: *"Is not mutual goodwill such a principle? What you do not want done to yourself, do not do to others."* This is strikingly like the form of the Golden Rule found in the first chapter of the "Teaching of the Apostles"—"All things so ever that you would not have done to yourself, do not do to another."[13]

In practice, the elements of Confucianism accumulated over time and matured into the following forms:

Rituals: Ritual originally signified "to sacrifice" in a religious ceremony. In Confucianism, the term ritual was soon extended to include secular ceremonial behavior and eventually referred also to the propriety or politeness that colors everyday life. Rituals were codified a nd t reated a s a comprehensive system of norms.[14] Confucius himself tried to revive the etiquette of earlier dynasties. It is important to note that ritual has developed a specialized meaning in Confucianism, as opposed to its usual religious meanings. Rituals are not necessarily regimented or arbitrary practices, but the routines that people often engage in, knowingly or unknowingly, the normal course of their lives. Shaping the rituals in a way that leads to a content and healthy society is one purpose of Confucian philosophy.

Loyalty: It is the equivalent of filial piety on a different plane. Confucius had advocated a sensitivity to the class relations in his time; he did not propose that might makes right. But a superior who had received the mandate of heaven should be obeyed because of his moral standing in the heavens. Loyalty was also an extension of one's duties to friends, family, and spouse. Loyalty to one's family came first, then to one's spouse, then to one's ruler, and lastly to one's friends. Loyalty was considered one of the greater human virtues.

Rén also has a political dimension. If the ruler lacks Rén, Confucianism holds, it will be difficult if not impossible for his subjects to behave humanely. Rén is the basis of Confucian political theory: it presupposes an autocratic ruler, will refrain from acting inhumanely toward his subjects. An inhumane ruler runs the risk of losing the "Mandate of Heaven," the right to rule. A ruler lacking such a mandate need not be obeyed. But a ruler who reigns humanely and takes care of the people is to be obeyed strictly, for the benevolence of his dominion shows that he has been mandated by heaven.[15]

The Gentleman: The term *jūnzǐ* (literally "nobleman") is crucial to classical Confucianism. Confucianism exhorts all people to strive for the ideal of a gentleman or perfect man. A succinct description of the perfect man is one who combines the qualities of saint, scholar, and gentleman. Elitism was bound up with the concept, and gentlemen were expected to act as moral guides to the rest of society.

In Confucianism, there is much to admire. It has taught a noble conception of the supreme heaven-god. It has established a remarkably high standard of morality. It has prompted the refining influence of literary education and of polite conduct. Confucius laid great stress on the cultivation of character, purity of heart, and conduct. He exhorted the people to develop a good character first, which is a priceless jewel, and which is the best of all virtues. The nature of man, according to Confucius, is fundamentally good, inclined toward goodness. Perfection of goodness can be found in sages and saints.

Every man should attempt to reach the ideal by leading a virtuous life, by possessing a very noble character, and by doing his duty unselfishly with sincerity and truthfulness. He who is endowed with a good character and divine virtue is a princely type of man. The princely man sticks to virtue, and the inferior man clings to material comfort. The princely man is just while the inferior man expects rewards and favors. The princely man is dignified, noble, magnanimous, and humble while the inferior man is mean, proud, crooked, and arrogant.

Basic Worship Service

"Aside from its important ethical principles, Confucianism does not prescribe any specific rituals or practices. These are filled by the practices of Chinese religion, Taoism, Buddhism, or other religion which Confucians follow."[16]

"The Chinese character for "rites," or "ritual," previously had the religious meaning of "sacrifice." Its Confucian meaning ranges from politeness and propriety to the understanding of each person's correct place in society."[17] Ritual can be seen as a means to find the balance between opposing qualities that might otherwise lead to conflict. It divides people into categories and builds hierarchical relationships through protocols and ceremonies, assigning everyone a place in society and a proper form of behavior.

Externally, ritual is used to distinguish between people; their usage allows people to know at all times who is the younger and who the elder, who is the guest and who, the host and so forth. Internally, rites indicate to people their duty amongst others and what to expect from them. Formalized behavior becomes progressively internalized, desires are channeled and personal cultivation becomes the mark of social correctness.[18]

Infant Baptism or Blessing

The *T'ai-shen* (spirit of the fetus) protects the expectant woman and deals harshly with anyone who harasses the mother to be. A special procedure is followed when the placenta is disposed of. The mother is given a special diet and is allowed rest for a month after delivery. The mother's family of origin supplies all the items required by the baby on the first, fourth and twelfth monthly anniversary of the birth.[19]

Initiation, Baptism, or Confirmation

The life passage called *Capping* is no longer being celebrated, except in traditional families. "Capping was a joyous ceremony, wherein the son was honored on reaching his twentieth year. In the presence of relatives and invited guests, the father conferred on his son a special name and a square cornered cap as distinguishing marks of his mature manhood. It was accompanied with a feast."[20]

Marriage

To the Confucians, marriage is of grave significance both in family and in society. In the perspective of family, marriage can bring families of different surnames (different clans) together and continue the family life of the concerned clans. Socially, a married couple is the basic unit of the population; sometimes, marriages can affect the country's political stability and international relations. For this reason, marriage can also be related to politics.

From the point of view of Confucian philosophy, one of the purposes of marriage is the cultivation of virtue. The Chinese have seen that marriage should be founded on love since the concept of monogamy is rooted in their mind-set. According to Zhang Yi's Guangya Shigu—a dictionary for ancient Chinese characters—friendliness, love, and harmony indicate the correct way of living for a married couple.[21]

The rule as laid down in the *"Li-Chi"* was that a young man should marry at the age of 30 and a young woman at 20. Due to the concept of filial piety and following rites of propriety, marriage was a costly affair. The use of a matchmaker ensured that the husband and wife were compatible with each other, but primarily worked in the families' best interests. The proposal and acceptance process pertained not to the young parties directly interested, but to their parents.

The parties could not be of the same surname, nor related within the fifth degree of kindred. " Monogamy was encouraged as the ideal condition, but the maintenance of secondary wives known as concubines was not forbidden. It was sometimes recommended when the true wife failed to bear male children and was too much loved to be divorced."[22] There were seven causes justifying the divorce of a wife besides infidelity, and one of these was the absence of male offspring. The will of the parents was declared to be supreme even to the extent that if the son's wife failed to please them, he was obliged to divorce her though it cut him to the heart.

Death and Afterlife

Confucius discouraged his students from worrying about the afterlife. Instead, he encouraged them to live in harmony and to help other people through government, service, teaching, or just being a good family member. Confucius thought that there was great joy to be found in everyday family life, participating in communal activities, enjoying music, and spending time with one's friends. He once said, *"Absorption in the study of the supernatural is most harmful. "*

Although Confucianism deals mostly with life here on earth rather than the afterlife, it does take into consideration mankind's ultimate concerns. One must remember the outlook of the people during the time of Confucius. Deceased ancestors were thought to exercise power over the living, sacrifice t o heaven w as a common occurrence, and observing the signs from heaven (thunder, lightning, the flight of birds, etc.), and all were prevalent. They obviously had a belief t hat spirits continued and that some force controlled nature. Heaven and its doings were assumed to be real rather than imaginary. However, Confucius taught not to place any great emphasis on this—he said that our lives and our purpose should be aimed at becoming sages and to strive for unity with *t'ien* (heaven).

Judgment and Salvation

Confucius regarded heaven (*T'ien*) as a positive and personal force in the universe; he was not, as some have supposed, an agnostic or a skeptic.

Special Doctrine

Is Confucianism a Religion? Most religions can be defined as having a God (monotheism) or group of gods (polytheism), an organized priesthood, a belief in a life after death, and established traditions. It is therefore "debatable whether Confucianism should be called a religion. While it prescribes a great deal of ritual, little of it could be construed as worship or meditation in a formal sense."

However, *t'ien* is sacred to many Confucians. "Its effect on Chinese and other East Asian societies and cultures has been immense, and parallels the effects of religious movements, seen in other cultures." Generally speaking, Confucianism is not considered a religion by Chinese or other East Asian people. Confucians maintain that Confucianism is not a religion but rather a moral code or philosophic world view. Those who follow the teachings of Confucius say that they are comforted by it. If religion is by definition worship of supernatural entities, the answer must be that Confucianism is not a religion. If, on the other hand, a religion is defined as a belief system that includes moral stances, guides for daily life, systematic views of humanity and its place in the universe, etc., then Confucianism qualifies.[23]

Moreover, religions in Chinese culture are not mutually exclusive entities: each tradition is free to find its specific niche, its field of specialization. One can practice religions such as Taoism, Christianity, Judaism, Sikhism, the Bahá'í faith, Jainism, Islam, Shintō, Hinduism, Buddhism, or Zoroastrianism and still profess Confucian beliefs. One might even call it a companion to all religions.

Confucianism and Government: His teaching was largely concerned with the problems of good government. He said, *"The Ruler himself should be virtuous, just, honest and dutiful. A virtuous ruler is like the Pole-star which, by keeping its place, makes all other stars to evolve round it. As is the Ruler, so will be the subjects."*

<u>Relationships are Central to Confucianism:</u> Particular duties arise from one's particular situation in relation to others. The individual stands simultaneously in several different relationships with different people: as a junior in relation to parents and elders, and as a senior in relation to younger siblings, students, and others.[24]

Confucius had one overwhelming message: if we are to achieve a state of orderliness and peace, we need to return to traditional values of virtue. These values are based entirely on one concept: jen, which is best translated as humaneness but can also mean humanity, benevolence, goodness, or virtue. Like his contemporaries, Confucius believed that the human order in some way reflected the divine order or the patterns of heaven.

"Filial piety is considered among the greatest of virtues and must be shown towards both the living and the dead (including even remote ancestors)."[25] This loyalty and devotion to the family was the top priority in Chinese life. Such duty to the family, particularly devotion to the elders, was continued throughout one's life. Such devotion was also extended to the dead, where the living stood as sons to their deceased family. This led to the veneration of ancestors.

<u>Ancestor Veneration:</u> A common feature of Chinese religion prevalent at Confucius's time was the veneration of ancestors. It is believed that the ancestors can control the fortunes of their families. If the family provides for the ancestors' needs, then the ancestors will in turn cause good things to happen to their relatives. In the days of Confucius, as at present, there was in every family home, a chamber or closet called the ancestral shrine, where wooden tablets were reverently kept, inscribed with the names of deceased ancestors. At stated intervals, offerings of fruit, wine, and cooked meats were set before these tablets, which the ancestral spirits were fancied to make their temporary resting place.[34] However, if the ancestors are neglected, it is believed that all sorts of evil can fall upon the living; consequently, the living sometimes live in fear of the dead.

Christianity and Confucianism: The Jen and the sayings of Confucius are very much parallel to the virtues and commandments of the Bible.

Jen: The nearest equivalent to this difficult word is *social virtue* . All those virtues that help maintain social harmony and peace, like benevolence, charity, magnanimity, sincerity, respectfulness, altruism, diligence, loving kindness, goodness, are included in jen. Followers of jen endeavor to display all the attributes of one who is Christlike, even without the knowledge or understanding of Christ. *"I no longer live, but Christ lives in me"* (Galatians 2:20).

With God in me, I am going to feed the hungry and give water to the thirsty, and not me, but Christ who lives in me. These are the same virtues that Confucius described. Confucius says,

"One should not be greatly concerned at not being in office, but rather about the requirements in one's self for that office. Nor should one be greatly concerned at being unknown, but rather with being worthy to be known. The superior man seeks what is right, the inferior one what is profitable. Those who are willing to forget old grievances will gradually do away with resentment. To prize the effort above the prize, that is virtue. These things weigh heavily upon my mind: failure to improve in the virtues, failure in discussion of what is learned, and inability to walk always according to the knowledge of what is right and just, and inability to reform what has been amiss." (The Ethics of Confucius by Miles Menander Dawson)

Notes

Notes

_____

_____

_____

_____

_____

_____

_____

_____

_____

_____

_____

_____

_____

Falun Gong

History

In China, the qigong arts used by Falun Dafa have an ancient history. (Technically, *Falun Gong* refers to the practice while *Falun Dafa* refers to the teaching of the movement, but the terms are now generally used interchangeably.) They were "passed down over the ages from a single master to a single disciple in each generation. The disciple would later have a disciple of his own, to whom he would pass on the teachings, thereby quietly passing the practice down throughout history." Some have speculated on Falun Gong as a cultural renewal of ancient Chinese cultivation forms starting from antiquity.

Qigong as we know it today was not, in fact, originally called qigong. The two-character term "qi gong" is nowhere to be found in the ancient texts. Qigong's original names were "great cultivation way of Buddha," and "great cultivation way of Tao." It had other names too, such as ninefold internal alchemy, way of arhat, vajra meditation, etc.

The term qigong was coined in the early 1950s as an alternative label to ancient spiritual disciplines rooted in Buddhism or Taoism, which promoted the belief in the supernatural, immortality and pursuit of spiritual transcendence. The new term was constructed to avoid danger of association with ancient spiritual practices which were labeled "superstitious" and persecuted during the Maoist era.[1]

Li Hongzhi claims to have started practicing self-cultivation after being trained by Quan Jue, the tenth heir to the Great Law of the Buddha School, at age four. He was then trained by a Taoist master from age eight to age twelve. He claims to have levitated and to have been able to control the actions of his playmates (specifically to stop them fighting) by the power of his thoughts alone. He claims to have been instructed by several masters in the mountains and to be enlightened and, who, like Jesus and Buddha, was dispatched to earth to offer salvation and teach the principles of moral cultivation.

Falun Gong ("Practice of the Wheel of Dharma") is a Chinese movement (introduced) by Li Hongzhi in 1992. Its adherents exercise ritually to obtain mental and spiritual renewal. The teachings of Falun Gong share the Asian religious traditions of Buddhism, Taoism, Confucianism, and Chinese folklore.

Li saw the original qigong movement as "rife with false teachings and greedy and fraudulent masters" and set out to rectify it. Li understood himself and Falun Gong as part of a "centuries-old tradition of cultivation," and in his texts would often attack those who taught "incorrect, deviant, or heterodox ways." A qigong scholar says Li "redefined his method a s aving entirely different objectives from qigong: the purpose of practice should neither be physical health nor the development of Extraordinary Powers, but to purify one's heart and attain spiritual salvation...Falun Gong no longer presented itself as a qigong method but as the Great Law or *Dharma* (*Fa*) of the universe."[2]

In twentieth century communist China, where spirituality and religion are looked down upon, the concept of qigong was tolerated because it carried with it no overt religious or spiritual elements, and millions flocked to it during China's spiritual vacuum of the 1980s.

Into the vacuum stepped Master Li Hongzhi, offering self-improvement, meditation, and, good health. More importantly, Falun Gong was offered free, to the annoyance of other qigong schools. The Falun Gong was perfectly suited to the many millions of older, semi-retired and unemployed Chinese, whose health benefits and pensions disappeared with the economic "rationalizations" of the new free-market economy. The old "iron rice bowl" of Chairman Mao, which had guaranteed employment, housing, food and health-care to all citizens for life, was a fading memory. Li offered health, rejuvenation and supernormal powers to the conscientious cultivator of Falun Gong.[3]

Neither Li nor Falun Gong was particularly controversial in the beginning. Li (referred to respectfully by practitioners as master or teacher) became an instant star of the qigong movement, with his practice method celebrated at the *Beijing Oriental Health Expos* of both 1992 and 1993 where its founder, Master Li Hongzhi, was credited with performing miracle cures in public. Falun Gong was welcomed into the *Scientific Qigong Research Association,* which sponsored and helped organize many of Li's activities between 1992 and 1994, including the fifty-four large-scale lectures given throughout China, in most major cities, to total audiences of twenty thousand or more, and later, places like New York and Paris. The scale of the activities was unprecedented at that time. At Falun Gong conferences, the stage was frequently decorated with a large photo of Master Li in Buddha mode. In 1993, Mr. Li Hongzhi was named the most welcomed qigong master in Beijing and bestowed by an official body with the *Award for Advancing Frontier Science.*

Sociological macroissues, such as economic insecurity, the collapse of moral standards, worries about health and medical care, and other factors, could be explanations for Falun Gong's rise. Falun Gong appeals to individuals on several levels of understanding. For beginners, health benefits seem to be a primary concern. Over time, as good health comes to be a given and as their study of Master Li's books deepens, the metaphysical system of Falun Gong seems to take precedence as cultivators work to shed their attachments and move to higher levels. Over time, followers appear to find in the teachings an intricate, orderly, and internally consistent understanding of the cosmos.

In a study of an Internet survey published in *Nova Religio,* practitioners understood the reason for Falun Gong's rapid growth within China to be related to family ties and community relationships, which still retain great power. In this context, whenever someone discovers something good, they automatically wish to pass it on to their family and friends. The tremendously positive word of mouth generated by practitioners naturally led to the rapid spread of the teachings within close-knit Chinese communities.

Li began to make his ideas more widely accessible and affordable, charging less than other qigong systems for lectures, tapes, and books and continued to teach for free. On January 4, 1995, Zhuan Falun, the main book on Falun Gong, was published and became a best seller in China. Many people learned Falun Gong by word of mouth, and it was usually practiced in the morning in parks like many other forms of exercise in China. It attracted many retired persons, factory workers, farmers, state enterprise managers, entrepreneurs, intellectuals, and students. For the first few years of spreading Falun Gong, Li was granted several awards by Chinese governmental organizations to encourage him to continue promoting what was then considered to be a wholesome practice.

Although Falun Gong had earned the support and commendation of various government agencies in the early 1990s, tensions soon began to appear between the practice and the Chinese Communist Party. The movement's growth in the 1990s was a great concern to the Chinese government, which viewed Falun Gong as a 100 million member

threat. In 1996, the state-run *Qigong Research Association* began urging Falun Gong to charge fees for the practice and establish a Communist Party branch. ... Li Hongzhi refused, and filed to withdraw from the Association, thus severing formal ties with the government. Later that year, Falun Gong books were banned from further publication, and practitioner began to face harassment by security forces.[4]

Shortly thereafter, he moved to the United States, where he now lives, and he has been well-received in cities throughout North America. Falun Gong clubs sprang up at *MIT* and *Columbia University*, which are active to this day.

As Falun Gong practitioners have no membership system or rosters, numbers are unknown. In 1998, the Chinese government published a figure of 70 million practitioners in China. *Clearwisdom.net,* a Falun Gong website, claims one hundred million practitioners in more than eighty countries.

On April 25, 1999, around ten thousand Falun Gong practitioners lined the streets near Zhongnanhai in silence, seeking legal recognition. Then later, on July 20, 1999, the Chinese Communist Party issued a statement banning Falun Gong. That same day, thousands of practitioners were arrested in the middle of the night, the media campaign to vilify the practice began, and the persecution was officially underway. The Ministry of Civil Affairs said that according to investigations, the *Research Society of Falun Dafa* had not been registered according and had been engaged in illegal activities, advocating superstition and spreading fallacies, hoodwinking people, inciting and creating disturbances, and jeopardizing social stability.

With the *"Regulations on the Registration and Management of Mass Organizations,"* it also affirmed that "the so-called 'truth, kindness and forbearance' principle preached by Li has nothing in common with the socialist ethical and cultural progress we are striving to achieve. Overall, Falun Gong was simply too big…and the government cannot understand how that many people can join in common cause and not be a threat to the state."[5] The Chinese authorities branded Falun Gong, along with some other practices, movements, or organizations, as *xiejiao,* which was translated into English with the somewhat inaccurate term cult or evil cult.

Since 1999, reports of torture, illegal imprisonment, beatings, forced labor, and psychiatric abuses have been widespread. Sixty-six percent of all reported torture cases in China concern Falun Gong practitioners, who are also estimated to comprise at least half of China's labor camp population, according to the UN special reporter on torture, Manfred Nowak, and the US Department of State, respectively.

While the Chinese government gained the cooperation of some (minor) Western anti-cult groups in its campaign to expose Falun Gong as a "cult," it was also criticized by human rights organizations who denounce the suspicious deaths, allegedly by accident, of some Falun Gong members detained in Chinese jails. According to *FalunDafa.org*, "To date [December 2005], there are more than 2794 documented cases of otherwise healthy practitioners being beaten and tortured to death while in detention."[6]

On July 30, 2008, the Chinese Communist Party foreign ministry spokesman confirmed that during the *Beijing Olympic Games*, Falun Gong websites would be blocked, censoring journalists' access to the Internet. For each death case, Minghui (Falun Dafa organization) records the victim's name, occupation, city, date of death, which institution they were detained at, sentence (if any), and abuses suffered at the hands of authorities. As of March 2015, Minghui has confirmed 3,859 deaths since the beginning of the persecution.

God or Gods

Master Li teaches, "The Buddhas, Taoist deities, and Gods we speak of exist in other dimensions that man cannot touch or see." If the universe is ordered, it is not the product of happenstance in the Falun Gong view. Rather, the existence of higher beneficent l i fe forms is basic to its teachings, and it is their presence and workings that are believed to inform and shape the world around us.

In Zhuan Falun, Li says that human life is not created in ordinary human society but in the space of the universe. When a life is created, it is assimilated into the characteristic of the universe as encapsulated by the values of truth, compassion, and tolerance. However, eventually a web of relations developed, and selfishness came about; gradually, the level of beings was lowered until, in the end, they reached this level of human beings. Li says in his book that the purpose of being human is to practice cultivation and return to the "original, true self." It has been interpreted as meaning that humans were originally gods of some sort who lost their status as life became complicated, and they engaged in immoral behavior. Presumably, humans can redeem themselves through cultivation and regain their divine status.

Christ

Falun Gong holds that Christ is a "mighty God in his realm," who was crucified to pay for the sins of his followers. He is believed to be one of several gods who have come to the world in various historical periods to impart upright teachings and offer salvation:

Great enlightened beings have emerged in all periods of prehistory. In the current civilization, beings such as Jesus, Shakyamuni, and Lao Zi came to tell things to people. In the civilized areas of different periods, there were different enlightened beings who were responsible for teaching people how to return to one's original, true self. They enabled those who could obtain the *Dao* to achieve Consummation; showed ordinary people how to cherish virtue; and required that mankind maintain its morality at a relatively level state, thus ensuring that the human mind would not degenerate so easily. (Li Hongzhi, Zhuan Falun, vol. 2, 1996)

Basic Doctrine

Terminology:

- *Falun Dafa. Fa* means the law and principles of the universe. Lun means wheel. *Da* means great. Falun Dafa may be translated as "the great law wheel." (Also known as the dharma wheel in Buddhism.)
- *Cultivation.* It refers to the improvement of one's heart and mind through the careful study of universal principles based on truthfulness, benevolence, and tolerance and transformation of one's entire being. This is true of any spiritual practice that teaches universal principles of truthfulness, benevolence, and tolerance and the transformation of one's entire being.
- *Falun.* The center of spiritual energy in the human body located in the lower abdomen, and it can be awakened (or "installed") through a set of exercises.
- *Gong.* A high-energy substance that manifests in the form of light that can be cultivated through the improvement of moral character.
- *Karma.* A type of black material that encompasses each person's body. If you have done wrong, your karma stays with you until your mistakes are corrected.
- *Milk-white body.* A person who has achieved a high level of enlightenment and has corrected his/her bad karma (which is black).
- *Ordinary person (normal person).* Someone who is not trying to reach enlightenment.
- *Practitioner or Cultivator.* A person who practices any spiritual path to enlightenment.
- *Qi* (pronounced chee). The internal energy force; all things have it.
- *Shifu.* Master or spiritual guide.
- *Third eye.* The enlightened can see other worlds and dimensions with this eye. (It is not a literal eye, but an ability to see.)

Falun Gong is also known as Falun Dafa. Falun Gong has claimed not to be an organized religion, and its texts speak of it as a practice rather than a religion. But it does contain teachings about the spiritual world, and it has a closely connected membership.[7] It has five sets of meditation exercises and teaches the principles truthfulness, compassion, and tolerance as set out in the main books *Falun Gong* and *Zhuan Falun.* The teachings deal with issues such as cultivation of virtue and character, moral standards for different levels, and salvation of all sentient beings.

"*Qi and Gong:* The *qi* we talk about nowadays was called *chee* by ancient people. They are essentially the same, as both refer to the qi of the universe—a shapeless, invisible kind of matter that permeates the universe."[8] The properties are said to be apart of all matter and life. The basic premise is that "the body itself, in keeping with traditional Chinese thought, is understood to be a receptacle of subtle energies. Such energies, when harnessed or refined, can be stored on a cellular level and utilized under certain, specific circumstances."[9]

It means that people who truly cultivate carry immense energy in their bodies. More simply put, *gong* is energy. Gong has physical characteristics, and practitioners can experience and perceive its objective existence through cultivation. Physical change in the body is predicated upon moral and cognitive change. "Without an elevation of the latter, the former is limited. If ordinarily 'you are what you eat,' in the psycho-physical realm of self-cultivation, you are what you think."

One hallmark of this process specific to Falun Gong is the importance granted to looking within. Master Li teaches that the cultivation of seeking a pure character will simultaneously enlighten and allow you to develop supernatural gifts and skills in the process. He also is adamant in the doctrine that if you pursue enlightenment just for the spiritual gifts and powers, your results will be hindered, and you will not progress because your motives are not of good character. Some abilities that have been mentioned are third eye, clairaudience, telepathy, precognition, etc. But not all of these abilities will appear as they vary with each individual. People with abilities are reluctant to use them for show since people who really do have great virtue are forbidden to use their abilities in public for recognition.

Cultivating Truth, Kindness, and Tolerance Simultaneously:
Their discipline cultivates truth, kindness, and tolerance simultaneously.
Truth is about telling the truth, doing things truly, and ultimately
becoming a true person. Kindness is about developing great
compassion, doing good things, and saving people. Only with tolerance
can a person cultivate into somebody with great virtue. Tolerance is a
powerful thing, and it surpasses truth and kindness. Throughout the
entire cultivation process, you are asked to tolerate, to mind your
character, and to exercise self-control.[10]

Practitioners should hold themselves to higher standards at all
times. The things that are encouraged on television, in the movies, and in
literature teach you to become a stronger and more practical person
among everyday people. Practitioners should have little or no involvement
with those vulgar and unhealthy things. You must remain unfazed no
matter how serious the challenges for your character among everyday
people may be. (This is the same concept as some Christian faith practices
that tell their member to live in the world, but not of it.) In the context of
Falun Gong, these principles require people to live upright lives, a
traditional morality—what has been called popular fundamentalism—a
supposed return to moral values that numerous Chinese feel have been
lost in the rush to modernization.

Ridding Yourself of Attachments: Li argues that having
material possessions itself is not a problem, but that the
problem is with developing attachments to those material things.
For Li Hongzhi, an attachment is literally any desire, emotion,
habit, or orientation that stands between a practitioner and the
pursuit of truth and cultivation. The stronger the feelings, the more
difficult they are to abandon and the more crucial abandonment
becomes.

Physical desires are also considered attachments. Falun Gong teachers
don't require you to become a monk or nun. What's key is that you get
rid of that attachment to sex. When you reach a higher level, you will
soon have no need or desire for those attachments. Anything that you
think you can't let go <u>must</u> be let go. So practitioners should take
all material gain lightly, pursue nothing, and let everything unfold
naturally, thus avoiding the emergence of new attachments. Once you
can let go of everything, your mind will naturally become clear and still.

<u>Hardship and Trials:</u> Falun Gong teaches that your gong potency will grow a bit higher with every problem you overcome. Small tests lead to small improvements; big tests lead to big improvements. You won't acquire real gong without expending effort. No principle exists that will let you gain gong comfortably without any hardship or effort. What's important is that we be compassionate. Your compassion emerges quickly in Falun Gong. They teach that you will become very compassionate of suffering around you. That is actually the heart of great compassion emerging.

It's hard when you are in the midst of an ordeal, but you must exercise self-restraint. Everything relies on whether you can improve your character. It doesn't matter what you have to go through in the short-term. At the same time, Law Bodies will look after you and protect your life, but you will still have to go through the ordeal.[11]

Your hardships are arranged according to your path as a cultivator. They are planned so as to improve your character. The lives of cultivators have been prearranged. You won't have too many or too few hardships. It is indeed tough. The divine beings will think of ways to make you give up all the things you find hard to let go, and that way, you improve your character with the hardships. Sometimes when you meet with hardship, you call out for help; it's possible they won't help you since that hardship is something you need to overcome. Li states that to practice cultivation, one must be considerate of others in all circumstances and always search within for the cause or the lesson when encountering tribulations.

<u>A Person's Underlying Base and Awakening Capacity:</u> "Underlying base" refers to the white matter a person brings along at birth. It is, in fact, virtue—a tangible form of matter and the opposite of karma. A person can transform his or her karma into virtue by suffering and doing good deeds and can transform virtue into karma by doing bad deeds, taking advantage of others, and so on. Through practice, a person gradually seeks to eliminate karma by transforming it into virtue and can thereby also improve their "awakening capacity" (also translated as "enlightenment quality"). People with a good underlying base more easily become enlightened. Once they hear about learning qigong or

about things related to cultivation, they immediately get interested and want to learn. In contrast, a person with a lot of the black matter makes it impossible for him to accept good things. The black matter will make him doubt good things when he encounters them.

Basic Worship Service

Falun Gong is not a worship service but a traditional Chinese spiritual discipline that is Buddhist in nature. It consists of moral teachings, a meditation, and five gentle exercises, which involve meditation and slow movements that resemble *tai chi* (a type of martial arts that is practiced for defense training or health benefits).

Through consistent and dedicated practice, the student of Falun Gong comes to achieve a state of selflessness, greater insight and awareness, inner purity, and balance—the inner workings of what might be called true health. Ultimately, he or she approaches what in the Asian tradition is known as enlightenment or attaining the *Tao* (or the "way").

Local assistants and veteran practitioners teach the exercises, always free of charge, at practice sites in cities and towns around the world. All books, lectures, and a complete library of audio and visual materials to help you learn the practice are available for free download on the Internet.

"Falun Gong has five sets of movements. They are the following exercises: Buddha Stretching a Thousand Arms, Falun Standing Stance, Coursing Between the Two Poles, Falun Cosmic Orbit, and Reinforcing Supernatural Powers."[12]

1. *Buddha Stretching a Thousand Arms.* The core of Buddha Stretching a Thousand Arms is stretching to open up all energy channels. This exercise is done as the foundational exercise of Falun Gong, and it is usually done first.

2. *Falun Standing Stance.* This is the second Falun Gong exercise. Falun Standing increases wisdom, raises a person's level, and strengthens supernatural powers.

3. *Coursing Between the Two Poles.* The purpose of this exercise is to mix and merge the universe's energy with the energy inside the body.

4. *Falun Cosmic Orbit.* This exercise enables the human body's energy to circulate from the entire yin side of the body to the yang side over and over again. This enables the human body to return to its original state and to have the whole body's energy circulate freely and smoothly.

5. *Reinforcing Supernatural Powers.* This is one of the serene cultivation exercises in Falun Gong. It is a multipurpose exercise intended to strengthen supernatural powers and abilities and gong strength by turning the Law Wheel using Buddha hand signs.

Infant Baptism or Blessing

Falun Gong does not practice baptism, nor does it adopt any other process of confirmation that differentiates the practitioner from nonpractitioner. The practice accords very little weight to formalities or displays of reverence or worship. Instead, it asks practitioners to focus on the genuine improvement of their moral standard.

Initiation, Baptism, or Confirmation

"The decision to practice cultivation is held to be a very serious and a very personal one. A person cannot oblige others to practice Falun Dafa, including one's children or family members" (Li Hongzhi, Zhuan Falun). There are no formal ceremonies with Falun Gong. Membership is open to all. People are free to affiliate and to leave the group. There are no prerequisites to learning Falun Dafa; there are no dues. Information is freely available on the Internet without charge. There is no paid staff or clergy. All work is done by volunteers. They do not maintain a list of members' names and other data.[13]

Marriage

They teach that marriage was arranged for human beings by divine beings. They believe that a person can have relations of husband and wife, but sexual relations outside of marriage, including the living together before marriage, are sins because they are not arranged and not allowed by divine beings. Modern people have been departing significantly from the arrangements made by divine beings.

A person's attitude toward marriage should acknowledge that marriage is a normal state of human life, and it carries with it responsibility for each other and the family, including responsibility for the emotional and financial aspects of the union and in m any other areas as well. When conflict arises, each should look within to find ways to improve and do their best for each other.

Beliefs about Homosexuality and Premarital Relations: The Falun Gong movement appears to treat homosexual behavior, not homosexual orientation, as a degenerate behavior at par with sexual promiscuity. When asked in Frankfurt, Germany, in 1998, whether gays could practice Falun Gong, Li answered, to a round of applause, "*You can cultivate, but you must give up the bad conduct.*"

Death and Afterlife

Li states that an important aspect of his system is its cultivation of the main spirit. He says that a person is made up of a primordial spirit, which could be composed of one's main spirit and one or more assistant spirits. Li states that the main spirit is the part of one's consciousness that one perceives as one's own self and is the spirit that humans must cultivate to ascend to higher levels. A person can also have one or more assistant spirits. Zhuan Falun says that upon death, all spirits split from the body and go their own ways.

Falun Gong teaches that the main spirit is locked in the cycle of rebirth, also known as samsara due to the accumulation of *Karma*. This is a negative, black substance that accumulates in other dimensions lifetime after lifetime, by doing bad deeds and thinking bad thoughts. Falun Gong states that Karma is the reason for suffering, and what ultimately blocks people from the truth of the universe and attaining enlightenment. At the same time, is also the cause of ones continued rebirth and suffering. Li says that due to accumulation of Karma the human spirit upon death will reincarnate over and over again, until the Karma is paid off or eliminated through cultivation, or the person is destroyed due to the bad deeds he has done.[14]

If, however, a person can extricate himself from delusion, suffer to repay karma, and improve his moral character, he can achieve liberation, being released from reincarnation and the suffering of the world and return to his divine origins.

Judgment and Salvation

Falun Gong teaches of a future judgment, in which all lives will answer for their actions and will be rewarded or punished in accordance with the level of their moral character.

Eliminating Karma: The laws in this world are the same as those in heaven. Eventually, you have to pay what you owe others. All the hardships and problems you encounter in your life result from karma.

In order to improve your realm of mind, you have to be tested by hardship in this world. If your character has really improved and stabilized, karma will be eliminated during the process, the hardship will pass, and your gong will develop. Li calls this "salvation of all beings." Enlightened beings must help followers to repay their sins and karma, teach them upright principles, and look after them until they are able to complete their cultivation and achieve reconciliation with the divine. "That is what they really have in mind; they are opening a door for you. Those who fail to return will have no choice but to reincarnate, with this continuing until they amass a huge amount of Karma and are destroyed."[15]

Special Doctrine

The Third Eye's Levels from Mankind's Perspective: Dimensions are quite complicated. Humankind knows only the dimension in which human beings currently exist, while other dimensions haven't yet been found or explored. When it comes to other dimensions, they say that the qigong masters have seen dozens of levels of dimensions. They can be explained theoretically, though they remain unproven by science. Even though some people don't admit the existence of certain things, they have actually manifested in our dimension.

They cite the example of the *Bermuda Triangle,* where ships and planes have disappeared in that area only to reemerge years later. No one can explain why as no one has gone beyond the confines of human thinking and theories. They believe the Triangle is a gateway to another dimension. The third eye has many different views depending on the practitioner's level of cultivation; at different levels, it sees different dimensions. The opening of your third eye doesn't mean that you can see everything in the universe. But you will gradually raise your level through further cultivation, right up until you reach enlightenment. At that point, you will be able to see more levels. According to Buddhism, there are five levels of vision for the third eye: flesh eyesight, celestial eyesight, wisdom eyesight, law eyesight, and Buddha eyesight. Only when someone is at or above the level of wisdom eyesight will other dimensions be observable.[16]

Healing: One of the more controversial issues is the teaching about medicine and healing. Falun Gong teaches that, through disciplined moral practice, a person's body can be purified. Moreover, its teachings hold that illness is a manifestation of karma, which is accrued by doing bad things. Through the process of suffering, one can repay karma, and therefore, Falun Gong discourages (but does not forbid) seeking medical treatment. In other words, living through the illness will allow you to release karma.

If your mind isn't steady as you cultivate and you adopt an attitude of doubt or of "let's try and see," then you will get nothing. You first have to believe if you are to see. In America, many may believe that qigong is a subjective, new age-style concept incapable of scientific proof; however, much of China's scientific establishment believes in the existence of qi. Controlled experiments by the *Chinese Academy of Sciences* in the late 1970s and early 1980s concluded that qi, when emitted by a qigong expert, "actually constitutes measurable infrared electromagnetic waves and causes chemical changes in static water through mental concentration."

Practitioners of Falun Gong indeed claim the practice has significant health benefits. For instance, in a 1998 survey conducted by medical health professionals in China's Guangdong province, over twelve thousand Falun Gong students were asked about the impact of the practice; 97.9 percent of them claimed their health had improved noticeably since taking up Falun Gong.

Richard Madsen, a professor of sociology at the University of California, says *"among the Falun Dafa practitioners I have met are Chinese scientists with doctorates from prestigious American universities who claim that modern physics (for example, superstring theory) and biology (specifically the pineal gland's functioning) provide a scientific basis for their beliefs. From their point of view, Falun Dafa is knowledge rather than religion, a new form of science rather than faith."*[17]

But critics of the movement not only ridicule such claims but regard its reliance on Falun Gong as an alternative to official medicine as hazardous to the members' health. But Falun Gong does not forbid anyone from taking medicine, and practitioners would not deny medical treatment to their children or families.

Conflict in China: Until 1999, Falun Gong had excellent public credibility in China. Practitioners talked enthusiastically of the benefits Falun Gong had brought to their lives, and this functioned as a powerful recruiting tool, especially within families and circles of friends.

Falun Gong has thus been the subject of many citations, awards, and proclamations as conferred by government officials and a variety of organizations. Many who practice Falun Gong have been the recipients of service awards in their communities. The practice's founder, Mr. Li Hongzhi, is a four-time *Nobel Peace Prize* nominee and was nominated by the European Parliament for the *Sakharov Prize for Freedom of Thought*. Few people today are aware that the practice and its followers received much in the way of official recognition in China during the 1990s, prior to a dramatic, and violent, change in political winds in 1999 which saw the practice banned.

At the time that Falun Gong became headline news in April 1999, Master Li claimed to have some one hundred million followers. The Chinese Communist Party officially has a mere sixty million members, so the sheer mass of Falun Gong devotees was seen as a cause for alarm. In addition to that was the fact that a large number of the Falun Gong were considered intellectuals, members of military organizations, and political party officials. It also threw into stark relief the incredible organizing power of the Internet, which was very new to China in 1999, and is now heavily policed there. Some 6,900 websites are listed in connection with Falun Gong, both for and against the practice.

Life as Falun Gong has thus taken on very different features in China. First, the practice of Falun Gong proper—its exercises, meditation, and study of teachings—has been driven underground by the repressive state apparatus... Gatherings in private are outlawed as well, as is any on-line discussion. This has effectively meant that networks of relations have shrunk and taken on new configurations; community has been reconfigured on a more local and perhaps personal scale.

One ironic, if unlikely, change is that China's Falun Gong contingent has had to become more international even as it becomes less public; the central community of adherents is now a virtual one, i.e., on line, in the form of a website (*Minghui.org*) that is hosted in West. But even the viability of this community is not ensured without great effort; just to access Falun Gong websites requires sophisticated technology, owing to the Communist Party's Internet censorship. The second major development is a remarkable campaign to remedy the oppression and its many ill effects. A grassroots effort of enormous—and still expanding—proportions has arisen in response to the unfair, and often brutal, treatment visited upon the group. Ordinary citizens have risen up to do extraordinary things in this capacity, often putting themselves at tremendous risk for the sake of principle.[18]

Organ Harvesting from Live Falun Gong Practitioners: From as early as December 2000, *Clearwisdom.net* has reported that Falun Gong practitioners' organs were stolen and sold for profit by the Chinese communist regime. The startling truth of live organ harvesting from Falun Gong practitioner only came to receive international attention in March 2006. On March 9, 2006, an informant revealed that more than six thousand Falun Gong practitioners have been detained in a concentration camp in Sujiatun, where practitioners' organs were harvested and bodies cremated. There is a lot more information on line with regards to this story. Due to space constraints, trying to write about it here would be unsatisfactory to the gravity of the story. The reader is encouraged to go on line and do detailed studying on the topic.[7][19]

Note: The books, lectures, and exercise materials have been translated into over forty languages and are available on the Internet free of charge.

"Any attempt to synthesize or summarize a body of teachings as vast and nuanced as those of Falun Gong is bound to come up short. Nor could it begin to account for the varied, and rich, interpretations of those teachings in the lives of its adherents."[20]

Notes

Notes

Hindu

Hindus have a saying, *"Ekam sataha vipraha bahudha vadanti ,"* which may be translated "The truth is one, but different sages call it by different names."

History

Ancient History: Hinduism is generally regarded as the world's oldest organized religion that is believed to have existed for over ten thousand years all over India and much of adjoining areas of Asia. Evidence that Hindu religion must have existed even circa 10,000 BC is available. Hindu sacred texts are perhaps the most ancient religious texts still surviving today. Numerous references to ancient rivers and astrological occurrences dating back to 10,000 BC in the *Rig Veda* (a collection of ancient Vedic Sanskrit texts) indicate that the *Rig Veda* was being composed well before 6,500 BC. The earliest literature of Hinduism is made up of the four Vedas: the *Rig Veda, Sama Veda, Yajur Veda* and the *Atharva Veda*. Of these, the Rig Veda is the oldest surviving work. These texts were created in the Bronze Age and Iron Age and transmitted through oral tradition. However, many Hindus believe that the Vedas have been around for perhaps eight thousand years as revealed by God to the *saptarshi* (meaning "seven sages"). The excavations of the pre-Vedic Indus Valley civilization have uncovered statues that seem to be images of modern-day Hindu deities.

When and how the word Hindu was coined is not precisely established. It was used by ancient Persians for the people inhabiting the lands of river Indus. Eventually, Hindu became equivalent and appropriate to anybody of Indian origin, thereby encompassing a wide range of religious beliefs and practices. Due to the wide diversity encompassed by Hinduism, there is no universally accepted definition on what a Hindu is, or even agreement on whether Hinduism represents a religious, cultural, or socio-political entity. Hinduism's religious doctrines, traditions, and observances are inextricably linked to the cultures of India.

Hinduism Spreads to Other Parts of Asia: During the first
century, the trade on the overland Silk Road increased just as
Romans were becoming extremely wealthy, and their demand for
Asian luxury was rising. This demand revived the sea
connections between the Mediterranean, China, and India. From
that time, through trade connection, commercial settlements, and
even political interventions, India started to strongly influence
Southeast Asian countries.[1] There are ancient ruins of Hindu
kingdoms dating back to this period in Malaysia, Thailand,
Cambodia, Indonesia, and Vietnam.

Buddhism and Hinduism are two closely related religions that are
in some ways parallel to each other, and in other ways are divergent in
theory and practice. The essential tenets of Buddhism and
Hinduism arose from similar ideas between the eighth and fourth
centuries BC. Almost every technical and religious Sanskrit term in
the Buddhist lexicon has a counterpart in Hindu philosophy. Some
Hindu scholars have also accepted Buddhism as a fulfillment of
Sanatana dharma philosophy. At the time of Adi Shankara's (the
first philosopher to consolidate one of the earliest Hindu
doctrines, 788–820 AD) life, Hinduism had begun to decline
because of the influence of Buddhism and Jainism.

Hinduism had become divided into innumerable sects, each
quarrelling with the others. The followers of Mimāmsa and
Sankhya philosophy had become polytheists in so much as they
did not believe in God as a unified being. Adi Shankara held
debates with the leading scholars of all these sects and schools of
philosophy to controvert their doctrines. He unified the theistic
sects into a common framework of Shanmata system. In his works,
Adi Shankara stressed the importance of the Vedas, and his efforts
helped Hinduism regain strength and popularity. He traveled on
foot to various parts of India to restore the study of the Vedas.
Even though he lived for only thirty-two years, his impact on
India and on Hinduism cannot be stressed enough.
He reintroduced a purer form of Vedic thought. He is the
main figure in the tradition of *Advaita Vedanta*. He is the founder of

the *Dashanami Sampradaya* (the ten sects of monastic groups) of Hindu monasticism and *Shanmata* tradition of worship. He traveled all over India three times over and was a major cause in the revival and integration of *Sanatana Dharma*.[2] The mathas (monasteries) he founded are very active today and form a major guiding force for Hinduism.

TheGupta Dynasty ruled northern India between the fourth and sixth centuries AD. The most accepted theory about the origins of the Guptas is that the Guptas originated from Bengal. The practice of dedicating temples to different deities came into vogue followed by fine artistic temple architecture and sculpture. Books on medicine, veterinary science, mathematics, astronomy, and astrophysics were written. The famous Aryabhata and Varahamihira belong to this age. The Gupta established a strong central government, which also allowed a degree of local control. Gupta society was ordered in accordance with Hindu beliefs. This included a strict caste system, or class system (see Special Doctrine).

"Muslim rulers began to extend their rule across Hindu populated lands in the eighth century AD and Islam began to spread across the Indian-subcontinent over several centuries. Most converts were from Hinduism or Buddhism; the two dominant local religions."[3] The prime drivers attributed to the conversions were duress by the invaders, political expediency, oppressive legal/legislative climate against Hindus and Buddhists, oppressive caste structure in Hindu society at the time, *jizya* (tax levied on the state's non-Muslim citizens), Sufi missionaries, intermarriage, and immigration from other Islamic lands.

<u>A More Loving Hindu Philosophy Develops</u>: It was during this period that the *bhakti* movements began. Bhakti are Hindu religious movements in which the main spiritual practice is the fostering of loving devotion to God, called bhakti. They were monotheistic movements generally devoted to worship of Shiva or Vishnu or Murukan or Shakti. Their teachings were that people could cast aside the heavy burdens of ritual, caste, and the subtle complexities of philosophy and simply express their overwhelming love for God.

South India's seventy-five apostles of *bhakti* (the twelve alvars and the sixty-three nayanars) nurtured the bhakti movement in India in the fifth to seventh centuries AD and were greatly influential in determining the expression of faith in South India. It was initially considered unorthodox as it rebelled against caste distinctions and Brahmanic rituals.

Bhakti was immediately accessible to all, calling to the instinct emotion of love and redirecting it to the highest pursuit of God and self-realization. In general a liberal movement and its denouncement of caste, offered recourse for Hindus from the orthodox Brahmanic systems. Of course, however, Bhakti's message of tolerance and love was not often heeded by those ensconced in the societal construct of caste.[4]

In the course of time, however, owing to its immense popularity among the masses (and even royal patronage), it became orthodox and continues to be one of the most important modes of religious expression in modern India.

Sri Ramakrishna and his pupil Swami Vivekananda led a reform in Hinduism in late nineteenth century. Their ideals and sayings have inspired numerous Indians as well as non-Indians, Hindus as well as non-Hindus.

The colonial period s aw the emergence o f various Hindu reform movements partly inspired as reactions against western civilization, including Spiritism and the national mysticism of the time. The *Partition of India* in 1947 was along religious lines, with the Republic of India emerging as the successor state of British India with a strong Hindu majority (about 80 percent). In the Republic of India, Hindu nationalism has emerged as a strong political force since the 1980s, the religious right *Bharatiya Janata Party* even forming the government of India from 1999 to 2004.

Dayananda started an *Arya Samaj* group in early twentieth century to bring back to Hinduism the people who had converted to Islam and Christianity. Dayananda claimed to be rejecting all non-Vedic beliefs altogether. Hence, the Arya Samaj unequivocally condemned idolatry, animal sacrifices, ancestor worship, pilgrimages, priestcraft, offerings made in temples, the caste system, untouchability, and child marriages on the grounds that all these lacked Vedic sanction. It aimed to be a universal church based on the authority of the Vedas. To this end, the Arya Samaj set up schools and missionary organizations, extending its activities outside India. It now has branches around the world.

Many *Dalit* (untouchables) have converted to Buddhism, Christianity, and other religions in recent years. This has often been motivated by a desire to escape the caste system. On November 4, 2001 one million low-caste Dalits were scheduled to meet in Delhi, India, for a mass conversion to Buddhism. According to Gospel for Asia, Dalits feel that: "The only way for our people to find freedom from 3,000 years of slavery is to quit Hinduism and Castism and embrace another faith." Mass conversions to Christianity have also occurred. This has generated massive anger and even instances of violence and murder directed at proselytizing religions by some Hindus.[5]

An important aspect of twentieth-century Hinduism has been its spread among non-Indians who have accepted the religion voluntarily. This perhaps began with the sojourn of Vivekananda (Sri Ramakrishna's pupil) to the *World Parliament of Religions in Chicago* in 1893, where he made a huge impact on the people. He founded the *Ramakrishna Mission* , which today operates temples, ashrams, charitable hospitals, and schools worldwide. In our times, transcendental meditation has become popular. And the *International Society for Krishna Consciousness* , inspired by the Vaishnavite strand of Bhakti, has established centers around the world. Modern Hinduism is the reflection of continuity and progressive changes that occurred in various traditions and institutions of Hinduism during the nineteenth and twentieth centuries. This continuity and adaptation to modern ideas is still a continuing process. Adherents.com estimates that there may be as many as 1.4 billion people who still consider Hinduism as part of their faith.

God or Gods

Most forms of Hinduism are *henotheistic* religions (the worship of one god without denying the existence of other gods). They recognize a single deity, and view other Gods and Goddesses as manifestations or aspects of that supreme God.

The idea that every deity whom men worship is the embodiment...of "The Absolute" is one of the most fundamental characteristics of Hinduism. It is this idea that makes Hinduism one of the most tolerant of religions, accepting alternate beliefs...All Hindus believe in the three levels of existence ...of the Divine power. However, in Hinduism it is the *Paramathma*, the Divine Supreme power who exists everywhere, the *Jivathma*, the Divinity residing inside every one of us, covered by our Karma and then the *Maya*, the Divine illusory cover that exists. The three important functions of the Supreme were Creation, Protection and Destruction or Dissolution—and came to be established in popular manifestations as the "Hindu Trinity"—*Brahma, Vishnu* (aka *Krishna*) and *Shiva*. (compare that to the Father, the Son and the Holy Ghost of western theology.)

The more intelligent among the people understood the various deities were in realities symbolisms of the Supreme Divinity, but to the masses, the symbols became "gods" in themselves. So, various levels of understanding are accepted.

The symbolism is common to all Hindus, but the exclusive emphasis on a particular god or goddess gave rise to the four major sects in Hindu Religious practice. They are *Shaiva* (worshipers of Shiva), *Vaishhnava* (worshipers of Vishnu) and *Shaakteya* (worshipers of Shakti). Those that do not belong to these three sects go by the ancient traditions and worship all gods without any exclusive preference and also follow the rituals of Vedas...However, all sects teach that the particular name and form of their deities are just one aspect of the Supreme Divinity, the All-pervading Brahman. [6]

Christ

He is not included in Hindu doctrine. But there are many scholars who try to compare the life of Jesus with the life of Krishna, the second person of the Hindu trinity, who took human form. Hindus believe that whenever profound evil spreads widely throughout the earth, the Supreme Being comes to earth in the form of a human person in order to uproot vice and to establish virtue so that the earth may get rid of sinners. Lord Krishna was just such an incarnation. Estimates of his birth date vary. Some are 1477, 3112, 3600, 5150, and 5771 BC. Krishna was the complete incarnate of Vishnu, the Godhead of the Hindu Trinity of deities. Of all the Vishnu Deities he is the most popular and the one closest to the heart of the mass[7]

Whether he was a human being or God incarnate, we cannot discount the fact that he has been ruling the hearts of millions for over three millennia. He is believed to have died at the advanced age of 125. In his final days on earth, he taught spiritual wisdom to Uddhava, his friend and disciple, and ascended to his abode after casting off his body.

Basic Doctrine

Hindu religion is not a true religion in the traditional sense but more a way of life or a *"Dharma"*—to live a life of purity with simplicity and with a sense of natural justice. It does not have any one founder, and it does not have one source book like a Bible or a Qur'an to which controversies can be referred for resolution. Consequently, it does not require acceptance of any one idea imposed on everyone. It encourages everyone to think, analyze, question and accept the faith with true knowledge and intuition. Since Hindu scriptures include not just books relating to spirituality but also secular pursuits like science, medicine, astronomy and engineering, it defies classification as a religion. In fact, one can almost identify Hinduism as a civilization and a culture.[8]

They believe that the prayers offered to every form of God is for the same almighty. "Many believe that multiplicity of deities makes Hinduism *polytheistic*. Such a belief is nothing short of mistaking the wood for the tree."[9] The faithful accepted the theory of one God with different names and varying forms or no form at all. Ekam sat, Viprāh bahudhā vadanti, says the Rig Veda or the Truth (God, Brahman, etc.) is one.

What the multiplicity of deities does indicate is Hinduism's spiritual hospitality as evidenced by two Hindu doctrines: *The Doctrine of Spiritual Competence* (Adhikaara) and *The Doctrine of The Chosen Deity* (Ishhta Devata). The Doctrine of Spiritual Competence requires that the spiritual practices prescribed to a person should correspond to his (or her) spiritual understanding. Each person studies, learns and follows a level of spiritual study that is proper for their needs. An illiterate villager who worships a stone image, and prays with simple songs, is no different from a well read scholar who meditates on the Supreme with all the knowledge of the Almighty. So, the different forms of the religious practice and images are to serve the masses according to each one's knowledge and understanding capacity. It is counter-productive to teach abstract philosophical concepts to a person whose heart hungers for faith in a higher power and vice versa.

The Doctrine of the Chosen Deity gives a person the freedom to choose a form of Brahman that satisfies his spiritual cravings and ability to understand.[10] In spite of this diversity in the forms of worship and practice, there is a subtle unity that is understood by all Hindu devotees. The true knowledgeable ones always finish their prayers with the statement, *"Like all the rain, waters that fall flow through the rivers to the same ocean; let all my prayers to various forms of the Divine ultimately flow to the same Almighty."*

All the sects and offshoots of Hinduism share the same basic moral ideals:

Ahimsa (non-violence)
Satya (truthfulness)
Brahmacharya (search for the Brahma)
Maitri (Friendship)
Dharma (fulfilling one's duty)
Karuna (Compassion)
Viirya (Fortitude)
Dama (Self Restraint—mental as well as physical)
Shaucha (Purity—mental as well as physical)

The basic discipline of a Hindu is following *Karma Yoga,* which is work or service without attachment to the benefits. Truth as a cardinal virtue in Hinduism is far more than mere truthfulness; it means eternal reality. Hinduism says that the pursuit of Truth, wherever it may lead or whatever sacrifices it may involve, is indispensable to the progress of man. Hence no Hindu scripture has ever opposed scientific progress or metaphysical and ethical speculations. Truth and non-violence are always associated with each other in the Hindu scriptures, and are considered to be the highest virtues. Mahātma Gāndhi describes Hinduism as a quest for Truth through non-violence. Notice that, in order to pursue non-violence, one must refrain from inflicting or tolerating violence on oneself. Therefore, non-violence is not passive resistance as many think: it is not the helplessness of the weak, but the calm strength of the mighty.[11] The common beliefs underlying a ll schools of thought in Hindu religion are beliefs concerning: 1) The evolution of the physical world; 2) The law of Karma and rebirth; 3) The four-fold goal of human life. The four-fold goal of human life is the *Purushhaarthas—Dharma* (Righteousness), *Artha* (Worldly Prosperity), *Kāma* (Enjoyment) and (Liberation). These are the f our types of human aspirations that will be the driving force of life and its purpose…Dharma, the righteous way of living according to Divine law codes without causing hurt to others is the most important.[12]

The real meaning of the religion becomes revealed to one who practices the spiritual discipline. It cannot be achieved by only the letter of law without meditation and prayer. One must have the faith in those writings and understand the teachings and then he must analyze and subject it to rigorous reasoning. After this, having been convinced of the soundness of the doctrine of the scriptures, one should meditate and experience the teachings in the depths of contemplation. This is the true spirituality, and this is the practice of Yoga, which means the union of the individual self with the Supreme Self. In the Vedic teachings, there are four different types of Yoga—each with special practices, and each designed to accomplish different things.

Basic Worship Service

Para-Bhakthi is the form of devotion with contemplation on the formless and unmanifested Brahman. It is the highest form of Bhakti suitable only for few learned people.

Gauni-bhakthi is the lower level of love and devotion to a manifested (Lord & master) and prayers to one of His forms accepted as...a personal God. There are many levels or many grades in this form of devotion. These are the various levels of search for the Supreme Truth as "God."

Ekantha-bhakthi is the purest form of devotion...Here, the devotee loves God for His own sake and not for His gifts. He sees the presence of God...in all places, at all times. This is the true monotheism that most Hindus try to achieve; all inclusive.[13]

Anyaya-bhakthi is a passionate form of monotheism which denies other forms and feels their form of monotheism is the only truth. In one way, it is part of the henotheism, recognizing only one form or aspect of the supreme divinity. "But, it shall not give rise to bigotry and cruelty toward those who have different concept of God and different methods of approach. Among Hindus, it is well recognized that the 'gods' whom others worship are only different forms o f one's own"[14] chosen manifestation of the supreme truth.

Bhaya-bhakthi is the very external form of worship of a Deity as God. It is the adoration paid to a form of God outside ourselves. It is the most basic form of a faith, based on the unenlightened form of feeling that God is external to us and dwells in a particular locality like the prayer room or Temple. The pilgrimages, worship of several images of God, symbols and sacred books are examples of this. Most popular religions do not rise above this level. This is the common simple blind faith of the "God-fearing"ones.

In the temple services, the statue of the deity in the temple "is woken up every morning with a morning service with ceremonial bath with water, milk and other perfumed substances...and Jewelry. The services are repeated four to six times or more every day, with offering of food as 'prasadam' and singing prayers and songs in praise of the Deity and reading of the Scriptures.

After this, 'Aarthi' of lighted camphor is performed for every one to see the Deity" in a Dharshan. "The devotees take what is given back to them as 'Prasadams,' let it be holy water, ashes, kumkum, a flower, a fruit or a full meal." Here, the prayer services are for the welfare of the community as a whole.

The prayer services at home are also very similar in practice. Often there is a prayer room. Sometimes, a special area is arranged to perform the home prayer services. Here, prayer services are offered to a picture, small icon or a lamp which is sanctified by rituals for the occasion. The Divine powers of the form of God offered prayer on that occasion is represented in this. The rituals are simple and they first invite God as a guest to the house. Then, they perform a ritualistic bathing and offering of clothes. Then, there will be prayers and singing of songs and offering of food which is then offered to members of the family and friends. Here the services are performed for the welfare of the individuals their family and friends.[15]

Infant Baptism or Blessing

Not applicable to Hindu religion.

Initiation, Baptism, or Confirmation

There is essentially no "initiation" ceremony in Hinduism. The closest thing is the coming of age ceremony. The "*Upanayana* is a kin to Bar Mitzvah in Jewish culture. This ceremony was performed before the boy went up to the Guru's *ashram* (school). In a ceremony administered by a priest, a young boy usually shaves his hair off as a measure of austerity (or just some portions, as deemed appropriate) and a cotton string is hung from around his shoulder to his waist line."[16] The ceremony varies from region to community and includes reading from the Vedas and special mantras and shlokas. It symbolizes a new birth or new eyes as a student. It does not resemble baptism; the new birth signifies the change in knowledge level and entry into a new stage in life. Hence, from this day onward, he belongs to the guru, who takes the place of mother and father in nurturing and training the young male.

The boy also swears to obey his guru and also takes oaths to confirm that he will not take intoxicants, he will speak the truth, serve the guru, and stay celibate throughout the education process.

While young females (prepubescent until married) do not have a similar ritual passage as young males, they follow annual monsoon austerity ritual of purification by not eating cooked food for one or two weeks, depending on age of child. This is known as *goryo* or *goriyo*. During this period, they cultivate from seeds of paddy, wheat, and mung beans in a small pottery to which they guard and nurture.[17]

Marriage

Wedding ceremonies and rituals vary in Hinduism. Most Hindu parents look for a prospective match for their children from their own community or caste. The ritual of matching the prospective *jathakam* or *janampatri* (Hindu horoscope), with the help of a holy priest, is also widely practiced by many Hindus. Modern-day couples usually approve each other before getting the elders of the family to approve their "arranged" marriage.

The important difference between a Hindu marriage and other types of marriage is that Hindu marriage is a three-party contract, as much as it is a two-party contract in the western civilization. The third party that needs to approve the marriage is essentially the elders of the family representing the interest of the clan. The elders' wishes still hold prominence and are not becoming obsolete even in modern marriages. Hindu marriage ceremonies are very colorful and elaborate. Families of the bride and the groom hold numerous festivities to celebrate the wedding. Marriage without a Brahman priest was traditionally not regarded as a religiously accepted marriage in Hindu society.

Death and Afterlife

Upon the death of a Hindu person, his or her body is ceremonially bathed and wrapped in clean, mostly white, cloth. At the ceremony of cremation all mourners usually wear only white clothes. An attending priest conducts the ceremony, sanctifying the body and pyre by sprinkling holy water and singing or chanting religious hymns or songs.

Hindus in India are cremated on open grounds upon wooden pyres. The ashes of the person's remains are gathered and placed in a pot, which may be ritually immersed or released in any of Hinduism's holy rivers, usually within three days.

"Hindus believe in the repetitious *Transmigration* of the Soul. This is the transfer of one's soul after death into another body. This produces a continuing cycle of birth, life, death and rebirth through their many lifetimes. It is called *Samsara* . Karma is the accumulated sum of ones good and bad deeds. Karma determines how you will live your next life."[18]

Judgment and Salvation

The doctrine of Karma emphasizes that God is not a judge who sits in a remote heaven meting out punishments and rewards, but an indwelling being (the Self) whose will works in us through the moral law here and now. While Karma Yoga is the highest form of application of this law, according to which one must live his life with a sense of detachment and perform such action as an offering to the Divine with a sense of pure Duty or *Dharma*...It is trying to attain perfection in whatever we do by concentrating on what is to be done rather than the anticipated results. Attachment to results leads to greed, jealousy and ultimately to grief.[19]

Special Doctrine

The colored dot on the forehead is variously referred to as a *"tilaka," "bottu," "bindiya," "kumkum,"* or *"bindi."* It is a sign of piety, and reveals to other people that the wearer is a Hindu. It symbolizes the third eye—the one focused inward toward God. Both men and women wear it, although the practice among men is gradually going out of style. In the past, many unmarried women wore black marks, whereas many married women wore red. But in recent times, women often wear dots that match the color of their saris (traditional Indian attire).[20]

The Caste System: The Rig Veda, a collection of ancient Vedic Sanskrit hymns dedicated to the Gods, defined four varnas (castes). In decreasing status, they are normally described as:

- *Brahmins* (the priests and academics)
- *Kshatriyas* (rulers, military)
- *Vaishyas* (farmers, landlords, and merchants)
- *Sudras* (peasants, servants, and workers in non-polluting jobs).

The *Dalit* were outcasts who are not even considered to be part of the caste system. They worked in what are considered polluting jobs. They were called the "untouchables" by the other four castes. In some areas of the country, even a contact with their shadow by a member of the Varnas was considered polluting.[21]

A person's caste determined the range of jobs or professions from which they could choose. There were rules that prohibited persons of different groups from intermarriage, eating, drinking, or even smoking with each other. About 500 BC to 500 AD, the system became even more rigid so that a person was born and died in the same group with no possibility of upward mobility. Although the caste system was abolished by law in 1949, and discriminating against a person because of their caste is now illegal, it remains a significant force among Hindus unchanged in some rural districts of India.

Hinduism in general does not encourage converting. This largely explains why there has never been any missionary activity in Hinduism. It is the belief of Hinduism that each person chooses their own path to reach God. You are never encouraged to stray from the path that you have chosen. Each religion is just a different path to the same God. Converting to another religion takes you to an entirely new path, which in Hinduism is seen as unnecessary. Modernity has led to an infusion of newer ideas into the Hindu religion, thereby making it more open, so that we find m any n on-Asians taking on Hinduism. Th is is particularly interesting because there is no large-scale proselytizing effort in Hinduism. The status of women is typically discussed on a nationwide basis. However, about eighty percent of the citizens of India are Hindu, fourteen percent are Muslim, and six percent are of other religions or no religion.

Most of the negative behavior toward girls and women across the country can probably be safely attributed to the practices of Hindus. Infanticide has been widespread in India for centuries. R. J. Rummel reported: "In India, for example, because of Hindu beliefs and the rigid caste system, young girls were murdered as a matter of course. When demographic statistics were first collected in the nineteenth century, it was discovered that in some villages, no girl babies were found at all; in a total of thirty others, there were 343 boys to 54 girls...In Bombay, the number of girls alive in 1834 was 603."[22]

A *Reuter's* article in July 2007 reported on the high level in India of:

- Female feticide. This is the practice of using ultrasound instruments to determine the sex of a fetus in order to abort fetuses that are found to be female.
- Infanticide. This involves the actual murder of a newborn female, typically because of her gender.
- Widespread neglect of girl children.
- Mob violence, including murders, victimizing women believed to be evil sorcerers.

Notes

Shintō

History

According to archaeological studies, the first records beginning in about 2000 BC were from the Jomon Period in Japan. Jomon peoples used natural housing, predated rice farming, and frequently were hunter-gatherers, the physical evidence for ritual practices are difficult to document. There are many locations of stone ritual structures and refined burial practices...that lend to the continuity of primal *Shintō*. The Jomon had a clan-based tribal system developed similar to much of the world's indigenous people. In the context of this clan based system, local beliefs developed naturally and when assimilation between clans occurred, they also took on some beliefs of the neighboring tribes. At some point there was a recognition that the ancestors created the current generations and the reverence of ancestors took shape. There was some trade amongst the indigenous peoples within Japanese islands and the mainland, as well as some varying migrations. The trade and interchange of people helped the growth and complexity of the people's spirituality[1] by exposure to new beliefs. The natural spirituality of the people appeared to be based on the worship of nature's forces, and the natural elements to which they all depended, which is similar to most ancient civilizations we have studied in these texts. (Though not often referred to today, the Japanese calendar year starts from 660 BC, the year of *Amaterasu's* (the sun goddess) accession. All the reigning emperors since then are considered to be the direct descendants of the sun goddess and are revered as living gods.)

Shintō has no founder or founding date. When the Japanese people and Japanese culture became aware of themselves... Shintō was already part of the culture. Among the primary Yayoi religious phenomena were agricultural rites and Shamanism. Early Shamans performed the ceremonies; eventually those of the Yamato tribe performed on behalf of the other tribes, and their chieftain assumed duties that led to headship of the Shintō state.[2]

Shintōism started to develop into a coherent religion starting approximately 500 BC. "It was originally an amorphous mix of nature worship, fertility cults, divination techniques, hero worship, and Shamanism."[3] Its name was derived from the Chinese words shin tao (the way of the gods). The Yayoi Period started round 400 BC, during which time the Japanese culture begins to develop in no small part due to influences from mainland trade and immigration from north east China. During this time in the pre-writing historical period, objects from the mainland start appearing in large amounts, specifically mirrors, swords, and jewels. All three of these have a direct connection to the imperial divine status as they are the symbols of imperial divinity and are Shintō honorary objects. Also the rice culture begins to blossom throughout Japan and this leads to the settlement of society, and seasonal reliance of crops. Both of these changes are highly influential on the Japanese[4] people's relationship to the natural world, and likely a development of a more complex system of religion.

The Yayoi culture, which originated in the northern area of the island of Kyushu around the third or second century BC, was a clan-based culture that lived in compounds with a defined leader who was the chief and head priest. They were responsible for the relationship with their gods (*kami*), and if one clan conquered another, their god would be assimilated.[5] The gradual introduction of methodical religious and government organizations from mainland Asia starting around 300 BC, seeded the reactive changes in primal Shintō over the next seven hundred years to a more formalized system. This is also the period that is referenced as the "beginning of the divine Imperial family."

The next period to continue the evolution of Shintōism was the Kofun Period (250–52 AD). This is the period of the development of the feudal state. This time period is defined by the increase of central power in Osaka, Japan, and the development of the feudal lord system. Much of modern Japan was under only fragmentary control by the imperial family and rival ethnic groups. In particular, the Asuka rulers of 552–645 AD s aw disputes between the more major families of the clan families.[6]

There were disputes about who would ascend to power and support the imperial family. The Soga family eventually prevailed and later helped assimilate Buddhist faith into Japan. The mythological anthologies, along with other poetry anthologies, like the collection of *Ten Thousand Leaves* and others, were intended to impress others with the worthiness of the imperial family and their divine mandate to rule. In the latter sixth century, there was a breakdown of the alliances between Japan and Korea, but the situation led to the codification of Shintō as the native religion. Up to this time, Shintō had been largely a clan-based religious practice, exclusive to each clan.

Confucianism reached Japan in the fifth century AD and spread among the people together with Chinese Taoism and *yin-yang* (harmony of two basic forces of nature) philosophy. All of these stimulated the development of Shintō ethical teachings.

In 552 AD, a Buddha image was given to the Yamato leader, who profoundly changed the course of Japanese religious history, especially in relation to the undeveloped native religious conglomeration that was Shintō. Greatly affected by the new religion, Japan's Prince Shotoku (574–622 AD) institutionalized Buddhism as a state religion and built many great temples. Buddhism started gaining in popularity among the Japanese people. The introduction of Buddhism was followed by a few initial conflicts, however. Buddhism and Shintōism were eventually able to coexist and even complement each other.

"Buddhism brought new theories on government, a means to establish strong centralized authority, a system for writing, advanced new methods for building and for casting in bronze and new techniques and materials for painting—and it allowed Japan to gain the benefits of joining the larger cultural sphere of mainland Asia."[7] The arrival of Buddhism from China marked the first use of the term *kami-no-michi* (the way of the kami). It distinguished native religion from those brought in by Chinese/Korean missionaries. Prior to this introduction, Japanese religious consciousness centered around a vast mythology of creation stories about the origin of the islands of Japan, indigenous occult forces or energies called kami, as well as a great reverence for ancestors and the well-being of their spirits.

But the Chinese traditions of Confucianism, Taoism, and Buddhism nevertheless had a profound and lasting effect on Japanese civilization. Having no written language of her own, Japan adopted the Chinese script as well as much of China's artistic heritage. Being a feudal culture, Japan adopted certain aspects of Confucian thought and ethics. Ancestor worship had always been practiced in Japan; therefore, the Confucianist-Taoist concept of filial piety was embraced as well. As far as Buddhism was concerned, its wide array of Buddhas and bodhisattvas were, to the Japanese, simply Chinese versions of the kami, so they were easily embraced as well.

By the seventh century, the Japanese court had aggressively accepted Buddhism, not only as a religious vehicle promising salvation for the upper classes, but also as an instrument to consolidate state power. Around the eighth century, Shintō traditions begin to imitate and blend with Buddhist influences. The Shintō-Buddhist syncretism of the period was actually formalized and pursued based on a theory called *honji suijaku* (the idea that imported Buddhist divinities manifested themselves as native Japanese kami in order to more easily bring salvation to the Japanese people).

One major center of Shintō-Buddhist merging that came later in the ninth century was the syncretic Mt. Hiei shrine-temple multiplex located near Kyoto (a note of interest because of the large numbers of temples and shrines in Kyoto, the city was off limits, out of respect, during World War II, and was never bombed), which came to prominence around the same time as another syncretic Buddha-Kami multiplex at Mt. Koya, also near Kyoto.

Eventually Buddhist temples were constructed alongside Shintō shrines on many sacred mountains, epitomized by the holy places throughout the Kumano mountain range. Pilgrimages to these sites were believed to bring double favor from both their Shintō and Buddhist counterparts. The number of deities proliferated. Syncretism was relatively smooth and marked by religious tolerance.[8]

"clan" Shintō had dominated and an organized form of *Imperial Shintō* did not exist as such. Due to increasing influence from Buddhism and mainland Asian thought, codification of the "Japanese"way of religion and laws begins in earnest. During this period, the *Kojiki* (the oldest-surviving book in Japan, 712 AD) and the *Nihon Shoki* (720 AD) were written. The Kojiki establishes the imperial family as the foundation of Japanese culture, being the descendants of Amaterasu Omikami, the sun goddess.[9] The Kojiki is the primary textual source for the mythological background of Japanese culture as well as the very origins of Japan itself.

The development of this text was (and is) a major component in the foundation of Japanese cultural heritage and religious identity. The Nihon Shoki was more interested in creating a structural system of government, foreign policy, religious hierarchy, and domestic social order. Shintō deities were not given anthropomorphic characteristics until after the appearance of these court-sponsored scriptures. The two texts were commissioned by Japan's leaders to demonstrate to the Chinese Emperor that the Yamato Dynasty (a.k.a. Japan) had a long and distinguished history, thereby proving that Japan was a sovereign kingdom.[10]

The establishment of the imperial city in partnership with *Taihō Code* (an administrative reorganization enacted in 701 AD, incorporating Confucianist ideas) is important to Shintō as the office of the Shintō rites becomes more powerful in assimilating local clan shrines into the fold and stabilizing the society through imperial power. It was a liturgy of rules and codifications, primarily focused on regulation of religion, government structure, land codes, criminal and civil law. All priests, monks, and nuns were required to be registered, as were temples. The Shintō rites of the imperial line were codified, especially seasonal cycles, lunar calendar rituals, harvest festivals, and purification rites. The creation of the imperial *Jingi-kan* or Shintō shrine office was completed. All of the grand shrines were regulated under Taihō and are now required to account for incomes, priests, and practices due to their national contributions.[11]

The period between eighth and ninth centuries hosted many changes to the country, government, and religion. There emerged tendencies to interpret Shintō from a Buddhist viewpoint.

The process of blending Buddhism with Shintō progressed uninterrupted. One notable example is a syncretic movement that combined Shintō with the teachings of Shingon Buddhism. This school believed that Shintō deities were manifestations of the Buddhist divinities. The Shintō Sun Goddess *Amaterasu,* for example, was identified with *Dainichi Nyorai* (the Great Sun Buddha).[12]

Bodhisattva names were given to kami, and Buddhist statues were placed even in the inner sanctuaries of Shintō shrines. In some cases, Buddhist priests were in charge of the management of Shintō shrines. By the ninth century AD, the distinctions between Shintō and the foreign religions began to fade into something of a syncretistic union. Along with other foreign influences and cultural forms, they were, in a sense, Japanized. The Japanese began to see the normal activities of day-to-day life as being the domain of Shintō, while the concerns of the afterlife were served by Buddhism.

During the Kamakura Period (1185–1333), power shifted from the isolated centrality of the royal court to the military-based government ruled over by a shogun (military leader). This is also the period of the *samurai* (meaning "to serve"), the elite warrior class who pledged themselves to the service of a *daimyo* ("great name,") a regional feudal landholder who served beneath a *Shogun*). "Shintō was emancipated to some degree from Buddhist domination by Japan's new military dictators (the Kamakura shogunate), and Shintō groups themselves proclaimed that Shintō divinities were not incarnations of the Buddha, but rather that Buddha himself was a manifestation of the Shintō deities."[13] A significant event in this historical period was the *kami no kaze* ("divine wind"): the storms that repelled the Mongol invaders from the western coast of Japan in 1274 and 1281. These miraculous events added credence to the assertion that divine spirits were indeed protecting the Japanese land and were Shintō kami and not Buddhist spirits.

In 1603, the Tokugawa shogunate was founded in Edo (Tokyo), and contact between Shintō and Confucianism was resumed after almost

1,000 years of lingering in the background. Scholars tried to interpret Shintō from the standpoint of Neo-Confucianism, emphasizing the unity of Shintō and Confucian teachings. Schools emerged based on the teachings of the Chinese philosophers Chu Hsi and Wang Yang-ming, and Neo-Confucianism became an official subject of study for warriors.[14]

A restoration of Shintō "began toward the end of the seventeenth century. Advocates of this school maintained that the norms of Shintō should not be sought in Buddhist or Confucian interpretations but in the beliefs and life-attitudes of their ancestors as clarified by philological study of the Japanese classics." In the eighteenth century, various Japanese scholars, in particular Motoori Norinaga, tried to tear apart the real Shintō from various foreign influences. When Shintō was reinforced by rulers, it quickly supplanted Buddhism. After the *Meiji Imperial Restoration of 1868* , the emperor gained control of the government and replaced the old feudal shogunate. Shintō became the official state religion. Policies were put into place against Buddhism and any other religions. The emperor was declared to be a living god and had supreme power.

However, since the people continued to embrace parts of Buddhism, in 1877, Buddhism was allowed to be practiced by the people with total religious liberty granted. But State Shintō was established and was to be regarded as a patriotic ritual by the citizens irrespective of their religion, requiring them to pay homage to the emperor. Then the Japanese government more rigorously enforced Shintō's position as the state religion with the enactment of the *Religious Organizations Law of 1939* , a move designed to impose stricter governmental controls over religions and began to demand that all citizens enshrine Shintō talismans in their homes.

As time went on, Shintō was increasingly used in the advertising of nationalist popular sentiments. "In 1890, the *Imperial Rescript on Education* was issued, and students were required to ritually recite its oath to 'offer yourselves courageously to the State' as well as to protect the Imperial family."[15] The ultimate offering was to give up one's life. It was an honor to die for Japan and the emperor. The fact is that innumerable soldiers, sailors, and pilots were determined to die, to become *eirei,* which are guardian spirits of the country. Young Japanese people were indoctrinated from an earliest age with these ideals. The practice of emperor worship was further spread by distributing imperial portraits for esoteric veneration. All of these practices were used to fortify national solidarity through patriotic observance at shrines.[16]

During the Second World War in the Pacific, the military leadership of Japan found in Shintō the rationalization for the conquest of East and Southeast Asia. This radical sense of ultra-nationalism resulted in the use of *kamikaze pilots* (suicide pilots) and a horrendous loss of life among both Japanese and Allied soldiers. This use of Shintō gave Japanese patriotism a special tint of mysticism and cultural introversion, which became more pronounced as time went on. Such processes continued to deepen throughout the period, when state Shintō became a main force of militarism, finally coming to an abrupt end in August 1945, when Japan lost the war in the Pacific.

Following Japan's surrender in 1945, the American occupation forces, realizing that Shintō had become such an intrinsic part of Japanese militarism, abolished state support for Shintō (the *Shintō Directive of December 1945*), and subsequently directed the emperor to issue an official statement declaring that he was not of divine origin. As the era of state Shintō came to a close with the end of World War II, most Japanese came to believe that the hubris of the empire had led to their downfall. In the postwar period, numerous new religions cropped up, many of them ostensibly based on Shintō; but on the whole, Japanese religiosity decreased.

However, the concept of religion in Japan is a complex one. The number of Japanese citizens identifying their religious beliefs as Shintō has declined a great deal, yet the general practice of Shintō rituals has not decreased accordingly, and many practices have persisted as general cultural beliefs. A survey conducted in the mid-1970s indicated that of those participants who claimed not to believe in religion, one-third had a Buddhist or Shintō altar in their home, and about one quarter carried an *omamori* (an amulet to gain protection by kami) on their person.[17]

Shintō currently has about 119 million known adherents in Japan, although a person who practices any manner of Shintō rituals is included. However, unlike many religious practices, Shintō and Buddhism typically do not require professing faith to be a believer or a practitioner, and as such, it is difficult to query for exact figures based on self-identification of belief within Japan. Shintō has shrines in many other countries, including the United States, Brazil, Canada, New Zealand, Australia, and the Netherlands among others, and is considered to be expanding to a global religion especially with the advent of international branches of Shintō shrines.

God or Gods

Shintō creation stories tell of the history and lives of the *kami* (deities). Among them was a divine couple, Izanagi-no-mikoto and Izanami-no-mikoto, who gave birth to the Japanese islands. *Amaterasu Omikami* (sun goddess) was their daughter. She is the ancestress of the imperial family and is regarded as the chief deity.[18] According to Japanese mythology, Amaterasu is the ruler of heaven. Some say Shintōism concurs with the Bible that God created everything in heavens and on earth, and every creature is beautiful and perfect, made that way by God. Others stress that Shintōism is definitely polytheistic.

Shintō teaches that everything contains a kami ("spiritual essence," commonly translated as god or spirit). Kami is a difficult concept to translate as there is no direct similar word in English. Kami is generally accepted to describe the innate supernatural force that is above the actions of man, the realm of the sacred, and is inclusive of gods, spirit figures, and human ancestors. All mythological creatures of the Japanese cultural tradition, of the Buddhistic tradition, the Christian God, Hindu gods, Islamic Allāh, various angels and demons of all faiths among others, are considered kami for the purpose of Shintō faith.

Christ

Not applicable.

Basic Doctrine

At its most fundamental level, Shintō refers to the spiritual consciousness and ritual practices that are indigenous to the people of Japan. While it embraces a wide variety of beliefs and practices, Shintō neither acknowledges a founder nor adheres to a particular creed or doctrine. Now, along with this, it must also be said that the Japanese language has no particular formal word for religion in and of itself.

The Japanese word *shukyu* was more or less a kind of nineteenth century construct that was created to refer to Western religions that are centered in formal doctrine and belief. This is in contrast to the idea of Shintō (the Way of the Gods) as just that—a "way" of doing something, a ritual action that is not a reflection of a doctrine, in the manner of Christianity, etc. In this sense, then, many Japanese will say that they are not "religious"[8] as their traditional practices do not reflect this doctrinal foundation that most Westerners take for granted.

Shintō has been called the religion of Japan, and the customs and values of Shintō are inseparable from those of Japanese culture. Many famous Japanese practices have origins either directly or indirectly rooted in Shintō. For example, it is clear that the Shintō ideal of harmony with nature underlies such typically Japanese arts as flower-arranging, traditional Japanese architecture, and the exquisite Japanese gardens.

A more explicit link to Shintō is seen in sumo wrestling, where, even in the modern version of the sport, many Shintō-inspired ceremonies must be performed before a bout, such as purifying the wrestling arena by sprinkling it with salt. The Japanese emphasis on proper greetings and respectful phrasings can be seen as a continuation of the ancient Shintō belief in *kotodama* (words with a magical effect on the world).[19]The kami reside in all things, but certain places are designated for the interface of people and kami (the common world and the sacred): sacred nature, shrines, and kamidana. There are natural places considered to have an unusually sacred spirit about them and are objects of worship.

---

[8]　Special thanks to Timothy D. Hoare, PhD, professor of humanities and religion for his input and advice.

In most cases, they are on or near a shrine grounds. The shrine is a building built to house the kami with a separation from the ordinary world. Each kami has a divine personality and responds to truthful prayers. The kami also guides people to live in accordance with truth and sincerity.

Shintō holds a generally positive view of human nature. A common Shintō saying is that "man is kami's child." First, this means that a person was given his life by kami and that his nature is therefore sacred. Second, it means that daily life is made possible by kami, and, accordingly, the personality and life of people are worthy of respect. An individual must revere the basic human rights of everyone as well as his own.[20]

Shintō teaches that certain deeds create a kind of ritual impurity that one should want cleansed for one's own peace of mind and good fortune, not because impurity is wrong in and of itself. Wrong deeds are called *impurity* as opposed to purity. Killing living beings (even insects) should be done with reverence for taking a life to continue one's own and should be kept to a minimum. Failure to show proper respect can be seen as a lack of concern for others and looked down on because it is believed to create problems for all. Those who fail to take into account the feelings of other people will find that kami will only bring ruin on their lives.

Purification rites are a vital part of Shintō. They are done on a daily, weekly, seasonal, lunar, and annual basis. In many ways, these purification rituals are the lifeblood of the practice of Shintō. While Shintō is not defined by a vast array of doctrinal ideas, a fundamental goal or aim of Shintō is the attainment of *makoto no kokoro* (true heart with sincerity) through the act of regular purification. When one has true heart, he/she is open to the subtle movements and presence of the spiritual forces.

Shintō's reverence for ancestors is family-oriented. The *kamidana* is a home shrine (placed on a wall in the home) that is a kami residence that acts as a daily substitute for a public shrine. It usually contains objects or symbols that hold a spiritual significance to that particular family. In each case, the object of worship is considered a sacred space that the kami spirit actually dwells, being treated with the utmost respect. Family members will make daily or weekly offerings of food and drink to the kami or to their ancestors.[21]

<u>Texts:</u> Shintō does not have any philosophical literature or official scripture that can be compared to texts like the Bible or the Qur'an. But the *Kojiki* (Records of Ancient Matters) and the *Nihongi* or *Nihon shoki* (Chronicles of Japan) are in a sense the sacred books of Shintō. They are compilations of the oral traditions, mythology, and ceremonies of ancient Shintō. But they are also books about the history, topography, and literature of ancient Japan. Also important is the collection of fifty books known as *Yengishiki* completed in 927 AD. These deal with the laws governing shrine ceremonies, the organization of religious leadership, and official prayers and liturgies.[22]

Shintō is described as a religion of continuity or community. The Japanese, while recognizing each man as an individual personality, do not take him as a solitary being separated from others. On the contrary, he is regarded as the bearer of a long continuous history that comes down from his ancestors and continues in his descendants. He is also considered as a responsible member of society. Shintō does not have the concept of the last day: there is no end of the world or of history. From the viewpoint of finite individuals, Shintōists also stress *middle present*. According to this point of view, the present moment is the very heart of all conceivable times. In order to participate directly in the eternal development of the world, it is required of Shintōists to live fully each moment of life, making it as worthy as possible.

In contrast to many monotheist religions, there are no absolutes in Shintō. There is no absolute right and wrong, and nobody is perfect. Shintō is an optimistic faith as humans are thought to be fundamentally good, and evil is believed to be caused by evil spirits. Consequently, the purpose of most Shintō rituals is to keep away evil spirits by purification, prayers, and offerings to the kami. Shintō priests perform Shintō rituals and often live on the shrine grounds. Men and women can become priests, and they are allowed to marry and have children. Priests are aided by younger women during rituals and shrine tasks. These women wear white kimono, must be unmarried, and are often the priests' daughters.

Basic Worship Service

The basic place for worship in Shintō is at one of the numerous shrines covering the country of Japan. A traditional Japanese home may have two family altars: one Shintō, for their tutelary kami and the goddess Amaterasu, and another Buddhist, for the family ancestors. Although many Shintōists have built altars in their homes, the center of worship is the local shrine. Many times, an offering of the food and wine is made to the seat of the kami. Many followers are involved in the "offer a meal movement," in which each individual bypasses a meal once per month and donates the money saved to their religious organization for international relief and similar activity,[23] which is similar to the "fast offerings" in many Christian faith practices.

There are a number of symbolic and real barriers that exist between the normal world and the shrine grounds including: statues of protection, gates, fences, ropes, and other delineations of ordinary to sacred space. Usually there will be only one or sometimes two approaches to the Shrine for the public and all will have the *Torii* (a traditional Japanese archway) over the way. Because believers respect animals as messengers of the Gods, a pair of statues of guard dogs that face each other within the temple grounds, will sometimes be at the entrance. In shrine compounds, there is a public hall of worship, hall of offerings and the innermost precinct of the grounds, the worship hall, which is entered only by the high priest or worshippers on certain occasions. The worship hall houses the symbol of the enshrined kami.[24]

Overall, shrine visitation pervades Shintō practice. There is a grand imperial shrine dedicated to the worship of Amaterasu at Ise, some two hundred miles southwest of Tokyo. This centralized place o f worship is the most sacred spot in all of Japan. The practice of worshipping at this particular spot began as early a 4 BC although the temple itself was constructed in the seventh century AD. It is here that the Shintōists made a pilgrimage to worship and remains important as a historically and culturally significant pilgrimage site. Today, shrne visitation is generally more personal and less national in nature. People will visit particular shrines prior to taking long journeys, prior to academic exams, at the outset of a new business, at the birth of a new child, etc.

About 80 percent of Shintō shrines in Japan belong to the Shrine Association, which was founded in February 1946.

The heart of the shrine is periodic rituals, spiritual events in parishioners' lives, and festivals. All of this is organized by priests who are both spiritual conduits and administrators. Shintō does not have weekly religious services. Some may go to the shrines during the month at their convenience and on the occasions of rites or festivals, which take place at fixed times during the year. Shrines are private institutions, and are supported financially by the congregation and visitors. The more well known shrines may have festivals that attract hundreds of thousands[25] including the spring festival, autumn or harvest festival, an annual festival, and the divine procession, and especially the New Year's season. New Year's Day is an important time for shrine visitation. Protective talismans, amulets, etc., that were obtained from a given shrine during the course of the previous year are returned to the shrine and burned. In turn, the pilgrim will receive new ones; these will most likely be taken home and placed on one's personal shrine in order to ensure a prosperous and healthful new year.

Matsuri (Festival or Festivals): Because of all the blending of various faiths over the centuries, there are now approximately 2,500 festivals in Japan. Some will be only observed by certain groups, and some observed by all of Japan. Because of the quantity and variation, there will be only a brief overview in this chapter. The annual schedule of matsuri seems to have been set early in the history of Japan. The original purpose of a matsuri (to learn what a kami had to tell) was gradually changed to the one-way request to the worshiped made through prayers. At the beginning of a year, matsuri are observed to pray for and celebrate in advance over a good harvest. In spring, the start of an agricultural season is reported to kami in matsuri. The summer matsuri is a prayer for stamping out noxious insects, and the autumnal matsuri is designed to be a thanksgiving affair.

The Divine Procession usually takes place on the day of the annual festival, and the kami is carried on the shoulders and transported through the parish.

The kami, on its way to the place of service, is carried by young men who are not supposed to provide the kami with a smooth, fast ride. Instead, they make it in a zigzag, swaying in all directions and pushing the mikoshi up and down, often very violently to amuse the kami. Music plays a very important role in the performance. Everything from the setup of the instruments to the most subtle sounds and the arrangement of the music is crucial to encouraging the kami to come down and dance. The songs are used as magical devices to summon the gods and as prayers for blessings.

Miko kagura is the oldest type of theatrical dance as performed by women in Shintō shrines and during folk festivals. The ancient miko were Shamanesses but are now considered priestesses in the service of the Shintō shrines. Miko kagura originally was a shamanic trance dance, but later, it became an art and was interpreted as a prayer dance. It is performed in many of the larger Shintō shrines and is characterized by slow, elegant, circular movements, by emphasis on the four directions and by the central use of fan and bells.

Marriage

Shinzen-kekkon (Marital Rites in the Presence of the Gods) is a term that broadly includes all nuptial rites conducted "before a kami," but in common usage today refers to wedding ceremonies performed at shrines or wedding halls by Shintō priests. In the late sixteenth century, there was a conscious association between marital observances and the gods; the schools of manners for the warrior class maintained set procedures for such rites, and these came to influence the customs of the common people in the towns and cities. The marriage of the Crown Prince (later the Emperor Taishō) in 1900 prompted the spread of shinzen-kekkon style marriage ceremony. For that event, the *Investigative Bureau of the Imperial Household System* set about researching and establishing a formal liturgy in August of 1899. That liturgy was codified in the April 1900 *Imperial Household Marriage Edict* and executed at the Crown Prince's wedding ceremony that May. After undergoing further revision at that shrine, the emergent liturgy spread and became the norm.

Whether the ceremony is performed at a shrine, at a wedding hall, or at home, it proceeds in the following order: 1) a purification rite; 2) a bow from the officiate; 3) the raising of food and sake as offerings to the deity; 4) a litany performed by the officiate and addressed to the gods; 5) the lowering of the now-blessed sake (rice wine) and the pouring of it for the bride and groom who drink it in a ritualized pattern; if the couple exchanges rings, the exchange typically occurs thereafter; 6) the marriage partners read their marriage vows; 7) the performance of music; 8) a sacred offering of evergreen branches from the officiate and the couple in turn; 9) the mutual pledge between families of the bride and groom and their partaking of the sacred sake; 10) the lowering of food offerings again; and 11) a bow from the priest to conclude the ceremony.

Shintō weddings are much less popular than they were a generation ago. Then 70 percent of Japanese chose a Shintō ceremony, now the number is less than 20 percent. "During recent decades, Japanese couples have introduced many Western elements to Japanese weddings. Many brides chose to wear white, Christian style dresses, and some religious ceremonies are even held completely in Christian style at a Christian church even though the couple may not be Christian. The ritual of cake cutting, the exchange of rings and honeymoons are a few other very common adopted elements." [26]

Infant Baptism or Blessing

Whenever a child is born in Japan, a local Shintō shrine adds the child's name to a list kept at the shrine and declares him or her a family child. Names can be added to the list without consent and regardless of the beliefs of the person added to the list. However, this is not considered an imposition of belief but a sign of being welcomed by the local kami, with the promise of addition to the pantheon of kami after death.[27] Various Shintō rites of passage are observed. The first visit of a newborn baby to the tutelary kami (thirty-first day for boys and thirty-second day for girls) is to initiate the baby as a new adherent. Parents and grandparents bring the child to a Shintō shrine to express gratitude to the deities for the birth of a baby and have a shrine priest pray for his or her health and happiness. The practice is not dissimilar to a Christian baptism.

Initiation, Baptism, or Confirmation

The *Shichi-go-san* (Seven-Five-Three) festival on November 15 is the occasion for boys of five years and girls of three and seven years of age to visit the shrine to give thanks for kami's protection and to pray for their healthy growth.

January 15 is Adults' Day. Youth in the village used to join the local young men's association on this day. At present, it is the commemoration day for those Japanese who have attained their twentieth year.

Death and Afterlife

Death is seen as polluting and conflicts with the purity of Shintō shrines. For that reason, cemeteries are never built on or near Shintō shrines. This results in most Japanese having Buddhist or secular funerals at a different location. The funerals are not conducted by priests because the contact with death would be too polluting for Shintō priests.

Because Shintō has co-existed with Buddhism for well over a millennium, it is very difficult to untangle Shintō and Buddhist beliefs about the world. Though Buddhism and Shintō have very different perspectives on the world, most Japanese do not see any challenge in reconciling these two very different religions, and practice both. Thus it is common for people to practice Shintō in life, yet have a Buddhist funeral. Their different perspectives on the afterlife are seen as complementing each other, and frequently the ritual practice of one will have an origin in the other.[28] Humans become kami after they die and are revered by their families as ancestral kami.

Shintōism does not divide life into a natural physical world and a supernatural transcendent world. Everything is a part of a single creation. They believe that spirit beings are still here, and human beings share the same world and they are intertwined in the life process.

Judgment and Salvation

In Shintō, human beings are believed to be born pure, with a gentle and clear disposition and sharing in the divine soul. Badness, impurity, or sin are things that come later in life, and that can usually be removed by simple cleansing or purifying rituals. Purity is at the heart of Shintō's understanding of good and evil. *Tsumi* (impurity) in Shintō refers to anything that separates us from kami and from the creative and harmonizing power.

The things which make us impure are pollution or sin. This pollution includes physical, moral, or spiritual effects. This concept is similar to sin, except that it includes things that are beyond the control of the individual and are believed to be caused by evil spirits. In ancient Shintō, tsumi also included disease, disaster, and error. Anything connected with death or the dead is considered particularly polluting. To be pure is to approach godliness; indeed, it is to become one with the state of the divine. It is Shintō's prayer, Shintō's heart, to return to that original human state and live a daily life, which is at one with the kami, indigenous folk deities of Japan.

Special Doctrine

Is Shintō a religion? The nature of Shintō as a faith can be easily misunderstood. Shintō has been called Japan's religion because of its influence on Japanese culture and values for the last two-thousand-plus years. But the heart of Shintō is ritual rather than belief.

Japanese people don't usually think of Shintō as a religion in the traditional sense—it's simply the way things are done and have been for centuries; it's the Japanese way of looking at the world. This has enabled Shintō to coexist happily with Buddhism, Confucianism, Taoism, and even Christianity for centuries. Shintō is involved in every aspect of Japanese culture. It has had an effect on every aspect of Japanese life from ethics, politics, family life and social structures, art, drama, and even sports, to say nothing of the spiritual lives of the Japanese people.

Shintōist rituals can often be observed among Japan's corporate groups. Many events that would be secular in the West involve a brief Shintō ritual in Japan—for example, whenever a new factory manager is appointed, he traditionally has to visit a minishrine installed at a cozy corner of the factory grounds, where he says a prayer for safety during his work day. At the groundbreaking ceremony or at the start-up of a new facility, be it a high-tech or a smoke-stack industry, a Shintō priest is always invited to perform the purification and exorcism rituals.

In the case of Toyota Motors, for example, top executives play out corporate rituals every autumn at the Ise Shrine in Mie Prefecture, the spiritual home of the Sun Goddess Amaterasu—here they unveil their newest models, making the three-hour drive from their headquarters near Nagoya. Shintō is thus firmly embedded in today's corporate society.[29]

Although most Japanese follow many Shintō traditions throughout life, they actually regard themselves as being devoted to their community's local shrine and kami rather than to a countrywide religion. So many Japanese don't think that they are practicing Shintō nor are followers of a Shintō religion, even though what they do is effected by concepts and teachings of Shintōism, just like any other faith practice we have studied.

Notes

_____

_____

_____

_____

_____

_____

_____

_____

_____

_____

_____

_____

_____

_____

Nature-Based Religions

These chapters will describe religions and practices that have an indelible connection to the Earth and the world around us. They focus upon the idea that gods and other supernatural powers can be found through the direct experience of natural events and natural objects and everything is interconnected. Keep in mind that some of these faith practices may in fact also fit into another category. This category was chosen as the primary source of the early years of the religion or practice. But during the process of evolving into what they are today, you will find some blending that is most interesting.

Native American
(First Nation)

"Brother, you say there is but one way to worship and serve the Great Spirit. If there is but one religion, why do you white people differ so much about it? Why not all agreed, as you can all read the Book? Brother, we do not understand these things. We are told that your religion was given to your forefathers and has been handed down from father to son. We also have a religion which was given to our forefathers and has been handed down to us, their children. We worship in that way. It teaches us to be thankful for all the favors we receive, to love each other, and to be united. We never quarrel about religion. Brother, the Great Spirit has made us all, but He has made a great difference between His white and His red children. He has given us different complexions and different customs. To you He has given the arts. To these He has not opened our eyes. We know these things to be true. Since He has made so great a difference between us in other things, why may we not conclude that He has given us a different religion according to our understanding? The Great Spirit does right. He knows what is best for His children; we are satisfied. Brother, we do not wish to destroy your religion or take it from you. We only want to enjoy our own." (Chief Red Jacket, 1757–1830, Seneca chief, Iroquois)

History

From their arrival on the continent at least fifteen thousand years ago until their encounter with Europeans, the indigenous peoples of North America lived primarily as hunters and gatherers. Until the end of the last ice age about ten thousand years ago, the peoples of North America shared a common culture with other Arctic peoples. As the ice caps retreated, and the ecosystems of North America began to take on their present characteristics, indigenous peoples spread out across the continent and settled in various environmental niches. These groups established culture areas and adapted to their physical surroundings. Eventually, millions of people were living in kinship communities throughout North America, producing their own food, clothing, and shelter and developing their own religious forms. The first religious ceremonies held in the Americas were conducted by the Holy Men of the tribes that originally settled these lands as far back as ten thousand years ago, perhaps even further.

The hundreds of tribal groups of North America maintained individual traditions that were adapted to their regional environments, although elements of these traditions were sometimes passed from one group to another through trade, migration, and intermarriage. Each community maintained its characteristic worldview, passed down its own myths, conducted its own rituals, and acted according to its own fundamental values. Because of this, the most distinctive aspect of American Indian religious traditions is the extent to which they are wholly community-based and may have no real meaning outside of the specific community in which the acts and ceremonies are conducted.

Unlike Euro-Americans, Indian people do not choose which tribal religious traditions they will practice. Rather, each of them is born into a community and its particular ceremonial life. For most Native Americans, there existed no institutionalized forms of social or political power—no state, no bureaucracy, and no army. Native American societies as a rule were egalitarian, without the kinds of centralized authority and social hierarchy typical of modern societies. Custom and tradition, rather than law and coercion, regulated social life. While there were leaders, their influence was generally based on personal qualities and not on any formal or permanent status. Authority within a group derived from the ability to make useful suggestions and knowledge of tribal tradition and lore.

The term American Indian is one that is veiled in controversy and sometimes even hostility. The term got its start when Christopher Columbus used the word Indian to describe the people he discovered on the islands of the Caribbean Sea. Unfortunately, Columbus's discovery of this New World brought an abrupt and tragic end to the lifestyle of the American Indian. The new European settlers brought with them the concepts of materialism and land ownership and soon began claiming lands the native tribes had lived on for thousands of years.

The settlers also brought smallpox and measles—diseases the indigenous peoples had never before seen. Their immune systems were not equipped to fend off these diseases, so epidemics followed the Europeans, killing off countless thousands of the tribal peoples.

In the sixteenth and seventeenth centuries, when the first European explorers and missionaries began to document the religious patterns of indigenous North America, they were confronted with cultures that had remained unaffected by developments in the civilizations of Europe and Asia. In particular, certain archaic religious characteristics were prevalent among the peoples of North America—namely, a preoccupation with the cycles of nature; a belief in the animate quality of all beings; the use of various techniques believed to control cosmic powers for personal and communal benefit; an emphasis on kinship as the metaphor for religious relations; a reliance on Shamans...; and a unified view of physical and spiritual sustenance expressed in an equivalence between economics and religion.

With the coming of these Europeans, Native Americans experienced a series of dislocations from which they are still struggling to recover. A large number of tribes migrated to the western part of the country, mostly due to Andrew Jackson's *Indian Removal Act of 1830*. In the midst of these crises, Native Americans turned to their own religious traditions to understand and ease their plight. At the same time, missionaries attempted to convert them from their traditional religions to Christianity.

Movements of *nativism* (the assertion of traditional values in the face of foreign encroachment) and revitalization (the revival of traditional culture)...have arisen, led by Native American prophets who claimed to have received revelation from the aboriginal deities, often in dreams and visions. These prophets have frequently shown evidence of Christian influence in their moral codes, their missionary zeal, and their concern for personal redemption and social improvement...The revivals of preachers such as the Iroquois Handsome Lake in 1799 and the Salish John Slocum in 1882 spawned new religions—part native, part Christian—that have endured in their respective communities to the present day.[1]

With roots in ancient tribal traditions, the Native American Church has evolved into a twentieth-century religion. It functions like other religions, offering spiritual guidance to its members, but it employs peyote as its sacrament. Anthropologists and archaeologists have documented tribal use of the peyote cactus ceremonially in pre-Columbian times in several tribes living along the coast of the Gulf of Mexico and the arid areas of northern Mexico.

Legends describe peyote as a gift that first came to American Indians in peril. Some stories tell of the spirit peyote speaking to a lone and despairing man or woman, advising the person to look under a nearby bush and eat a small cactus to be found there, after which the person would find renewed strength and the knowledge that would permit a return home. Suppression of the use of peyote began early in the contact of Indians with Europeans. The king of Spain issued an edict in 1620 against the use of peyote. Beginning in 1886, federal Indian agents requested prohibition of peyote, and congressmen attempted to pass the necessary national legislation. Indian agents lobbied the Oklahoma Territorial Legislature, which adopted a law (repealed in 1908) prohibiting peyote by name.

Peyote was accepted as a remedy and inspiration by members of many tribes…during an era of agonizing cultural disintegration, which reached a peak during the 1880s. By 1874, the Kiowa and Comanche, once proud warriors of the southern Plains, were confined to reservations in Oklahoma. The loss of liberty, intrinsic to reservation life, brought great pain and suffering to all Native Americans.[2]

Quanah Parker is credited as the founder of the Native American Church Movement, which started in the 1890s. Parker adopted the Peyote religion after reportedly seeing a vision of Jesus Christ while suffering from a near-fatal wound following a battle with federal troops. Peyote is reported to contain hordenine and tyramine, phenylethylamine alkaloids that act as potent natural antibiotics when taken in a combined form. Parker was given peyote by an Ute medicine man to cure the infections of his wounds. During the peyote experience, Parker claimed he heard the voice of Jesus Christ who then appeared to him and told him in order to atone for his many killings and misdeeds, he must forsake a life of violence and take the Peyote religion to the Indian peoples. Parker's words and teachings comprise the core of the Native American Church doctrine and the Peyote Road.

Parker taught that the sacred peyote medicine was the sacrament given to all peoples by the Creator and was to be used with water when taking communion in some Native American Church medicine ceremonies. Healers and singers achieve a union with their Creator as incarnated in peyote. Peyote speaks through them. One such tribe is the Huichol. Huichol religion parallels Christianity in that the Creator, out of compassion for His people, subjects Himself to the limitations of this world.

In Christianity, He incarnates Himself as a man who dies but is resurrected to save human beings; in Huichol, they believed He dies and is reborn in the peyote plant to give His people wisdom. The rituals of the Native American Church allow believers to experience a revelation of mystical knowledge from the Creator. When the Creator is acknowledged as the Christian God, the Peyote ritual blends traditional native beliefs and Christianity. Perhaps because it provided a powerful alternative to both ancient tribal religions and missionary-controlled versions of Christianity, the Peyote religion spread like wildfire.

The Peyote meeting is a genuinely intertribal institution. Reservations established in Indian Territory, which subsequently became the State of Oklahoma, containing tribes that had formerly been scattered across the country. In the early 1880s, after the railroads reached Laredo, Texas, in the heart of the area where Peyote is gathered, the stage was set for rapid communication between Oklahoma tribes and all other Native Americans. The railroads made it easier for Native Americans to obtain their sacrament and share their religious traditions.[3]

The Peyote religion allowed members to establish a new identity, which combined native and Christian elements. Except for the secular powwow, Peyote meetings are now the most popular Native American gatherings.

The rituals of the Native American Church spread rapidly in the years before World War II. Faced with the suppression of many traditional rituals, native people welcomed the advent of ceremonies that took place quietly and with some legal protection. Battling alcoholism and poverty, many followers were attracted to the church's strict avoidance of alcohol and its call for monogamy and hard work. Many older religious leaders among the Navajos and elsewhere opposed the new faith, but it continued to gain adherents.

The Indians bravely defended their religious freedom in their respective states and in Congress. One of the most eloquent of these defenders was Albert Hensley, a Winnebago educated at the Carlisle Indian School. By 1908, Hensley and the Winnebago had come to regard Peyote as both a Holy Medicine and a Christian sacrament. *"To us it is a portion of the body of Christ,"* Hensley said, *"even as the communion bread is believed to be a portion of Christ's body by other Christian denominations. Christ spoke of a Comforter who was to come. It never came to Indians until it was sent by God in the form of this Holy Medicine."*—Peyote Religion: A History (Norman: University of Oklahoma Press, 1987). [4]

Intense antagonism to the Peyote religion and to Indian religions in general forced members of the *Native American Church* to organize formally to protect themselves. Accordingly, on October 10, 1918, the Native American Church incorporated itself in the state of Oklahoma. Led by Frank Eagle, the group's first president, the church stated its intention to promote Christian religious belief using "the practices of the Peyote Sacrament" and to teach Christian morality and self-respect.

The 1918 charter of the Native American Church was changed through amendments in 1944 and a new charter in 1950 and further amended in 1955. Most of the changes reflected the expansion of the group from Oklahoma and Mexico to the Midwest, the Great Plains, the Southwest, and even into Canada. Peyotists chartered their churches in states where the religion became active. In addition, Peyotists gained the recognition of the Texas Department of Public Safety so that they could gather the cactus in that state, the only place in the United States where it grows.

In August 1964, the California Supreme Court held that prohibiting their use of peyote was a violation of the First Amendment's ban on state infringement of religious freedom. As a result of this ruling, federal authorities thereafter generally protected the ceremonial use of peyote, even though several states continued to list the substance as a narcotic, subject to state drug laws. To formally protect the Indian religion, Congress passed the *Native American Religious Freedom Act* of August 11, 1978, as an official expression of good will toward Native American spirituality.

Though the law pledged that Indian people would enjoy the free exercise of religion, it contained no enforcement provision. In 1994, in the aftermath of conflicts between federal policy and state drug laws, Congress amended the 1978 law to include a new section that states, *"Notwithstanding any other provision of law, the use, possession, or transportation of Peyote by an Indian who uses Peyote in a traditional manner for bona fide ceremonial purposes in conjunction with the practice of a traditional Indian religion is lawful, and shall not be prohibited by the United States or any State ."* In the wake of this legislation, many religious practices once considered on the verge of disappearing were revived. These include Pipe Ceremonials, Sweat Lodges, Vision Quests, and Sun Dances (see Special Doctrine).

After years and years of struggle, American Indians are finally getting the much-deserved respect that they should have received a long time ago. Museums have been erected all over the country showing tribute to this great people and educating the public about their history and rich heritage. While the number of American Indians still living today is much fewer than it was centuries ago, their people still remain strong and proud of who they are and what they have become.

Many mainline churches have begun to realize the harm that was done by their ancestors, and the long drawn-out period of negotiations for settlements and healing have had a profound impact on all those involved. An expression of the new understanding regarding the relationship of the Catholic missionaries with the *First Nations* peoples in the past can be found in the apology given by the Missionary

Oblates of Mary Immaculate to the First Nations peoples at Lac-Ste-Anne, Alberta, Canada in July 1991:

We apologize for the part we played in the cultural, ethnic, linguistic, and religious imperialism that was part of the mentality with which the peoples of Europe first met the Aboriginal peoples and which consistently has lurked behind the way the Native peoples of Canada have been treated by civil governments and by the churches. We were, naively, part of this mentality and were, in fact, often a key player in its implementation. We recognize that this mentality has, from the beginning, and ever since, continually threatened the cultural, linguistic, and religious traditions of the Native peoples.[5]

Other church groups involved in operating residential schools have apologized to First Nations peoples as well and have endeavored to make amends in various ways for instances of abuse or general cultural damage and to assist with the healing process. This part of the story of the relationship of the Christian churches with First Nations peoples, many of whom are devout and active Christians themselves, will continue to unfold in the coming years. Certainly, much has been learned by everyone, and the approach of the Christian community in spreading its gospel has changed, as respect for and solidarity with others of differing religious beliefs have become essential cornerstones of interfaith and intercultural relations.

Native American Church of North America is one important place where Christianity and indigenous beliefs intersect, although some Native American Church chapters avoid Christian references and rely entirely on traditional tribal ways.

Tens of thousands of Native Americans now identify Christianity as their traditional religion. Their families have heard Christian stories, sung Christian hymns, seen Christian iconography, and received Christian sacraments for generations. In the mid 1990s, more than two-thirds of Native Americans characterized themselves at least nominally as Christians. Others have combined Christian beliefs and practices with their native religions or have practiced two faiths —Christian and native—side by side but separately. In many cases,

Native Americans have reshaped Christianity, assimilating Jesus Christ as a cultural hero and interpreting Holy Communion as a medicine. In other cases, the forms of native religions have been retained while their contents have been thoroughly Christianized.[6]

The Native American Church of North America (NACNA) has tribal, regional, national, and two international organizations, with local churches, called chapters, in twenty-three states, Canada, and Mexico. The Church sponsors semiannual conferences as well as quarterly area meetings. Its Council of Elders, composed of past presidents, assists the organization. In addition, the presidents or chairmen of the *Native American Church of North America*, the *Native American Church of Navajoland, Inc.*, and the *Native American Church of the State of Oklahoma* have formed a national council to provide leadership for the entire membership.

With followers and practitioners across North America, the NACNA can rightfully claim to be the oldest traditional religious organization in the Western Hemisphere. "Today the Native American Church of North America has 80 chapters and members belonging to some 70 Native American Nations. In the continental United States, every state west of the Mississippi has at least one chapter. The steady proliferation of its membership among diverse North American tribes has made it Native America's largest religious organization."[7]

Basic Doctrine

Note: First Nations is the term for Indigenous peoples of the Americas. The term emphasizes the sovereignty and originality of diverse and numerous indigenous cultures. There are more than five hundred indigenous nations and tribes in the United States alone, with distinctive cultures, languages, histories, and religions. Religious patterns vary tremendously, especially as related to traditional life ways (e.g., wild rice farming along the Great Lakes, nomadic hunting on the central plains, desert mesa top villages, and maize farming in the Southwest, etc.) and current living situation (e.g., reservation, urban, traditional, assimilated, and blends of these).

Given the great diversity of the sacred ways of First Nations peoples, a basic overview of sacred beliefs and ceremonies of a selected number of First Nations peoples is all that can be attempted here. The indigenous peoples of North America perceived themselves as living in a cosmos pervaded by powerful, mysterious spiritual beings and forces that underlay and supported human life. Native Americans believed that in order to survive as individuals and communities, it was necessary to acknowledge these spiritual powers in every aspect of their lives—by addressing the powers in prayer and song, offering them gifts, establishing ritual relationships with them, and passing down knowledge about them to subsequent generations, primarily through myths and legends.

Despite the great variety of spiritual ways, there are some themes that are broadly shared among traditional First Nations peoples. Below are some examples:
Humans and the many other animal, plant, insect, bird, and spirit beings of earth and sky are relatives. Humans should treat them all with respect. The entire created world is, in turn, seen as alive, sentient, and filled with spiritual power, including each human being. The sense of the interrelationship of all of creation, of all two-legged, four-legged, winged, and other living, moving things (from fish and rivers, to rocks, trees, and mountains) may be the most important contribution Indian peoples have made to the science and spirituality of the modern world.

The everyday life of the American Indian is thought to have been one closely associated with earth elements—plants, animals, wind, water, and weather. Their reverence for the world of nature dominates their art and folklore, including tales of the creation of the earth and its people. All things in nature were considered sacred and conservation practices were instinctive to these Native Americans.

"Well-being is nurtured through lifestyles that harmonize with the cycles of human birth through death, and the cycles of moon and sun and seasons. Individuals have their identity within the context of their family, community, and place."[8] Native Americans have a sense of holism wherein establishing and maintaining a circle of right relationships between and among humans, as well as between the human and natural worlds, is absolutely critical. What Christian missionaries and others often dismissed as animism or polytheism was actually a way of seeing in the entire world, a wondrous creation in which humanity has a special responsibility to uphold the circle.

Christian missionaries often completely missed the sense of a single creating Spirit that permeates most First Nations' sacred systems. Animals such as the buffalo, which played a central function in the survival of the northern plains peoples, assumed a key role in the spirit world. First Nations peoples prayed to the spirits of these animals for help, even as these animals were killed for human use. Their use was not simply for consumption: they were regarded as an integral part of the kinship of all creation. Prayers of intercession and supplication were not made for the sake of one person alone but for the entire community. Thus, the spirituality of the community was defined not only by humans, but also by the entire spectrum of nature and reality as it appeared to the indigenous peoples.

<u>Relating with the land in a sacred way is crucial to health</u>. Each Indigenous tradition includes wisdom about the healing and helping qualities of plants and animals and sacred places and spirits in the area of habitation. In addition, Indigenous cultures include specialists of healing, such as herbalists, midwives, Shamans, and many others. Many contemporary Native people blend traditional healing practices with conventional health and social service systems.

Nearly every human act was accompanied by attention to religious details, sometimes out of practiced habit and sometimes with more specific ceremony. In the northwest, harvesting cedar bark would be accompanied by prayer and ceremony, just as killing a buffalo required ceremonial actions and words dictated by the particularities of tribal nation, language, and culture. Among the Osage Indian, the spiritual principle of respect for life dictated that the decision to go to war against another people usually required an eleven-day ceremony, allowing time to reconsider one's decision and to consecrate the lives that might be lost as a result of it. Because to be successful, the hunt required acts of violence, it was also considered a type of war. Hence, the semi-annual community buffalo hunt, functioning on the same general principle of respect for life, also required a ceremony—one that was in all respects nearly identical to the war ceremony.

"Native Americans lived in a world of spirits who made their presence known primarily through natural phenomena. Most Native Americans believed in a Great Mystery or Great Spirit that under lays the complexity of all existence, as well as in many other spiritual powers that influenced the whole of life."[9] The identification of places of particular spiritual power points to yet another important aspect of Indian religious traditions: these places are experienced as powerful because they are alive. Not only are they sentient; they are intelligent manifestations of the sacred mystery or the sacred power.

The sacred mystery, sometimes translated as the Great Spirit, is typically described first of all as a great unknown. Yet this unknown becomes known as it manifests itself to humans in a particular place, in a particular occurrence, in an astronomical constellation, or in an artifact such as a feather.

At times of crisis, Native Americans turned to powerful spirits to acknowledge their dependence on these spirits and to seek help. Such crises included drought and disease, the suspicion of witchcraft, and the failure to track and kill game. Each tribal group conceived of the spirit world in its own particular way, and there were variations of belief and ritual practice within each community.[10]

In a world filled with both helpful and harmful forces, Native Americans tried to locate repositories of spiritual power. (If you have ever been out in nature and felt a strong sense of peace or closeness to God, you will know what types of sacred places they found.) Uncanny phenomena such as geysers, trees struck by lightning, and deposits of rare minerals, as well as dangerous locales such as waterfalls and whirlpools, became sites of pilgrimage where indigenous peoples hoped to collect spiritual power. They gathered herbs and pollen, oddly shaped stones and horns, bones, teeth, feathers, and other body parts of animals and placed them in medicine bundles—collections of objects believed to heal disease and to ward off ghosts, witches, foes, and destructive spirits. Many Native Americans kept these medicine bundles for personal, household, and community protection.

God or Gods

In many cases, a supreme being could be conceptualized in more than one way due to cultural differences. Among the Sioux, *wakan tanka* (great mystery) was pictured both as a single entity and as an assemblage of deities—including sun, winds, earth, and rock. In practice, many Native Americans interacted less with a supreme being than with various subordinate powers believed to be useful in particular circumstances. The Ojibwa believed in *kitche manitou* (great spirit) but developed personal relations with guardian spirits who appeared to individuals in visions and dreams.

The Hopi referred to *Masau* as their chief god, yet their ritual life focused on scores of kachinas, the spirits of ancestors, and the forces of the environment that made fertility possible. The Navajo venerated the sun and the changing woman, a figure who personified creative power, but there were also hundreds of monsters, holy people (creators and cultural heroes), and other forces to be evoked or exorcised in blessings and curative chants.[11] However, during the assimilation of Christianity, many of these practices could be compared to worshiping the one true God, but praying to angels and saints. In fact, within the various cultures, there were legends that align themselves quite easily to Christian interpretation.

In Blackfoot mythology, there is also a supernatural world, dominated above the natural world by the sun. The sun or the creator (*nah-too-si*, superpowered or holiness) created the earth and everything in the universe. Nah-too-si is sometimes personified by the mystical Napi or old man. Napi was sent by the Nah-too-si to teach us how to live a sinless life like He and his wife, *Ksah-koom-aukie,* earth woman.

Tirawa was the creator god and taught the Pawnee people tattooing, fire-building, hunting, agriculture, speech and clothing, religious rituals (including the use of tobacco), and sacrifices. He was associated with most natural phenomena, including stars and planets, wind, lightning, rain, and thunder. The lesser solar and lunar deities were Shakuru and Pah, respectively. (Could this not be easily assimilated to represent God, Jesus and the Holy Spirit?)

The Cherokee revered the great spirit, called the *Yowa* (a name so sacred that only a priest could say it; notice the similarity with the Jewish name for God for YHWH and the fact that it was "never pronounced"), who presided over all things and created Mother Earth. This would have made it very easy for them to accept the Christian view of God later on. The Cherokee believed that every aspect and thing had a spirit presiding over it but did not hold a belief in multiple gods. All figures identified as gods were simply greater beings in the Cherokee belief, whose names were so great there were no English words for them, and thus they were misinterpreted as the Indians' gods by Englishmen. However, the Cherokee paid direct respect to and worshipped only Yowa. They held that signs, visions, dreams, and powers were all gifts of the spirits and that their world was intertwined and presided over by the spirit world.

In yet another culture, it was believed that the *thunder beings* that lived close to the earth's surface could and did harm the people at times. The thunder beings were viewed as the most powerful of the servants of the Apportioner (creator spirit) and were revered in the first dance of the Green Corn Ceremony held each year. There were three thunders beings from the West in the ancient legends, a greater spirit and his two sons.

The legend from the Navajo tradition describes the story of creation: The Creator with the help of the holy people created the natural world. They created humans, birds, and all of the natural world was put in Hozjo. This *Hozjo* (harmony, balance, and peace) is dependent on interconnectedness. All of the natural world depends on another. The Navajo say they are glued together with respect, and together they work in harmony.

A Hopi Indian legend states that at the beginning of this cycle of time, long ago, the Great Spirit came down and He made an appearance and He gathered the peoples of this earth together they say on an island which is now beneath the water and He said to the human beings, "*I'm going to send you to four directions and over time I'm going to change you to four colors, but I'm going to give you some teachings and you will call these the Original Teachings and when you come back together with each other you will share these so that you can live and have peace on earth, and a great civilization will come about.*" And he said, "During the cycle of time I'm going to give each of you two stone tablets. When I give you those stone tablets, don't cast those upon the ground. If any of the brothers and sisters of the four directions and the four colors cast their tablets on the ground, not only, will human beings have a hard time, but almost the earth itself will die."[12] Members of The First Nation Church in the fullness of their Christian teachings believe that the Creator (God) is the one and only eternal and self-existent one. They believe that the Creator (God) exists as the three-in-one (Trinity) known as the Father, the Son, Christ Jesus, and the Holy Spirit. They believe that all people need to actively seek and pursue, striving to maintain, a close personal relationship with the Creator (God) through His Son, Jesus Christ and by the power of the Holy Spirit.

Christ

In 1969, the elders of Dhyani Ywahoo's Cherokee group decided to release teachings that have been kept in secret since the conquest. Through books, lectures, and workshops, Dhyani Ywahoo is disseminating that knowledge. She claims that her own Ywahoo lineage was founded by a legendary prophet called the *Pale One*, who rekindled the sacred fires throughout the Americas. She says,

"The Pale One is a cyclically incarnating being. He comes when the people have forgotten their sacred ways, bringing reminders of the Law, recalling all to right relationship. He is expected soon again, and he may be alive even now. It is good."

Hopi prophecies speak of the return of *Pahana*, their true white brother, who left them in ancient times, promising to return. They wear their hair in bangs to form a window, they say, by which to see their elder brother when He returns. It is also an identifying mark for the elder brother to recognize them.

Basic Worship Service

Rituals may vary within tribes and from chapter to chapter. In the last decade of the nineteenth century, Quanah Parker developed a major ritual for the modern religion as it spread among his tribesmen. Ministers of the Native American Church, called *road men*, officiate at prayer meetings, aided by other officials, firemen, drummers, and others. Services of the Native American Church also accompany weddings, funerals, thanksgivings, and healings.

Singing to the accompaniment of a gourd rattle and small drum occupies about 60 percent of the Church's devotional ritual. Singing is often in the local "Native American language, but English phrases like 'Jesus only' and 'He's the Savior' are likely to erupt. Worshipers sing, drum, pray, meditate, and consume Peyote during all-night meetings. Most meetings are held to mark a particular event such as a birthday, healing, baptism, marriage, or funerals"[13] by offering prayer, thanksgiving, praise, and appeals for spiritual guidance. At the heart of each ceremony is the attempt to understand the paradox of suffering amidst the joy of life. These ceremonies often blend indigenous and Christian beliefs and symbols.

Peyote is regarded as a gift from God. It is not eaten to induce visions. It heals and teaches righteousness. It is eaten, or consumed as a tea, according to a formal ritual. Reverently, it is passed clockwise around the circle of church members a number of times in the course of all-night prayer vigils. Peyotist beliefs, which combine Indian and Christian elements, vary from tribe to tribe. They involve worship of the Great Spirit, a supreme deity who deals with humans through various other spirits. In many tribes, Peyote is personified as Peyote Spirit and is associated with Jesus. The rite often begins on Saturday evening and continues through the night. *The Peyote Road* is a way of life calling for brotherly love, family care, self-support through work, and avoidance of alcohol.

The Church has no professional, paid clergy. Members are free to interpret Bible passages according to their own understanding. Morality is basically Christian and stresses the need to abstain from alcohol and be faithful to one's spouse. Other prominent values include truthfulness, fulfilling one's family obligations, economic self-sufficiency, praying for the sick, and praying for peace.

Infant Baptism or Blessing

While the birth ceremonies vary within each culture, there are some similarities. Each marks the proper start of the child down the path of life. This introduction into the clan and the sacred rituals will result in a healthy, harmonious, and balanced life.

Initiation, Baptism, or Confirmation

The ceremonies involved were more like initiations into the tribe, and many are no longer practiced. *Vision Quest* was used for young boys before or at puberty. They are encouraged to enter into a period of fasting, meditation and physical challenge. He separates himself from the tribe and goes to a wilderness area. The goal is to receive a vision that will guide his development for the rest of his life. They also seek to acquire a guardian spirit who will be close and supportive for their lifetime. Girls are not usually eligible for such a quest.[14]

Marriage

It is their belief that love, not law, is the basis and the foundation of marriage. They teach that no government should be allowed to legislate for or against any person based upon their gender, race, sexual orientation, or religious belief. First Nation Church, its members and ministers, believe that marriage is a covenant between two adults and their God, based upon their love for one another. They believe that love for each other, for nature and for all things created by God, materializes from the heart, not from legislative bodies. There are many old traditions that are sometimes incorporated into a more modern ceremony. One tribe, the Cheyenne, forbid the new husband from having any contact with his mother-in-law or his wife's sisters.

Death and Afterlife

In general, native religions have no single belief about life after death. Some believe in reincarnation, with a person being reborn either as a human or animal after death. Others believe that humans return as ghosts, or that people go to another world. Others believe that nothing definitely can be known about one's fate after this life.[15] Combinations of belief are common. Most, however, believe that death is the beginning of a journey into the next world. There were various rituals performed to ensure the safe passage or comfort of the person on their journey. There is also a mingling of traditional and Christian customs when it comes to their beliefs.

Judgment and Salvation

It is difficult to find any documentation regarding their beliefs. But with the assimilation of Christianity, the beliefs could be along the same lines as those Christian faiths, but that is purely speculation.

Special Doctrine

<u>Sweat Lodge Ceremony:</u> The Sweat Lodge Ceremony is practiced by many First Nations people across North America. It is used for rituals of purification, for spiritual renewal and of healing, for education of the youth, and can be performed by itself or as a prelude to other ceremonies such as the Sun Dance. The site of the lodge is usually chosen with great care. A fire pit is dug in the center, where specially chosen rocks are heated. The builder then gathers supple saplings, which are bent to form a dome; amongst many First Nations, this dome represents the womb of Mother Earth. The saplings are covered with layers of blankets, and sometimes, canvas tarpaulins are placed over the blankets (in earlier times, furs and bark were used). The opening of the lodge usually faces east. Once the ceremony is ready to begin, one person will remain on the outside to look after the heated rocks and put them in the central pit during the ceremony.

The ceremony usually takes place in the late afternoon, and sometimes lasts until dawn of the next day. There are two styles; one where only heated rocks are used and another where water is poured on the rocks. Either will produce the desired effect of sweat. When the rocks are heated to the point where they are considered ready, the participants strip naked or to light undergarments. The host then enters the lodge on hands and knees; the others follow in the same manner and sit in a circle around the centre pit. Once all the participants are inside the lodge, the fire-tender begins to pass in the heated rocks, which are placed in the pit. Once a number of heated rocks are passed into the Lodge, the entry is closed and the host begins to pray. Participants can say prayers in their own way during this time. After some time, everybody leaves the lodge and then goes back in so as to prevent any health hazard of overheating. This process can be repeated as many as four times, depending on the needs of the participants. At the end of the ceremony, everyone wishes everyone else a good life. After the ceremony is over, a traditional feast is often held by the family of the host.

Pipe Ceremony: The pipe is very sacred to First Nations' people. In the past, it was used to open negotiations between different nations as a way for good talks to take place. You may recall the term "peace pipe." This ceremony was also regarded as the way by which participants would be truthful, respectful and abide by the decisions and agreements that were made during the meeting time. The participants sit in a circle with the pipe carrier. Amongst some First Nations, the men sit in an inner circle and the women sit in an outer circle; in others, all sit in one circle. The pipe carrier, who is the host of the ceremony, says prayers to seven cardinal points: the Four Directions; the Above or Spirit World; the Below or Mother Earth; and the Center or all living things. The pipe is then passed to the participants for them to either touch or smoke it. After this, the pipe carrier may speak a few words of gratitude about life and expectations; each participant is also invited to speak such words; and the ceremony is considered closed.

Smudging: Smudging is a sacred ceremony of most First Nations. Many First Nations people understand that there are negative forces which can cause harm: smudging is a method to protect oneself from these. Smudging should be done starting the burn at the tip of the plant. The plant should be used until about 5 cm, including the roots, are left; this part is to be returned to Mother Earth to assist in replenishing her. During the smudging, people through motions of their hands cover their body with the smoke; completion is indicated by turning the palms of the hands down. After each person has carefully smudged, the smoke is allowed to stop burning.

Sun Dance: The Sun Dance, also called Rain or Thirst Dance, is a sacred ceremony of First Nations peoples who live in the grasslands. It fulfilled many religious purposes: to give thanks to the Creator, to pray for the renewal of the people and earth, to promote health, etc. The host can use any one of the three names, depending upon the reason for doing the ceremony. This ceremony, which lasts from four to eight days, can take place from early spring to mid-summer. The participants usually begin with the Sweat lodge ceremony, and gather to celebrate the renewal of life, good growing seasons, a safe community, good health, and so on. The Sun Dance lodge is built in a circle with the entry facing east, signifying the coming of light. Prior to this, the host will have chosen the centre pole, and a selected group of males will bring the pole to the site where the ceremony is to be held. The pole is not allowed to touch the ground until it is placed standing in the centre of the lodge. At the top of it sits the Thunderbird nest, for it is the Sacred Thunderbird as represented by the mighty Eagle who is the messenger for prayers sent to the Great Mystery. The host and the participant dancers continue to dance in shifts for several days, while stepping to the beat of the drum and saying prayers which are carried to the Creator. This sacred ceremony is one method for traditional Plains Indians to reaffirm their belief in their sacred ways. During the actual dance, the participating dancers will always face the centre pole with their eyes on the Thunderbird nest; they will continue until dusk of the final day, dancing and saying prayers for the good of family, community, and Mother Earth. [16]

Rituals were meant not only to communicate with spiritual beings but also to pass down tribal traditions. One of the most common rituals among Native Americans was the recounting of myths, which contained a wealth of religious knowledge. Myths provided communities with a cosmogony, a story of how the world came to have its present form; a worldview, a picture of how the various aspects of the world are related to one another; and an ethos, a code of behavior for human beings.

Native American Humor

2000 BC—Here, eat this root

1000 AD—That root is heathen. Here, say this prayer.

1850 AD—That prayer is superstition. Here, drink this potion.

1940 AD—That potion is snake oil. Here, swallow this pill.

1985 AD—That pill is ineffective. Here, take this antibiotic.

2000 AD—That antibiotic doesn't work anymore. Here, eat this root.

Below is a Hopi Indian prophesy for you to ponder:

But there's going to come a time when the earth itself will rise up and purify itself and this will be announced. It will be announced by the speaking of more than 16 Great Ones on the West Coast of this land. And when the 16 Great Ones speak, the purification will have begun. There was five years ago when Mt. Saint Helens, one of the 16 great volcanoes on the West Coast of this land, "spoke." Four years and four days later, Mt. Saint Helens erupted the second time (May 1980)... That was our grace period. We could have still done something really good. But now things are going to speed up. Now things are going to really happen fast. Time is going to go so fast. The more we share the Message, the more we will cushion the Third Shaking of the Earth (first and second "shakings" were WW I and WW II), and the easier it will be on ourselves and others. We are now within the purification of all things. Non-Natives call this the "Apocalypse." The Native elders call this the "Purification." But don't despair. It sounds terrible, but we will survive it. We will live through it. I don't think there's anyone chosen to live through it, but some people will. So, in closing I would like...

to call on each and every person, regardless of who you are, young or old, Native or non-Native, to arise now, and to awake, to embrace this time, to learn everything you can about the Teachings and the Writings, to arise and awake and go forth, all the peoples of the earth. Peoples everywhere are now receptive to the Message. This year is the year when that is really going to start, I believe, myself. Arise and awake. There are people out there waiting to hear, waiting to hear...[17]

Notes

Notes

Shamanism

History

The term Shamanism comes from the Manchu-Tungus word *šaman*. The noun is formed from the verb ša- "to know"; thus, a Shaman is literally "one who knows." The Shamans recorded in history have included women, men, and transgender individuals of every age from middle childhood onward. Further ethnologic investigations show that the true origin for the word Shaman can be traced from the Sanskrit initially, then through Chinese-Buddhist mediation "indicating a much deeper but now overlooked connection between early Buddhism and Shamanism generally. In Pali it is *schamana*, in Sanskrit *sramana* translated to something like "Buddhist monk, ascetic." The intermediate Chinese term is *scha-men*.[1]

Cultural anthropologists have in the past defined Shamanism as an initial stage of the institutionalized religious systems. In reality, shamanism was actually the beginning steps toward human spiritual development. Shamanistic practices are sometimes claimed to predate all organized religions, dating back to the paleolithic (two million BC) and certainly to the neolithic (9500 BC) period. Shamanism in Scandinavia may be represented in rock art dating to the neolithic era and was practiced throughout the Iron Age by the various Teutonic tribes and the Fino-Baltic peoples. There are currently no historically verifiable accounts that compare the practices of the druids of Britain to shamanistic practices, but the connection has been speculated.

Archaeological evidence does exist for Mesolithic Shamanism. In November 2008, researchers announced the discovery of a 12,000-year-old site in Israel that they regard as one of the earliest known Shaman burial sites. The elderly woman had been arranged on her side, with her legs apart and folded inward at the knee. Ten large stones were placed on the head, pelvis and arms. Among her unusual grave goods were 50 complete tortoise shells, a human foot, and certain body parts from animals such as a cow tail and eagle wings. Other animal remains came from a boar, leopard, and two martens.

"It seems that the woman …was perceived as being in a close relationship with these animal spirits," researchers noted. The grave was one of at least 28 at the site, located in a cave in lower Galilee and belonging to the Natufian culture, but is said to be unlike any other among the Natufians or in the Paleolithic period.[2]

Most archeologists agreed that Shamanism originated with hunter-gatherers, gradually transforming into herding and farming societies after the origins of agriculture. Shamanism also seems to have gone hand in hand with animism, a belief system in which the world is home to a plethora of spirit-beings that may help or hinder human endeavors.

"In the remote part of an ancient mountain range, high above the tree line, a group of modern day hikers stumbled across the body of a man frozen to death in the snow, fully dressed in clothes of a tribal nature, his body nearly intact and almost perfectly preserved. Incredibly, tests showed the man had been frozen 5,000 years before, sometime between 3350-3140 BC. After a rather intensive investigation over a period of years by a team of scientific experts from a variety of fields, it was concluded that the man appeared to have been a Shaman, presumably dying of exposure when caught out in the open during a mystical retreat on the side of the treacherous mountain. Several associated facts presented themselves for such speculation. Like many Shamans from many cultures the body was tattooed; his weapons, consisting of a roughly-hewn bow made of yew, several unfinished arrows, and an all wood dagger, resembled "dummy weapons" associated with Shamans in other cultures; he carried a medicine bag containing, among other things, a leather thong on which was threaded two pieces of a common birch fungus Piptoporus betulinus which contains polyporic acid C, an effective antibody, especially against stomach micro-bacteria, which would indicate, if not a specific knowledge of herbs and natural ingredients, at least a general acceptance of their use. A similar fungus, also closely associated with the birch, Amanita muscaria, is not only hallucinogenic but has been used by various Shamans' cultures as an aid to "ecstasy" before the dawn of history. It is possible that, if not authentically hallucinogenic, the ones the frozen iceman carried, could at least have been believed to be so; he also carried with him, and unusually so, a copper-headed axe. Last, an item not discussed at any length in the numerous reports on the frozen man was a net he carried, an object not typically found in hunting as much as used to trap spirits and seen in various forms today as a "dream catcher." Taken together, the fact that he carried only what he needed and not a variety for wider Shamanistic use, again underscores his mountain sojourn as having a more "mystical retreat" aspect to it. The body was well above known trails, high in the mountains above the 10,400 foot level, and alone it seems, suggesting the possibility that he had traveled there to be closer to the gods."[3]

Aspects of Shamanism are encountered in later, organized religions, generally in their mystic and symbolic practices. Greek Paganism was influenced by Shamanism, as reflected in the stories of Tantalus, Prometheus, Medea, and Calypso among others, as well as in the Eleusinian Mysteries…Some of the shamanic practices of the Greek religion were later adopted into the Roman religion.

Some scholars suggest similarities between Christianity and Shamanism. One such comparison includes the transubstantiation of bread and wine in the Catholic religion. There have also been several speculative articles, suggesting that Moses was in fact a Shaman, with the help of *ayahuasca*, a psychoactive potion made from plants that are found in the Middle East and was commonly used at that time.

The shamanic practices of many cultures were marginalized with the spread of Christianity. Shamanism in Europe can be traced most recently through Celtic and Germanic cultures, but unfortunately, any remnant remains of Shamanism that was not eliminated by the annihilation of the early tribes was successfully stamped out many years later by the Inquisition.

In Europe, starting around 400 AD, the Christian Church was instrumental in the collapse of the Greek and Roman religions. Temples were systematically destroyed and key ceremonies were outlawed or appropriated. Beginning with the Middle Ages and continuing into the Renaissance, remnants of European Shamanism were wiped out by campaigns against so-called "witches." These campaigns were often orchestrated by the Catholic Inquisition.

In Scandinavia, Shamans were forbidden, and many were burned at the stake during the seventheenth century. The repression of Shamanism continued as Christian influence spread with Spanish colonization. In the Caribbean, and Central and South America, Catholic priests followed in the footsteps of the Conquistadors and were instrumental in the destruction of the local traditions, denouncing practitioners as 'devil worshippers' and having them executed.[4]

In North America, with the arrival of foreign European settlers and colonial administration, the practice of Shamanism was discouraged. During the late nineteenth century, a mass shamanistic-type belief became popular amongst many tribes of Native Americans' First Nations, also known as ghost dance. The belief was that through the ghost dance, a great flood would come, and all white men would die in it. This form of Shamanism was brutally suppressed by the United States government's military.

Thousands of surviving Native American youngsters from many cultures were sent into Indian boarding schools to destroy any tribal, shamanistic or totemistic remnants from their mind-sets. Though many Native American cultures have traditional healers, ritualists, singers, mystics, lore-keepers, and medicine people, none of them ever used, or currently use, the term Shaman to describe these religious leaders. Rather, like other indigenous cultures the world over, their spiritual functionaries are described by words in their own languages and, in many cases, are not taught to outsiders.

When the People's Republic of China was formed in 1949 and the border with Russian Siberia was formally sealed, many nomadic Tungus groups that practiced Shamanism were confined in Manchuria and Inner Mongolia. These include the Ewenki and the Oroqen. The last Shaman of the Oroqen, Chuonnasuan (Meng Jin Fu), died in October 2000. In many other cases, Shamanism was in decline even at the beginning of twentieth century. In North America, the English Puritans conducted periodic campaigns against individuals perceived as witches. As recently as the 1970s, historic petroglyphs were being defaced by missionaries in the Amazon. A similarly destructive story can be told of the encounter between Buddhists and Shamans in Mongolia. "It has been postulated that modern state campaigns against the use of entheogenic substances are the offshoot of previous religious campaigns against Shamanism."⁵ More recently, attacks on shamanic practitioners have been carried out at the hands of Christian missionaries to third-world countries and by the US Drug Enforcement Administration (DEA) here in the United States based on their use of hallucinogenics.

In many areas, former Shamans ceased to fill the functions in the community they used to, as they felt mocked by their own community, or regarded their own past as a deprecated thing, sometimes even unwilling to talk about it. Moreover, besides personal communications of former Shamans, even some folklore texts narrate directly about a deterioration process. For example, a Buryat epic text details the wonderful deeds of the ancient "first Shaman" Kara-Gürgän: he could even compete with God, create life, and steal back the soul of the sick from God without his consent. A subsequent text laments that Shamans of older times were stronger, possessing capabilities like omnividence, fortune-telling even for decades in the future, moving as fast as bullet; the texts contrast them to the recent heartless, unknowing, greedy Shamans.⁶

In the most affected areas, shamanistic practices ceased to exist when authentic Shamans died and their personal experiences were lost. There are former Shaman apprentices unable to complete the learning among some Greenlandic Eskimo peoples. Variants of Shamanism among Eskimo peoples were once a widespread (and very diverse) phenomenon, but today are rarely practiced, and they were already in the decline among many groups even in the times when the first major ethnological researches were done (e.g., among Polar Eskimos). At the end of nineteenth century, Sagloq died—the last Shaman who was believed to be able to travel to the sky and under the sea.

In many cultures, the entire traditional belief system has become endangered (often together with a partial or total language shift), the other people of the community remembering the associated beliefs and practices (or the language at all) became old or died; many folklore memories, songs and texts went forgotten—this threatens even such peoples which could preserve their isolation until the middle of the twentieth century, like the Nganasan ...The isolated location of Nganasan people allowed Shamanism to be a living phenomenon among them even in the beginning of twentieth century, the last notable Nganasan Shaman's séances were recorded on film in the 1970s.

After exemplifying the general decline even in the most remote areas, let us mention that there are some revitalization or tradition-preserving efforts as a response, sometimes led by authentic former Shamans. "Attempts are being made among Sakha people and Tuvans to preserve and revitalize Shamanism; some former authentic Shamans have begun to practice again, and young apprentices are being educated in an organized way."[7]

Today, Shamanism, once possibly universal, survives primarily among indigenous peoples. However, Shamanism is also used more generally to describe indigenous groups in which roles such as healer, religious leader, counselor, and councilor (member of local government/ leadership) are combined. In this sense, Shamans are particularly common among other Arctic peoples, Australian Aborigines, and those African groups, such as the San, that retained their traditional cultures well into the twentieth century. This is especially true in South America, where mestizo Shamanism is widespread.

Shamanic practice continues today in the tundras, jungles, deserts, and other rural areas, and also in cities, towns, suburbs, and shantytowns all over the world. Traces of Shamanism may be found among peoples who have been converted to other religions, as in the Fino-Ugric peoples who became Christians, Turkic peoples in Central Asia and Asia Minor who became Muslim, and Mongols who became Buddhists. Among groups that have converted to Christianity, Islam, or another world religion, former shamanistic practices may be revealed through an analysis of folklore and folk beliefs.

There is a growing revival of interest in Shamanism in many of the western countries. There are currently an indigenous tribal people inhabiting Mexico. The Mazatec, the tribe occupying the mountain region of north-east Oaxaca, is estimated to number from 18,000 to 20,000. Huantla, their chief town, with its dependent villages, has a population of about 7,000. The Mazatec retain most of their ancient beliefs and many of their ceremonies. By tolerance of the Mexican Government they maintained their tribal autonomy under their hereditary chiefs up to 1857, the last of whom, a descendant of their ancient kings, died in 1869. Their native cult is still kept and based around animal worship; the snake, panther, alligator, and eagle being most venerated. Maria Sabina the first contemporary Mexican *curandera* (healer), defined in New Age parlance as a native Shaman, is probably the most famous of the Mazatecs.[8]

American youth began seeking out Sabina and the "holy children" as early as 1962, and in the years that followed, thousands of counterculture mushroom seekers, scientists, and others arrived in the Sierra Mazateca, and many saw her. By 1967, more than seventy people from the United States, Canada, and Western Europe were renting cabins in neighboring villages. Many of them went there directly after reading the May 13, 1957, *Life Magazine* article written by R. Gordon Wasson about his experiences.[9]

The New Age movement has imported some ideas from Shamanism in general and core Shamanism in particular, as well as beliefs and practices from Eastern religions and Native American cultures. As with other such appropriations, the original practitioners of these traditions frequently condemn New Age use as misunderstood, sensationalized, or superficially understood and/or applied.[10] "At the same time there is an endeavor in occult and esoteric circles to re-invent Shamanism in a modern form, drawing from core Shamanism, various indigenous forms of Shamanism and chaos magic."[11]

Sometimes people from western cultures claim to be Shamans. Most commonly, they will claim Cherokee or Sioux ancestry because of all the western movies, especially *Dances with Wolves*. The risk for studying under such people varies from simply losing money to even death in an ill-fated sweat lodge as happened in Arizona in 2009.

This is considered offensive by many indigenous medicine men, who view these New Age western "Shamans" as hucksters out for money or affirmation of self. Many shamanistic cultures feel there is a danger that their voices will be drowned out by self-styled "Shamans"; citing, for example, the fact that Lynn Andrews has sold more books than all Native American authors put together.[12]

Moreover, according to Richard L. Allen, research and policy analyst for the Cherokee Nation, they are overwhelmed with fraudulent Shamans. In fact, there is no Cherokee word for Shaman or medicine man. Besides tradition-preserving efforts, there are also neoshamanistic movements; these may differ from many traditional shamanistic practice and beliefs in several points.[13] With all the various types and versions of Shamanism today,*Adherents.com* estimates there are 12 million people involved in Shamanism at this time, however, another site suggests that there may be as many as 230 million. As with all religions, the term involvement represents different things to different people.

God or Gods

God has created us with a free will to choose Him or to succumb to evil.

<u>Great Shaman/Celestial Shaman</u>: This numinous figure is found in various shamanic traditions, particularly in Siberia and Central Asia. The great or celestial Shaman is the highest source of shamanic initiation.

<u>The Polestar</u>: In Siberian shamanic tradition, the North Star is sometimes called the peg in the sky or the Nail of Heaven. It is the visible point in the sky where the axis mundi connects the earth with the heavens. It may also represent the great or celestial Shaman.

<u>Cosmic pillar/Universal Tree</u>: A symbolic representation of spirit as the axis mundi or center of the world. With its roots deep in the earth, and its uppermost branches reaching out into the heights of the heavens, the World Tree symbolizes the presence and flow of spirit upon which Shamans and other esoteric practitioners are said to ascend and descend in their journeys.

<u>The Sacred River</u>: Another representation of spirit, the river may be both seen and heard. It represents the flow and presence of spirit in the varied realms of the heavens, the earth, and the underworld.

Christ

Not applicable.

Basic Doctrine

The term Shaman wears a halo of mystery and can evoke diverse and even contradictory realities. While much of the focus of shamanic studies has been on the shamanic complexes of North and Central Asia, shamanism is a universal phenomenon not confined to any particular region or culture. In contemporary historical or traditional shamanic practice, the Shaman may at times fill the role of priest, magician, physician, or healer.

The Shaman lives at the edge of reality as most people would recognize it and, most commonly, at the edge of society itself. Few indeed have the stamina to venture into these realms and endure the outer hardships and personal crises that have been reported by or observed of many Shamans.

A common experience of "the call" to Shamanism is a psychic or spiritual crisis, which often accompanies a physical or even a medical crisis, and is cured by the Shaman him or herself... The Shaman is often marked by eccentric behavior such as periods of melancholy, solitude, visions, singing in his or her sleep, etc. The inability of the traditional remedies to cure the condition of the Shamanic candidate and the eventual self cure by the new Shaman is a significant episode in development of the Shaman. The underlying significant aspect of this experience, when it is present, is the ability of the Shaman to manage and resolve periods of distress.[14] (see Initiation section)

Because there is a belief that the Shaman communicates with the spirits, they are treated with great respect and authority in their communities. Generally, they do not get involved in menial work; therefore, the Shaman must be supported by the community, which considers his gifts and skills necessary.

Generally, the Shaman was never contradicted nor was any unfavorable opinion expressed about him behind his back. Such an economic and social position resulted, in some instances, in giving the Shaman political power as well. During the sixteenth through the eighteenth centuries, it was not unusual to see a Shaman being the leader of the clan, and many times, the Shaman led the fight in a war. The ruler of one domain among the Vadeyev Samoyed in northern Siberia was a Shaman as well as the reigning prince.[15]

Shamans have been credited with the ability to control the weather, divination, the interpretation of dreams, astral projection, and traveling to upper and lower worlds. Shamanistic traditions have existed throughout the world since prehistoric times. Shamanism is based on the premise that the visible world is pervaded by invisible forces or spirits that affect the lives of the living...Shamans are not, however, organized into full-time ritual or spiritual associations, as are priests.

Each Shaman acts on his/her own gifts and powers. In engaging in this work, the Shaman exposes himself to significant personal risk from the spirit world, from any enemy Shamans, as well as from the means employed to alter his/her state of consciousness. Certain of the plant materials used can kill, and the out-of-body journey itself can lead to nonreturning and physical death.[16] Spells of protection are common, and the use of more dangerous plants is usually very highly ritualized.

Systems of religious and spiritual practice of Shamans become traditions over time, and are passed on from Shaman teacher to Shaman apprentice. These usually contain the a s pecialized k nowledge a nd understanding of the lore of the community being served; recognizing the presence of spirit and of natural and elemental forces, guiding, helping, ancestor and teaching spirits; blessings, charms, wards and ceremonies; methods of divination; the means for creating or obtaining the clothing and equipment necessary for the performance of Shamanic responsibilities, initiatory rites; and techniques of shamanic flight and access to other realms and states of consciousness. In addition, there are some aspects of these traditions which may also be learned in dreams or while in trance state or from direct observation of nature and of life in the community. In some instances, a community may be without a Shaman to pass on these traditions. When this occurs, and direct instruction by experienced Shamans is not possible, the new Shaman must re-acquire the continuity of the shamanic tradition from dreams, inner journeys and observation as the primary sources of his or her training. (*soc.religion.Shamanism FAQ* by Dean Edwards)[17]

There may be found among some traditional cultures persons who appear to practice Shamanism. But similar traits does not necessarily indicate that a culture is shamanistic, as the central figures in these cultures—sorcerers, medicine men, or healers—have attained their position through deliberate study and the application of knowledge, not through the involuntary call that a Shaman has. Although they perform ceremonies, hold positions of authority, and possess magical abilities, they can be entirely different from that of the Shaman. Some examples below are:

Medium vs. Shaman: Both affirm they have a relationship with the spirits. In both, there is a change in the state of consciousness, a modification that can be searched for voluntarily by both. In the Shaman's case, the control of the relationship with the spirits is generally more energetic while the medium acts in a more passive way. Once done, the Shaman is capable of remembering it. The medium doesn't necessarily remember what he did or what happened during the trance.

Healer vs. Shaman: The healer shows himself as a person capable of treating diseases that are particularly feared by people and for which medicine still does not own the most efficient therapeutic methods. The healer's activity can be varied and unusual. He is found more commonly in rural than in urban surroundings. The Shaman can be considered a type of healer, but not all healers are Shamans.

Wizard vs. Shaman: They share the following attributes, they both produce a feeling of the extraordinary, break with life routines, and intervene over space and time. Shamans are the physical and spiritual healers of aboriginal cultures (the original and indigenous people of any certain region) over the entire world. Wizards are their mirror image in today's cultural traditions. The wizard we know today can arouse the same surprise as the Shaman, and perhaps, he can trace his origin back. However, he lacks the healing projection essential to Shamanism.

Outside of academic circles a growing number of people have begun to make serious inquiries into ancient shamanic techniques for entering into altered states of consciousness...These methods for exploring the inner landscape are being investigated by a wide range of people. Some are academics, some come from traditional societies and others are modern practitioners of non-traditional Shamanism or neo-Shamanism. Along with these techniques, the NDE or "near-death-experience" has played a significant role in shamanic practice and initiation for millennia. There is extensive documentation of this in ethnographic studies of traditional Shamanism. With this renewed interest in these older traditions these Shamanic methods of working with dreams and being conscious and awake while dreaming are receiving increased attention.[18]

Guardian Spirit or Spirit Guide: A spirit which protects, instructs or assists a Shaman...while journeying, carrying out shamanic responsibilities or training. Encounters with these numinous beings may occur in trance, dreams, and visions or in observing and interpreting the events and circumstances of daily life...Spirit guides are usually attached to particular individuals on a personal basis. Sometimes, a spirit guide may be an ancestor or relative.

Power Animal: A spirit perceived as taking an animal form which instructs, guides and protects an individual or Shaman and usually becomes closely identified with the individual concerned. Unlike the clan or group totem, this is a distinctly personal relationship with an individual or collective animal spirit-being. The presence of a Power Animal is thus unique to an individual, rather than being shared by a group, family or clan. These spirit beings are prominent in many shamanic traditions. The first item of business for a potential Shaman is to learn to travel in the other worlds, then to discover his power animal. That knowledge is necessary in order to start the long process of learning. Power animals are usually a reflection of your deepest self and also represent qualities that you need in this world, but which are often hidden or obscured. "Michael Harner in '*The Way of the Shaman*,' defines a Power Animal as: "a spirit being that not only protects and serves the Shaman, but also becomes another identity or alter ego for him."[19]

Basic Worship Service

Dress and equipment: A Shaman wears regalia, some part of which usually imitates an animal—most often a deer, a bird, or a bear. It may include a headdress made of antlers or a band into which feathers of birds have been pierced. The footwear is also symbolic—iron deer hooves, birds' claws, or bears' paws. An important device of the Shaman is the drum, which always has only one membrane. During the trance brought on by the sound of the drum, the spirits move to the Shaman—into him or into the drum—or the soul of the Shaman travels to the realm of the spirits. The sound of his drum excites not only the Shaman but also his audience. An integral characteristic of this drama is that those who are present are not mere objective spectators but rather faithful believers, and their belief enables the Shaman to achieve results, as in healing physical or mental illnesses.

Drama and Dance: Shamanic symbolism is presented through dramatic enactment and dance. The Shaman, garbed in regalia, lifts his voice in song to the spirits. This song is improvised but contains certain obligatory images and similes, dialogue, and refrains. The performance always takes place in the evening. The theatre is a conical tent or a yurt; the stage is the space around the fire where the spirits re invoked. The audience consists of the invited members of the clan, awaiting the spirits in awe. [20] Just like shamanism itself, music and songs related to it in various cultures are diverse. In some cultures, some songs related to Shamanism intend to imitate natural sounds. Due to diversities, Shamans may have differing kinds of paraphernalia as well, such as feathers, rattles, gongs, or clap sticks. In order for Shamans to do their work, they must effect, firstly, a change of consciousness in themselves.

The Shaman enters into an ecstatic trance, either autohypnotically or through the use of entheogens, during which time, they are said to be in contact with the spirit world or enter a separate reality. Some of the methods for affecting this consciousness shift are fasting, sweat lodges, and the use of power plants with hallucinogenic capabilities.

Shamanic Ecstasy: From the Greek *ekstasis*, ecstasy literally means "to be placed outside." This is a state of exaltation in which a person stands outside of, or transcends, his or herself.

These experiences may occur in either the dream state or the awakened state, or both. In order to journey to the other dimensions of existence, a Shaman induces an altered state of consciousness in himself similar to a state of self-hypnosis. While in this Shamanic trance he is in complete control; able to take his consciousness and subtle bodies into nonphysical reality where he visits the heavens and hells of existence, communicates with and controls spirits, gains information, retrieves souls, and makes subtle changes in reality which may affect the physical world. (Joseph Bearwalker Wilson, 1978)[21]

Shamanic Healing: Healing via Shamanic methods can include journeying, working with spirit helpers, extraction, soul retrieval, etc. Shamanism can be used to perform spiritual/psychological and sometimes physical healing on a person...Shamanic healing usually involves...a series of journeys to determine what forms of healing are necessary; a journey to contact the spirit resources necessary for the healing, and a ritual to perform/honor the healing. Note that Shamanic healing may not cure physical or psychological illness, but it may help gain psychic energy that will allow one better to handle illness. Shamanic healing therefore is best used in conjunction with other treatments, not as a substitute for them.

Soul Retrieval: "A part of one's life essence can leave one's body during a trauma of short or long duration." Such loss of life force may result in physical or psychic illness or distress. The retrieval of lost or stolen life essence or psychic life force of an individual can be accomplished by a Shaman or shamanic counselor. It involves a shamanic healing ritual whereby "a Shaman journeys on behalf of someone who may have experienced soul loss. The Shaman retrieves the life essence that was lost and returns it to the person."[22]

Psychopomp: The shaman will sometimes act as a spirit or individual or "divine entity which accompanies the soul of the recently deceased to a place in another world...The practice is based on the belief that sometimes if a person dies suddenly or dies in state of confusion or senility, the soul does not realize that it has been separated from the body and needs to move on."[23]

Marriage

There is wide variation regarding marriage within Shamanism. If a marriage is allowed, to marry the Shaman would be highly honored. Because of the difficult life leading up to the calling, many do not marry, or some will have a spirit spouse. The spirit spouse of dreams is one of the most widespread elements of Shamanism, distributed through all continents and at all cultural levels. The spirit spouse visits in dreams. The person dreaming will habitually dream of having, in the dream, a spouse accounted as divine. That spouse able to assist in waking-world activities by controlling categories of events, which may in the waking-world impinge on the life of the dreamer.

Gender and Sexuality: In some societies, Shamans exhibit a two-spirit identity, assuming the dress and attributes, role or function of the opposite sex, gender fluidity, and/or same-sex sexual orientation from a young age. This may include a man taking on the role of a wife in an otherwise ordinary marriage. Indeed, these two-spirited Shamans were so widespread as to suggest a very ancient origin of the practice. Such two-spirit Shamans are thought to be especially powerful and Shamanism so important to ancestral populations that it may have contributed to the maintenance of genes for transgendered individuals in breeding populations over evolutionary time through the mechanism of kin selection. They are highly respected and sought out in their tribes as they will bring high status to their mates. Duality and bisexuality are also found in the Shamans of the Dagara people of Burkina Faso (Africa).[24]

Infant Baptism or Blessing

Not applicable. The Shaman's assistance is necessary at the three great life passages: birth, marriage, and death. If a woman has not borne a child, for instance, then, according to the belief of the Nanai, in the Amur region of northeastern Asia, the Shaman ascends to heaven and sends her an embryo soul from the tree of embryos. Among the Buryat, the Shaman performs libations after birth to keep the infant from crying and to help it develop more quickly.

Initiation, Baptism, or Confirmation

Tradition holds that a Shaman is chosen by the spirits, not by the people. Shamanism begins with an inner calling, which is actually the call of the spirit who has chosen the Shaman and who oppresses them until they accept this vocation. Known as *Shaman illness*, the spirits' torments will anguish them for months, and in some cases, for years—that is, for as long as the human avoids the inevitability of their calling. *"Had I not become Shaman, I would have died,"* said a Nivkh (southeastern Siberia).[25]

A Shaman may be initiated via a serious illness, by being struck by lightning, or by a near-death experience, and there usually is a set of cultural imagery expected to be experienced during Shamanic initiation regardless of method. Such imagery often includes being transported to the spirit world and interacting with beings inhabiting it, meeting a spiritual guide, being devoured by some being and emerging transformed, and/or being "dismantled" and "reassembled" again, often with implanted amulets such as magical crystals. The imagery generally speaks of transformation and granting powers or of traveling to the other world and making useful contacts with spirits there. [26]

Dream and trance initiations and experiences with spirits are also common experiences of those being called to become a Shaman. Sometimes psychic distress may be experienced as sudden and significant mood swings or periods of lengthy melancholy, loss of affect, incoherency, or even loss of consciousness. When signs of shamanic tendencies are recognized by other shamans or members of the Shaman's family, clan, or community, the individual who appears to have been called may be advised to seek training and begin to gather the necessary equipment of a Shaman, which is appropriate to that community and cultural milieu. Some may choose to avoid this call to become a Shaman; others may deliberately seek it out.

Death and Afterlife

Infinity is everything that surrounds us: the spirit, the dark sea of awareness. It is something that exists out there and rules our lives (Castaneda, The Active Side of Infinity).

Of course, the infinity of which Castaneda speaks is synonymous with the emptiness referred to in ancient texts as *sunyata* , and it is not just out there, as Castaneda implies. Sunyata is the whole, encompassing, encompassed, and the encompassing.

Judgment and Salvation

In shaman-based communities, they are taught that justice is not postponed. A perfect equity adjusts its balance in all parts of life. *Oichusoi Dios aei enpiptousi* ,—The dice of God are always loaded. The world looks like a multiplication-table, or a mathematical equation, which, turn it how you will, balances itself...Every secret is told, every crime is punished, every virtue rewarded, every wrong redressed, in silence and certainty. The more pure and spiritually developed a person is (especially if they are actively working towards real spiritual advancement) the more attention they will attract from the negatives to pull them down. In other words, the potential of any aspirant generates their level of negative opposition, plus their level of positive assistance, as set by Karmic Law. This is the natural way of things, and is part of the reason why real long-term spiritual development is so difficult. And this is also why those that achieve any significant level of spiritual/psychic development usually live fairly difficult lives, or have a painful past.[27]

Special Doctrine

Shamans claim to control the weather, know the future, and be able to expose the perpetrators of thefts, and so on. A Shaman enjoys considerable prestige and authority as a healer, as the intermediary between humans and the gods or spirits, and, in certain regions, as the guide of souls of the dead to their new abode. They also guarantee that ritual observances are properly conducted, defend the tribe against evil spirits and sorcery, point out places for fruitful hunting and fishing, increase wildlife, and ease childbirth.

South American Shamans can also fill the role of sorcerer; they can, for example, become animals and drink the blood of their enemies. It is probable that a certain form of Shamanism was infused on the two American continents with the first waves of immigrants from Asia. Later contacts between Northern Asia and North America made Asian influence possible well after the penetration of the first immigrants.

The local cultures show great diversity. The myths concerning the role of Shaman had several variants, and also the name of their protagonists varied from culture to culture. Also the soul conceptions (e.g., the details of the soul dualism showed great variability, ranging from guardianship to a kind of reincarnation). Concepts of spirits or other beings had also many variants. There are a large number of cultures that still exhibit some form of Shamanism today.

The largest concentration of these cultures a re located i n some Eskimo cultures, from Eastern Siberia through Alaska and Northern Canada to Greenland; the Mayan people of Guatemala, Belize, and Southern Mexico; cultures in Argentina, Brazil, Panama, Ecuador, and Peru. There are also cultures in central Asia, Nepal, and Northern India; in Vietnam, and on the Ryukyu Islands (Okinawa, Japan); Australia, New Guinea, Borneo, and last but not least, Africa.

In the Caribbean are the most powerful, the most dreaded, and the most feared Shaman called the *Obeah*—a once very powerful and celebrated secret religious order emanating from a remote age that has long since been watered down, with the less powerful versions of Obeah incorporating various modifications of occult spellcraft as once practiced mostly by tribal people from West Africa. It is a dying breed shrouded in secrecy, with the most powerful versions known and practiced only by a select few.

One theologian suggests that despite really astonishing similarities, there is no unity in Shamanism. The v arious f ragmented s hamanistic practices and beliefs coexist with other beliefs everywhere. There is no record of pure shamanistic societies.

Different Forms of Shamanism

Historical Shamanism: Traditional native systems and traditions of Shamans and Shamanism, which existed in the past. Historical Shamanism is believed to extend back many millennia and to be among the oldest human religious and spiritual practices.

Nontraditional Shamanism: "Often at least loosely based on one or more traditional shamanic systems, non-traditional Shamanism is usually a hybrid of ecstatic techniques of shamanic journeying and other aspects of contemporary psychological, religious and spirituality." Nontraditional practitioner focuses on utilizing the ancient techniques of the Shaman in ways appropriate to a modern audience.

Neo-Shamanism (a.k.a. Core Shamanism): A movement which has grown out of a combination of environmentalism, popular anthropology and a growing desire for more open non-institutionalized forms of religion and spirituality. Since the early 1970s it has been gaining adherents in many western and more recently in former communist countries. Each individual is believed capable of becoming their own Shaman usually under the instruction of a shamanic instructor or counselor. These new shamanic practices, termed *"neo-Shamanism"* by Piers Vitebsky, (PhD, anthropologist and head of the Scott Polar Research Institute, University of Cambridge, England), in his book, *"The Shaman,"* (1995), have been influenced by popularization of certain aspects of Native American religious practices including spirit helpers and power animals.[28]

"Among the leading instructors in the neo-Shamanic movements are Michael Harner and Kenneth Meadows, authors of various books and who offer workshops and courses of study. Michael Harner is an anthropologist and a founder of *The Foundation for Shamanic Studies.*"[29]

Harner synthesized shamanic beliefs and practices from all over the world into a system now known as *"Core* Shamanism." It does not hold a fixed belief system, but focuses on the practice of trance travel and may, on an individual basis, integrate indigenous Shamanism, the teachings of Carlos Castaneda (a Peruvian-born American anthropologist who wrote a series of books that describe his training in Shamanism) and other spiritualities. Those who practice core Shamanism do not usually refer to themselves as Shamans, preferring "Shamanic practitioner" out of respect for indigenous peoples.

Harner has faced much criticism for implying that pieces of diverse religions can be taken out of context to form some sort of universal shamanic tradition.

Notes

Notes

Vodoun
(Commonly Known as Voodoo)

History

Although its essence may go back six thousand years in Africa, today's Vodoun can be directly traced to the West African Yoruba people who lived in eighteenth and nineteenth century Dahomey. That c ountry occupied parts of today's Togo, Benin, and Nigeria. Slaves brought their religion with them when they were forcibly shipped to Haiti and other islands in the West Indies. The i nformation a vailable m ost r eadily i s that of the Haitians and the Yoruba. Although there are some cultural differences due to language and location, the basics have a connecting thread that runs throughout.

To fully understand Vodoun, you must study the people, the language and examine Vodun at its roots in Africa, and how it began and evolved on the islands. Vodoun history belongs to the millions of people, whose ancestors were brought in bondage from Africa to the "Caribbean islands of the Dominican Republic and Haiti. This b lack population of millions encompassed members from the Bambara, Foula, Arada or Arda, Mandingue, Fon, Nago, Iwe, Ibo, Yoruba, and other Congo tribes."[1] Although its essence originated in distinct regions of Africa long before the Europeans started the slave trade, Vodoun as we know it today was born in different r egions o f t he w orld d uring the European colonization. Ironically, it was the forced immigration of African slaves from different tribes that provided the circumstances for its development. These stories of African roots, enslavement and hard-fought freedom, comprise the history of Vodoun.

The religion of the slaves fascinated their masters at first, but soon the whites became fearful of the strange practices and forbade the slaves from their religious practices and from gathering in any type of congregations. Penalties for violations were sadistic and severe, including mutilation, sexual disfigurement, flaying alive and burial alive.

Any slave found possessing a *fetish* (an object believed to have spiritual significance) could be imprisoned, hanged or flayed alive.[2] Even today, the word fetish has negative connotations. Slaves often experienced confiscation of fetishes before and after reaching America. Their holders, or even Priests, would take these images from the frightened slaves, telling them that they should not put trust in these idols, but in Jesus Christ who would help them. No one ever thought in most cases that these frightened slaves hardly knew, or did not know at all, who Jesus Christ was; the only thing being accomplished was that this frightened individual was being stripped of the last security that he or she had.[3]

Vodoun continued to be actively suppressed during colonial times. "Many Vodoun Priests were either killed or imprisoned, and their shrines destroyed, because of the threat they posed to Euro-Christian/Muslim beliefs. This forced some to form Vodoun Orders and to create secret societies, in order to continue the veneration of their ancestors, and the worship of their powerful gods."[4] Much the same as Christians and Jews have done during periods of persecution. The slavery trade started to take its toll on African populations.

In the course of a century, the slave population swelled from a few thousand to over half a million. This growing slave population became very diverse, and many African nations, languages, and belief systems were represented within its people. It is during this period of French colonization that much of Vodoun developed. In an attempt to keep their beliefs alive, the Africans began to not only invoke their own spirits but to practice the rites of other African nations. Colonists thought that by separating tribe members, individuals would not come together as a community. However, in the misery of slavery, the transplanted Africans found a common thread in their faith. These mixed, intermingled religions are the basis of Vodoun.

An inaccurate and sensational book (S. St. John, "*Haiti or the Black Republic*") was written in 1884. It described Vodoun as a profoundly evil religion, and included lurid descriptions of human sacrifice and cannibalism. This book caught the imagination of people outside the West Indies, and was responsible for much of the misunderstanding and fear that is present today. Hollywood found this a rich source for "Voodoo" screen plays.

Horror movies began in the 1930s and continue today to misrepresent Vodoun. It is only since the late 1950s that accurate studies by anthropologists have been published.[5]

The Vodoun went underground to some extent, but it grew in popularity, in large measure because of the oppression. Christianity and European influence also played another role (to some extent) in the development of Vodoun. During the French occupation period, the Roman Catholic Church required the recognition of African slaves as human beings and required that all slaves should be baptized and instructed in the Catholic faith.

This and other practices of saveholders quickly forced the slaves to take their native practices underground. They practiced Catholicism in front of their masters even attending Mass regularly, but whenever they could, they secretly gathered together to worship the gods of their ancestors. Occasionally rites were held deep in woods, while prayers were transmitted into work songs and the worship of saints became a secret prayer to their previous gods. Secretly through unique variations, old traditions were kept alive.

Over time, the Africans began using Catholicism as a means to mask their religious practices. This is how the syncretism or perceived assimilation of African deities with Catholic saints developed. The Africans incorporated Catholic prayers into their services and used images of Catholic saints as representations of their spirits.

As for example, this worked well with St. Patrick, who supposedly banished snakes from Ireland. A slave could publicly be thought to be begging the intercession of St. Patrick while secretly praying to the snake-god *Danbhalah-Waldo*. Fetishes became unnecessary, even masters were tolerant of slaves keeping a tame snake and lighting candles for the saints. A syncretism evolved: a blending of the traditional Catholic worship of the saints and Christ with the gods of Africa. Eventually Vodounists did not regard this as profaning either Christianity or Vodoun but as an enrichment of their faith.[6]

The twentieth century had not been so kind to the Vodoun, and the culture once again fought for its own survival when evangelical Protestant missionaries became bitter enemies of Vodoun and deemed it satanism.

Many of these people claimed that the people's misery was because they were being punished by God for the sins of their Vodoun servitude. However, these efforts have not been successful. In May 1991, a symposium of the great leaders of the Vodoun cults was held with the aim of restoring a certain degree of legal recognition for this traditional religion. Recently, there have been moves to restore the place of Vodoun in national society, such as an *Annual International Vodoun Conference* held in the city of Ouidah, in Benin, that has been held since 1991. Its effect was to foster its renewal.

In the same year, Pope John Paul II's visit and his highly media-enhanced meeting with Vodoun leaders were taken by many Vodoun followers, not as a sign of dialogue, but as the indication that the Church at last recognizes that the Vodoun faith has its place. This combination of circumstances means that in Benin, Africa, Vodoun is currently organizing and structuring itself more and more as a traditional religion, with a national feast and a national hierarchy.[7]

Vodoun was formally recognized as Benin's official religion in 1996. It is also followed by most of the adults in Haiti. It can be found in many of the large cities in North America, particularly in the south. Presently, Adherents.com notes there are an estimated sixty million worshippers worldwide (this does not count the Traditional African Religion). Vodoun is almost universally practiced in Haiti but also is practiced in many cities of the United States such as New York, New Orleans, Houston, Charleston, South Carolina, and Los Angeles. In the United States, it is recognized as a legitimate religion.

God or Gods

Contrary to modern beliefs and preconceived notions, Vodoun is a *monotheistic* religion. Similar to Catholicism, there is one God, with many helpers. "This God, recognized as the Supreme Being, as Transcendent, is referred to by the term *Mawu*...That God is the creator of the universe, of mankind and of all that exists is generally accepted." Ultimately, it is to this God that all worship is given, He who alone is worthy of being adored. Indeed, in this same view, it is the one God who created all men and all these vodouns (spirits) and gave them to men as intermediaries. It is clear that to speak of Vodoun in the context of polytheism is hardly correct. Rather, it appears to be *polyhedral* (multi-sided) monotheism, which highlights an active relationship with the cosmos, nature, phenomena, and deceased human beings, in contrast with a direct relationship with God. Neither can one say absolutely that they are in the presence of a pantheist (God in everything), it is rather pan-**in**-theist (everything in God).

For the people of South Benin, Mawu is God, but He does not concern Himself directly with man; He is omnipotent but has delegated his power to the vodouns. Hence, the vodouns, recognized as Mawu's creatures, are Mawu's representatives among men. For this reason, they are explicitly distinct from Mawu. But we find that there is no actual worship of the spirits in the tradition, except certain spontaneous prayers or references such as *'Mawu na blo* " (God will act), *'Kpê Mawu ton* " (may God decide thus) used on different occasions. The vodouns receive the worship because of their proximity to Mawu compared to man.[8]

Divine qualities are attributed to them, characterized as spirits; they are considered to be above all natural laws. The faithful believe that the work of the spirits is present in all aspects of man's daily life, and that, pleasing God, will gain them health, wealth, and spiritual commitment. It is often believed that it is these aspects of the religion, similar in many ways to the intercession of saints and angels, which made Vodoun so compatible with Christianity, especially Catholicism in the New World, and produced such strongly syncretistic religions as Haitian Vodoun. The pantheon of the Vodoun is quite large and complex. In one tradition, there are seven daughters and sons of Mawu, which are interethnic and related to natural phenomena or historical or mythical individuals, as well as dozens of ethnic vodouns, defenders of a certain clan, tribe, or nation. There are a hierarchy of these lesser creations, which range in power from major deities governing the forces of nature and human society, to the spirits of individual streams, trees, and rocks—the more impressive of which may be considered sacred. Since all of creation is considered divine, it therefore, contains the power of the divine.

This is a concept vital to medicine, such as herbal remedies, and explains the ubiquitous use of mundane objects in religious ritual.

There are hundreds of minor spirits. Some of the most prominent are:

- serpent spirit
- protector
- spirit of the forests
- spirit of the sea
- rainbow spirit
- spirit of agriculture
- evil spirit taking the form of an animal
- guardian of the grave
- spirit of streams
- spirit of storms
- female spirit of waters
- female spirit of love
- spirit of creation
- spirit of healing
- spirit of war

Christ

Even though it is believed that *Danbhalah* represents the ancestral knowledge of Vodoun, it is acknowledged that no communication may occur between the gods and worshipper without the offices of *Legba*. He is the Orient, the East, the sun and the place the sun rises. He controls gates, fences, and entryways; no deity may join a Vodoun ceremony unless Legba has been asked to open the "door." He governs all actions of the spirits. Legba is depicted both as a man sprinkling water and as an old man walking with a stick or crutch. He personifies the ritual waters and the consolidation of the Vodoun mysteries. He is called Papa; and through syncretism has become identified with St. Peter, the gate keeper, the man to whom Christ gave the keys to the Kingdom. Still others liken Legba to Christ, a *mulatto* (a person of mixed ancestry) man born of the sun and moon.[9]

Basic Doctrine

Note: Vodoun capitalized is the religion; vodoun in lower case is a spirit.

Let us recognize that defining Vodoun is not an easy task even for Vodoun adepts. Vodoun is more than just a faith practice; it is a way of life. For those it touches, it is impossible to define. Vodoun is religion, culture, heritage, and philosophy. It is also art, dance, language, medicine, music, justice, power, storytelling, and ritual. Vodoun is a way of looking at and dealing with life. It heals and destroys—it is both good and bad; simple in concept and complex in practice. Vodoun is seen in daily life, and every detail of life has meaning in Vodoun. It is open to all yet holds many secrets and mysteries to those who are uninitiated.

Contrary to its reputation, Vodoun did not develop to be used for evil. However, there is a dark side to Vodoun practice. Sorcerers and sorceresses called Botono are believed to cast hexes on the enemies of supplicants. The Botono claim to call upon evil vodoun (spirits) to bring misfortune or harm to others. The black magic aspects of this religion play a very minor role and are not typical of Vodoun. In the early to mid-1900s, there were exaggerated claims about the practice, and movies portrayed followers as ignorant people who were obsessed with evil.

Werewolves, zombies, the casting of spells, and the use of "voodoo" dolls were sensationalized as the common practices of these people. In actuality, the use of black magic is rare, but this stereotype remains with us even today. The use of "voodoo" dolls is unheard of in Haiti and most places where the religion is practiced. The only recorded serious use of the dolls among Vodoun worshippers was in the New Orleans area in the early 1900s. Hexes were cast to bring either good or bad luck to another person. The doll was used to symbolize that person. The sticking of pins into the doll was to reinforce and direct the spells that were cast.

<u>The Universe:</u> In the created universe, there is a vodoun of the earth, a vodoun of the sky, a vodoun of the sea, and voduns representing the ancestors. Indeed, all the elements of the universe are involved in the Vodoun phenomenon. Vodoun is thus neither the generator nor the

creator of the universe. But its link to everything in nature is one of mediation and of the protection of man. In fact, Vodoun's link with universe only finds its meaning through its connection with man.

The essential acts of worship in the Vodoun religion are sacrifices (of propitiation or thanksgiving), offerings and prayers. Communion meals and annual purification rites complete the vast range of forms of ritual worship. The Vodoun rules establish a life of solidarity among these individuals. In addition, "Vodoun tolerates no transgression of its prohibitions. This maintains among sincere Vodoun adepts a permanent culture of fidelity. The total commitment of ex-Vodoun adepts who have converted to Christianity is a proof of this."[10] The features to be focused on, therefore, are the values of fraternity, solidarity, communion, and religious fidelity.

Family's disagreements, discords between employer and employee, disputes concerning land ownership, differences of opinion and of point of views, problems created by birth, education, health, work, and death, find their solutions in Vodoun. That system of belief is the interpersonal as well as the collective mediator of the…people. For implicitly enfolded in the entire Vodoun system is a "Code of Ethics" which serves as an instrument of peace and harmony for everyone.[11]

The teachings are revealed to many, and the precepts are instructive to all who naturally see the well-founded grounds for them. This explains why Vodoun, whenever and wherever it is practiced, gathers the adhesion of the majority of the population. Religious conviction gives meaning to behavior and moral choices.

Mecca: Guinea represents the symbolic homeland of the African people. The most sacred city of Guinea is Ife (an ancient Yoruba city in southwestern Nigeria, where the founding deities *Oduduwa* and *Obatala* began the creation of the world as directed by the Supreme Being). It is the mecca of Vodoun. Since Africa is east of the New World, Ife represents the celestial position of the sun. Devotees gain spiritual strength from Ife; they are sent to Ife in a very solemn ceremony signifying death, burial, and resurrection.

Prayer: For most people, well-balanced living, meditation, and sincere veneration sufficiently strengthen one's being. Being well-balanced, it is believed that you are in a position to make use of the simplest form of connection between the spirits and the Supreme Being in the form of petition/prayer for divine support. The divine messenger, without partiality for good or for bad, negotiates communication and navigates your prayers to the Supreme Being. It is thought that spirits are called upon whilst in times of major decision-making; whatever the offering, the line of advice is commonly used to draw conclusions that would not have been first thought.

The mode of transmission of Vodoun's precepts isn't limited to individual and group revelations. There are also, carried through the tradition, a whole oral literature in the form of prayers, litanies, religious songs, mythological stories, charades, maxims, proverbs and even some anecdotes about boys and girls that everyone repeats across the country. They too carry the norms of behavior as well as the philosophical reflections about God, the Great Master, or the Great Mistress Who govern the Universe; Nature, which is man's environment; and reflections concerning the human being.[12]

Basic Worship Service

Patterns of worship follow various dialects, vodouns, practices, songs, and rituals. In Vodoun, the practice of offering an animal sacrifice is common as a way to show respect and thankfulness to the gods. Worshippers also believe in ancestor veneration and hold the idea that the spirits of the dead live side by side in the world of the living. They also utilize items that hold spiritual properties. Vodoun talismans called *fetishes* are objects such as statues or dried animal parts that are sold for their healing and spiritually rejuvenating properties.

Most Vodoun activities center in the temple divided into a ceremonial space called the paristyle, and adjacent altar rooms or sanctuaries that are used for private healings and devotions.

Ceremonies in the paristyle move to the rhythm of the drum. Servitors sing and dance around a central pillar which acts as a lightning rod for divine energies. Induced by sound and glitter, the spirit may possess their servitors, or as Haitians say, "ride their horses." When possessed, servitors are dressed and fed to please the spirit, or "divine horsemen." In return, the spirits offer counsel to their human family. Vodoun ceremonies can be extravagant and beautiful; but they are comparatively rare. More commonly the temple serves as a kind of community center, where members of the Vodoun family seek medical help, psychological counseling, legal advice, commercial assistance, and other services offered by the Vodoun Priest or Priestess. The temple also serves as popular theater and museum, where sacred drama and art flourish.[13]

The drum is the most sacred of the objects used in service to the spirit, for it speaks with a divine voice. Without it there would be no Vodoun. But the sacred arts of Vodoun include hundreds of other object types as well. Certain objects are present in nearly every temple or home altar. Others reflect the personal history or tastes of the servitor and his or her spirits. Almost anything can be dedicated to a spirit and then set upon an altar or incorporated into some larger religious work. All these objects can possess magical powers, for they are all capable of transforming the natural into the supernatural.[14]

There are several rites and practices in Vodoun. These come from tribal rites and display or honor different manifestations of the spirits. The two main rite of Vodoun are *Rada* or *Petro*. Rada rites follow the more traditional African patterns emphasizing the gentler, more positive attributes of the spirits. Devotees wear all white clothing during these ceremonies. Animal sacrifices, which represent the "partaking of the blood," include chicken, goats, and bulls. Three ox hide-covered drums provide the rhythms for the chanting, representing three atmospheres of the sun. These drums provide the resonant combinations of musical rhythm of any rite and are struck with drumsticks. The Petro rites appear to have originated in Haiti during the slavery days. The name Petro allegedly comes from Don Juan Felipe Pedro, a Spanish Vodoun Priest and former slave who contributed a rather violent style of dance to the ceremonies. Many of the Petro practices include more violent worship services and the use of red in the ceremonial clothing and on the face; which came from the Awak and Carib Indians who then lived on Saint Dominique. The Petro spirits tend to be more menacing, deadly, and ill-tempered than other spirits; many of their names simply have the appellation *GeRouge* (Red Eyes) after a Rada name to signify the Petro form. Pigs are the animals generally chosen to be sacrificed for the benefit of the Petro spirits.

Some aspects of the Vodoun worship appear fairly constant, with local variations for all rites. The temple, which can be anything from a formal structure to a designated place behind a house …Within the temple, also known as the "holy of holies," is the altar and perhaps rooms for solitary mediation by initiates. The altar stone is covered with candles and small jars believed containing spirits of ancestors. Offerings of food, drink, and money may also grace the altar, as well as ritual rattles, charms, flags, sacred stones, and other paraphernalia…The walls and floors are decorated in elaborated colored designs, symbolizing the gods. These drawings can be permanent or created in cornmeal, flour, powdered brick, gun powder, or face powder just before a ceremony. They are quite beautiful and incorporate the symbols and occult signs of the spirits being worshipped…Usually drawn around the center post, or the place of sacrifice, the drawings serve as a ritual "magnet" for the spirit's entrance, obliging the spirit to descend to the earth.

Outside the main temple is the paristyle, the roofed and sometimes encircled courtyard adjacent to the holy of holies. Since the structure probably cannot accommodate all of the Vodoun participants and onlookers most of the ceremonies are held in the open-air paristyles, as is the treatment of the sick. A low wall encircles the area, allowing those who are not dressed properly, or merely curious, to watch less conspicuously. Holding up the paristyle is the center post. The post symbolizes the center of Vodoun from the sky to hell and is the cosmic axis…of all Vodoun magic. Usually made of wood it is set in a masonry base. The post bears colorful decorations and designs…The post symbolizes *Legba Ali-Bon* ("wood of justice" or Legba Tree-of-the-Good), "The Way" of all Vodoun knowledge and communion with the gods (See Christ Section). Geometrically the placement of the center post forms perfect squares, circles, crosses and triangles with the base adding to its magical powers. All Vodoun temples have a post, or center, even if the post exists symbolically and is not necessary structurally.

Outside the paristyle, the trees surrounding the courtyard serve as sanctuaries for gods. Vodoun devotees believe that all things serve the spirit, and are by definition expressions and extensions of God, especially the trees. They are revered as divinities themselves, and receive offerings of food, drink, and money. Like cathedrals they are places to be in the presence of the Holy Spirit; banana trees are particularly revered."[15]

<u>Calling the Spirit:</u> The followers of Vodoun believe that true "communion" comes through divine possession. When summoned, the gods may assume a person's mind or body...The possessed loses all consciousness, totally becoming the possessing spirit with his or her desires and eccentricities. Young women possessed by older spirits seem frail and decrepit, while the infirm possessed by young, virile gods dance and cavort with no thought of their disabilities. Even facial expressions change to resemble those of the god or goddess.

Although there exists a sacred interaction between the spirit and devotee, possession is taken very seriously and approached with caution. "The spirits manifest to protect, punish, confer skills and talents, prophesy, cure illness, exorcise spirits, give counsel, assist with rituals, and take sacrificial offerings. The priest or priestess is an intermediary to summon the spirit and helps the spirit depart when his or her business is finished. The priest or priestess receives total authority from the spirits, and therefore, their roles could be compared to that of the pope. Indeed, the priest is often called *papa* or *papa-spirit*, while the priestess is called *mamman* or *mama*. The priest or priestess serves as healers, diviners, psychologists, counselors, and spiritual leaders.[16]

Like the ruler's scepter, the most important symbol of the priest's or priestess' office is a large ritual rattle made from a type of squash with a bulbous end and a long handle. Symbolically, the rattle represents the joining of the two most important magic principles: the circle at the round end and the post at the handle, symbolizing the central post of the temple. Inside the dried squash are sacred stones and serpent vertebrae, considered bones of African ancestors. Eight different stones in eight different colors are used to symbolize eight ancestor gods (eight signifies eternity).

Chains of colored beads symbolizing the rainbow of Aida-Wedo or more snake vertebrae encircle the round end of the squash. When the vertebrae rattle, making the rattle "speak," the spirits come down to the faithful through Danbhalah, the oldest of the ancestors. Once the priest or priestess has attracted the spirit through the deity's symbol, appealed to Legba (see Christ) for intercession, and performed the water rituals and prayers, shaking the rattle or striking it releases the power of the spirits and brings them into the ceremony.

"Other important members of the worship are the masters of ceremonies who orchestrate the flag waving ceremonies, and frequently the choral singing, the chanting, and the drum beating. Another person carries the ritual sword usually decorated with geometrical symbols and designs. The sword is called *ku-bah-sah* meaning 'cutting away all that is material'."[17] The sword is waved east to west, cutting away all that is material so the worshippers might more freely come into the divine presence.

The purpose of rituals is to make contact with a spirit, to gain their favor by offering them animal sacrifices and gifts, to obtain help in the form of more abundant food, higher standard of living, and improved health. The Vodoun faith teaches that human and spirit depend upon each other. Rituals are held to celebrate lucky events, to attempt to escape a run of bad fortune, to celebrate a seasonal day of celebration associated with a Spirit, for healing, at birth, marriage and death… Animal sacrifice … are humanely killed by slitting their throat and blood is collected in a vessel. The possessed dancer may drink some of the blood. The hunger of the Spirit is then believed to be satisfied. The animal is usually cooked and shared. Animal sacrifice is a method of consecrating food for consumption by followers of Vodoun, their gods and ancestors.[18]

The initiate who obtains the sacrificial animals oversees the distribution of sacrificial food not reserved for the spirits, much the same way a priest would oversee the sacrament in a Christian faith.

The central and key aspect of Vodoun is healing people from illness. Such healing activities probably constitute 60 percent of all Vodoun activity. Healers heal with herbs, faith healing (with the help of spirit and other spirits) and, today, even with western medicine.

Magic, used for both good and evil purposes, is an integral part of Vodoun. The followers recognizes no dichotomy between good and evil, as expressed within the Judeo-Christian philosophy, but sees evil as the mirror image of good. Devotees feel that the magic of the spirits is there to be used, if that magic is evil, so be it; they make no judgments. A (priest or priestess) who practices more black magic sorcery than healing is referred to "one who serves the spirit with both hands."[19]

Marriage

Weddings can be very elaborate, involving feasting and dancing for days within a community; they can be very simple, or they can even be performed in huge marriage ceremonies involving many different couples. Weddings are a family affair and involve the combining of two lives, two families, and even two communities. There are many different wedding traditions. However, in all the communities, the bride plays a very special role and is treated with respect because she is a link between the unborn and the ancestors. A bride might eventually bear a very powerful child. In some areas, the groom's family would even move to the bride's village and set up a whole new house there. There are many steps that take place before marriage, starting at a very young age, where training takes place in how to be a suitable partner. Many times, girls will go to schools where adult women teach them what is involved in marriage and, in some ethnic groups, even learn secret codes and languages so that they can communicate with other married women.

Infant Baptism or Blessing

The *Àgabasa-yiyi* (access to the living room) is of capital importance in the lives of the Vodoun people. It is the first of a series of three rites of initiation and is fundamentally the most important of the three through which everyone must pass. The Àgabasa-yiyi ceremony has no rigorously fixed date. It never takes place before at least three lunar months after birth. The purpose of Àgabasa-yiyi is to introduce the child to the family community in the living room of the representative of the ancestor. It is the rite of the integration of a child or of several children of the same generation within the family community, including the deceased members, the living, and the spirits that protect the family.[20]

The consultation by the diviner healer reveals the child's *joto* (personal spirit) or the ancestor, sometimes deified who, in him, is sent to the family by the Supreme Being. The joto is a reference to a protective force. It is a dynamic element that intervenes in the constitution of the individual's personality. The joto is "Father of the coming into existence," the direct collaborator of *Mawu* (Supreme Being) in the life of the child (like a guardian angel). In principle, the child does not take on the name of his joto. He can, however, be addressed by this name from time to time in order to remind him of it.

Through the *Àgabasa-yiyi* rite, the individual is recognized as a true member of his family. The Agbasa rite has two dimensions: while the possession of a joto confers a social status on a person, the determination of his *dù* (oracle) recognizes his individual character. Thus, there is reciprocal interaction between social status and the status of the individual. Those who have not been through the rite of Àgabasa-yiyi have neither personal nor community status. If the joto and the dù are not known by their families, they remain strangers, men without roots.[21]

Until a child reaches the age of reason, it is the mother who respects the ordinances of his oracle. In general, mothers take upon themselves the responsibility and the concern to follow these ordinances for the rest of their lives, for and with their offspring, even after the children are adults. By this gesture, they demonstrate that the life preserved in a family member is a gain in vitality for all and that everyone must cooperate in maintaining it.

Initiation, Baptism, or Confirmation

The young follower is faced with his religious responsibilities as soon as he reaches the age of twelve or thirteen years. His parents teach him to know his joto (divinity) and his dù (oracle). Until this point, he has been allowed not to observe the ordinances of his dù, given his young age. His mother acted on his behalf. But now, it is up to him to respect these ordinances, even if his mother continues to do so for him.

Agoo-ma-yi-sogwé is the stage that marks late adolescence (around the age of twenty). At this time, the second initiation takes place, known as *Fá-sinsên* (adoration of the Fá) or *Fá-yiyi* (reception of the Fá). He or she must receive and adore the Fá; in other words, in a public religious act, conform to his or her will to that of the Supreme Being of whom the Fá is the messenger. Youthful freedom struggling for self-control must utter the most profound "yes" to the will of God in order to become stronger. A divine healer offers the sacrifice that clears their lives of obstacles, accidents, and misfortunes, much like the cleansing away of sins through baptism in a Christian faith. They are given the Fá, and they receive it; it is the word of God for each one as he definitively leaves childhood to enter adult life. (This concept could be seen as being similar to confirmation in some Christian faith practices.)

The third initiation to the Fá is reserved for adult male candidates alone. It is the door to the consultation of the Fá: a rite through which the man "receives the revelation of the whole of his destiny." The candidate is no longer only the one for whom the consultation is made but also the one who consults for himself. This is where the man officially has a personal line of communication with the Supreme Being through the Fa'. It is very sacred, and non-initiates and women are not even admitted as spectators.

Throughout the initiation period, the Initiate is not allowed to have sex; he is in a period of close and special relationship with the sacred. Sexual continence disposes the candidate to preserving all his vital energy for the benefit of his encounter with the "divine power"; it enables the sacred energy to operate effectively on the candidate, free of any hindrance.

The lifting of the sex ban happens on the third day after he has returned from the *Fázun* (the wood of the Fá). It happens after a further consultation of the Fá to make sure that the Initiate's oracle came for his good ...Finally the man is clothed in a brand new white loincloth, and then he goes home with his Fá. He is a full initiate with regards to the stages reserved to common man. Henceforth, he knows "the meaning of life" and the meaning of his own life; he knows his personal destiny.[22]

<u>Vodoun School for Priesthood:</u> The very day a child enters the Vodoun convent, the Vodoun takes possession of the child, girl or boy, who has chosen it. For three months, he or she will be a neophyte. What we call novitiate is therefore the process by which they will be made to become what they already are mystically. The neophytes are supervised by the head of house in charge of discipline; then there are the novice master and mistress, respectively. The convent is a harsh school of renunciation and endurance. Within it, the elect are initiated to the understanding of the Vodoun to which they are consecrated for their whole life. Initiation to Vodoun is a particularly important moment that deeply marks the life of the individual. Its aim is gradually to lead the profane individual from non-existence to their existence as sacred persons; the novice undergoes a series of separations which are each a death to the previous profane life. Before anything else, the novice must make a solemn vow of absolute discretion as regards what they have seen and heard or will see and hear in the convent. Any novice who cannot keep quiet about what is to remain secret, and act with the veneration that is due...will be a traitor. Failure to observe the rules of initiation... is considered a threat to the authority, not of men, but of the Divinity.

During the process of initiation, the neophyte is required to prove his capacity for endurance in the formation trials; these formation trials are themselves a condensed form of the trials of life. Discipline and tenacity are essential, and corporal punishment serves to develop these. In this respect, it can be said the body records knowledge. Each novice stores up in his body the soil in which the initiatory word is sown by means of gestures, attitudes, and rhythms. Mind, heart, and body work together to build the total man.

Apart from learning the Vodoun language, cultural chants, and dances to satisfy the material needs of the convent and the high priest, the young must devote themselves at fixed times to working in the fields and manual tasks. There is no relaxation in the initiation period; laziness is to be hated like the plague. The novice, male or female, must show maturity and be serious in matters of religion. In this way, they are to contribute to the balance and order, social, cultural, and religious integrity, of their community and people.[23]

There are three degrees of initiation that defines a person as a part of the spiritual lineage of the priest or priestess. The next degree places the initiate on the level of junior priest or priestess. At this degree of initiation, you can use herbal magic, lucid dreaming, spell casting, invocation of the spirit, and various divination systems. This is an appropriate level of initiation for those who plan to practice the Vodoun religion without becoming a full priest. The final level of initiation confers senior priesthood upon the initiate, who then is fully trained and eligible to be called a priest or priestess. Initiation into the Vodoun faith is not something to be taken lightly or done on a whim. It involves much responsibility and some sacrifice, and once you have been initiated, you have made a lifetime commitment to celebrate, practice, and uphold the tenets of this unique and profound religion.

Death and Afterlife

Despite the confusing terminology encountered in the formulation of the term joto (see Infant Baptism or Blessing), any idea of reincarnation should be absolutely discarded; even though the joto becomes a part of the child, the child is not the reincarnation of his joto ancestor. Vodoun belief holds that the individual is immortal. When a person dies and enters the world of the spirits, the individual goes back to the Supreme Being, in other words, to his origins, his original state, at which time he too becomes a joto for another living person. In his role as joto, it is he who places his hand on the head of the candidate to life to take him under his protective shadow.

There is no reincarnation in the proper sense, but a transmission of the personality. The individual soul of the joto does not become incarnate in his protégé, but the joto transmits to the latter his sociological part, his status, and his role. A proof of this is that several persons living at the same time can have the same joto. Throughout all the stages of life—from birth and through the different existential situations—the faithful will feel enfolded in the omnipresence of Vodoun and will constantly benefit from the watchful and protective eye of his or her joto.

But curiously and paradoxically, the joto does not accompany a faithful in death, to the beyond. At the funeral of a Vodoun adept, a rite exists to remove the joto that has been with him, so as to leave the individual to his own fate. Here there are perhaps two meanings that are important to note: Firstly, the vodoun takes care of the living and not of the dead. Secondly, vodoun is essentially an intermediary between man and the Supreme Being, to whom the joto simply delivers the man when he dies.

Judgment and Salvation

It is in the Vodoun philosophy that all humans have manifest destiny to become one in spirit with the Supreme Being and source of all energy. Each person in the physical realm uses thought or action energies to impact the community of all other living things, including the earth, and so to move toward destiny. As such, one's destiny is in one's own hands. To attain transcendence and destiny in the spiritual realm of those who do good and beneficial things, one's behavior and spiritual consciousness here on earth must be elevated. Those who stop improving are destined for the spiritual realm of the forsaken.

Special Doctrine

Magic and Sorcery: With the functionality of Vodoun, one might say that it is simply a naturalist religion. However, the whole power of the phenomenon is based on two realities: magic and sorcery....What is even worse is the sometimes malicious use that is made of its power...

whoever knows how to make the charm that is supposed to protect from evil spells, has also known the poison…But there is nothing more dangerous than this inextricable world where evil takes the shape of good and imposes a code of conduct.[24] That statement can also be made in many other walks of life.

Falsely equated with savage superstitions…Vodoun is one of the world's least understood and most maligned religious traditions… So powerful are the negative stereotypes of Vodoun, that some may be surprised to learn of its progressive stands on religious tolerance, feminism, the key role of women as religious leaders, the right to use contraceptives, and equality for gays and lesbians.[25]

First and foremost Vodoun is a religion. Many of the practices and descriptions of Vodoun beliefs may sound to us like superstition, but then, imagine the beliefs of Christianity to people who know nothing about it. Tell them about the Trinity—three gods in one— or the resurrection—someone being raised from the dead—or the presence of Jesus in the Eucharist—eating and drinking His body & blood. Any of these practices which Christians believe in, would seem no less superstitious and perhaps bazaar to someone unfamiliar with Christianity. Thus we urge you to recognize that Vodoun is taken very seriously, not merely by uneducated or primitive peasants. Many intelligent and learned members of their society believe as sincerely in Vodoun as do theology professors in Christianity. In no way do we expect you to believe in Vodoun; no more than we would expect you to convert to Islam. But, please do consider that it is, to its followers, every bit as real a religion as the other religions of the world.[26]

Notes

Notes

Other Religions and Faith Practices

The chapters in this category of faith practices stand on their own for varying reasons. Perhaps they are a compilation of all practices, or perhaps they merely have little common doctrine with the other religions we read about in previous chapters. That being said, each faith practice does have a large number of adherents and bears further exploration and comparison.

Atheist/Agnostic

Note: Atheists don't think of atheism as a religion, but since it is often compared to religions or sometimes labeled as a lack of religion, it is worth trying to understand fully for the purpose of this study.

History

In early Ancient Greek, the adjective *atheos* meant "godless." The word began to display more-intentional, active godlessness in the fifth century BC, acquiring definitions of "severing relations with the gods" or "denying the gods; ungodly." Western Atheism can be dated back to pre-Socratic Greek philosophy, but was not a distinct world-view until the late Enlightenment Period. The fifth century BC Greek philosopher Diagoras is known as the "first Atheist," and strongly criticized religion and mysticism. Some philosophers viewed religion as a human invention used to frighten people into following moral order. Socrates (471–399 BC) was accused of impiety because he inspired questioning of the state gods. Although he denied that he was a "complete Atheist," saying that he believed in spirits, he was ultimately sentenced to death. Euhemerus (330–260 BC) had written that the gods were only human rulers, conquerors and founders of the past that had been deified. Although not strictly an Atheist, he was later accused of having "spread Atheism over the whole inhabited earth by obliterating the gods." The Roman poet Lucretius (99–55 BC) believed that, if there were gods, they did not care about humanity and could not affect the natural world. For this reason, he believed humanity should have no fear of the supernatural. The Roman philosopher Sextus Empiricus held that one should not judge any belief systems; that nothing was inherently evil, and that peace of mind is attainable by withholding one's judgment. His relatively large volume of surviving works had a lasting influence on later philosophers.

The meaning of atheist changed over the course of history. The early Christians were labeled atheists by non-Christians because of their disbelief in their pagan gods. During the Roman Empire, Christians were executed for their rejection of the Roman gods in general, and emperor worship in particular. When Christianity became the state religion of Rome, atheistic views became rare in Europe during the Middle Ages. Then, during the Renaissance, there was an expansion of free thought and skeptical inquiry. Individuals such as Leonardo Da Vinci sought experimentation as a means of explanation and opposed arguments from religious authority.

In English, the term atheism was derived from the French *athéisme* in about 1587. The term atheist, in the sense of one who denies or disbelieves the existence of God, was coined in about 1571.

Karen Armstrong writes that *"The term 'Atheist' was an insult. Nobody would have dreamed of calling himself an Atheist."* Atheism was first used to describe a self-avowed belief in late eighteenth century Europe, specifically denoting disbelief in the monotheistic Abrahamic god. In the twentieth century, globalization contributed to the expansion of the term to refer to disbelief in all deities, though it remains common in society to describe Atheism as simply 'disbelief in God'.[1]

Most recently, there has been a push in certain circles to redefine atheism as the "absence of belief in deities" rather than as a belief in its own right.

Criticism of Christianity became increasingly frequent in the seventeeth and eighteenth centuries. Some Protestant thinkers, such as Thomas Hobbes, espoused a materialist philosophy and skepticism toward supernatural occurrences. Practically all the philosophers of eighteenth-century France and England held to some form of deism, which was to say that one did not need any sort of religion to tell them there was a Supreme Being. Despite their ridicule of organized Christianity, many deists held atheism in scorn as well. But the transition from deism to atheism was a short one for some.

The first known atheist who threw off the mantle of deism, bluntly denying the existence of gods, was Jean Meslier, a French priest who lived in the early eighteenth century. He was followed by other openly atheistic thinkers, such as Baron d'Holbach, who appeared in the late eighteenth century, when expressing disbelief in God became a less dangerous position.

Between the eighteenth century and the mid-twentieth century, Atheism became more accepted by those with intellectual or philosophical dispositions. There has been a movement among the atheist society to stop what they consider infringements on their rights to not believe.

A court case that was begun in 1959 by the Murray family challenged prayer recitation in the public schools. That case—*Murray v. Curlett*—was a landmark in American jurisprudence on behalf of our First Amendment rights. It began:

> *Your petitioners are Atheists, and they define their lifestyle as follows. An Atheist loves himself and his fellow man instead of a god. An Atheist accepts that heaven is something for which we should work now—here on earth—for all men together to enjoy. An Atheist accepts that he can get no help through prayer, but that he must find in himself the inner conviction and strength to meet life, to grapple with it, to subdue it and to enjoy it. An Atheist accepts that only in a knowledge of himself and a knowledge of his fellow man can he find the understanding that will help lead to a life of fulfillment.*

Out of this court case, an organization called *American Atheists* was founded in 1963 by Madalyn Murray O'Hair, the noted atheist activist. Now in its fourth decade, American Atheists is dedicated to working for the civil rights of atheists, promoting separation of state and church and providing information about atheism. There still exists discrimination against atheists in the United States today. Part of this may be based on the historical linkage between Communism and atheism. Many communists are atheists. But many people do not realize that most atheists in North America are not communists. Another reason for discrimination against atheism is the common belief that a person cannot be motivated to lead a moral life unless they hope for the reward of heaven and fear the punishment of hell. Many atheists were also conscientious objectors opposed to participating in warfare and were thrown in jail, but their opposition was to killing other humans and not based on their lack of belief in God.

It is difficult to quantify the number of atheists in the world. Not everyone defines atheism in the same way. In addition, people in some regions of the world refrain from reporting themselves as atheists to avoid social stigma, discrimination, and persecution. A 2006 study by researchers at the University of Minnesota involving a poll of two thousand households in the United States found atheists to be the most distrusted of minorities, more so than Muslims, recent immigrants, gays and lesbians, and other groups. Statistics on atheism are often difficult to represent accurately for a variety of other reasons. Atheism is a position compatible with other forms of identity. Some atheists also consider themselves agnostic, Buddhist, Jains, Taoist or hold other related philosophical beliefs. Adherents.com tallies the top fifty countries' approximate totals of atheists worldwide at approximately 240 million, with the highest numbers in China (over 100 million) and Japan (82 million), and between 8.8 million and 26.8 million in the United States.[3]

God or Gods

Perhaps the most common characteristic of religion is a belief in supernatural beings of some sort, including gods. Few religions lack this characteristic, and most religions are founded upon it. Atheism is the <u>absence</u> of belief in gods, but it does not necessarily exclude some atheists from belief in other supernatural beings. But most atheists in the West do not believe in any. Atheists believe that the only reason religions teach prayer and other rituals is because their members feel a need to communicate with their gods. Because atheists don't believe in gods, they obviously don't try to communicate with any.

An atheist who believes in some type of supernatural being might try to communicate with it, but such communication is completely incidental to that individual but not to atheism as a whole. People who believe in gods often come up a common theological argument known as Pascal's wager: If the believer is wrong and God doesn't exist, then nothing has been lost; on the other hand, if the atheist is wrong, and God does exist, then the atheist risks going to hell. Therefore, it is wiser to take a chance on believing than to take a chance on not believing, and then the atheist is in a bad spot.

Atheists believe there are a number of problems with this argument. For one thing, it assumes that believing or not believing is a choice that a person can make rather than something determined by circumstances, evidence, reason, experience, etc. Wagering requires the ability to choose through an act of will, and belief is not something which you can choose through an act of will. Most atheists do not <u>choose</u> atheism. They just are. Atheism is not chosen but rather the automatic consequence of circumstances as they understand them. It is true that many atheists are highly intelligent and look to define their "belief" by some concrete measure. If that measure doesn't exist, they logically can't justify the belief.

The other fallacy they find with Pascal's wager is the assumption that there are only two options: either the believer is wrong or the atheist is wrong. In fact, both could be wrong because there could be a god, but not the god of the believer. Perhaps it is an entirely different god. The atheist logic is such, if there is a god, and it is moral and loving and worthy of respect, then it won't mind if people have rational doubts about it and rational reasons for not believing in it. This god won't punish people for exercising their critical thinking skills and are skeptical of the claims of other fallible humans. Thus, you wouldn't lose anything.

And if there is a god who punishes people for rational doubt, why would you want to spend an eternity with it anyway? Such a capricious, egotistical, and nasty god wouldn't be much fun. If you can't trust it to be as moral as you are, you can't trust it to keep its promises and make heaven nice or even let you stay for long. Not spending eternity with such a being doesn't sound like much of a loss to an atheist.

Christ

"You must be an atheist because you've never heard about Jesus and the Gospel." There seems to be a belief on the part of many theists —especially Christians and some Muslims—that the only reason why a person would not be a member of their religion is because they are simply unfamiliar with it, or to put it in Christian terms, because one hasn't heard the Good News (which they, of course, now wish to share). As a result, it is common for these believers to immediately launch into preaching in order to rectify that situation.

Of course, it is possible some random atheist really hasn't heard about Jesus or God or Islam, but that is exceedingly unlikely. In fact, it is much more likely that the atheist you are talking to was at one time a Christian, Jew, or Muslim. Although some atheists were raised without belief in any gods, most seem to have started out in a religious household and only later became atheists. Moreover, in a great many cases, it is actually the knowledge of religion that has been a key factor in leading a person to atheism. Many atheists have studied religion extensively, and the more they have learned, the less accepting they have been of what religious authorities have traditionally taught.

Basic Doctrine

<u>What is atheism?</u> Most people already have their own ideas about what atheism is, and what atheists are. Theists usually define atheism incorrectly as a belief system. Atheism is not a belief system. Atheism is not a religion. Atheism does not have a doctrine at all, and atheists certainly do not "deny" a belief in God. Atheism does not know there is a god, but refuses to believe in him. That would be like saying that you know that your mother exists, but you refuse to believe in her. Atheism is the philosophical position that deities do not exist. In the broadest sense, it is the absence of belief in the existence of deities.

Many atheists say they are modern mater*iali sts* (not to be confused with mater*ialism*) and are linked with the everyday experience of people. It is in social life that man develops his mind and emotions, will and conscience, and puts meaning and purpose into life. A materialist lives a full social life and is inspired by progressive ideals; he is concerned with the problems and joys of life, not death. He is deeply involved with shaping his life as a useful member of society and contributing what he can to its progress.

Materialists believe not to hope for happiness beyond the grave but to prize life on earth and strive always to improve it. They put their faith in the human intellect, in the power of knowledge in man's ability to fathom all the secrets of nature and to create a social system based upon reason and justice. The faith is in man and his ability to transform the world by his own efforts. It considers the struggle for progress as a moral obligation and impossible without noble ideals that inspire men to struggle, to perform bold, creative work.

Atheists do not believe in a supernatural power or powers. Atheism does not have a spiritual leader, and it does not have any rites or practices around such a spiritual leader. Atheism requires no initiation, no baptism, no atheist Bible to read, no rituals that atheists must go through to join an atheist church (which in fact does not exist), and no central beliefs that all atheists must adhere to in order to be true atheists. The common thread that ties all atheists together is a lack of belief in gods and supernatural beings.

Every atheist is as unique as a fingerprint when it comes to his or her individual philosophy, convictions, and ideals. There are many reasons why people become atheists. When asked this question during debates or discussions, people assume atheists were driven from religion because of some psychological crisis associated with the churches, religions, or gods that they may have had when younger; or that atheists had some major event happen in their personal lives that made them hate gods. In most cases, that is not true. It is not that complicated. In order to hate gods, atheists would have to believe in gods.

The majority of atheists began by simply questioning some of the core beliefs of their religion. These questions led them to ask their religious leaders. The religious leaders' answers left them unsatisfied. They would then go out and learn on their own, researching their theology, and often, the theology of other religions. For some, that journey took months or a few years; and for some, that journey took decades. Some religions have shown themselves to be a poor example of what they preach. Some religions have impeded scientific progress, liberty, and reformation. And many horrific things have been done in the name of religion over the centuries. It is sometimes these thoughts that drive a person to question their religious upbringing.

Atheism and Morality. Atheists can hold any number of spiritual beliefs because they are never told what to believe. For the same reason, atheists can hold a wide variety of ethical beliefs, ranging from the moral universalism of *humanism*, which holds that a moral code should be applied consistently to all humans, and at the other end of the spectrum, moral *nihilism*, which holds that morality is meaningless. For most religious theists, their faith practices provide the basis for their entire understanding of morality and moral values. Many are convinced that atheists who don't believe in any gods and who have no religion couldn't possibly have a basis for morality or even understand what true moral behavior is. Many go further and argue that it leads to immoral behavior.

The book *Positive Atheism* by Gora, first published in 1972, introduced an alternative use for the phrase. Having grown up in a hierarchical system with a religious basis, Gora called for a secular India and suggested guidelines for a positive atheist philosophy, meaning one that promotes positive values. Positive atheism entails such things as a being morally upright, showing an understanding that religious people have reasons to believe, not proselytizing or lecturing others about atheism, and defending oneself with truthfulness instead of aiming to win any confrontations with outspoken critics.

"Philosophers Susan Neiman and Julian Baggini assert that behaving ethically only because of divine mandate is not true ethical behavior but merely blind obedience. Baggini argues that Atheism is a superior basis for ethics,"[4] claiming it is necessary to evaluate the morality of the imperatives themselves to be able to discern, for example, that "thou shalt not steal" is moral without someone else telling you that.

Atheists believe that much of what passes for Christianity today seems to be more culturally determined than scripturally determined. Their argument is that Christianity is what Christians do, and what Christians do doesn't necessarily correspond to the alleged teachings of Christianity. And the fact that Christians themselves can't agree on one truth, makes athiests doubt it even more.

Logically speaking, atheists feel that most people in North America could be considered atheists. Christians consistently deny the existence of the Hindu, Ancient Roman, Ancient Greek, Ancient Egyptian, and many hundreds of other gods and goddesses. Thus, the difference between a typical Christian and a typical atheist is numerically small. The strong atheist believes that none of the many thousands of gods and goddesses exist; the Christian believes that one God exists, whereas all of the other thousands of deities are nonexistent artificial creations by humans. Undoubtedly, most people think that knowledge is good, and some have tried to reconcile faith and reason, but in the end, to one who believes in gods, faith is always more important. To an atheist, knowledge is more important.

Basic Worship Service

Myth: Most people believe that everyone worships something. Because of the central importance of their religion and worship to their own lives, they view the atheist through the prism of their own belief systems. They assume whatever is "important" to atheists must hold a similarly central position in atheists' lives. Below are some of the suggested candidates for what atheists must worship, but none of them are true.

Myth: Atheists are Materialistic and Worship Money, Material Goods, Comforts. The belief that Atheists are more materialistic than theists isn't one that is founded on any evidence, but it is a popular one. A survey done by researchers in the University of Minnesota's department of sociology found that Atheists are the most despised and distrusted minority in America. The most popular reasons cited were "moral indiscretions" like criminal behavior, rampant materialism, and cultural elitism.[5]

Myth: Atheists Worship Science, Evolution, and Darwin. Technology is their church, evolution is their creed, Darwin is their prophet, and scientists are their high priests. The idea that evolution is a creed for atheists and Charles Darwin a prophet is based on the popular belief among conservative evangelical Christians that evolution is anti-Christian and anti-God. Atheists don't place any greater importance on evolution than on other aspects of science. It is fair to say that atheists place a lot of trust and confidence in science, but this isn't faith in the religious sense and how religious theists typically use the concept. Atheists place their confidence in science because it has repeatedly demonstrated how reliable it is.

Myth: Atheists Worship Satan. Although it's not as common as it once was, there are still people who believe that atheists both believe in and worship Satan, the evil opponent of God. Since atheists profess in an absence of belief in all deities, that would of course include a lack of belief in Satan.

Myth: We All Worship Something Larger, So Atheists Worship Humanity. The idea that Atheists worship themselves in any manner like religious theists worship their god is absurd enough to dispense with quickly. Perhaps because of this some religious theists think it is easier to claim that atheists worship something similar, but larger: all of humanity, the human intellect, or perhaps human government. If everyone has a religion and everyone worships something, then these must seem like plausible candidates. This is just a myth, though, and is not true.[6]

Atheism's Holidays and Rituals: One issue that affects pretty much all atheists is how or, even, if, they might celebrate local religious holidays (or secular holidays with an important religious component). It might seem obvious to say that if you no longer adhere to a particular religion, then it would logically follow that you would also not observe the relevant holidays. Some atheists do take this position, but the matter is a bit more complicated.

Many, albeit not all, religious holidays are a great deal more about the social levels than simply acknowledging religious beliefs. Holidays can serve to form a connection to your own past by evoking memories of past celebration. Holidays can form and reinforce connections with the friends and family with whom you celebrate. But are holidays exclusively for religion and theism? One of the biggest losses in not attending religious ceremonies at a church and not participating in religion-themed rituals is the loss of joint family activities and the diminishing of a family tradition.

<u>Do Any Atheists Go to Church?</u> The idea of atheists attending church services seems contradictory. Doesn't that require belief in God? Doesn't a person have to believe in a religion in order to attend its worship services? Isn't freedom on Sunday morning one of the benefits of atheism?

Although most atheists don't count themselves as part of religions, which require regular attendance at churches or other houses of worship, you can still find some who do attend such services from time to time or even regularly. The reasons for such attendance are varied. Some atheists do count themselves as members of religious groups that encourage attendance at Sunday morning meetings or services.

Being an atheist means not believing in any gods—it doesn't mean not being religious in any fashion. In the United States, there are several groups that count themselves as religious but either don't require belief in any gods or actually discourage belief in the traditional god of orthodox Christianity. These groups include *Ethical Culture*, the *Unitarian-Universalist Church*, and a variety of religious humanist organizations. Many, many atheists are members of these groups and regularly attend meetings or services on Sunday mornings (or at some other time during the week).

There are also atheists who can be found at the services of even traditional theistic religious faiths. Some enjoy the music. Some attend for the sake of harmony and unity within their families. Others appreciate the chance to take time out of their hectic schedules in the context of something that challenges them to think differently about some of life's more enduring mysteries. Granted, they don't actually agree with many of the premises and conclusions offered during the sermons, but that doesn't stop them from being able to appreciate the positions described and from finding interesting insights into human nature and life's journey. This brings us to another reason why an atheist might attend religious services: to learn firsthand what members of different religious faiths really believe and how they express those beliefs. You can learn quite a lot from books and magazines, but in the end, you can miss a lot if you don't try to develop at least some firsthand experiences. And as we stated earlier, knowledge is very important to an atheist.

An atheist seeking to learn more probably won't be involved with regular attendance at a particular church; instead, they are more likely to be involved with attending a number of churches, mosques, temples, and such on an irregular basis in order to find out what they are like at different times of the year. This doesn't mean that they are considering abandoning their skepticism or critical stance vis-à-vis religion and theism; it just means that they are curious about what others believe and think that they might be able to learn something, even from those they disagree with quite strongly.

How many religious theists can say the same? How many religious theists take the time to attend religious services at other denominations and groups within their own faith tradition (e.g., Catholics going to Quaker services or white Episcopalians attending a black Baptist church)? How many go outside their tradition (e.g., Christians going to a mosque on Friday or Jews going to Hindu ashram)? How many people from any of these groups attend meetings of skeptics or services at a Unitarian church, which hosts primarily humanist viewpoints?

Infant Baptism, Blessing

Not Applicable

Initiation, Baptism, or Confirmation

There are an increasing number of atheists who are "debaptizing" themselves as a statement of their feelings. They state that they were baptized as infants and didn't have a choice. Many are finding it more of a challenge than they expected to get their names off church roles.

The *National Secular Society's Debaptism Certificate* caused a sensation in the blogosphere and around the BBC after it was reported by Robert Pigott, the BBC's religious affairs correspondent. It turned into the most viewed news story of the day.

The Certificate of Debaptism declares: I _____ having been subjected to the Rite of Christian Baptism in infancy (before reaching an age of consent), hereby publicly revoke any implications of that Rite and renounce the Church that carried it out. In the name of human reason, I reject all its Creeds and all other such superstition in particular, the perfidious belief that any baby needs to be cleansed by Baptism of alleged Original sin, and the evil power of supposed demons. I wish to be excluded henceforth from enhanced claims of church membership numbers based on past baptismal statistics used, for example, for the purpose of securing legislative privilege.[7]

Marriage

Atheists are human too, and so of course atheists are just as likely as anyone else to participate in many of the common social experiences that mark a society. One of them is, of course, weddings—their own and those of friends and relatives. It isn't always easy to cope with the widespread religiosity one can encounter in society, especially when it comes to significant events, which are supposed to be happy and/or meaningful. It is, however, important to understand that just because religion plays such an important role for other people doesn't mean it must play a similar role for all people.

Atheists consider marriage a commitment to another individual, just as theists do. Marriage is one of the most intimate and serious relationships a person can have in their lives; consequently, it is understandable that people wonder to what degree the differences between atheism and theism affect that relationship. An atheist, in fact, has more to consider than many other people getting married as they make this lifelong commitment. Can atheists and theists make a marriage work? And, of course, more questions can arise as a marriage develops, for example: What do you do when your in-laws are very religious? Do you even tell them about being an atheist?

Problems also develop because people develop—they may become more or less religious as time goes on, thus altering the nature of the marriage. Basically, the trials of marriage are the same for atheists as they are for theists.

Death and Afterlife

Dying in America is a complex and distasteful process for most American families and often a taboo subject. As Timothy Leary puts it, *"Most human beings are taught to face death, like life, as victims—helpless, fearful, resigned."* He goes on,

In America all of these threatening perceptions of death, and the fears that they engender, have become integral to the development of a high-income death industry; pre-death medical treatment, cadaver dressing including makeup, artificial under skin inserts, wigs, freezing, embalming, burials, cremations, urn-production, casket-building, funerals, home visiting, soul saving and church/temple services are all part of this.

As Robert Hatch says, *"For once we complete life's passage, we enter a realm where two divergent forces control our destiny; the undertaker our body, and God our soul."*[8]

But atheists must face this multiple-layered challenge with an additional concept that there are no gods and there is no afterlife. And as atheists, they must come to terms with this position, not only as an intellectual exercise, but as part of their emotional well-being and their scientifically defined way of living and viewing life. To face death is to be able to prepare for this last part of living, to embrace it as an end and not to fear it. It is a fundamental part of who they have chosen to be—an atheist.

Death in America is tightly interwoven with religious ritual and political regulation. So there is another hurdle the atheist has to deal with in preparation for death. Obviously, atheists are not interested in having prayers said over their corpses or some kind of processional cemetery burial. But the problems go much further than this. It is during dying that the first problems begin. An atheist believes that he or she is a biological machine whose purpose is to make a difference here and now. There is no afterlife. Therefore, life itself is very valuable. But they also believe that if their existence is no longer going to benefit anyone, they should be allowed to cease to exist. And so when they are physically and mentally at weak or vulnerable moments, atheists are faced with a fight whose rules are created by people who don't necessarily look at life through the same prism as they do. Choices in dying must be carefully considered by atheists long before that time comes.

How do they create an environment to exercise control over where you die, when you die, how you die, how much you suffer when you are dying, and how to maintain your atheist tenets throughout the process? Many atheists have additional verbiage added into their living wills:

If I am in a medical facility/hospital that is supported by a religious denomination I must be moved to an alternative secular facility immediately, regardless of my condition. It must be made clear to all medical staff dealing with me that I do not believe in a god; therefore I do not believe in miracles or "acts of god." It must also be made clear to all medical staff that my non-beliefs, as they affect my treatment, supersede their beliefs, therefore, they may not impinge their beliefs on their choice of treatment for me. I don't fear death at all. As a committed Atheist I have come to terms with the end of my life as a natural, anticipated process. I think about it and talk about it as an everyday item. Dying and death have always seemed to be something final, simple, and very commonplace. Atheism is to me, a way of life—I and others like me should be able to make it our way of dying and death, too. And of course there is the Atheist's life: "As a well-spent day brings happy sleep, so life well lived brings happy death."

I don't fear death, but what I do fear, desperately, is the way my fellow non-Atheist humans are going to abuse me as I approach death and after I die. Even though death is final, I feel so sad that my wishes as an Atheist will probably not be taken into consideration. At the end of my life, my non-beliefs will be superseded by others' beliefs because I will no longer have a voice. Because of the insidious involvement of formal religions in every facet of dying and death and instead of continuing to help my species after death—as my Atheism demands—I will be thrown away.[9]

Atheists also attempt to avoid all expenses and ceremony of the traditional funeral. Many try to find a way to have their bodies disposed of in a way that is in line with their atheism. As an atheist and a supporter of scientific advancement for the good of the species and the improvement of life, they may bequeath their body to a medical college. Hopefully, it will have helped science in a small way to further benefit humankind.

Judgment and Salvation

"One of the first questions Atheists are asked by true believers and doubters alike is, 'If you don't believe in God, there's nothing to prevent you from committing crimes, is there? Without the fear of hell-fire and eternal damnation, you can do anything you like, can't you?'"

From a treatise by an atheist.

The answer to the questions posed above is, of course, "Absolutely not." The behavior of Atheists is subject to the same rules of sociology, psychology, and neurophysiology that govern the behavior of all members of our species, religionists included. Moreover, despite protestations to the contrary, we may assert as a general rule that when religionists practice ethical behavior, it isn't really due to their fear of hell-fire and damnation, nor is it due to their hopes of heaven. Ethical behavior—regardless of who the practitioner may be—results always from the same causes and is regulated by the same forces, and has nothing to do with the presence or absence of religious belief. [...] As human beings, we are social animals. [...] Among our kind, emotions are contagious, and it is only the rare (individuals) among us who can be happy in the midst of a sad society. It is in our nature to be happy in the midst of happiness, sad in the midst of sadness. It is in our nature, fortunately, to seek happiness for our fellows at the same time as we seek it for ourselves. Our happiness is greater when it is shared. [...]

This should not surprise us when we consider that among the societies of our nearest primate cousins, the great apes' social behavior is not chaotic; even if gorillas do lack the Ten Commandments. The young chimpanzee does not need an oracle to tell it to honor its mother and to refrain from killing its brothers and sisters. Of course, family squabbles and even murder have been observed in ape societies, but such behaviors are exceptions, not the norm. [...] It is further cheering to learn that socio-biologists have even observed altruistic behavior among troops of baboons. More than once, in troops attacked by leopards, aged, post reproduction-age males have been observed to linger at the rear of the escaping troop and to engage the leopard in what often amounts to a suicidal fight.

As the old male delays the leopard's pursuit by sacrificing his very life, the females and young escape and live to fulfill their several destinies. [...] So too it is in human societies, everywhere and at all times. [...]

Let us bring this essay back to the point of our departure. Because we have the nervous systems of social animals, we are generally happier in the company of our fellow creatures than alone. Because we are emotionally suggestible, as we practice enlightened self-interest we usually will be wise to choose behaviors which will make others happy and willing to cooperate and accept us—for their happiness will reflect back upon us and intensify our own happiness. [...] Thus it happens, when the Atheist approaches the problem of finding natural grounds for human morals and establishing a non-superstitious basis for behavior; that it appears as though nature has already solved the problem to a great extent. Indeed, it appears as though the problem of establishing a natural, humanistic basis for ethical behavior is not much of a problem at all. It is in our natures to desire love, to seek beauty, and to thrill at the act of creation.[10]

Special Doctrine

Practical Atheism: In practical or pragmatic atheism, also known as apatheism (individuals live as if there are no gods and explain natural phenomena without resorting to the divine. The existence of gods is not denied, but may be designated unnecessary or useless; gods neither provide purpose to life nor influence everyday life, according to this view).

A form of practical atheism with implications for the scientific community is methodological naturalism—the "tacit adoption or assumption of philosophical naturalism within scientific method with or without fully accepting or believing it." Practical atheism can take various forms: absence of religious motivation (belief in gods does not motivate moral action, religious action, or any other form of action); active exclusion of the problem of gods and religion from intellectual pursuit and practical action; indifference (the absence of any interest in the problems of gods and religion); or unawareness of the concept of a deity.

<u>Theoretical Atheism:</u> Theoretical, or contemplative, atheism bases its arguments against the existence of gods on various psychological, sociological, metaphysical, and epistemological forms.

<u>Epistemological Atheism:</u> Epistemological atheism argues that people cannot know God or determine the existence of God. This form of atheism holds that gods are not discernible as a matter of principle and, therefore, cannot be definitely known to exist. Skepticism, based on the ideas of Hume, asserts that certainty about anything is impossible, so one can ever know the existence of God.

<u>Metaphysical Atheism:</u> Metaphysical atheism is based on metaphysical monism—the view that reality is homogeneous and indivisible. Absolute metaphysical atheists subscribe to some form of physicalism; hence, they explicitly deny the existence of nonphysical beings.

<u>Theodicean Atheism:</u> Theodicean atheists argue that an omniscient, omnipotent, and omnibenevolent God is not compatible with a world where there is evil and suffering, and where divine love is hidden from many people. A similar argument is attributed to Siddhartha Gautama, the founder of Buddhism.

<u>Logical Atheism:</u> Logical atheism holds that the various conceptions of gods, such as the personal god of Christianity, are ascribed logically inconsistent qualities. Such atheists present deductive arguments against the existence of God, which assert the incompatibility between certain traits, such as perfection, creator-status, immutability, omniscience, omnipresence, omnipotence, omnibenevolence, transcendence, non-physicality, justice and mercy.

<u>Axiological or Constructive Atheism:</u> Axiological or constructive atheism rejects the existence of gods in favor of a "higher absolute," such as humanity. This form of atheism favors humanity as the true source of ethics and values, and permits individuals to resolve moral problems without resorting to God.[11]

<u>Atheism vs. Agnosticism:</u> What's the difference? A variety of categories have been proposed to try to distinguish the different forms of atheism. It was suggested that the man who is unacquainted with theism is an atheist because he does not believe in a something he is not familiar with. The fact that a child does not believe in God because he has never heard of God qualifies him as an atheist. Hence, the term *implicit atheism* refers to "the absence of theistic belief, without a conscious rejection of it." *Explicit atheism* refers to the more common definition of conscious disbelief.

Philosophers such as Antony Flew, Michael Martin, and William L. Rowe have contrasted *positive atheism* with *negative atheism*. Positive atheism is the explicit affirmation that gods do not exist. Negative atheism includes all other forms of nontheism. According to this categorization, anyone who is not a theist is either a weak or a strong atheist. Under this demarcation of atheism, most agnostics qualify as negative atheists or implicit atheists. *Agnosticism* is a recent concept introduced by Thomas Huxley, the famous friend and advocate of Darwin, to describe his own concerns about knowledge and belief. It is derived from the Greek roots *a* (without) and *gnosis* (knowledge).

Most agnostics see their view as distinct from atheism, which they may consider no more justified than theism or requiring an equal conviction. The supposed unattainability of knowledge for or against the existence of gods is sometimes seen as indication that atheism also requires a leap of faith. Agnostics are supposedly people who claim to be undecided about religious questions or possibly uninterested in them. They are not sure or noncommittal; they do not have enough information, and hypothetically, they are waiting, actively or passively, for some basis on which to settle the two claims of theism versus atheism.

Persons who declare themselves to be agnostics allegedly say, "I don't know." Many people who claim they are agnostic discount the idea that they are also an atheist. It is common to believe that agnosticism is a more "reasonable" position while atheism is more "dogmatic."

People who are brave enough to state that they do not believe in any gods are still despised in many places, while an agnostic is perceived as more respectable. This may be a mistake because some atheists do not necessarily deny any gods and may indeed be an atheist because they do not know for sure—in other words, they may be an agnostic as well.

Agnosticism was originally used to describe a person who did not know for sure if any gods exist or not. But many find it confusing. A person can believe in a god (theism) without claiming to know for sure if that god exists: the result is *agnostic theism*. On the other hand, a person can disbelieve in gods (atheism) without claiming to know for sure that no gods can or do exist: the result is *agnostic atheism*.

In the end, the fact of the matter is a person isn't faced with the necessity of only being either an atheist or an agnostic. Quite the contrary, not only can a person be both, but it is in fact common for people to be both agnostics and atheists. An agnostic atheist won't claim to know for sure that nothing warranting the label "God" exists, or that such cannot exist; but they also are unsure that such an entity does indeed exist.

This is all very intellectual and philosophical, but the bottom line is that, right or wrong, atheists have feelings that should be honored and discussed with an open mind. We may have to agree to disagree in the end, but looking for common ground is still worth the effort.

Notes

Notes

Church of Scientology

The Creed of the Church of Scientology says: We of the Church believe:"... "That a ll men h ave inalienable rights to their own religious practices and their performance." The Church of Scientology believes "that Man is basically good, that he is seeking to survive, [and] that his survival depends on himself and upon his fellows and his attainment of brotherhood with the universe.

History

The Church of Scientology sprouted from the creative genius of Lafayette Ronald Hubbard. Born in 1911, he spent much of his childhood on his grandfather's Montana ranch while his parents served abroad in the US Navy. During the 1920s, Hubbard started to visit his parents as a teenager in Asia, where he was introduced to Taoism, Buddhism, and other Eastern philosophies.

As a child, he read extensively, and by the age of twelve was studying the theories of Freud. "Hubbard always claimed that his ideas of *Dianetics* originated in the 1920s and 1930s. By his own account, he spent a great deal of time in the Oak Knoll Naval Hospital's library, where he would have encountered the work of Freud and other psychoanalysts."[2]

In 1929 he returned to the United States and in 1930 enrolled in George Washington University, studying mathematics, engineering, and nuclear physics. Hubbard wanted to answer the basic questions relating to the human being's nature, and decided to do further research on his own. To finance this, he began a literary career in the early 1930s, publishing numerous stories and screen plays in various genres, including adventure, mystery, and science fiction. Hubbard continued his travels and then served in the United States Navy during World War II. He suffered near fatal wounds during the war, and used some of his own theories concerning the human mind to assist in his healing.[3]

In 1938, L. Ron Hubbard authors a manuscript called *Excalibur*, which contains ideas that were later incorporated into Scientology.

In 1949, his first published work on the theory of dianetics appeared in the winter/spring issue of the *Explorers Club Journal* entitled "*Terra Incognita: The Mind.*"

Two of Hubbard's key supporters at the time were John W. Campbell Jr., the editor of *Astounding Science Fiction,* and Dr. Joseph A. Winter. Winter, hoping to have Dianetics accepted in the medical community, submitted papers outlining the principles and methodology of Dianetic therapy to the *Journal of the American Medical Association* and the *American Journal of Psychiatry* in 1949, but these were rejected.[4]

In April 1950, Hubbard and four others, "an attorney, a publisher, a doctor and an engineer" established the *Hubbard Dianetic Research Foundation* in New Jersey to coordinate work related for the forthcoming publication. Hubbard wrote *Dianetics: The Modern Science of Mental Health* at that time, allegedly completing the 180,000-word book in six weeks. This book described mental techniques designed to clear the mind of unwanted sensations, irrational fears, and psychosomatic illnesses.

His book entered the New York Times bestseller list in June and stayed there for twenty-six consecutive weeks.[5] Dianetics appealed to a broad range of people who used instructions from the book and applied the method to each other, becoming practitioners themselves. Hubbard found himself the leader of a growing dianetics movement. He became a popular lecturer and began training his first dianetics counselors or "auditors."[6]

The success of selling *Dianetics, The Modern Science of Mental Health* brought in a flood of money, which Hubbard used to establish Dianetics foundations in six major American cities. The scientific and medical communities were far less enthusiastic about Dianetics, viewing it with bemusement, concern, or outright derision. Complaints were made against local Dianetics practitioners for allegedly practicing medicine without a license. This eventually prompted Dianetics advocates to disclaim any medicinal benefits in order to avoid regulation. Dianetics continued to meet criticism. Morris Fishbein, the editor of the Journal of theAmericanMedical Association (and well-known at the time as a debunker of quack medicine) dismissed Hubbard's book.

An article in Newsweek stated that *"the Dianetics concept is unscientific and unworthy of discussion or review."* In January 1951, the New Jersey Board of Medical Examiners instituted proceedings against the *Hubbard Dianetic Research Foundation* for teaching medicine without a license, which eventually led to that foundation's bankruptcy.[7]

Because of a sale of assets resulting from the bankruptcy, Hubbard no longer owned the rights to the name dianetics, but its philosophical framework still provided the seed for Scientology to grow.

Also in 1951, Hubbard introduced the *Electropsychometer* (E-meter for short) as an auditing aid. Based on a design by Hubbard, the device is held by Scientologists to be a useful tool in detecting changes in a person's state of mind.

Some practitioners of Dianetics reported experiences which they believed had occurred in past lives, or previous incarnations. In early 1951, reincarnation became a subject of intense debate within Dianetics. Campbell and Winter, who were still hopeful of winning support for Dianetics from the medical community, championed a resolution to ban the topic. But Hubbard decided to take the reports of past life events seriously and postulated the existence of the thetan, a concept similar to the soul. This was an important factor in the transition from secular Dianetics to the religion of Scientology.[8]

Scientologists refer to the book *Dianetics: The Modern Science of Mental Health* as book one. In 1952, Hubbard's research soon led him into a spiritual realm; Hubbard published a new set of teachings as Scientology, a religious philosophy. Scientology did not replace Dianetics but extended it to cover new areas. Where the goal of Dianetics is to rid the individual of his reactive mind engrams, the stated goal of Scientology is to rehabilitate the individual's spiritual nature so that he may reach his full potential. Hubbard publicly announces the formal establishment of the philosophy of *Scientology* and the formation of the *Hubbard Association of Scientologists International.* He demonstrates the first E-meter and moves to Phoenix, Arizona; then shortly after, *A History of Man* was published. In 1954, the first *Church of Scientology* was established in Los Angeles, California.

In 1955, Hubbard established the Founding Church of Scientology in Washington, DC. In 1957, the Church of Scientology of California was granted tax-exempt status by the United States Internal Revenue Service (IRS), and so, for a time, were other local churches. In 1958 however, the IRS started a review of the appropriateness of this status. In 1959, Hubbard moved to England, remaining there until the mid-1960s.[9]

The religion continued to grow during the 1950s and 1960s, and the movement quickly spread, both in the United States and other English-speaking countries such as England, Ireland, South Africa, and Australia. In the mid-sixties, the Church of Scientology was banned in several Australian states, starting with Victoria, in 1965. The ban was based on the *Anderson Report*, which found that the auditing process involved command hypnosis, in which the hypnotist assumes positive authoritative control over the patient. The church experienced other challenges as well. The United States Food and Drug Administration began an investigation concerning the claims the Church of Scientology made in connection with its E-meters. On January 1963, they raided offices of the Church of Scientology and seized hundreds of E-meters as illegal medical devices. The devices have since been required to carry a disclaimer saying that they are a purely religious artifact.

In the course of developing Scientology, Hubbard presented rapidly changing teachings that were often self-contradictory. For the inner cadre of Scientologists in that period, involvement depended not so much on belief in a particular doctrine but on absolute, unquestioning faith in Hubbard. In 1966 Hubbard stepped down as executive director of Scientology to devote himself to research and writing. The following year, he formed the *Sea Organization* or Sea Org, which was to develop into an elite group within Scientology. The Sea Org was based on three ships, the Diana, the Athena, and the Apollo, which served as the flag ship. One month after the establishment of the Sea Org, Hubbard announced that he had made a breakthrough discovery, the result of which were the *"OT III"* materials purporting to provide a method for overcoming factors inhibiting spiritual progress. These materials were first disseminated on the ships, and then propagated by Sea Org members reassigned to staff Advanced Organizations on land.

In 1967 the IRS removed Scientology's tax-exempt status, asserting that its activities were commercial and operated for the benefit o f Hubbard, rather than for charitable or religious purposes. The decision resulted in a process of litigation that would be settled in the Church's favor a quarter of a century later, the longest case of litigation in IRS history.[10]

In 1981, Scientology took the German government to court for the first time in order to obtain religious status there. On January 1, 1982, the *Religious Technology Centre* (RTC) was established to oversee and ensure the standard application of Scientology technology. On January 24, 1986, L. Ron Hubbard died at his ranch near San Luis Obispo, California, after spending most of his last years traveling around quietly on his yacht. David Miscavige became the head of the organization. Hubbard had completed all his research before his death in 1986 and left all his materials and copyrights to the Church of Scientology's Religious Technology Centre along with most of his personal estate.

The Church of Scientology has pursued an extensive public relations campaign for the recognition of Scientology as a religion. A number of governments now view the Church as a religious organization entitled to protections and tax relief, while others continue to view it as a pseudoreligion or cult. The differences between these classifications have become a major problem when discussing religions in general and Scientology specifically. Scientology is officially recognized as a religion in the United States. Recognition came in 1993, when the IRS stated, after previously rescinding tax-exempt status, that Scientology is "operated exclusively for religious and charitable purposes." In 2000, the Italian Supreme Court ruled that Scientology is a religion for legal purposes. In the years that followed, many other countries granted religious status to the Church, with Germany fighting the longest battle, finally giving up in 2007. Other countries, notably Canada, France, Greece, Belgium, and the United Kingdom, refuse to grant Scientology religious recognition.

On May of 2004, David Miscavige announced the *"Golden Age of Knowledge,"* a church program intended to make all Scientology materials available. It started with the release of eighteen congresses. The new head of the church also began the process of revising all books and lectures.

In July 2007, a re-release of all of Hubbard's basic books and tape recordings on Dianetics and Scientology was announced. The announcement was made in a speech given by David Miscavige at the Flag Land Base. In an almost three hour briefing he claimed that many errors had been found in previous versions of the books, and that a large-scale project was undertaken to locate the original Dictaphone recordings and annotated transcriptions of the books and restore each work to its original, pure form.[11]

The latest edition of the organization's publication, *What Is Scientology?*, lists 373 churches and missions (plus hundreds of related organizations, which are not directly comparable to congregations) in 163 countries. In 2007, a church official claimed 3.5 million members in the United States. But *Adherents.com* estimates there are less than 750,000 continuing members. In 2008, the American Religious Identification Survey estimated that there are only 25,000 active members in the United States. The actual membership of the Church of Scientology is difficult to assess. Scientologists tend to disparage general religious surveys on the grounds that many members maintain cultural and social ties to other religious groups and will, when asked their religion, answer with their traditional and more socially acceptable affiliation to prevent ridicule. There are others who have not converted from their original faith and feel that Scientology has increased their awareness of the spiritual nature of man and the religious life in general so they feel comfortable with both and believe that their two faiths enhance each other.

God or Gods

Scientology says they believe in "the Supreme Being, whatever you believe that to be." They do not really worship God in the same senseChristians do. "Scientology considers the belief in a God or gods as something personal and therefore offers no specific dogma. The nature of the Supreme Being is revealed personally through each individual as s/he becomes more conscious and spiritually aware. There exists a life energy or force (*Theta*) beyond and within all."[12]

Christ

Quote from a website developed by a Scientologist: "I do not know any Scientologist who believes Jesus Christ didn't exist. Each individual Scientologists belief in Christ is personal to them. There is no Church of Scientology doctrine instructing one how to view Christ."

Although there are some references on some websites to the belief in Christ and Christianity as being part of a mental implant that happened in the very distant past.[13]

Basic Doctrine

The word scientology literally means "the study of truth." It comes from the Latin word *scio,* meaning "knowing in the fullest sense of the word" and the Greek word *logos,* meaning "study of." Scientology has a defined creed, which was composed in 1954, the year Scientology was established as a religion. This creed states that all church members believe that people "of whatever race, color, or creed were created with equal rights." It holds that all people "have inalienable rights to their own religious practices and their performance," as well as their lives, sanity, and defense, and that they have inalienable rights to "choose, assist or support their own organizations, churches and governments," and "to think freely, to talk freely, to write freely their own opinions and to counter or utter or write upon the opinions of others." According to the creed, God forbids people to destroy each other, to destroy another's sanity or to "destroy or enslave another's soul," and "to destroy or reduce the survival of one's companions or one's group." Lastly, it states the belief "that the spirit can be saved and that the spirit alone may save or heal the body."[14]

They teach that man consists of three parts. The first of these is the spirit, called in scientology the *thetan* (from the Greek letter theta, meaning "thought" or "spirit"), which is the individual himself. It is the most important of the three parts of man. The second of these parts is the mind. The thetan uses his mind as a communication and control system between himself and his environment. The third of these parts is the body. The body is not the person.

<u>The Dynamics of Existence:</u> Through Scientology, a person realizes that his life and influence extend far beyond himself. He becomes aware also of the necessity to participate in a much broader spectrum. By understanding each of these dynamics and their relationship, one to the other, he is able to do so and, thus, increase survival on all these dynamics. Scientology states that the basic principle of existence is survival. Survival is considered as the single and sole purpose, and it is subdivided into eight dynamics:

- *Dynamic One* is the urge toward survival as an individual. It includes one's own body and one's own mind. This dynamic includes the individual plus his immediate possessions.
- *Dynamic Two* is creativity in making things for the future and includes any creativity. The second dynamic contains the family unit and the rearing of children as well as anything that can be categorized as a family activity.
- *Dynamic Three* is the urge toward survival for the group. It is group survival, the group tending to take on a life and existence of its own. "A group can be a community, friends, a company, a social lodge, a state, a nation, a race or in short, any group." (Based on the belief that you cannot free yourself spiritually without working to free others, Scientology has founded and supports many organizations for social betterment, particularly in the areas of drug abuse, crime, psychiatric abuse, and government abuse of law, human rights, religious freedom, education, and morality. Scientology strongly favors the use of their methodology for spiritual/mental healing over the use of conventional treatment.)

- *Dynamic Four* is the urge of the individual toward survival for all of mankind.
- "*Dynamic Five* is the urge to survive as life forms and with the help of life forms such as animals, birds, insects, fish and vegetation. This includes all living things whether animal or vegetable, anything directly and intimately motivated by life."
- *Dynamic Six* is the urge to survive as part of the physical universe and includes the survival of the physical universe itself.
- *Dynamic Seven* is the urge toward survival as a spiritual being. This is separate from the physical universe and is the source of life itself. Thus there is an effort for the survival of life source.
- *Dynamic Eight* is the urge toward survival as a part of the Supreme Being and "is commonly called God, the Supreme Being or Creator, but it is correctly defined as infinity." It actually embraces the allness of all.[15]

The optimum solution to any problem is that solution that brings the greatest benefit to the greatest number o f dynamics. Actions are considered "good" if they promote survival across all eight dynamics or realms of action. Goodness is conceived in terms of constructive survival action, as construction may also require a degree of destruction for new construction to take place, construction must outweigh destruction in order for something to be considered good.

Through Scientology, a person realizes that his life and influence extend far beyond himself. By understanding each of these dynamics and their relationship, one to the other, he is able to increase survival on all of these dynamics.

While Scientology believes that many social problems are the unintentional results of people's imperfections, it states that there are also truly malevolent individuals. Hubbard believed that approximately 80 percent of all people are what he called social personalities—people who welcome and contribute to the welfare of others. The remaining 20 percent of the population, Hubbard thought, were suppressive personalities. According to Hubbard, only about 2.5 per cent of this 20 percent are hopelessly antisocial personalities; these make up the small proportion of truly dangerous individuals in humanity: "the Adolf Hitlers and the Genghis Khans, the unrepentant murderers and the drug lords."

Scientologists believe that any contact with suppressive or antisocial individuals has an adverse effect on one's spiritual condition, necessitating disconnection.[16]

Scientology and Dianetics place a heavy emphasis on understanding word definitions. Hubbard wrote a book entitled "*How to Use a Dictionary,*" in which he defined the methods of correcting "misunderstoods" (a Scientology term referring to a "misunderstood word or symbol"). It is believed in Scientology that complete understanding of a subject matter requires first complete understanding of the words of that subject matter. Hubbard also assembled the *Technical Dictionary*, a lexicon of hundreds of words, terms, and definitions that are used by Scientologists. Hubbard modified definitions for many existing English words, such as "*clear*" and "*static.*" "Clear" was borrowed from early computer science during his 1948 research. He likened the human mind to a perfect computer that needed to be "cleared" of erroneous data enforced upon it from engrams or painful memories. Soon after the word "*clear*" as a noun meant a person who had attained such a state. He also coined many terms that are variants on standard English words, such as "*enturbulate*" (to make turbulent) and "*havingness*" (the state of having). Critics of Scientology have accused Hubbard of "loading the language" and using Scientology jargon to keep Scientologists from interacting with information sources outside of Scientology.[17]

"Scientology describes itself as the study and handling of the spirit in relationship to itself, others, and all of life. One purpose of Scientology, as stated by the Church of Scientology, is to become certain of one's spiritual existence and one's relationship to God, or the "Supreme Being."[18] Scientologists believe that an individual should discover for himself that Scientology works by personally applying its principles and observing or experiencing desirable results.

Scientology claims that its practices provide methods by which a person can achieve greater spiritual awareness. Two primary methods of increasing spiritual awareness are referred to in Scientology as "auditing" and training. Within Scientology, progression from level to level is often called the bridge to total freedom. Scientologists progress from preclear to clear and ultimately operating thetan.

Scientology has a series of techniques called "assists" which are believed to alleviate injury, trauma or discomfort. These techniques used are based on the belief that the spirit can solve the body's difficulties by putting the spirit in communication with the body. Scientology oversees a program referred to as the *"Purification Rundown,"* which is promoted as a method of "detoxification" developed by L. Ron Hubbard. It involves the use of saunas, exercise, vitamins, the drinking of oils, as well as light jogging. The Purification Rundown is usually the first step taken by a Scientologist attempting to attain a state of "Clear" and is promoted as a health regimen within Scientology and in Scientology's drug rehabilitation program Narconon.[19]

<u>The Auditing Session:</u> Scientology presents two major divisions of the mind. The reactive mind is thought to absorb all pain and emotional trauma, while the analytical mind is a rational mechanism, which is responsible for consciousness. The reactive mind stores mental images that are not readily available to the analytical (conscious) mind; these are referred to as engrams.

Engrams are believed to be painful and debilitating; as they accumulate, people move further away from their true identity. To avoid this fate is the scientologist's basic goal. Dianetic training is the tool through which the scientologist progresses toward the clear state, winning gradual freedom from the reactive mind's engrams and acquiring certainty of his or her reality as a thetan. The primary way that Scientology's principles are applied to an individual is called *auditing*—from the Latin word audire, meaning "to listen."

Auditing in the context of Dianetics and Scientology is an activity where a person trained in "auditing" listens and gives auditing commands to a subject, (a "preclear") which seeks to elevate the mind to a state of Clear, one of freedom from the influences of the reactive mind. By doing this, the subjects are said to be able to free themselves from unwanted barriers that inhibit their natural abilities. Scientologists state that the person being audited is completely aware of everything that happens and becomes even more alert as auditing progresses.

Scientology asserts that people have hidden abilities which have not yet been fully realized. Through auditing, it is said that people can solve their problems and free themselves of *engrams*. This restores them to their natural condition as thetans and enables them to be more effective in their daily lives, responding rationally and creatively to life events rather than reacting to them under the direction of stored engrams.

Auditing is a one-on-one session with a Scientology counselor or auditor. It bears a superficial similarity to confession or pastoral counseling, but the auditor does not dispense forgiveness or advice the way a pastor or priest might do. Instead, the auditor's task is to help the person discover and understand engrams and their limiting effects for themselves. Most auditing requires an *electropsychometer* or E-meter that measures the mental state or change of state of a person, helping the auditor locate areas of spiritual distress or travail so they can be addressed and handled in a session. [20]

The E-meter does not in itself do anything to a person. It is a highly sensitive instrument that reacts to changes in mental activity. Scientology teaches that individuals are immortal souls or spirits and are not limited to a single lifetime. The E-meter is believed to aid the auditor in identifying ingrained memories (engrams, incidents, and implants) of past events in a thetan's current life and in previous ones.

In such Scientology publications as *"Have You Lived Before This Life?,* Hubbard wrote about past life experiences dating back billions and even trillions of years. According to the Church of Scientology's official guidelines, all communications during auditing are confidential. The auditor is obliged by the church's doctrine to maintain a strict code of conduct toward the preclear called the *Auditor's Code.* Auditing is said to be successful only when the auditor conducts himself in accordance with the code. A violation of the Auditor's Code is considered a high crime under Scientology law. Auditors are required to become proficient with the use of their E-meters. A training simulator able to recreate all manner of E-meter reactions is used to assist in auditor training. Auditors do not receive final certification until they have successfully completed an internship and have demonstrated and proven ability in the skills they have been trained in.

Scientologists believe that material must be learned in a definite order, never skipping to material which is overly complex before it is called for. The Church of Scientology publishes a particular sequence of study which must be followed in progression of Scientology. A Scientologist must receive the newer and higher levels only upon completion of the previous level. Scientology calls this concept a "gradient: breaking down a complicated idea into smaller pieces so that someone who could not grasp the whole idea at once can learn it piece by piece." Scientologists say that approaching information on a gradient keeps people from becoming confused.[22]

The Church of Scientology holds that at the higher levels of initiation (*OT levels*), teachings are imparted which may be considered mystical and potentially harmful to unprepared readers. These teachings are kept secret from members who have not reached these levels. The Church states that the secrecy is warranted to keep its materials' use in context, to protect its members from being exposed to materials they are not yet prepared for.[23]

The OT level teachings include accounts of various cosmic catastrophes that befell the thetans. Hubbard described these early events collectively as "space opera." The highest level, OT VIII, is only disclosed at sea, on the Scientology cruise ship *Freewinds*. It was released in the late 1980s. Since being entered into evidence in several court cases beginning in the early 1980s, synopses and excerpts of these secret teachings have appeared in numerous publications.

In Scientology, founder L. Ron Hubbard used the science fiction term space opera to describe what he said were actual extraterrestrial civilizations and alien interventions in past lives. It is a basic belief of Scientology that a human being is actually an immortal spiritual being—termed a thetan—that is presently trapped on planet earth in a "meat body."[24] Hubbard described key incidents on the "whole track: the moment to moment record of a person's existence in this universe in picture and impression form" in his writings and lectures.

He also gave details of alien civilizations, their roles and their histories—most of which seem to have involved the mass brainwashing of thetans with *implants* (false memories). Each thetan has had innumerable past lives, and it is accepted in Scientology that the thetan's arrival on earth came from extraterrestrial cultures. "Descriptions of space opera incidents are seen as nonfiction in the beliefs of Scientology; they appeared in the online *Glossary for Dianetics and Scientology*, although they were later removed from it."[25] Descriptions of space opera incidents are seen as true events by Scientologists. Although incidents can literally be any incident that occurs anywhere on the whole track, Hubbard's writings dwelled almost exclusively on fanciful ones from earth's prehistory because these key incidents are crucial to auditing. Many of them first appeared in Hubbard's book *What to Audit* (later retitled A History of Man). Scientology auditing practices often have to do with addressing implants that have taken place prior to one's current lifetime.

Hubbard said that the modern-day science fiction genre of space opera is merely an unconscious recollection of real events that took place millions of years ago, leaving destructive engrams behind. Other important aspects in Scientology doctrine include the Helatrobus implants, which Hubbard claimed occurred 382 trillion years ago to 52 trillion years ago by an alien nation. These implants are said to linger in the subconscious minds of humans today and are said to be responsible for the current concept of heaven.

In many cases, current life engrams or implants are also addressed. In his writings and lectures, Hubbard describes many key incidents said to have occurred to thetans during the past few trillion years. Not all incidents deal with implants; some are simply unusual and traumatic events said to have happened to thetans millions of years ago. This trauma is said to linger for trillions of years and causes unresolved psychological problems in the present day. According to Hubbard, only scientology methods can resolve the burdens left by such traumas.

Members of the Church of Scientology have objected to Scientology being painted as a science fiction fantasy. Space opera is defined in the official *Scientology and Dianetics Glossary* as:

> *of or relating to time periods[...]millions of years ago which concerned activities in this and other galaxies. Space opera has space travel, spaceships, spacemen, intergalactic travel, wars, conflicts, other beings, civilizations and societies, and other planets and galaxies. It is not fiction and concerns actual incidents and things that occurred on the [whole] track [in the past].*

In its public statements, the Church of Scientology has been notably reluctant to allow even a public mention of some of the doctrine. A passing mention by a trial judge in 1997 prompted the church's lawyers to have the ruling sealed, although this was reversed. In the relatively few instances in which it has acknowledged the space opera, the church has stated the story is a religious writing that can be seen as the equivalent of the Old Testament in which miraculous events are described that are unlikely to have occurred in real life, assuming true meaning only after years of study. They complain of critics using it to paint the religion as a science fiction fantasy.[26]

The material contained in the OT levels have been characterized as bad science fiction by critics but in fact bears similarities to gnostic thought and ancient Hindu myths of creation and cosmic struggle. J. Gordon Melton (a research specialist in religion and new religious movements with the *Department of Religious Studies* at the University of California) suggests that like biblical mythology, these elements of the OT levels may not have been intended as descriptions of historical events and adds that on "whatever level Scientologists might have received this mythology, they seem to have found it useful in their quest to become spiritual beings."

Although many of us would find it easy to make light of the church's teachings, it appears as though the church takes them very seriously and has spent millions of dollars to preserve them.

The *Church of Spiritual Technology,* also known as CST, incorporated in 1982, owns all the copyrights of the estate of L. Ron Hubbard. The

CST is doing business as L. Ron Hubbard Library. The organization receives its income from royalty fees paid to it by licensing of the copyrighted materials of Dianetics and Scientology to Scientology-connected organizations approved by the *Religious Technology Center,* and from its wholly owned for-profit subsidiary *Author Services Inc.,* which publishes and promotes Hubbard's fiction works. In a 1993 memorandum by the Church of Scientology International, the role and function of CST has been described as follows: an autonomous church of the Scientology religion outside of the international Scientology ecclesiastical hierarchy.[26]

The CST oversees the Scientology scriptural archiving project, which aims to preserve the works of Hubbard on stainless steel tablets and encased in titanium capsules in especially-constructed vaults throughout the world. The most famous example is the Trementina Base, an underground vault built into a mountainside near Trementina, New Mexico, and can be seen from outer space. The project began in the late 1980s. The base includes a number of dwellings and the archives themselves, the latter in a network of underground tunnels. The base also has its own private concrete airstrip, the San Miguel Ranch Airport. It is not shown on FAA sectional charts or in navigation databases by the organization's request.

Basic Worship Service

All Scientology services bring people closer to the Eighth Dynamic, and the congregational services especially focus on this. It is a bringing together of many beings in a joint spiritual experience and an occasion to recognize the ultimate which is the Eighth Dynamic, or God. The Church of Scientology Sunday service consists of a reciting of the Creed of the Church, a sermon based on the writings of the Scientology Founder L. Ron Hubbard, congregational group auditing and prayer. There may also be music and singing, as well as announcements of Church events and programs.[27]

At the first level of the Scientology ecclesiastical hierarchy are the individual ministers of Scientology who do not serve on the staff of a church or mission. These field ministers provide introductory religious services to their families, friends, and members of their communities. They minister auditing and provide their parishioners marriage counseling, help in overcoming drug problems, assist in dealing with basic distress of life, and are involved in the many other aspects one traditionally associates with a community ministry.

Field auditors sometimes join together to form auditors associations or Dianetics counseling groups, thereby expanding their activities to include organized lectures, seminars, and other means of proselytization. Scientology churches are sustained through the contributions of their parishioners, much in the same way that Christians support their churches with pledges or tithes. They are supported by the donations their parishioners make in order to participate in specific religious services. These donations are used exclusively to advance the religious charitable and other public benefit activities that churches of Scientology carry out.

Churches and missions are licensed franchises; they offer services for a fee and return a proportion of their income to the mother church. They are also required to adhere to the standards established by the *Religious Technology Center* (RTC), which supervises the application of Scientology tech and owns the trademarks and service marks of Scientology. The organization's chairman is David Miscavige, who, while not the titular head of the Church of Scientology, is believed to be the most powerful person in the Scientology movement.

Holidays: There are many holidays, commemorations, and observances in the Church of Scientology. Most all of them mark some important day in church history. There are none of the holidays traditionally found in any other world religion, except the celebration of New Year's Eve. Scientologists also celebrate religious holidays, depending on other religious beliefs, as Scientologists very often retain their original affiliations with faiths in which they were raised. Scientology states that it is compatible with all major world religions. However, due to major differences in the beliefs and practices between Scientology and especially the largest monotheistic religions, a simultaneous membership in Scientology is not always seen as compatible. Scientology only allows a passive formal membership in a second religion.

Marriage

The Church of Scientology describes marriage as "an essential component of a stable family life." In 2005, a spokeswoman for the church told the *New York Daily News* that the church had "not taken an official position on gay marriage and that members prefer not to talk about it."

Women are encouraged to be as silent as possible and avoid taking drugs during childbirth. They can only make sounds but must not utter any words, and neither must the birthing staff, unless absolutely necessary. Newborns are deemed especially vulnerable to induced engrams and trauma transmitted from their mother or acquired from their environment.

Infant Baptism or Blessing

There are no specific ceremonies for baptism; however, there are special rules for childbirth. The followers of Scientology believe what is said and done to a person when unconscious and in pain is recorded in the mind below one's awareness. These recordings c an p lay b ack l ater i n life, causing a person to react inappropriately or even to suffer f rom unwanted psychosomatic illnesses, lowered IQ, and disabilities.

Thousands of case studies of those undergoing Dianetics counseling prove that what was said by others present during the trauma of birth is recorded in the reactive mind. The idle chatter of doctors and nurses or loud remarks and laughter have been recorded by the person when being born, affecting emotional and spiritual well-being later in life. Modern Science of Mental Health in May, 1950, states that expectant mothers should be extremely gentle on themselves during pregnancy. He also advocated that people assisting a woman giving birth maintain silence during delivery "so a child should have a very quiet prenatal period, and should have a silent, and painless as possible, birth" and "the delivery itself should carry as little anesthetic as possible, be as calm and no-talk as possible."

This viewpoint was in stark contrast to the practices of the day, where delivery rooms were brightly lit, noisy places and women were heavily drugged.

In the 1960s and 1970s, alternative, popular natural childbirth methods evolved from principles of a calm, quiet, and relaxed birthing environment and little or no anesthesia. These methods also promote that a positive emotional attitude on the part of the mother is an essential component of a better delivery. Founder of the *Bradley Method,* Robert A. Bradley, MD, urged darkness and solitude, quiet physical comfort and relaxation, and closed eyes. Adherents of the Bradley Method encourage the use of midwives rather than technical-oriented doctors. Parents should take the responsibility for the birthplace, procedures, and emergency backup. Bradley teaches conditioning exercises and muscle relaxation in labor. A slow, deep breathing, take-your-time approach is advocated in a quiet, unlit, pillow-laden environment.

Initiation, Baptism, or Confirmation

The Church of Scientology requires that every member sign a legal waiver that covers their relationship with the Church of Scientology before engaging in Scientology services.

Scientology claims that its beliefs and practices are based on rigorous research, and its doctrines are accorded a significance equivalent to that of scientific laws. "Scientology works 100 percent of the time when it is properly applied to a person who sincerely desires to improve his life," the Church of Scientology says. Conversion is held to be of lesser significance than the practical application of Scientologist methods.

Death and Afterlife

They believe that we are each an eternal spiritual being called a thetan. According to Scientology, when we die, we drop our (physical) body and go to heaven (which is actually a mental implant/processing station where our memories are erased), after which we return to earth and attach ourselves to new bodies. Thetans are believed to be reborn time and time again in new bodies through a process called assumption, which is comparable to reincarnation. Like Hinduism, Scientology suggests a causal relationship between the experiences of earlier incarnations and one's present life, and with each rebirth, the effects of the *MEST universe* (Matter, Energy, Space, and Time) on the thetan are believed to become stronger.

Scientology's emphasis on the importance of present (or future) consequence of past actions also resembles the concept of karma.

Rebirths continue until one consciously confronts all pre-birth, current-life, and previous-life traumas and realizes one's true nature as a thetan, immortal spirit—transcending matter, energy, space, and time. His experience extends well beyond a single lifetime. His capabilities are unlimited, even if not presently realized—and those capabilities can be realized. The images of experiences collected over many lifetimes are referred to as "engrams" in Scientologist terminology. Engrams are believed to be painful and debilitating; as they accumulate, people move further away from their true identity as thetans. To be saved from this fate and restore the thetan is the Scientologist's basic goal. The thetan could be compared with the *Ātman* (the true self of an individual) of Hindu mythology. Dianetic training is the tool through which the Scientologist progresses towards the "Clear" state, winning gradual freedom from the reactive mind, and acquiring certainty of his or her reality as a spiritual being, or thetan. Achieving this state enables the spirit to escape the cycle of birth and death—to operate independently of the physical universe and become one with God (or Supreme Being).[28]

Judgment and Salvation

In common with most religions, Scientology is basically concerned with the origin and nature of the universe. In Scientology, the cosmic source or life force is represented by the Greek letter *theta* (Θ). Theta is meant to represent life or the life source; it is not part of the physical universe, but it can control the universe.

The individual expression of theta is called the thetan. This is held to be the true identity of every human being—intrinsically good, all-knowing, nonmaterial, and capable of unlimited creativity. As thetans, people are pure spirit, immortal and godlike, outside of space and time. Thus, the thetan concept is similar to the western concept of the soul, with the distinction that the latter does not usually go so far as to assert a godlike true nature for human beings.

Salvation is achieved through the practices and techniques of Scientology, the ultimate goal of which is to realize one's true nature as an immortal spirit, a thetan. The path to salvation, or enlightenment, includes achieving states of increasingly greater mental awareness— Pre-Clear, Clear, and ultimately *Operating Thetan*. An Operating Thetan is a spirit who can control matter, energy, space, time, thought, and life.[29]

Special Doctrine

A number of Scientology organizations specialize in promoting the use of Scientology technology as a means to solve social problems.

Narconon is a drugeducation and rehabilitation program. The program is founded on Hubbard's belief that drugs and poisons stored in the body impede spiritual growth, and was originally conceived by William Benitez, a prison inmate who applied Hubbard's ideas to rid himself of his drug habit. Narconon is offered in the United States, Canada and a number of European countries; its Purification Program uses a regimen composed of sauna, physical exercise, vitamins and diet management, combined with auditing and study.

Criminon is a program designed to rehabilitate criminal offenders by teaching them study and communication methods and helping them reform their lives. The program originally grew out of the Narconon effort and today is available in over 200 prisons. It has experienced steady growth, based on a good success rate, with low relapse percentages.

Applied Scholastics promotes the use of Hubbard's educational methodology, known as study tech. Originally developed to help Scientologists study course materials, Hubbard's study tech is now used in some private and public schools as well. Applied Scholastics is active across Europe and North America as well as in Australia, Malaysia, China and South Africa. It supports literacy efforts in American cities and Third World countries, and its methodology is sometimes included in management training programs.

The Way to Happiness Foundation promotes a moral code written by Hubbard, to date translated into more than 40 languages.

The Association for Better Living and Education (ABLE) acts as an umbrella organization for these efforts.

The World Institute of Scientology Enterprises (WISE) is a not-for-profit organization which licenses Hubbard's management techniques for use in businesses.

The Citizens Commission on Human Rights (CCHR). Founded in 1969, it has a long history of opposing psychiatric practices such as lobotomy, electric shock treatment and the use of mood-altering drugs.

The National Commission on Law Enforcement and Social Justice, devoted to combating what it describes as abusive practices by government and police agencies, especially Interpol.[30]

Notes

Notes

Unitarian Universalism*

History

Unitarian Universalism emerged from two different religions: *Unitarianism* and *Universalism*. Both Unitarianism and Universalism started in Europe hundreds of years ago.

Traditionally, Unitarianism was a form of Christianity. Unitarians trace their history back to the apostolic age and claim for their doctrine prevalence during the ante-Nicene period. Many Unitarians believed their Christology most closely reflected that of the original Christians. The term may refer to any belief about the nature of Jesus Christ that affirms God as a singular entity and rejects the doctrine of the Trinity. The early Unitarian Church not only rejected the Trinity, but also predestination, original sin, and substitutionary atonement. There were several different forms of Christology in the beginnings of the Unitarian movement; ultimately, the variety that became prevalent was that Jesus was a man, but a man with a unique relationship to God.

In the Nicene Creed, adopted at the First Council of Nicaea in 325, the issue was considered settled, and the adoption of Constantine's view became the orthodox doctrine, and all other views were considered heresy and officially suppressed. Later, Theodosius I out lawed all non-Trinitarian forms of Christianity. Unitarianism was rebuffed by orthodox Christianity, but it resurfaced subsequently in church history, especially during the theological turmoil of the Protestant Reformation.

---

* The main website for this denomination declined to allow me to use any information from their site (www.uua.org). I did have a retired UU pastor of thirty-five years, read it over and I have tried to find information elsewhere. But with this key website not represented, there may be some areas that could be incomplete. The explanation is as follows by Rachel Walden, information assistant of Unitarian Universalist Association: *"Not only is this not our mission, but the UUA does not have the resources to help all others who wish to describe or explain our faith do so accurately. But it is the right of our Association to protect how we are represented. To this end, we ask that you do not include information from our website and instead refer people to the website or to me at the Association. If your wish is truly to bring people closer together by showing the similarities among religions, then we hope you will give us the opportunity to explain our faith in our own words."*

In the early 1500s, a Spanish physician Miguel Servetus studied the Bible and concluded that the concept of the Trinity was not biblical. His books on the errors of the Trinity and christianismi restitutio caused much uproar. Servetus was eventually arrested, judged, and burned at the stake in Geneva in 1553 at the same time that John Calvin was leading the Reformation there. Nowadays, most Unitarians see Servetus as their pioneer and first martyr, even though his views on Jesus Christ are quite different from what many Unitarians believe today.

King John Sigismund of Transylvania (now a part of Romania and Hungary), in 1568, issued the first edict of religious freedom. This allowed citizens to hold diverse religious beliefs and still be loyal to the state, and the earliest organized Unitarian movements were founded in the sixteenth century in Poland and Transylvania. The term *Unitarian* first emerged in 1682 and was construed in a broad sense to cover all who, with whatever differences, held to the unipersonality of the divine being.

An organized Unitarian movement started to emerge in the late eighteenth century. The first true Unitarian congregation in Britain was opened by Theophilus Lindsey in London, in 1774. Benjamin Franklin was said to have attended the first service there. On June 19, 1785, Lindsey used the revised *Book of Common Prayer* based upon that of Dr. Samuel Clarke, removing the Trinitarian Nicene Creed and references to Jesus as God and to allow a more Unitarian interpretation. The object "in the new liturgy was to leave out all such expressions as would wound the conscience of a Unitarian, without introducing any which should displease a Trinitarian." His efforts met with substantial criticism by the more conservative priests and bishops who held sufficient power within the Church of England to stifle Lindsey's attempts at reform. John Priestley, a close friend of Theophilus Lindsey, attended Lindsey's church regularly in the 1770s and occasionally preached there. He continued to support institutionalized Unitarianism for the rest of his life, writing several defenses of Unitarianism and encouraging the foundation of new Unitarian chapels throughout Britain and the United States.[1]

Joseph Priestley became a minister at Mill Hill Chapel, one of the oldest and most respected Unitarian congregations in England. Priestley believed that by educating the young, he could strengthen the bonds of the congregation. In his magisterial three-volume, Institutes of Natural and Revealed Religion, (1772–74), Priestley outlined his theories of religious instruction. The doctrines he explicated would later become the standards for Unitarians in Britain. The Institutes shocked and appalled many readers, primarily because it challenged basic Christian orthodoxies, such as the divinity of Christ and the miracle of the Virgin Birth.

In demanding that his readers apply the logic of the emerging sciences and comparative history to the Bible and Christianity, he alienated religious and scientific readers alike; scientific readers did not appreciate seeing science used in the defense of religion, and religious readers dismissed the application of science to religion. Because of his continued outspokenness and failure to back down from any of his teachings, Priestley finally had to flee to America after his home was torched, and he became a leading figure in the founding of the church on American soil.

In the United States, The first official acceptance of the Unitarian faith on the part of a congregation was by King's Chapel in Boston. (King's Chapel was the first Episcopalian Church in New England.) James Freeman, a Harvard graduate (and the first preacher in America to call himself a Unitarian) had preached at various Boston pulpits. In 1782, King's Chapel asked Freeman to officiate as their reader for six months. Freeman was well-liked at King's Chapel, and when his six months were concluded on Easter, 1783, the proprietors asked him to be pastor of the church. Before he accepted the position of pastor at King's Chapel, he requested that he not have to read the Athanasian Creed. As the Episcopalians were not particularly fond of the creed, the congregation readily consented. After reading Joseph Priestley's "*A History of the Corruptions of Christianity* " and Theophilus Lindsey's "*An Historical View of the State of the Unitarian Doctrine and Worship from the Reformation to our own Times,*" Freeman began to further doubt the doctrine of the Trinity and became increasingly uncomfortable with the liturgy in the Book of Common Prayer. Having adopted the Unitarianism of Priestley and Lindsey, he rejected the pre-human existence of Jesus. He told his closer friends at the Church that he could not conscientiously perform the service as it stood. He wondered if he should relinquish his position as pastor. One of his friends suggested that he present his dilemma to the congregation, and let them decide.[2]

Beginning in 1784 Freeman preached a series of sermons on the unity of God, stating his dissatisfaction with certain parts of the liturgy, and giving his reasons for rejecting the Trinity. He thought that these would be the last sermons he would ever give there. To his surprise he was heard patiently, attentively, and kindly. He persuaded the Church to alter the liturgy, eliminating all references to the Trinity and addressing all prayers to God the Father. The Chapel was the first church in America to make such changes, on the grounds it might be considered the first Unitarian church in the country. In 1785 the people of the Church altered their Prayer Book in accordance with Freeman's views and officially became the first *Unitarian Church* in the United States.[3]

Although Freeman still considered the church to be Episcopalian, Bishop Seabury of Connecticut, who represented the Anglican Church, refused to ordain him. On November 18, 1787, Freeman was ordained by the senior warden of King's Chapel, in the name of the congregation, in words still used in ordinations at King's Chapel today: "to be the Rector, Minister, Priest, Pastor, Public Teacher and Teaching Elder." He remained rector of King's Chapel for thirty-nine years.

The Unitarian movement began to spread primarily in the Congregational parish churches of New England. In the late eighteenth century, conflict grew within some of these churches between Unitarian and Trinitarian factions. In 1819, William Ellery Channing preached the ordination sermon, outlining the Unitarian position, and the dispute culminated in the foundation of the *American Unitarian Association* as a separate denomination in 1825.

After the schism, some of those churches remained within the Congregational fold, while others voted to become Unitarian. In the aftermath of their various historical circumstances, some of these churches became member congregations of the Congregational organization (later the *United Church of Christ*),others became Unitarian and eventually became part of the UUA. Today, the UUA and the United Church of Christ cooperate jointly on social justice initiatives such as the *Sexuality Education Advocacy Training* project. In the nineteenth century, under the influence of Ralph Waldo Emerson (who had been a Unitarian minister), Unitarianism began its long journey from liberal Protestantism to its present, more pluralist form

Universalism was a fairly commonly held view among theologians in early Christianity. In the first five or six centuries of Christianity, there were six known theological schools, of which four were Universalist. One accepted conditional immortality, and one (in Rome) taught the endless punishment of the lost. Universalism developed from the influence of various Pietist and Anabaptist movements in Europe, including Quakerism, Moravians, Methodists, Lutherans, Brethren, and others. The first General Society was held in 1778. Annual conventions started in 1785 with the New England Convention. In 1804, this convention changed its name to *"The General Convention of Universalists in the New England States and Others ."* At its peak in the 1830s, the Universalist Church was around the ninth largest denomination in the United States.[4] On June 25, 1863, Olympia Brown, from Racine, WI, became the firstwoman in the United States to receive ordination in any national denomination. By 1920, there were eighty-eight Universalist women ministers, the largest group in the United States.

The Universalist Church had its origins in pietistic, evangelistic movements with a liberal bent. However, the development of modern science somewhat sapped the Universalists' power to claim that they were the true possessors of revealed Christian truth. Stuck in an uneasy compromise, the Universalist Church gradually lost influenceand evangelical zeal to spread itself. Unitarians and Universalists often have had a great deal of common interests and communication between them. Eventually, the church came to the conclusion that the only way to deal with the threat of humanism and secular liberalism was to embrace it and merged with the *American Unitarian Association* to form the *Unitarian Universalist Association*.

In 1961, the *American Unitarian Association* (AUA) was consolidated with the *Universalist Church of America* (UCA) to form the new religion of *Unitarian Universalism*. The UUA contains a considerably looser set of beliefs than the Universalists of the 1800s as a noncreedal religion. In 1995, the UUA helped establish the *International Council of Unitarians and Universalists* (ICUU) to connect Unitarian and Universalist faith traditions around the world. As of 2009, the UUA comprised of 1,041 congregations with 164,656 certified members and 61,795 church school enrollees served by 1,623 ministers. In 2009 Adherents.com listed the faith with 600,000 members worldwide.[5] But most other more recent stats suggest the membership is currently less than 200,000. The UUA was given corporate status in May 1961, under special acts of legislature of the commonwealth of Massachusetts and the state of New York.[5]

God or Gods

A belief in God is welcomed but not required within Unitarian Universalism; many Unitarian Universalists believe in God, and some do not believe in God. Types of theism include monotheism, pantheism, polytheism, and deism. Deists believe in a God but believe that logic and reason are the only sources of true knowledge. They also believe that the divine does not intervene in the workings of the world. Deist thought is quite common within Unitarian Universalism. Some believe that God is a metaphor for a transcendent reality. Some believe in a female god (goddess), a passive god (deism), a Christian god, or a god manifested in nature or the universe as revealed by science. Many UUs reject the idea of deities and instead speak of the spirit of life that binds all life on earth.[6]

Christ

Traditionally, Unitarians did believe in God, and they adhered to strict monotheism, and maintain that Jesus was a great man and a prophet of God, perhaps even a supernatural being, but not God himself. They believed Jesus did not claim to be God, and that his teachings did not suggest the existence of a triune God. Unitarians believe in the moral authority, but not necessarily the divinity, of Jesus. Their theology is thus opposed to the Trinitarian theology of other Christian denominations.[7]

But after the merging of the two groups, the doctrine has pretty much been replaced by a freedom to believe in Jesus, or not. UUs do consider His teachings as a good source for life lessons. As the Bible says, "*if you don't believe in me, believe in what I do*" (John 10:37–38). For many Unitarian Universalists, Jesus and Christian teachings provide insight into understanding how to live our lives. One of the shared sources of their faith is "Jewish and Christian teachings which call all to respond to God's love by loving our neighbors as ourselves." As one Unitarian Universalist wrote: "*Jesus' message remains strong in our efforts to create a beloved community here on earth; impelling us to witness to the injustices of this time.*" And Rev. Anita Farber-Robertson says, "*Jesus gives us the strength to fight, the courage to love, and hearts that do not give up on anyone.*"[8]

Basic Doctrine

There is no single unifying belief that all Unitarian Universalists hold, aside from complete and responsible freedom of speech, thought, belief, faith, and disposition. Unitarian Universalists believe that each person is free to search for his or her own personal truth on issues, such as the existence, nature, and meaning of life, deities, creation, and afterlife. UUs can come from any religious background, and hold beliefs and adhere to morals from a variety of cultures or religions.[9]

Unitarian Universalism is a liberal religion that encompasses many faith traditions. Unitarian Universalists include people who identify themselves as Christians, Jews, Buddhists, Hindus, Pagans, atheists, agnostics, humanists, while others hold to natural theism, pantheism, and other beliefs. As there is no official Unitarian Universalist creed, Unitarian Universalists are free to search for truth on many paths. Although they uphold shared principles, individual Unitarian Universalists have varied beliefs about everything from scripture, to rituals, to God. They generally do not hold the Bible— or any other account of human experience—to be either an infallible guide or the ultimate authority in matters of faith.

Unitarian Universalists view the individuals depicted in such works in much the same way. For example, many UUs believe that Jesus of Nazareth probably existed, and they respect him for many of the values he stood for and for his fearless campaign for what he believed in. Most Unitarian Universalists, however, do not believe that Jesus is the Son of God or the Messiah. They have respect for the sacred literature of all religions but do not necessarily accept them as infallible. UUs view these sacred texts as historically significant literary works that should be viewed with an open mind, a critical eye, and an appetite for good literature. Contemporary works of science, art, and social commentary are valued as well. Unitarian Universalists aspire to truth as wide as the world—they look to find truth anywhere, universally.[10]

Whatever their theological perspective, Unitarians attempt, in their style of worship and their community life, to combine personal integrity with a willingness to share and learn from others. Most choose to attach no particular theological label to their beliefs. This diversity of views is considered a strength in the Unitarian Universalist movement.

Many UU congregations have study groups that examine the traditions and spiritual practices of other faiths. Some UU ministers, such as the Reverend James Ford, are also ordained Zen teachers. Other UU ministers, such as the Reverend David Miller, are atheists. There are Buddhist meditation teachers, Sufi teachers, as well as agnostic and persons who have been consecrated as Christian bishops outside the structures and canon law of the established churches. While Sunday services in most congregations tend to espouse Humanism (a philosophy that usually rejects supernaturalism and stresses an individual's dignity and worth), it is not unusual for a part of a church's membership to attend Pagan, Buddhist, or other spiritual study or worship groups as an alternative means of worship.[11]

Regardless of their orientation, most congregations are fairly open to differing beliefs. They seek to provide a creative alternative to the rigidity of dogma, which encumbers so many branches of organized religion.

In a survey done in 2005, Unitarian Universalists in the United States were asked which provided term or set of terms best describe their belief. Many respondents chose more than one term to describe their beliefs. The top choices were:

- Humanist—54%
- Agnostic—33%
- Earth-centered—31%
- Atheist—18%
- Buddhist—16.5%
- Christian—13.1%
- Pagan—13.1%

Although only 6 percent of the UU membership participated, these statistics are published in many places on the Internet, including an archived document by Rev. Rudra Vilius Dundzila, PhD, DMin, that was available on uua.org but is no longer available. Unitarian Universalism believes that there are many sources that play an important part in their beliefs and practices: man's personal experiences, the words and action of men and women who cause us to challenge and evaluate our lives, the wisdom and teaching from all religious practices around the world, the Judeo-Christian teachings that guide man to love one another, the guidance of reason and the results of science, teachings of earth-centered traditions that stress the circle of life and the connectivity of nature. There are principles which Unitarian Universalist congregations affirm and promote:

- We believe in the freedom of religious expression. All individuals should be encouraged to develop their own personal theology, and to present openly their religious opinions without fear of censure or reprisal.
- We believe in the toleration of religious ideas. All religions, in every age and culture, possess not only an intrinsic merit, but also a potential value for those who have learned the art of listening.

- We believe in the authority of reason and conscience. The ultimate arbiter in religion is not a church, or a document, or an official, but the personal choice and decision of the individual.
- We believe in the never-ending search for Truth. If the mind and heart are truly free and open, the revelations which appear to the human spirit are infinitely numerous, eternally fruitful, and wondrously exciting.
- We believe in the unity of experience. There is no fundamental conflict between faith and knowledge, religion and the world, the sacred and the secular, since they all have their source in the same reality.
- We believe in the worth and dignity of each human being. All people on earth have an equal claim to life, liberty, and justice and no idea, ideal, or philosophy is superior to a single human life.
- We believe in the ethical application of religion. Good works are the natural product of a good faith, the evidence of an inner grace that finds completion in social and community involvement.
- We believe in the motive force of love. The governing principle in human relationships is the principle of love, which always seeks the welfare of others and never seeks to hurt or destroy.
- We believe in the necessity of the democratic process. Records are open to scrutiny, elections are open to members, and ideas are open to criticism—so that people might govern themselves.
- We believe in the importance of a religious community. The validation of experience requires the confirmation of peers, who provide a critical platform along with a network of mutual support. These principles and sources of faith are the backbone of their religious community.[12]

Note: Some websites only list Seven Principles.

Basic Worship Service

As in theology, Unitarian Universalist worship and ritual are often a combination of elements derived from other faith traditions alongside original practices and symbols. Religious services are usually held on

Sundays and might be difficult to distinguish from those of a Protestant church, but they vary widely among congregations.[13]

At the opening of Unitarian Universalist worship services, many congregations light a flame inside a chalice. This flaming chalice has become a well-known symbol of the denomination. It unites members in worship and symbolizes the spirit of their work. Many Unitarian Universalist families light a chalice as part of their dinner-table ritual, sort of a UU version of saying grace. Many wear chalice necklaces and pendants like Christians wear crosses.

Hans Deutsch, an Austrian artist, first brought together the chalice and the flame as a Unitarian symbol during his work with the Unitarian Service Committee during World War II. The design of a stylized chalice, with the flame of freedom burning inside, w as adopted by the *Unitarian Service Committee* because of the challenges of language, culture, and religion in those dangerous days and was used in aiding the escape of countless refugees from Nazi oppression. Safe houses were marked by chalices scratched in the dirt; clandestine notes using the symbol were understood to be trustworthy.

Each Unitarian Universalist congregation holds its own style of religious services. Most UU services contain religious music, a chalice lighting, a sermon, prayers or meditations, and readings. Sermon topics range from current events to theological concepts like earthly justice to reflections on the seasons and might be read y the minister or a lay leader. Since Unitarian Universalists do not recognize a particular text or set of texts as primary or inherently superior; inspiration can be found in many different religious or cultural texts as well as the personal experiences of the speaker. [14] Many congregations collect money in offering plates during the service, but people are not required to give. The service also includes hymn singing accompanied by organ, piano, or other available instruments and possibly led by a song leader or choir.

Many UU congregations no longer observe the Christian sacraments of baptism, communion, or confirmation, at least in their traditional forms or under their traditional names. Congregations that continue these practices under their more traditional names are often federated churches or members of the *Council of Christian Churches* within the Unitarian Universalist Association (CCCUUA), or may have active chapters associated with the Unitarian Universalist Christian Fellowship or similar covenant groups. Annual celebrations of Water Communion and Flower Communion may replace or supplement Christian-style communion (though many pluralist and Christian-oriented congregations may celebrate or otherwise make provisions for communion on Christian holy days).

The Water Communion is a ritual service common in Unitarian Universalist congregations. It is usually held in the fall. Due to the nature of Unitarian Universalism, traditions vary from one congregation to another; however, most Water Communions follow the same general idea. Throughout the year, members of the congregation collect samples of water from various places they go to, ranging from vacations to homes; film canisters are often used as containers for this purpose. At the service, the samples of water are placed in a bowl and allowed to mix. This water is often used for ceremonial purposes at other times of the year. The symbolism can be interpreted in various ways. The classic life-related symbolism of water is apparent. The rejoining of many waters can also symbolize the rejoining of the congregation after summer travels.[15]

The Flower Communion is a ritual service common in Unitarian Universalism, though the specific practices vary from one congregation to another. It is usually held before summer, when some congregations recess from holding services. The Flower Communion was initiated by Norbert Capek, who was also the founder of the Unitarian Church in Czechoslovakia. He saw the need to unite the diverse congregants of his church, from varying Protestant, Catholic, and Jewish backgrounds, without alienating those who had left these traditions. The Flower Communion instead borrows from the universal beauty of nature. The first Flower Communion was held in Prague on June 4, 1923. The Flower Communion was reportedly introduced in the United States in 1940 by Norbert's wife, and was widely adopted by the American Unitarian churches, and their successor Unitarian Universalist congregations.

The Flower Communion involves each congregant bringing a flower to be used in the service; congregants leave their flowers in a central location either as they enter or during the service. At the end of the service, the flowers are distributed when each person chooses a flower different from the one they brought. Other service elements might include a sermon, the blessing of or a prayer over the flowers, a reading by Dr. Norbert Capek, the story of the Flower Communion, hymns, etc. Many congregations include a formalized blessing to consecrate the flowers before they are passed to or distributed among the people. There is no single interpretation of the Flower Communion. The beauty and diversity of flowers is seen as symbolic of the beauty and diversity of life.

Pastoral elements of the regular Sunday service may include a time for sharing joys and sorrows/concerns, where individuals in the congregation are invited to light a candle (similar to the Catholic practice of lighting a candle) and/or say a few words about important events in their personal lives. Many UU services also include a time of meditation or prayer led by the minister or service leader, both spoken and silent. Responsive readings and stories for children are also typical. There is often an opportunity for attendants to gather and socialize after the service. Coffee hour usually consists of cookies and casual conversation but occasionally includes organized discussion groups and full luncheon buffets.

Unitarian Universalism believes in learned individuals in addition to called clergy. Because of this, lay leaders are also highly respected within the congregations. Each congregation chooses its own leaders. Because of the diversity of belief within Unitarian Universalism, ministers must undergo a great deal of training before being ordained. A Unitarian Universalist minister is generally required to have a masters of divinity degree from an approved school, a ministerial internship, many interviews, and final approval from the Ministerial Fellowship Committee.

Infant Baptism or Blessing

Unitarian Universalist congregations generally have *Child Dedication"* services for infants, young adopted children, or young children whose families have recently joined the congregation. The dedication ceremony celebrates the blessing of new life, expresses the parents' hopes for their child, and a call to all members to lead and nurture the child's spiritual life. Adults do not need to be baptized when joining the Unitarian Universalist faith.

Initiation, Baptism, or Confirmation

Unitarian Universalist teenagers usually become official members of their congregations with a special *"Coming of Age"* Ceremony. Most require a year-long curriculum, helping them to learn more about Unitarian Universalism faith. It is not required that people convert to Unitarian Universalism when they join the church, nor is it necessary to revoke their previous faith. Many congregations, instead, hold new member ceremonies. Anyone is welcome to visit a Unitarian Universalist congregation. You don't have to be a member to participate in most of the life of the congregation. Each Unitarian Universalist congregation determines its own rules and policies, so there is no one official definition of membership. In most congregations, you are considered a member when you sign the membership book and pay a pledge to the congregation. While each congregation relies on financial pledges from their members to support the congregation's continued life and work, some don't require any financial commitment. Some do require participation in a "new member" class before joining.[16]

Marriage

There is no standard wedding service. Each service is developed by the couple. Unitarian Universalist congregations and ministers bless same-sex unions, even in the states where they are not yet legally recognized. Many congregations have undertaken a series of organizational and practical steps to welcome and integrate gay and lesbian members. Some UU ministers have been performing same-sex unions since at least the late 1960s and now same-sex marriages in states where they are legal. On June 29, 1984, the Unitarian Universalists became the first major church to officially approve religious blessings on homosexual unions. Unitarian Universalists have been in the forefront of the civil rights work to make same-sex marriages legal in their local states and provinces as well as on the national level. In May 2004, Arlington Street Church was the site of the first state-sanctioned same-sex marriage in the United States. The official stance of the UUA is for the legalization of same-sex marriage.

Unitarian Universalists hold that divorce is entirely a matter for conscientious decision on the part of the persons involved. They view divorce as an *Ending Rite of Passage*, corresponding to the *Partnering Rite* that is marriage. Both are viewed as life choices, which are supported as long as they are healthy for all concerned. Because of this flexibility, the Unitarian church was actually creating "divorce rituals" as far back as the 1960s, and there are a few standard ceremonies that ministers draw upon today, adapting each to personalize the event.

Unitarian Universalist divorce ceremonies transmit a message of hope and love in a public setting, acknowledging the role of society in the couple's lives. The ceremony can be held at any time the participants are ready, before or after the civil divorce. The couple, a minister, and friends and family (a more intimate group than for a wedding, but large enough to reflect the community in which the family has lived) gather for the ceremony. Congregants generally don't participate but are present to bear witness to the couple's desire to begin anew. As a community event with a message of affirmation and hope, they believe it would be a good ceremony for including children, who may also feel the relief (expressed in the text of the ceremony) at the resolution of the tensions they've felt in their parents' marriage. Having the ceremony take place in a church setting is important in this ritual. This reflects the couple's determination to divorce in a manner as sacred (and public) as that in which they got married.

The minister reminds them that they were married within the community, and that the community is now present for their divorce. The individuals are then led in an affirmation that, though their marriage is ending, they will endeavor to value the past and enter a new, respectful relationship that transcends the pain and bitterness of the recent past. At this point, the wedding rings are returned, and the minister releases the couple from their vows, proclaiming that they're free to enter a new life and to love again: "Go forth, not in the hurt of ties wrenched and faith unachieved, but with hope and belief in love yet possible." The minister calls on society to acknowledge and support the couple in their decision to separate. "It is to peace that God has called you. We your families and friends, (as well as the law of the land—if applicable), now recognize that your marriage is ended...May God bless your separate lives and homes." The couple shakes hands, and those who are gathered depart.[17]

Death and Afterlife

One theological issue many people are curious about is Unitarian Universalism's view of the afterlife. Historically, Unitarians believed in a traditional Christian Heaven and Hell, while Universalists believed in Universal Salvation; that is, that everyone will go to Heaven. Today, some Unitarian Universalists believe in Heaven, some in reincarnation and some in no afterlife at all. Unitarian Universalism is primarily directed toward this life, not the next.

More than 150 years ago, the Unitarian forbearers rejected the theological doctrine of original sin. They believed that people are inherently good, and that our most precious gift—free will—allows us sometimes to act wrongly, rather than predestination or external temptation. While the traditional concept of sin is no longer part of Unitarian Universalist theology, a small number of Unitarian Universalists believe there are divine consequences attached to all of one's actions.

Others believe in general karmic effects or the principle of reciprocity, that all actions have corresponding consequences. Still others find no compelling evidence for any direct external spiritual repercussions for either good or bad behavior. Many people ask how they can have religious morals without agreeing on whether heaven, hell, judgment, sin, and damnation exist. Most Unitarian Universalists would probably tell you that their own moral code has little to do with their ideas of the afterlife and more to do with their belief in right actions in this life. Despite these variations in beliefs, all Unitarian Universalists share a deep obligation to act with justice and compassion in accordance with Unitarian Universalist values.

Judgment and Salvation

There are diverse beliefs, but most believe that heaven and hell are not places but are symbolic. Some believe heaven and hell are states of consciousness, either in life or continuing after death. Some believe in salvation through faith in God and Jesus Christ along with doing good works and doing no harm to others. Many believe all will be saved as God is good and forgiving. Some believe in reincarnation and the necessity to eliminate personal greed or to learn all of life's lessons before achieving enlightenment or salvation. For some, the concepts of salvation or enlightenment are irrelevant or unnecessary as right actions in this life are all that really matters.

Special Doctrine

Historically, Unitarian Universalists have often been active in political causes, notably the civil rights movement, the gay rights movement, the social justice movement, and the feminist movement. In the nineteenth century, Unitarians and Universalists were active in abolitionism, the women's movement, the temperance movement, and other social reform movements. Susan B. Anthony, a Unitarian and Quaker, was extremely influential in the women's suffrage movement.

Unitarian Universalists and Quakers still share many principles, notably that they are creedless religions with a long-standing commitment to social justice. It is therefore common to see Unitarian Universalists and Quakers working together. UUs were and are still very involved in the fight to end racism in the United States. John Haynes Holmes, a minister and social activist at the Community Church of New York, Unitarian Universalist, was among the founders of both the NAACP and the ACLU.

Notes

Appendix I
Comparative Charts

Religion or Faith Practice	Atheism Page 375	Amish and Mennonite Page 23
God or Gods	The absence of belief in Gods	The Holy Trinity Three in One
Christ	The absence of belief in Gods	Son of God
Behavior Specifications	To meet life and to live life in a way to benefit all of the earth & mankind	Pattern everyday life after Him. Concern for others. Limit outside contact
Baptism or Blessing	Some Atheists are becoming "debaptized" from their old churches	Infant Consecration. Blessing for child & parents
Initiation, Confirmation	None	Pour water over head—at the age of accountability
Marriage	Believe in marriage as a serious commitment to another individual	Instituted by God Parental approval required. No Divorce.
Death or Afterlife	No life after death. Prize life on earth & strive always to improve	Heaven and hell. Christ will create a new earth after the resurrection
Judgment and Salvation	None	Judged on your life and works. Only *they* will get to heaven

Assemblies of God and Pentecostal Volume 2	Bahá'í Volume 2	Baptist Volume 2
The Holy Trinity Three in One	A personal God, the source of all revelation; eternal, omnipresentand almighty	The Holy Trinity Three in One
Son of God	Prophet of God along with seven others	Physical incarnation of God the Father
To carry God's work into every aspect of your life. Strongly suggest no alcohol or tobacco.	Treat everyone as equal in all things. Prayer and fasting. Moderation in all things. No alcohol.	Must witness to the world at all times. SBC–No alcohol
Dedication as an infant. Parental commitment to Christian life.	Christ was not in need of baptism. Baptism is with the *spirit* ofGod, not by water.	Dedicated as an infant. Parental commitment to teach Christian life
Baptism by immersion at age eight to ten at the age of accountability	Signing what is called a "Declaration Card" professing your belief	Baptism by immersion at age nine to twelve at the age of accountability
Instituted by God. No same-sex unions. Lifetime commitment	Encouragemixed unions. Marriage is eternal. Divorce after "one year of patience"	Instituted by God; committed for life. No same-sex unions
Righteous will be resurrected or raptured. New earth and new heaven.	Not a "specific place" more a Unity with God. Soul is eternal.	Righteous spirits return to God right away. Wicked must await judgment day.
Righteous with Christ forever. Wicked will burn in Hell	No actual judgment. Soul's distance to God is the "heaven or hell"	Righteous with Christ forever. Wicked will burn in hell

Religion or Faith Practice	Buddhism Volume 2	Catholic (Roman Catholic) Page 37
God or Gods	Ranges from irrelevant to many, depending on what sect	The Holy Trinity. Three in One. Mary also revered.
Christ	Not part of the faith Mixed views on Jesus	Physical incarnation of God the Father
Behavior Specifications	Right thoughts and actions in all things. Dietary restrictions and guidelines	Christlike behavior. Eucharist and Confession. Concern for others.
Baptism or Blessing	None	Six to eight weeks. Water on head.
Initiation, Confirmation	None (except in Japan)	Between ages seven to eighteen. Confirms faith and strengthens grace
Marriage	Principal of non-harming each other. Divorce allowed only due to vast differences.	No divorce and no same-sex unions
Death or After Life	Once fully enlightened, one is liberated from rebirths, reaching a state of absolute selflessness results in Nirvana—the deathless state.	Purged in purgatory before going to heaven. Sinners to eternal hell.
Judgment and Salvation		Salvation and judgment based on works, faith, and grace.

Charismatic Movement Page 55	Christian Science Page 77	Church of Jesus Christ of Latter-Day Saints Volume 2
A personal God, the source of all revelation—eternal, omnipresent, & almighty	God the Father is infinite. The creator of all that is spiritual	God the Father, Jesus Christ, & the Holy Ghost are three separate beings. God & Jesus have physical bodies
Son of God	Did not die for sins but to show us the illusion of death—Way Shower	Jesus is the Son of God. Died for our Sins
To share the gospel with all mankind. To endeavor to bring all faith into one united belief.	To understand life is an illusion. The spiritual reality is the only reality	Live Christ-like life. Service to fellow man. Temple ordinances
May vary by denomination. Parental commitment to raising in a Christian life	No service since the physical birth is an illusion	Babies are blessed at infancy. Baptism is at age 8, considered the age of commitment
Baptism by water in most. *All* believe in a second baptism of the Holy Spirit that bestows "gifts"	Membership at age 12. Graduates from Sunday school at age 20	Baptism is at age 8, considered the age of commitment
Instituted by God. Other perimeters may vary by denomination	Nothing specific since all of material life is an illusion	Temple marriage for time and all eternity. Divorce is very difficult to get. No same-sex union
May vary slightly by denomination but most all believe final salvation is based on "works"	Death is not inevitable but an illusion that can be overcome	All go to Prison or Paradise after death to be taught. Remain till judgment day

Religion or Faith Practice	Confucianism Page 227	Congregational (United Church of Christ) Volume 2
God or Gods	Spirits of mountains, rivers, land, grain, the sun, moon, and stars are all subordinated to the Supreme Heaven, god	The Holy Trinity Three in One
Christ	Not applicable	Son of God. His atonement is the only way to be saved
Behavior Specifications	To make oneself as good as possible; this was the main purpose of life	Strive to be holy in all things. Desire for unity of all Christian faiths. No gambling or pornography
Baptism or Blessing	None	Baptism by water at any age—immersion or sprinkling
Initiation, Confirmation	Capping: son was honored on reaching his twentieth year. Only currently practiced in most traditional circles.	Varies by congregation. Baptism *does not* save. It is only an outward sign of your commitment to Christ.
Marriage	The purpose of marriage is the cultivation of virtue. Marriage should be founded on love	Same-sex unions accepted
Death or After Life	Heaven as a positive and personal force in the universe	Soul continues in a spiritual state after death. They all will be raised and judged by their lives
Judgment and Salvation	For us to become one with cosmos, virtues must be cultivated and shared with others.	Believers must *continue* to live God's word, or you *can* fall from grace

Episcopal Volume 2	Falun Gong Page 247	Han Volume 2
Holy Trinity, "Three and yet one"	Deities are working to help us achieve enlightenment	Many different gods and goddesses. Some ancestor worship
Jesus Christ is fully human and fully God	Not part of the faith. Master Li is at the same level as Jesus and Buddha	Some have incorporated Jesus into their other beliefs
To live out their faith on a daily basis; to be guided by tradition, reason, and scripture	Truth, compassion, and tolerance in all things. No attachments to anything in this world	The primary concern is how to lead a good life on earth. Must venerate and care for ancestors
Holy Baptism by water and the Holy Spirit. Generally done as an infant	None	None
Confirmation is done later when a mature commitment can be made. Generally done by a bishop	None	None
Marriage is a sacred vow. Same-sex "blessings" are allowed. Divorce allowed	Marriage designed by deities for us. No same-sex marriage or premarital relations	Many arranged marriages. Women obey men. No same-sex unions
No real information available that can be corroborated	Souls are reborn over and over till they are rid of karma	The dead could influence the quality of life for those still in this world
By the grace of God, we are saved if we accept Jesus as our Savior	Enlightenment is the salvation of all sentient beings	Transform into a being with special powers to aid and assist others

Religion or Faith Practice	Hinduism Page 267	Islam Page 91
God or Gods	One superior truth can take on many forms	*Allāh* is God, the one and only
Christ	Not included in teachings. Sometimes compared to Krishna	Not the son of God, but a prophet of God & the Messiah
Behavior Specifications	The pursuit of truth, nonviolence, & compassion, purity, & self-restraint	Prayer 5 times per day. Fasting thru Ramadan. Modest clothing, Dietary restrictions
Baptism or Blessing	None	Words used in prayer are the first that the baby will hear
Initiation, Confirmation	Upanayana. Boy "belongs" to his guru while he goes thru "school"	Shahada or "witnessing." A Muslim repeats the Islamic declaration of faith
Marriage	Elders arrange marriage or at least must approve.	Polygamy is legal. Divorce strongly discouraged
Death or After Life	Constantly dying & being reborn into a new body	Paradise & hell are actual physical places that we will be for all eternity
Judgment and Salvation	Your behavior affects your next life through karma	Judged on your works & your faith. Only Muslims will be saved

Jainism Volume 2	Jehovah's Witness Page 117	Juche Volume 2
No Creator. Universe is eternal. Each person can become a god	Jehovah is the one God. Holy Ghost is His "force"	Founder Kim Il Sung is venerated and worshiped
Not included in teachings	Jesus is the *literal* firstborn of God, and a separate being	Not included in teachings
Prayers and activities. Fasting required for long periods. Do no harm to any even an insect	Follow JW rules. No smoking. Bible study. Proselytizing and spending five hours a week in meetings	Each person should work for the common good of the country
Ten days of cleansing and rituals. Naming ceremony on eleventh, thirteenth, or twenty-ninth day	None	None
None	Baptized by immersion at age of accountability after questioning	None
Nine rituals on wedding day. No same-sex unions	No same-sex unions. Divorce condemned except for adultery	No information available
Cremation of body. Soul awaits rebirth	Soul expires with body; Christ will restore the righteous only	Heaven is not the afterlife but a situation of complete order
Transform into a being with special powers to aid and assist others	Righteous will live forever. Wicked will remain dead with no existence	No information available

Religion or Faith Practice	Judaism **Page 133**	Lutheran *Volume 2*
God or Gods	First being, without beginning or end, who brought all things into existence	One person of the Father, another of the Son, and another of the Holy Ghost. But they are one
Christ	Jesus, not the Son of God; not the messiah. Did not die for us	Jesus is the Son of God. All God and all man. Died for our sins
Behavior Specifications	To strive to live rightly everyday by obeying the laws that have been given.	Partaking in the sacraments. Good works are caused by faith
Baptism or Blessing	Circumcision for boy infants at eight days old. Girl babies have a name-giving ceremony	Six to eight weeks. Water on head. Or for converts as adults
Initiation, Confirmation	Bar Mitzvah (boys) and Bat Mitzvah (girls) at ages twelve to thirteen	Usually at adolescent age confirms faith and strengthens "grace"
Marriage	A private contractual agreement. Divorce is allowed. Polygamy in some countries	Instituted by God. Same-sex unions are under evaluation
Death or After Life	Righteous brought back to life but wicked will not be, and they are punished for one year	Christians are taken to the presence of Jesus where they await the resurrection
Judgment and Salvation	Not focused on how to get into heaven. Judaism is focused on how to live this life	By grace through faith in Christ and doing God's will, all will be saved

Monophysitism Page 155	*Moravian* *Volume 2*	*Native American* *(First Nations)* Page 305
The Trinity is God the Father, Son, and Holy Spirit. One in essence and is undivided.	The Holy Trinity God is the creator, Father of Jesus Christ	The Great Spirit who created all things
Jesus has only one nature. God and man infused into one new entity	Jesus is All. He is the only authority	Jesus is the Son of God. Died for our Sins
Fasting and attendance at all the important feasts. Must spend time in private worship.	Unity with all other Christian faiths. Live and behave just like Christ.	Tolerance of other cultures, hard work, honesty, and truth
Washing the baby by immersion eight days after birth to wash away original sin	Infant baptism. Sponsor involved in spiritual education	Can vary by group. Welcomes infant into tribe.
Chrismation when the baptized are anointed with oil and received the Holy Ghost	Two-year class at ages twelve to thirteen. Laying on of hands for confirmation	Some still practice vision quest for young boys
A unity in God as Christ and His church. Both must be Orthodox. No same-sex unions	Marriage is a union with God. Counseling required. No same-sex unions	Marriage governed by God and love, not by law
No specific information available. Prayer on the third day at home of deceased	Buried in "God's Acre" by age and sex. All graves identical for unity and equality	All will travel to the next world
Good deeds practiced through faith are necessary and essential for salvation	Most believe that eventually all will be saved	No information available

Religion or Faith Practice	Orthodox Volume 2	Paganism Volume 2
God or Gods	The Holy Trinity is three distinct persons, without overlap or modality among them, who share one divine essence	Many are willing to accept the presence of the divine in all things or other gods and goddesses
Christ	A physical incarnation of God the Father. Of one being with God. Died for our sins	Some believe he was a great spiritual teacher, but not a god
Behavior Specifications	To be willing to sacrifice even as Christ sacrificed for us.	If what they do or what they say would harm anyone, they should not do or say it
Baptism or Blessing	Infant baptism by immersion	The naming ceremony and blessings of the parents during the pregnancy
Initiation, Confirmation	*Chrismation* by anointing with oil to bestow the gift of the Holy Spirit	The parents of the child will often ask for divine guidance and protection for their child
Marriage	God joins man and woman into one. No same-sex unions. Priest can marry before ordination.	Not a legally binding ceremony; either member of the couple may choose to end it at any time
Death or After Life	Separated from the body, spirit escorted either to paradise or the darkness of Hades	The pagan afterlife is a place for reunions, rest, and reconnection with the divine
Judgment and Salvation	Salvation based on your works and unity with the Orthodox Church	Heaven is a final resting place; hell is a place of rest from where souls may choose to rebirth

Presbyterian Page 177	*Quaker (Religious Society of Friends)* Volume 2	*Scientology* Page 397
The Father is God, the Son is God, and the Holy Spirit is God—but they are one God.	Trinity of the Father, the Son, and the Holy Spirit. One God	God or Supreme Being left up to personal interpretation.
Fully human, fully God. Died for our sins so that we will be saved	Most believe He is the Son of God and died for our salvation	Not part of the official doctrine, although some do agree He existed.
Evangelism, justice, compassion, spirituality, leadership, and support through Christ. Encourages no alcohol	Peace equality, integrity, simplicity, plainness in clothing and possessions	The spirit can be saved and that the spirit alone may save or heal the body.
Infant baptism with pouring or sprinkling. All baptized accepted	Baptism is an individual spiritual thing, not a ritual.	NA. However, they do believe in a totally silent birth environment
Adolescence confirms faith and strengthens commitment. Thirty-five week course required	None	NA. They do have to sign a waiver to keep confidential doctrine a secret from nonmembers
Sacred but is not considered a sacrament. Same-sex "blessing"	Must be approved through the meeting. No officiate. No same-sex unions.	No special service or beliefs
Soul leaves body and goes to God to await judgment	It is more important to worry about how you are living now.	Soul goes to a holding station, where the conscious memories are erased for next life
No speculation. Believe it is a mystery that God will work out.	People are saved on the basis of their faith in God even if they have never heard of Jesus	The path to salvation includes achieving states of greater enlightenment.

Religion or Faith Practice	Seventh-day Adventists Volume 2	Shamanism Page 329
God or Gods	The Father is God, the Son is God, and the Holy Spirit is God—but they are one God.	The great or celestial shaman is the highest source of shamanic initiation
Christ	Forever truly God, He became also truly man. Died for our sins.	Not part of the doctrine
Behavior Specifications	Think, feel, and act in harmony with the principles of heaven in all things. No Alcohol, drugs, or tobacco.	The shaman lives for the needs of his people. All acts revolve around their needs
Baptism or Blessing	Infants are dedicated and baptized when they are older.	None
Initiation, Confirmation	Baptism by immersion with required baptismal vows.	Shamans are called or chosen. It is not a personal option
Marriage	Marriage commitment is to God as well as to spouse. No same-sex unions.	Hermaphrodites are revered or some dress in the opposite sex's clothing.
Death or After Life	Death is an unconscious state. God grants immortality based on His choice.	Shaman will escort the spirit to the next world to make sure they arrive safely.
Judgment and Salvation	God will destroy or annihilate the wicked. The righteous will live on in immortality.	Everything you do is returned to you.

Shintoism Page 283	*Sikhism* Volume 2	*Soka Gakkai* Volume 2
Everything has a kami (spirit). The sun goddess, Amaterasu, is chief deity.	God is omnipresent and infinite, formless and beyond the human reach.	A universal law (dharma) underlies everything in the universe.
Not part of doctrine	Not part of the doctrine. Some compare Christ to a guru	Not part of the doctrine
Shinto emphasizes right practice, sensibility, and attitude.	To live a good life, do good deeds as well as meditating on God.	Create value, work for the happiness of oneself and others with respect for the sanctity of all life
Baby is taken to a shrine at one month to be blessed by a priest.	Naming ceremony at temple within forty days of birth.	None
Boys aged five; girls aged three and seven go to be blessed by priest for protection and healthy growth.	"Holy nectar" is sprinkled on head, into eyes and is drunk by devotee.	Inducted at a modest ceremony with participation of family, friends, and/ or local members
Modern Shinto marriage is similar to Christian marriage in many ways.	Commitment to God with guru as spiritual witness. No same-sex unions.	There is no standard marriage ceremony
Death is considered impure, all funerals are done by Buddhists away from Shinto shrines.	Departure of life from a body, then rebirth based on stage of spirituality.	Life is eternal; death is an integral part of life likened to the wake/sleep states
Be pure to approach godliness; indeed, it is to become one with the state of the divine.	No such place as heaven/ hell, but spiritual union with God, which results in salvation.	Upon death, good go to heaven at once, and very bad persons fall into hell immediately.

Religion or Faith Practice	Spiritism Page 197	Taoism Volume 2
God or Gods	God is the supreme intelligence & primary cause of all things.	Tao is all things before & after. Tao cannot be explained or seen, only lived.
Christ	Jesus was on earth as a special envoy from God.	Not a specific part of the doctrine.
Behavior Specifications	Charity is the supreme law. Love each other as brothers and sisters.	Reestablish the original balanced wholeness of human nature & society.
Baptism or Blessing	None	None
Initiation, Confirmation	None	None
Marriage	Divorce is possible because the union by God is spiritual, not legal.	No info on ceremony, but much on sexual interaction, relating to life energy.
Death or After Life	Death is simply the destruction of the body, the shell of the Spirit. Spirits are reborn into new bodies based on their spiritual need.	Life & death are merely two aspects of the same reality.
Judgment and Salvation	Destined for perfection. Good spirits are getting better & bad spirits are doing it over.	The departed have gained in deeper knowledge & interact with the living.

Traditional Religions of Africa *Volume 2*	*Unitarian/Universalism* Page 421	*Vodoun* Page 352
The Supreme Being is the creator and sustainer of all that is.	81 percent believe in a single God (no Trinity); 19 percent believe in many gods or no God at all.	The Supreme Being who created everything. Lesser spirits are mediators between us and God.
Not a specific part of the doctrine	The supreme teacher and leader of humankind. But not divine.	No spirit may join a ceremony unless *Legba* opens the "door."
The moral obligation to collaborate with the ordered harmony in creation.	It is our deeds, not our creeds, that are most important.	The moral obligation to collaborate with the ordered harmony in creation.
Offers sheep as an offering to those who were keeping the child's soul before.	Dedication as an infant. Parental commitment to raise child in a spiritual life	Divine healer reveals baby's divinity or ancestor, who protects and guides it through life.
Rites of passage help the individual to attain to the goals of his or her destiny.	Coming of age ceremony for teenagers preceded by classes.	Rites of passage help the individual to attain to the goals of his or her destiny.
Marriage has a foremost place in the social economy.	No set ceremony. Same-sex unions, okay. Special divorce ceremony.	The combining of two lives, two families, and sometimes even two communities.
Practitioners attain superpowers and gain residence in wondrous otherworldly paradises.	Varies. They teach that *this* life is more important than the next.	Person's immortal spirit goes back to the world of spirits at death.
No one can attain ancestral status without having led a morally good life.	Varies. They teach that *this* life is more important than the next.	To get to heaven, one must be spiritually elevated. The realm of the forsaken is for others.

This chart <u>barely</u> touches the surface of each faith practice. It is not inclusive of all aspects and should not be taken as such.

Endnotes

Abrahamic Religions and Faith Practices

Amish and Mennonite

1. "Beliefs," Amish Studies, http://www2.etown.edu/amishstudies/Beliefs.asp.
2. "Amish Religion—tightly knit religious and ethnic group,"Religious Beliefs, http://www.religious-beliefs.com/amish-religion.htm.
3. "Ausbund," Wikipedia, last modified March 04, 2016, http://en.wikipedia.org/wiki/Ausbund.
4. "The Dordrecht Confession of Faith," Bibleviews, last modified September 20, 2012, http://bibleviews.com/Dordrecht.html.
5. "Beliefs of the Amish," Religious Tolerance, last updated July 08, 2013, http://www.religioustolerance.org/amish3.htm.
6. "Amish Religion—tightly knit religious and ethnic group."
7. "Beliefs."
8. Ibid.
9. Ibid.
10. "Beliefs of the Amish"
11. "Beliefs of the Amish."
12. "Beliefs."
13. Ibid.

Roman Catholic

1. "Catholic Church,"Wikipedia, last modified March 30, 2016, http://en.wikipedia.org/wiki/Catholic_church.
3. http://www.anawim.pair.com/CATHOLICS/INFO.htm, © 2007 dead link. Retrieved October 2009
4. "Catholic Church."

5. "Catholic Church and the Age of Discovery" Wikipedia, last modified on 22 March 2016, https://en.wikipedia.org/wiki/Catholic_Church_and_the_Age_of_Discovery

6. "Catholic Church" info retrieved October 2009 is no longer available, Modified April 1, 2016

7. "Pope John Paul II and Judaism" Wikipedia, last modified on 27 January 2016, https://en.wikipedia.org/wiki/Pope_John_Paul_II_and_Judaism

8. "Catholic Church" info retrieved October 2009 is no longer available, Modified April 1, 2016

9. "Pope Francis: Church is in a love story," Vatican Radio, last modified April 24, 2013, http://www.news.va/en/news/pope-francis-church-is-in-a-love-story.

10. "Catholic Church."

11. Ibid.

12. Ibid.

13. http://www.anawim.pair.com/CATHOLICS/INFO.htm,© 2007dead link. Retreived October 2009

14. "On the Last Judgment and the Resurrection, Hell, Purgatory, and Heaven", http://www.catholic.net/index.php info no loger available, retrieved October 2009. Can be accessed at: http://biblehub.com/library/kinkead/baltimore_catechism_no_4/lesson_37_on_the_last.htm

15. "Catholic Church."

16. http://www.anawim.pair.com/CATHOLICS/INFO.htm,   © 2007dead link. Retreived October 2009

17. "Catholic Church."

Charismatic Movement

1. The Chrisitian and Psycology," http://www.rapidnet.com/~jbeard/bdm/Psychology/char/more/hist.htm; Adapted by Gary Gilley, Pastor, Southern View Chapel, Springfield, IL Article no longer available, retrieved April 2009

2. "Charismatic Christianity"Wikipedia, last modified on 9 September 2015, http://en.wikipedia.org/wiki/Charismatic_Christianity

3. "The Charismatic Movement—35 Doctrinal Issues" last modified Jan 1999, http://www. middletownbiblechurch.org/doctrine/charis35.htm
4. "Charismatic Christianity"
5. "The Chrisitian and Psycology,"
6. "Charismatic Christianity" http://www.casagrandebaptistchurch.com/charisma.html http://www3.telus.net/thegoodnews/charismatic.htm

First Church of Christ, Scientists (Christian Science)

1. "Christian Appologetics & Research Ministry", http:/ www.carm.org/christian science.htm
2. "Beliefs and Teachings", http://christianscience.com/ what-is-christian-science/beliefs-and-teachings; Special thanks to Joe Farkas from Christian Science Committee on Publication for Wisconsin
3. "Church of Christ, Scientist," Wikipedia, last modified on 25 December 2015, https://en.wikipedia.org/ wiki/Church_of_Christ,_Scientist
4. Eddy, Mary Baker"Science & Health," retrieved October 2011, http://christianscience.com/the-christian-science-pastor/science-and-health,
5. Excerpts used with permission from Healing Unlimited, www.ChristianScience.org, heal@christianscience.org, 800.962.1464
6. Grekel, Doris, The Forever Leader (1900-1910) Vol. 3 in the Womanhood of God Series, published by Healing Unlimited, © Doris Grekel 1999
7. Christian Science Church Manual, pg. 334
8. "Christian Science Heals through Spiritual Law," Copyright © 2012, http://www.christianscience.org/index.php/items-previously-published/82-christian-science-a-religion-that-heals-through-spiritual-law
9. Eddy, Mary Baker, Science and Health page 35
10. "Beliefs and Teachings"
11. "Christian Science Heals Through Spiritual Law"

12. Eddy, Mary Baker"Science & Health," pages 496-497 http://www.tfcs.org/

Islam

1. Ismail Nawwab, Peter Speers & Paul Hoye, "A Brief History of Islam" (edited by IslamReligion.com) Pub on 19 Apr 2006, http://www.IslamReligion.com/
2. Ibid.
3. Ibid.
4. "Islam", Wikipedia, last modified April 2016, https://en. wikipedia. org/wiki/Islam
5. "A Brief History of Islam"
6. "Islam"
7. Ibid.
8. Ibid.
9. "70,000 Muslim Clerics Issue Fatwa Condemning Terrorism," Posted December, 2015. http://www.forwardprogressives. com/70000-muslim-clerics-issue-fatwa-condemning-terrorism/
10. "Islam"
11. M. Abdulsalam, Jesus in Islam (© 2006 IslamReligion.com), http://www.IslamReligion.com/
12. "Islam"
13. AbdurRahman Mahdi, "The Family in Islam" (© 2006 Islam Religion.com) Pub on 7 Aug 2006, http://www.Islam Religion. com/
14. "Islam"
15. Ibid.
16. AbdurRahman Mahdi, "The Pleasures of Paradise" (© 2006 Islam Religion.com)
17. "The Journey into the Hereafter" by IslamReligion.com (co-author AbdurRahman Mahdi) Pub on 25 Sep 2006, http://www.Islam Religion.com/
18. "A Description of Hellfire" by IslamReligion.com Pub on 15 May 2006, http://www.IslamReligion.com/
19. "Islam"

20. Ibid.

21. http://www.IslamReligion.com/

22. http://www.jamaat.org/islam/WomanDivorce.html   =Non-Englishwebsite, referenced by a blogger commenting on Islamic Divorce

23. "An Introduction to Polygamy" in Islam by IslamReligion.com, Pub on 25 Apr 2006, http://www.IslamReligion.com/

24. "Islam"

25. "Modesty", by IslamReligion.com, Pub on 16 Jan 2006, http://www.IslamReligion.com/

26. "Ahmadiyya", last modified April 2016, https://en.wikipedia.org/wiki/Ahmadiyya

http:/ www.religionfacts.com/islam/index.htm

http://timesofindia.indiatimes.com/india/70000-clerics-issue-fatwa-against-terrorism-15-lakh-Muslims-support-it/articleshow/50100656.cms

Jehovah's Witnesses

1. "Jehovah's Witnesses", Wikipedia, last modified April 2016, http://en.wikipedia.org/wiki/Jehovah%27s Witnesses

2. Ibid.

3. Ibid.

4. "Facts About Jehovah's Witnesses," retrieved January 2011, http:/ www.jwfacts.com/

5. Ibid.

6. http://www.watchtower.org/, retreived January 2011, [redirects to https://www.jw.org/en/] Original info available at: http://www.utahvalleyinterfaith.org/religions/jehovahs-witnesses.php

7. "Jehovah's Witnesses"

8. http://www.watchtower.org/, retreived January 2011, [redirects to https://www.jw.org/en/]

9. "Jehovah's Witnesses"

10. "Beliefs and practices of Jehovah's Witnesses," Religion Wikia, retreived January 2011

11. http://www.watchtower.org/, retreived January 2011, [redirects to https://www.jw.org/en/]
Original info available at: "Jehovah's Witnesses"

12. http://www.watchtower.org/, retreived January 2011, [redirects to https://www.jw.org/en/]

13. http://www.watchtower.org/, retreived January 2011, [redirects to https://www.jw.org/en/] Original info available at: "Facts About Jehovah's Witnesses"

14. "Jehovah's Witnesses"

15. http://www.watchtower.org/, retreived January 2011, [redirects to https://www.jw.org/en/]

16. "Paedophilia", last modified 2006, http://jehovah.net.au/pedophilia.html

17. Ibid.

18. Ibid.

19. Ibid.

20. Ibid.
http://www.4jehovah.org/bible-answers/
jehovahs-witness- beliefs-and-practices/
http://www.beliefnet.com/ep/jehovah-witness-religion.asp   http://www.jwfiles.com/index.htm

Judaism

1. "Judaism: beliefs, practices, Jewish-Christian relations, news…"
Last modified May 2015, http://www.religioustolerance.org/judaism.htm

2. "Jewish History," last modified March 2016, https://en. wikipedia. org/wiki/Jewish_history

3. Ibid.

4. "Judaism: beliefs, practices, Jewish-Christian relations, news…"

5. "Jewish History,"

6. "Judaism: beliefs, practices, Jewish-Christian relations, news…"

7. "Jewish History,"

8. "Islam & Jewish Relations", last modified March 2016, https:// en.wikipedia.org/wiki/Islamic%E2%80%93Jewish_relations

9. "Judaism: beliefs, practices, Jewish-Christian relations, news…"

10. "Blood Libel", Last modified March 2016, https://en.wikipedia.org/wiki/Blood_libel

11. "Persecution of the Jews", last modified March 2016, https://en.wikipedia.org/wiki/Persecution_of_Jews

12. "Jewish History,"

13. "Persecution of the Jews"

14. "Judaism", Last modified March 2016, https://en.wikipedia.org/wiki/Judaism

15. "Principals of Faith", last modified Febraury 2016, https://en.wikipedia.org/wiki/Jewish_principles_of_faith#Principles_of_faith_in_Modern_Judaism

16. "Shabbat", last modified April 2016, https://en.wikipedia.org/wiki/Shabbat

17. "Judaism: beliefs, practices, Jewish-Christian relations, news…"

18. "Olam Ha-Ba: The Afterlife", http://www.jewfaq.org/olamhaba.htm; © 5756-5771 (1995-2011), Tracey R Rich; approved for educational purposes.

19. Ibid.

20. "Judaism"

21. Ibid.

22. "Judaism and Dietary Laws", last modified March 2016, https://en.wikipedia.org/wiki/Judaism#Dietary_laws:_kashrut
http://www.beliefnet.com/ep/jewish-religion.asp
http://judaism.about.com/od/judaismbasics/a/Jewish-View-Of-Jesus.htm
http://www.jewishvirtuallibrary.org/jsource/Judaism/

Monophysitist

1. "Monophysitism" BELIEVE", http://mb-soft.com/believe/txc/monophys.htm
—Dead Link. Info available at http://www.gotquestions.org/monophysitism.html

2. "Monophysites and Monophysitism," Copyright © 2012, last modified April 2016, http://www.newadvent.org/cathen/ 10489b. htm
3. "Monophysitism" BELIEVE"
4. "History of the Christian Church," retrieved July 2011, http://www. ccel.org/ccel/schaff/hcc3.iii.xii.xxix.html;
5. Ibid.
6. Ibid.
7. "The Coptic Church and Worship" 1998-2014, retrieved July 2011, http://www.copticchurch.net/ topics/thecopticchurch/church2-1.html
8. Ibid.
9. Ibid.
10. "The Coptic Feasts", http://www.copticchurch.net/topics/the copticchurch/church2-1.html
11. Ibid.
12. "Fasting and the Church Order", 1998-2014, retrieved July 2011, http://www.copticchurch.net/ topics/thecopticchurch/church2-2.html
13. "Private Worship in the Coptic Church" 1998-2014, retrieved July 2011, http://www.copticchurch.net/ topics/thecopticchurch/church2-2.html
14. "The Coptic Church and Worship"
15. Ibid.
16. "The Christian Coptic Orthodox Church of Egypt," last modified January 2006, http://www.coptic.net/EncyclopediaCoptica/
17. "The Coptic Church and Worship"
18. Ibid.
19. "The Christian Coptic Orthodox Church of Egypt,"
20. Ibid.
    http://orthodoxwiki.org/Monophysitism
    http://en.wikipedia.org/wiki/Monophysitism
    http://www.coptic.net/articles/Monophysitism Reconsidered.txt
    Wahba, Fr. Matthias F. "Monophysitism: Reconsidered"—dead link 9-2011

Presbyterian

1. "Presbyterian Church History", http://www. presbyterianmission.org/ministries/101/history/
2. "Presbyterianism," http://en.wikipedia.org/wiki/Presbyterian
3. "Presbyterians believe Jesus was", http://www. presbyterianmission.org/ministries/101/jesus/
4. Ibid.
5. "Presbyterianism,"
6. "The Brief Statement of Faith", http://www.presbyterianmission. org/ministries/101/brief-statement-faith/
7. "Social issues: Alcohol and Gambling", http://www. presbyterianmission.org/ministries/101/social-issues/
8. "Sexuality and Same-Gender Relationships," http://www.presbyterianmission.org/ministries/101/homosexuality/
9. "Learn about the mission and ministry of the Presbyterian Mission Agency", http://www.presbyterianmission.org/ministries/
10. "Prebyterian Worship", last modified April 2016, https://en. wikipedia.org/wiki/Presbyterian_worship
11. Ibid.
12. "Sacraments," http://www.presbyterianmission.org/ministries/ 101/sacraments/
13. "Presbyterian Church in America", last modified April 2016, https://en.wikipedia.org/wiki/ Presbyterian_Church_in_ America#Marriage
14. "Sin and Salvation" http://www.presbyterianmission.org/ministries/ 101/sin-salvation/
15. "What We Believe," http://www.fpcdallas.org/ index.cfm/Page ID/830/index.html
16. "Sin and Salvation"
17. Ibid.
18. "Predestination," http://www.presbyterianmission. org/ministries/ 101/predestination/
19. Ibid.

20. "Learn about the mission and ministry of the Presbyterian Mission Agency"
21. "Anti-Zionism," last modified April 2016, https://en.wikipedia.org/wiki/Anti-Zionism#Presbyterian_Church_of_USA
http://www.westpca.com/
http://pcanet.org/general/aboutPCA.htm
http://www.reformedonline.com

Spiritist

1. "Spiritism" last modified April 2016, http://en.wikipedia.org/wiki/Spiritism
2. "Before WWI" (Witchcraft), https://en.wikipedia.org/wiki/Spiritism#Before_World_War_I
3. "Emanuel Swedenborg" https://en.wikipedia.org/wiki/Spiritism#Swedenborg
4. "Leon Denis", last modified March 2016, https://en.wikipedia.org/wiki/L%C3%A9on_Denis
5. "Fox sisters" https://en.wikipedia.org/wiki/Spiritism#Fox_ sisters
6. Ibid.
7. "Talking boards" https://en.wikipedia.org/wiki/Spiritism# Talking_boards
8. "Spiritism", by A. Kardec, 2nd ed., FEESP (1989) http://www.allankardec.org.nz/index.php?option=com_content&view=article&id=48&Itemid=2
9. "Fox sisters"
11. "Spiritism—Background"https://allankardecsandiego.org/about/spiritism/
12. "Leon Denis"
13. "Leon Denis—The Consolidator of the Spiritist Doctrine", based on the book "Pages from Léon Denis" by Sylvio Brito, http://www.explorespiritism.com/historydenis.htm
14. "The Triple Aspect of Spiritism" http://www.explorespiritism.com/SCIENCE%20start.htm
15. "Spritism Today", http://www.explorespiritism.com/historytoday.htm

16. "God, the Universe, and the Laws of Nature" http://www.explorespiritism.com/BASICS%20start.htm

17. "God's Nature and Attributes", http://www.explorespiritism.com/RELIGION%20start.htm

18. "Spiritist views of Jesus" https://en.wikipedia.org/wiki/Spiritism#Spiritist_views_of_Jesus;
"Jesus" http://www.explorespiritism.com/basicswhatteaches_jesus.htm

19. "The Triple Aspect of Spiritism"

20. "Reincarnation" http://www.explorespiritism.com/basicswhat teaches_reincarnation.htm

21. "Spiritism" http://www.paul-stephen.org.au/spiritism.htm

22. "The Gospel According to Spiritism" last modified April 2015, https://en.wikipedia.org/wiki/The_Gospel_According_to_Spiritism

23. "Without Charity, There is No Salvation" http://www.explorespiritism.com/RELIGION%20start.htm

24. "Practicing Spiritism", http://www.explorespiritism.com/basicspracticing.htm
"Meetings" https://en.wikipedia.org/wiki/Spiritism#Meetings

25. "Prayer" http://www.explorespiritism.com/basicswhatteaches _ prayer.htm

26. "The Universe Evolves: Stages of Inhabited Worlds" http://www.explorespiritism.com/PHILOSOPHY%20start.htm

27. "Divine Justice—Equality in Creation & Opportunity" http://www.explorespiritism.com/PHILOSOPHY%20start.htm

28. "Spiritual Evolution" https://en.wikipedia.org/wiki/Spiritism#Spiritual_evolution; "Worlds of Trials and Purifications" http://www.explorespiritism.com/PHILOSOPHY%20start.htm
http://www.seedoflight.org.au/content/spiritism
http://www.usSpiritistcouncil.com/Spiritism.htm
http://www.answers.com/topic/Spiritist-doctrine
http://www.snu.org.uk/spiritualism/pioneers/fox_sisters

Eastern Philosophy Religions and Faith Practices

Confucianist

1. "Confucianism", retreived July 2011, http://www.newadvent.org/cathen/04223b.htm Copyright © 2012,
2. "What is Confucianism?" last modified November 10, 2015, http://www.religionfacts.com/a-z-religion-index/confucianism.htm
3. "Confucianism", retreived July 2011, http://www.crystalinks.com/confucianism.html
4. "Confucianism: a world religion founded by K'ung Fu Tzu (a.k.a. Confucius)", Copyright © 1995 to 2009, last modified February 15, 2011, http://www.religioustolerance.org/confuciu.htm
5. "Confucianism", Wikipedia, last modified on 4 April 2016 http://en.wikipedia.org/wiki/Confucianism
6. "History of Confucianism", last modified April 2016, https://en.m.wikipedia.org/wiki/History_of_Confucianism
7. "What is Confucianism?"
8. "Confucianism", [crystalinks]
9. "Confucianism: a world religion founded by K'ung Fu Tzu (a.k.a. Confucius)"
10. "Confucianism", http://cs.mcgill.ca/~rwest/wikispeedia/wpcd/wp/c/Confucianism.htm
11. "Confucianism", [newadvent]
12. Ibid.
13. Ibid.
14. "Confucianism", [cs.mcgill]
15. "History of Confucianism
16. "What is Confucianism?"
17. "Confucianism", [cs.mcgill]
18. "Confucianism", [crystalinks]
19. "Confucianism: a world religion founded by K'ung Fu Tzu (a.k.a. Confucius)"
20. "Confucianism", [newadvent]

21. "Confucian view of Marraige" Wikipedia, last modified December 2013, https://en.wikipedia.org/wiki/Confucian_ view_of_marriage
22. "Confucianism", [newadvent]
23. "Confucianism", [cs.mcgill]
24. "Confucianism: a world religion founded by K'ung Fu Tzu (a.k.a. Confucius)"
25. "Confucianism", [newadvent]
   http://www.wsu.edu:8080/~dee/—access disabled as of 8- 2011
   "Confucionism", http://confucianism.freehostingguru.com/

Falun Gong

1. "Brief Introduction to Falun Dafa", http://en.falundafa.org/introduction.html
2. http://falungong.org, dead link, retrieved September 2009
3. "Falun Gong", Wikipedia, last modified on April 2016, http://en.wikipedia.org/wiki/Falun_Gong
4. "What is Falun Gong?" last modified November 2015, http://www.religionfacts.com/a-z-religion-index/falun_gong.htm
5. "Peaceful Resistence," http://www.faluninfo.net/, Special Thanks to Caylan Ford, Editor for Falun Dafa Information Center
6. "Introduction to Falun Gong & Falun Dafa," last modified October 2015, http://www.religioustolerance.org/falungong1.htm
7. "Brief Introduction to Falun Dafa"
8. "Brief Introduction to Falun Dafa",
9. http://www.faluninfo.net/, articles retrieved September 2009- now archived
10. "Brief Introduction to Falun Dafa",
11. Ibid.
12. Ibid.
13. "What is Falun Gong?"
14. Ibid.
15. Ibid.
16. "Brief Introduction to Falun Dafa",
17. "What is Falun Gong?"
18. http://www.faluninfo.net/, articles retrieved 2009- now archived

19. By David Matas, Esq. and Hon. David Kilgour, Esq., January 2007 "Bloody Harvest, Revised Report into Allegations of Organ Harvesting of Falun Gong Practitioners in China," http://organharvestinvestigation.net/ http://www.clearwisdom.net/emh/articles/2007/8/6/88367.html

Hindu

1. "History of Hinduism," Wikipedia, last modified on March 2016, http://en.wikipedia.org/wiki/History_of_Hinduism
2. Ibid.
3. "Hinduism: The world's third largest religion," last modified October 2015, http://www.religioustoleran ce.org/hinduism.htm
4. Ibid.
5. Ibid.
6. "Beliefs, Prayers and Rituals for One God in many forms," with sub-links, http://www.bnaiyer.com/Hindu-Part-1/bas-07.html. Used with permission from Dr. Bala N. Aiyer, M.D.
7. "An Over-view of the Teachings of Hindu Faith and the Beleifs" with sub-links http://www.bnaiyer.com/Hindu-Part-2/Philosophy- 00-Title.htm
8. Ibid
9. "Beliefs, Prayers and Rituals for One God in many forms,"
10. Ibid.
11. "An Over-view of the Teachings of Hindu Faith and the Beleifs"
12. "Prinipals and Practices of Hindu Dharma," with sub-links http://www.bnaiyer.com/sadhana.html
13. "Beliefs, Prayers and Rituals for One God in many forms,"
14. Ibid.
15. Ibid.
16. "History of Hinduism"
17. "Beliefs, Prayers and Rituals for One God in many forms,"
18. "History of Hinduism"
19. "The Knowledge of Dharma & Karma," http://www.bnaiyer.com/Hindu-Part-2/Philosophy-67.htm
20. "Hinduism: The world's third largest religion,"
21. Ibid.

22. Ibid.
    http://hinduism.about.com/od/basics/a/hinduism.htm

Shintō

1. "Shintō", last modified April 2016, http://en.wikipedia.org/wiki/ Shinto
2. "Shintō", last modified November 2015, http://www.religionfacts. com/shinto, Posted articled archived, info available at http://www. crystalinks.com/shinto.html
3. "Shintō, an ancient Japanese religion", last modified July 2013, http://www.religioustolerance.org/shinto.htm
4. "Shintō", Wikipedia
5. "Kami", last Modified April 2016, https://en.wikipedia.org/wiki/ Shinto#Kami
6. "Shintō", Wikipedia
7. "Early Japanese Buddhism", http://www.onmarkproductions.com/ html/early-japanese-buddhism.html
8. "Blending of Shintō and Buddhist Traditions", http://www. onmarkproductions.com/html/shinto.shtml
9. "Shintō", Wikipedia
10. "Scriptures, Sacred Texts, Shinten", http://www. onmarkproductions.com/html/shrine-guide-2.shtml#scriptures
11. "Shintō", Wikipedia
12. "Blending of Shintō and Buddhist Traditions"
13. Ibid.
14. "Shintō", last modified November 2015, http://www.religionfacts. com/shinto, Posted articled archived, info available at http://www. crystalinks.com/shinto.html
15. "State Shintō" last Modified April 2016 https://en.wikipedia.org/ wiki/Shinto#State_Shinto
16. "Shintōism", http://psychology.wikia.com/wiki/Shintoism
17. "Home Altars" last Modified April 2016, https://en.wikipedia.org/ wiki/Kamidana
18. "Shintō Deities" (Kami), http://www.onmarkproductions.com/ html/shinto-deities.html

19. "Kotodama", last Modified April 2016 https://en.wikipedia.org/wiki/Kotodama
20. "Kami"
21. "Home Altars"
22. "Scriptures, Sacred Texts, Shinten"
23. "Shintō, an ancient Japanese religion"
24. "Shrines", last Modified April 2016 https://en.wikipedia.org/wiki/Shinto#Shrines
25. "Shintō, festivals, rites and ceremonies", http://www.onmarkproductions.com/html/shinto-festivals.html
26. "Weddings", last modified February 2016, http://www.japan-guide.com/e/e2056.html
27. "Shintō", Wikipedia
28. "Afterlife", last Modified April 2016 https://en.wikipedia.org/wiki/Shinto#Afterlife
29. "Shintō Guidebook", http://www.onmarkproductions.com/html/shinto.shtml
(*) Special thanks to Timothy D. Hoare, PhD, Professor of Humanities & Religion for his input and advice
    http://www.bbc.co.uk/religion/religions/Shinto/beliefs/
    http://www.greatcom.org/resources/handbook_of_todays_ religions

Nature-Based Religions

Native American

1. "Native American Religions" Microsoft® Encarta® Online Encyclopedia © 1997-2001, http://www.angelfire.com/realm/shades/nativeamericans/nativeamericanreligions4.htm; Dead Link.
2. "Native American Religions"
3. Fikes, Jay, A Brief History of the Native American Church from One Nation Under God. ©1996 by Huston Smith, http://www.csp.org/communities/docs/fikes-nac_history.html;
4. A Brief History of the Native American Church from One Nation Under God

5. "Native American Spirituality", Copyright © 1995 to 2015, last modified September 2015, http://www.religioustolerance.org/nataspir.htm
6. "Native American Religions" Dead Link. Information can be found at: https://archive.org/stream/americanindianre02unit/americanindianre02unit_djvu.txt
7. A Brief History of the Native American Church from One Nation Under God
8. http://www.socwel.ku.edu/candagrant/Gallery/HFC-Thumbnail/First%20Nations%20of%20North%20America/First%20Nations%20of%20North%20America%20page.htm; Edward R. Canda, MA, MSW, PhD; Article moved to University of Kansas Archives.
9. http://www.socwel.ku.edu/candagrant/ Article moved to University of Kansas Archive.
10. "Native American Religions"
11. Ibid.
12. "Native American Spirituality"
13. A Brief History of the Native American Church from One Nation Under God
14. Ibid.
15. Ibid.
16. "Native American Religions" Dead Link. Information can be found at: https://archive.org/stream/americanindianre02unit/americanindianre02unit_djvu.txt
17. "Sweatlodge Ceremony", Canadian Plains research Center Copyright 2006, retrieved November 2009, http://esask.uregina.ca/entry/sweat-lodge_ceremony.html
http://www.crystalinks.com/
http://encarta.msn.com/content_761580498/Native_American_Religions.html

Shamanist

1. "Shaman's and Shamanism", retreived July 2011, http://sped2work.tripod.com/shaman.html

2. Milstein, Mati, "Oldest Shaman Grave Found", for National Geographic News, November 4, 2008, http://news.nationalgeographic.com/news/2008/11/081104-israel-shaman-missions.html

3. "Ancient Shamanism", retreived July 2011, http://the-wanderling.com/how.html

4. http://deoxy.org/ retreived June 2011,–Dead link. Info can be found at "History", http://www.crystalinks.com/Shamanism.html

5. "Shamanism," last modified March 2016, http://en.wikipedia.org/wiki/Shamanism

6. "Shamanism", http://psychology.wikia.com/wiki/Shamanism

7. "Decline and Revitilization", last modified March 2016, http://en.wikipedia.org/wiki/Shamanism

8. "Maria Sabina", last modified February 2016, https://en. wikipedia.org/wiki/Mar%C3%ada_Sabina

9. "Psilocybin" last modified April 2016, https://en.wikipedia.org/wiki/Psilocybin

10. "Neo-Shamanism", http://deoxy.org/ Retreived June 2011,–Dead link. Info can be found at "Shamanism and the New Age", http://www.crystalinks.com/Shamanism.html

11. "Decline and Revitilization", http://en.wikipedia.org/wiki/Shamanism

12. "History", http://www.crystalinks.com/Shamanism.html

13. "Neoshamanism", last modified March 2016, https://en.wikipedia.org/wiki/Neoshamanism

14. "Shamanism", last modified March 1994, http://www.sacred-texts.com/bos/bos613.htm

15. "Social Role" retreived July 2011, http://www.britannica.com/topic/shamanism

16. "Death Had a Face": NDE, retreived July 2011, http://the-wanderling.com/death.html

17. "Shamanism-General Overview", By Dean Edwards, last modified November 1996, used with permission 2011, http://www.faqs.org/faqs/shamanism/overview/

18. "Shaman's and Shamanism"

19. "Shamanism-General Overview"
20. "Practice and Method", http://www.crystalinks.com/Shamanism. html
21. "Shaman's and Shamanism"
22. "Shamanism-General Overview"
23. "Psilocybin"
24. "Gender & Sexuality", http://www.crystalinks.com/Shamanism. html
25. "Selection", http://www.britannica.com/topic/shamanism
26. http://deoxy.org/ Retreived June 2011,–Dead link. Info can be found at "Selection", http://www.britannica.com/topic/shamanism
27. "Shaman's and Shamanism"
28. "Shamanism-General Overview"
29. Ibid.
      http://www.angelfire.com/electronic/awakening101/Shamanism. html;
      http://www.scribd.com/doc/2231000/Moses-the-Shaman
      http://www.sacred-texts.com/sha/sis/sis05.htm
      http://rampant-griffon.net/Paganplace/Shaman.html

Vodoun

1. "Vodoun (also Voodoo)" Guiley, Rosemary Ellen, The Encyclopedia of Witches and Witchcraft. 1989 [ISBN 0-8160-2268-2] http://www.themystica.com/mystica/articles/v/vodoun_also_voodoo.html
2. Ibid.
3. Ibid.
4. "Vodun (a.k.a. Voodoo) and related religions", last modified February 2010, Copyright © 1998 to 2010, http://www.religioustolerance.org/voodoo.htm
5. Ibid.
6. "Vodoun (also Voodoo)"
7. "Vodoo" http://afrikaworld.net/afrel/zinzindohoue.htm—article no longer available, Information available at http://www.africanholocaust.net/news_ah/vodoo.htm
8. Ibid.

9. "Vodoun (also Voodoo)"
10. "Vodoo"
11. "What is the Temple of Yehwe" http://www.Vodou.org/whatis. htm; © Max G. Beauvoir–1998 -2005
12. Ibid.
13. http://www.amnh.org/exhibitions/Vodoun/tools. html (American Museum of Natural History—articles archived) From Fowler Museum Exhibit UCLA Information can now be found at http://www.fowler.ucla. edu/curriculum/sacred-arts-of-haitian-vodou/lesson-7
14. Ibid.
15. "Vodoun (also Voodoo)"
16. Ibid.
17. Ibid.
18. "Vodun (a.k.a. Voodoo) and related religions",
19. "Vodoun (also Voodoo)"
20. http://afrikaworld.net/afrel/zinzindohoue.htm—article no longer available, Information available at http:// www.africanholocaust.net/news_ah/vodoo.htm
21. Ibid.
22. Ibid.
23. Ibid.
24. Ibid
25. "What is Vodoun?" http://coat.ncf.ca/our_magazine/links/ 63/63 _6.htm
By Richard Sanders, editor, and coordinator, Press for Conversion! Coalition to Oppose the Arms Trade
26. "Introduction to Voodoo in Haiti" http://faculty.webster.edu/ corbetre/haiti/voodoo/overview.htm
Bob Corbett, Professor Emeritus of Philosophy. Webster University March 1988
http://en.wikipedia.org/wiki/West_African_Vodoun
http://encyclopedia.farlex.com/Vodoun
http://www.neuereligion.de/ENG/Wolf/pg15.htm
http://mamiwata.com/index8/index12.html

Other Religions and Faith Practices

Atheist/Agnostic

1. "Atheism," Wikipedia, last modified March 26, 2016, http://en.wikipedia.org/wiki/Atheism.
2. "Stand Up for Your Rights," American Atheist, http://www.Atheists.org/Atheism/.
3. "43,941 adherent statistic citations: membership and geography data for 4,300+ religions, churches, tribes, etc." Aherents.Com Last modified 9 August 2007, http://www.adherents.com/Na/Na_42.html#314]
4. "Atheism."
5. Ibid.
6. "Myth: We All Worship Something Larger, So Atheists Worship Humanity", http://atheism.about.com/od/atheismatheistsworship/a/WorshipHumanity.htm, retrieved October 2009
7. "Churches gloomy as atheists rush to debaptise themselves", http://freethinker.co.uk/2009/03/28/churches-gloomy-as-atheists-rush-to-debaptise-themselves/ Retreived March 2016; note Original link dead, retrieved October 2009
8. "Stand Up for Your Rights."
9. http://www.secularism.org.uk/livingwill/atheism, dead link—retrieved October 2009
10. "The Probing Mind", http://www.Atheists.org/Ethics_Without_Gods. February 1985
11. "Atheism."

Church of Scientology

1. "What is Scientology?" http://www.scientology.org/what-is-scientology.html, Quotations from the Church of Scientology's website © 1996-2011 by Church of Scientology International, used with permission
2. "Dianetics," last modified March 2016, http://en.wikipedia.org/wiki/Dianetics

3. "Foundation for Religious Freedom" (800) 556-3055 David Hinkley ©1999, 2004 http://www.forf.org/news/2004/scientology. html—Dead link, retrieved June 2011

4. "Scientology." Last modified April 2016, http://en.wikipedia.org/wiki/Scientology

5. "What is Scientology?"

6. "Auditing", last modified April 2016, https://en.wikipedia.org/wiki/Auditing_(Scientology)

7. "Dianetics,"

8. "Scientology"

9. "Classified as Church, or Business," last modified April 2016, https://en.wikipedia.org/wiki/Church_of_Scientology#Classification_as_church_or_business

10. Ibid.

11. "Restoring Ron L. Hubbard's Lectures", http://www.scientology.org/david-miscavige/restoring-1-ron-hubbards-lectures.html

12. "What do Scientologists Believe?" –Diety, http://www.beliefnet.com/Faiths/Scientology/What-Do-Scientologists-Believe.aspx?p=3

13. "Jesus in Scientology," last modified March 2016, https://en.wikipedia.org/wiki/Jesus_in_Scientology

14. "Scientology Creeds and Codes"

15. Ibid.

16. "Scientology"

17. Ibid.

18. "Dianetics,"

19. "List of Scientology Organizations" last modified August 2015, https://en.wikipedia.org/wiki/List_of_Scientology_ organizations

20. "Auditing"

21. "Scientology"

22. Ibid.

23. "Scientology Creeds and Codes",

24. "Space cpera in Scientology," last modified April 2016, https://en.wikipedia.org/wiki/Space_opera_in_Scientology

25. "Dianetics,"

26. "Space cpera in Scientology,"

27. "Church of Spiritual Technology," last modified April 2016, https://en.wikipedia.org/wiki/Church_of_Spiritual_Technology
28. "Religious Ceremonies", http://www.scientology.org/what-is-scientology/scientology-religious-ceremonies.html
29. "After Death", http://www.beliefnet.com/Faiths/Scientology/What-Do-Scientologists-Believe.aspx?b=1&p=6
30. "List of Scientology Organizations" http://www.freedommag.org/scientology_religious_recognitions http://www.scientologyhandbook.org/ http://www.acceptedscientology.net/ http://www.allaboutreligion.org/church-of-scientology.htm

Unitarian Universalist

1. "History of Unitarianism", last modified April 2016 https://en.wikipedia.org/wiki/History_of_Unitarianism#United_ States
2. "Universalism" last modified April 2016 https://en.wikipedia.org/wiki/Unitarian_Universalism# Universalism
3. Ibid.
4. "Universalism"
5. "Integration", https://en.wikipedia.org/wiki/Unitarian_ Universalism#Integration_1825.E2.80
6. http://www.docstoc.com/docs/15217101/Unitarianism, dead link
7. "Christology", https://en.wikipedia.org/wiki/Unitarianism#Christology
8. "Rev. Dr. Anita Farber-Robertson", http://www.reverendanita.com/
9. "Diversity of practices" https://en.wikipedia.org/wiki/ Unitarian_ Universalism#Diversity_of_practices
10. Ibid.
11. "Worship and ritual" https://en.wikipedia.org/wiki/Unitarian_ Universalism#Worship_and_ritual
12. "Seven Principles and Purposes" https://en.wikipedia.org/wiki/ Unitarian_Universalism#Seven_Principles_and_Purposes
13. "Services of Worship" https://en.wikipedia.org/wiki/Unitarian_ Universalism#Borrowing_from_other_religions
14. "Approach to sacred writings"

https://en.wikipedia.org/wiki/Unitarian_Universalism#
Approach_to_sacred_writings

15. "Services of Worship"
16. Ibid.
17. http://www.beliefnet.com/story/75/story_7566_1.html, dead link,
    Information available at
    "Unitarian Ceremony of Hope", http://www.beliefnet.com/Faiths/
    Unitarian-Universalist/Unitarian-Ceremony-Of-Hope.aspx
    "Adherents by religion" © 2014 http://www.adherents.com/
    Religions_By_Adherents.html
    http://uua.org
    http://archive.uua.org/re/reach/fall01/curriculum/unitarian_
    views_of_jesus.html
    http://www.rosslynhillchapel.com

Bibliography

- Grekel, Doris, *The Forever Leader* (1900-1910), Volume 3 Womanhood of God Series, Healing Unlimited, 1990, Science in Education
- Harner, Micael, *The Way of the Shaman*, 1990, HarperCollins Publishers
- Kardec, Alan, *The Gospel According to Spiritism*, 2008, International Spiritist Council
- Kardec, Alan, *The Spirit's Book*, 2012, Spastic Cat Press
- Magida, Arthur [editor], *How To Be a Perfect Stranger*, 1996, Jewish Lights Publishing
- Schaff, Philip, *History of the Christian Church, Volume III*: Nicene and Post-Nicene Christianity. A.D. 311-600, 2009, VFMI, LLC.
- Telushkin, Joseph, Jewish Literacy, 1991, William Morrow
- The *Holy Bible*, Authorized King James Version

CPSIA information can be obtained
at www.ICGtesting.com
Printed in the USA
FFHW02n0026270818
48001536-51707FF